The energy question

EDITED BY EDWARD W. ERICKSON
AND LEONARD WAVERMAN

The energy question
An international
failure of policy

VOLUME 1 THE WORLD

UNIVERSITY OF TORONTO PRESS

© University of Toronto Press 1974
Toronto and Buffalo

Volume 1
ISBN 0-8020-2134-4 (cloth)
ISBN 0-8020-6238-5 (paper)

Volume 2
ISBN 0-8020-2140-9 (cloth)
ISBN 0-8020-6240-7 (paper)

LC 73-91565

Printed in the United States of America

Contents

Contents

EDWARD W. ERICKSON AND LEONARD WAVERMAN

Introduction

SCENARIO OF THE CRISIS

Table 1 shows data on world oil production, exports, and imports for 1972. The US produced 21 per cent of world oil and consumed 30 per cent. Western Europe consumed 27 per cent of oil produced, Japan 11. Middle East oil was shipped primarily to Western Europe (47 per cent) and Japan (21 per cent), and the US took only a small percentage of Mid East production (5 per cent).[1] Venezuelan oil goes mainly to North America (65 per cent) and Europe (12). It is clear from these figures that the US is central to any discussion of energy, since 30 per cent of world production and consumption and 20 per cent of world oil trade involves the US. Moreover, of the eight major international petroleum companies (Exxon, Texaco, Standard Oil of California, Mobil, Gulf, British Petroleum, Shell, and Compagnie Française de Pétroles (CFP)), five are American-based.

It is equally clear from Table 1 that, if the US becomes self-sufficient in oil, a significant portion of the world market will be lost to present oil producers and exporters, primarily Venezuela and the Middle East; currently, the US market takes some eight million barrels per day or three billion barrels per year. Eight years ago, US imports of oil were only 2.5 million barrels per day, while Europe and Japan together imported 10 million barrels per day.

The rapid growth in international trade in petroleum products is then a product of two trends – the rapid rate of growth in the industrial west with its related growth in energy consumption – and the increasing reliance of the US on imported petroleum products.

TABLE 1

World oil 1972 (1965) '000 bd

	Production		Consumption		Imports		Exports	
	1972	1965	1972	1965	1972	1965	1972	1965
United States	11,180	9,015	15,980[b]	11,300	4,740	2,465	225	185
Western Europe	435	440	14,205	7,730	14,060	7,725	325	165
Canada	1,835	925	1,665	1,150	915	555	1,085	325
Mexico	500	385	610	360				
Caribbean[a]	3,650	3,810	1,195	720	1,170	195	3,620	3,250
South America	825	475	1,495	920	880	480	100	60
Middle East			1,145	660	120	25	16,950	7,610
Saudi Arabia	5,735	2,025						
Iran	5,050	1,905						
Kuwait	3,000	2,170						
Abu Dabi	1,050	30						
Other	3,140	2,210						
North Africa	3,745	1,895						
Sub-Saharan Africa	2,085	315	950	680	130	400	5,390[e]	2,140
South East Asia	1,295	600	7,460	3,030	6,420[c]	3,000	1,130	460
USSR	7,890	4,800						
Eastern Hemisphere (excl. USSR)	1,510	610	7,990	4,500	380	265	1,260	900
TOTALS	52,925	31,700	52,695	31,050	29,575[d]	15,110	30,085[d]	15,110

a Venezuela, Columbia, and Trinidad
b Processing gain excluded from domestic demand
c Japanese imports are 4.8 Mbd
d Does not equate because of minor unrecorded shipments
e North African exports are 3.5 Mbd

SOURCE: BP *Statistical Review of the World Oil Industry*, 1972, 1965.

Japan and Europe have imported far larger percentages of their energy needs than has the US. Yet it is American government officials – not Japanese or European – who in seeing oil imports grow from zero to 10 per cent of requirements, a level that officials in other countries dream fondly of, began to fear an energy shortage.

The energy question is a complex one. There are many diverse actors – consuming nations who act independently of each other; producing nations; multinational producing companies; smaller independent companies, diverse substitutes, etc. The energy question must be analyzed against the backdrop of growing awareness in underdeveloped nations of the power of taxes, heightened Arab nationalism, tax policy in consuming countries, western industrial national policies for indigenous energy sources. *There is no simple answer.* To look for a scapegoat or simplistic solution to a complex problem is psychologically appealing but irrelevant. To understand the nature of today's problems and possible solutions, let us consider some of the individual events which together make up the energy question of the 1970s.

A C T I O N

The world petroleum market has recently been in turmoil; long-standing relationships have been changing rapidly, and at a time when many other aspects of the energy economy are also under stress. For example:

The delivery and installation of nuclear power plants have not been as prompt as scheduled.

Once installed, nuclear power plants have not, in general, had the reliability that was anticipated.

Growth in electricity demand, together with the two factors above, has caused power companies to prolong the life of aging (on average less dependable) equipment, to use older equipment more intensively than normally would have been the case, and to expand effective capacity with fuel-intensive internal combustion turbines.

Artificially low ceiling prices for natural gas in the United States have created a regulation-induced shortage of natural gas reserves and production.

Environmental considerations have delayed the construction of the trans-Alaska pipeline, the availability of oil from that source, and drilling on the Alaskan North Slope to discover the approximate magnitude of the oil and gas reserves there.

The maneuvering surrounding the issue of the trans-Alaska pipeline in turn clouded discussions of the Mackenzie Valley pipeline through Canada and delayed intensive exploratory drilling in the Canadian Arctic.

Serious environmental problems caused drilling programs to be curtailed in a number of world locations.

Oil producers in the United States were made very nervous by the deliberations of the Cabinet Task Force on Oil Import Control and were left in a state of uncertainty concerning when and how the mandatory import control program would be relaxed, the prospects for the state conservation regulation system under which they were accustomed to operate, and the landed price, source, and volume of foreign oil against which they would have to compete.

Price controls in the United States distorted normal economic incentives with regard to the product mix of refinery output, kept the price of crude oil below the market clearing level, and evolved into a two-tier price system for 'old' and 'new' crude oil with various categories of exemptions and incentives.

Uncertainty about the future course of the United States oil import program and refinery-siting problems caused a hiatus in US refinery construction at a time when substantial new refining capacity needed to be initiated.

Power plant emissions controls, land reclamation standards, and mine safety laws simultaneously affected the demand and supply conditions for coal.

Non-price rationing and end-use priority controls to allocate the shortage of natural gas, together with restrictions on the production and use of coal, shifted fuel demands to low-sulfur fuel oils at the same time that refining capacity has been becoming more and more pinched.

Automobile emission controls caused a decrease in gasoline mileage and an increase in gasoline demand.

Challenges to the US Bureau of Land Management postponed lease sales and delayed the discovery and development of new oil and gas reserves in the Gulf of Mexico.

Alarmists marching to the beat of an imaginary drummer – in the face of new oil and gas strikes in Indonesia, China, Russia, Nigeria, South America, the North Sea, Australia, Alaska, Canada, and elsewhere – proclaimed that the world was in imminent danger of 'running out' of fossil fuels.

As a result of all of the above factors but the last, the United States became a significant and unexpected source of temporary incremental demand in world refined-product and low-sulfur crude oil markets. The United States and other consuming countries adopted the role of supplicants in dealing with the oil merchants of the Persian Gulf. European countries acted in independent self-interest to attempt to 'tie up' long-term contracts with Persian Gulf producers. Japan and France actively supported the policies of some producing countries to end concession rights to existing firms and re-offer these rights to new firms which happened to have Japanese or French interests.

European nuclear strategy could not be developed. Countries could not (and still have not) decided on options which include developing new breeder capacity, adopting or modifying the Canadian heavy water reactor, or adopting the enriched US nuclear capacity. Even in adopting enriched reactors, Europe is divided on the appropriate enriching process, France and Britain moving in separate directions. Because of these problems, delays in nuclear investment have been experienced, with the same effects as described above in the US.

When 'wolf' is cried often enough, even the wolf believes it. Producers could not let consumers, who believed in shortages, enjoy low prices. Prices began to march up in 1970. It is important to note that much of the early price increases were due to actions in Venezuela and in Nigeria. Nigeria did not join OPEC until late 1971.

As the price continued to rise, governments in consuming countries had two rational policies available:
1 let domestic prices rise to limit consumption, limit demand, thus limiting imports and so Persian Gulf production
2 band together to face the cartel. Instead, most consuming countries, expecting even higher prices for oil, scrambled for short- and long-term contracts with producing countries, increasing the demand for oil as the price rose. The oil market began to show deep signs of disequilibrium as perverse action prevailed. The Arab-Israeli war of October 1973 precipitated a complete embargo of nations friendly with Israel, a 25 per cent reduction in production and hefty price increases by Persian Gulf producers. It is important to distinguish the *political* from the *economic* actions of the Arabs. To embargo the US and Holland was political, although such action could have little impact on these countries' foreign policies. Nor could the embargo have a major impact on the US, which, depending on which numbers you read, imports from 6 to 10 per cent of its energy requirements from the Middle East. Increasing the price to friend and foe alike is *not a political move*, but is clearly economic. No votes are gained by charging India an extra $150 million per year. The embargo, the political actions, will soon end. The economic actions will continue.

A QUESTION OF CRISIS
OR A CRISIS OF QUESTION

The net result of the above factors (and probably other factors which have been overlooked) is what is called the 'energy crisis.' Most of the contributing circumstances cited above involve dimensions of energy policy in the United States and Europe, primarily the US. The emphasis on the United States in these volumes is not just a result of the ethnocentricity of one of the editors. The United States is simultaneously the biggest consumer and the biggest producer of energy in the world. When supply and demand get out of balance in the United States, the effects are felt throughout the world; as an old aphorism proclaims, when the United States sneezes, the world catches pneumonia. The recent and continuing convulsions in the world energy markets are evidence that this same rule applies there. Moreover, care must be exercised that the cure for the US does not kill the world.

What then of the energy crisis? The energy crisis is policy-induced. The consensus of the contributors to this volume is that the crisis does not represent some abrupt change in the fundamental relationships between man and nature. The world is not on the verge of running out of fossil fuels. Relative costs and prices are changing. But the price changes are initially more related to the effects of policy inconsistencies and policy failures than they are to changes in real resource costs on a world basis. After a period of adjustment, the marginal real resource costs of some fuels from some sources will rise to meet prices. Nevertheless, on a worldwide basis, policy-created price changes will have led cost changes. The abrupt price changes do not reflect discontinuity in the incremental cost of incremental world supplies of fossil fuels.

The touchstone of modern economic analysis is Alfred Marshall's *Principles of Economics*, first published in 1890. Marshall thought he was writing a primer on economic analysis for businessmen. Instead he wrote the basic text for nearly a half a century of graduate education in microeconomics. Indeed, much of Marshall's analytical framework is still the appropriate context within which to examine contemporary economic problems. Perhaps no single line of Marshall's text is more relevant to the problems addressed in these volumes than the epigraph. That inscription is: *natura non facit saltum*. The approximate translation is, 'nature does not proceed by leaps.'

In early 1971, crude oil was in excess supply, especially in Europe, and prices fell. Since nature does not proceed by leaps, since growth in world oil consumption could not in two years outpace supply, especially since Saudi Arabia alone increased production nearly 40 per cent in two years, how did today's shortages occur. More importantly, how did the price rise and what is the outlook for the future?

Just as we now live in the cities of the twenty-first century, so we are now operating in the energy economy of the twenty-first century. This is basically a fossil-fuel economy. If the energy crisis is policy-induced, then for the foreseeable future the critical policy responses are going to be those about fossil fuels, and oil and natural gas are the premier fossil fuels in this regard.

The basic questions and root causes of the energy crisis necessitate that we delineate energy policy options and choose among them. To facilitate this, most countries are in the process of establishing a national Energy Administration to coordinate and administer energy policy. In this context, a legitimate question is the extent to which the energy crisis overall or even for any individual country is simply a result of uncoordinated policies – a case where either policy X or policy Y in isolation might be appropriate, but where the combined effects of policies X and Y together are undesirable. Alternatively, we must identify and rectify fundamentally inappropriate policies, each with separate effects unambiguously detrimental to smoothly functioning energy economies, and with combined effects which can only exacerbate imbalance in the system. In the current state of affairs, creation of single national energy agencies and reorganization of executive departments and administrative agencies is unlikely by itself to bring order out of chaos. Some of the policies which are important determinants of the energy crisis lie outside the feasible jurisdiction of a national energy administration. Moreover, coordination on a national basis alone is unlikely to be sufficient to remedy the current ills. In addition, fundamental review is required. Coordination and review must be a continuing process with well established feedback and consistent principles of coordination and bases for review. In the sense that it will require continuing policy decisions, the energy crisis is apt to be with us for a long time. This is because one definition of a crisis is a change in relative costs and prices. As they have in the past, relative costs and prices can be expected to continue to change in the future.

What should be the principles for coordination and the bases for review? Economists would almost universally recommend that the principles should be those of supply and demand, and that the basics should be accommodation to the market mechanism.

THE BASIC LAWS: SUPPLY, DEMAND, PRICE, AND PROFITS

It is worthwhile, then, to review what these ideas entail. Demand is the valuation of benefits from consumption. Supply is the valuation of the costs of production. The underlying assumption is that individual consuming and producing units are their own best judges of the benefits to them of additional consumption or production at going and expected market prices. Supply and demand determine price. On the basis of price, there is decentralized evaluation of costs and benefits by those best able to make the judgments. To the extent that policy formulation and administration prevent this process from working, queues and surpluses develop which must ultimately be resolved by discontinuous jumps in market variables. It is these discontinuities which create a crisis atmosphere.

To economists, profit is not a dirty word. Profit realization and the potential it indicates are the signals which cause resources to flow in a responsive market system. It is crucial to distinguish between the process and the result of behavior motivated by the attempt to maximize profits. Profit maximization requires cost minimization for any rate of output. Cost minimization is required for the conservation of real resources. Profit maximization also requires a balance to be struck between production and use now and production and use in the future. Thus, profit maximization is consistent with the conservation of energy resources.

The market system, however, cannot always be relied upon to produce socially optimal results. Two situations which are important in this regard are: (*a*) the existence of market power in less than competitive markets; and (*b*) the presence of externalities in production and use.

The externalities problem is central to the consideration of the environmental consequences of energy supply and demand. The textbook example of an externality is the case of a papermill which imposes costs on downstream water users as a result of effluent discharges into a stream which is treated as a free waste sink by the papermill. These downstream costs have often not been included in the accounting of the costs of producing paper and are thus 'external' to the decisions of the papermill operators and the consumers of paper.

In the list of policy factors which have contributed to the energy crisis presented at the beginning of this introduction, a number of policies associated with environmental protection were included. This was not because we feel that environmental protection is a fundamental cause of the energy crisis. (Neither do we feel that all environmental protection policies are necessarily optimal.) Environmental protection policies have aggravated energy supply and demand adjustment processes; however, these environmental policies are at best second- or perhaps third-order factors in the energy crisis. The consensus of the contributors to these volumes is that it is possible to have enhanced environmental protection – at some cost – without immediate and drastic changes in either the level or rate of growth of real income. (In fact, the kind of flexibility and iterative adaptation that seems to be developing in the environmental policy area might serve as a model for energy policy.)

Bigness is often mistaken for monopoly. At the present time, this misconception is nowhere more apparent than with regard to the petroleum industry.

Monopoly is in the eyes of the beholder
The structure of the petroleum industry is consistent with an effectively competitive industry. The individual firms are very large, but so is the industry. Exxon

xiv

occupies about the same relative position in the petroleum industry as Burlington Industries does in the US textiles industry. Definitions of what is a 'major' petroleum company vary. The US Federal Trade Commission pinpoints eight major petroleum companies in its *Investigation of the Petroleum Industry*.[2] Other definitions list twenty-odd major companies. Either figure is revealing, but consider the twenty-odd companies. Most industrial-organization economists consider twenty firms to be a sufficient number for competitive results. Moreover, there are substantial numbers of intermediate and still smaller sized companies which are active and successful on a worldwide basis. If the more restrictive definition of eight 'majors' is used, then the competitive 'fringe' correspondingly expands to include such significant and active companies as BP, Amerada-Hess, Phillips, Continental, Union Oil of California, Sun Oil, etc. In addition, national petroleum companies operate in both producing and consuming countries. On a structural basis, the petroleum industry is probably effectively competitive.

Many individuals and agencies allege that the conduct of the petroleum industry is cooperative rather than competitive. It is also alleged that there are barriers to entry for non-integrated, independent refiners. The combination of these circumstances is alleged to affect competition adversely. As an example, consider, as does the FTC, gasoline marketing in the United States. Between 1955 and the latter half of 1973, the real price of gasoline and the market share in gasoline sales of the majors fell. At this same time, as a result of both growth in demand because of higher real incomes and the changing structure of transportation demand due to suburbanization, it is likely that gasoline demand became more price inelastic. In such a situation, the profit-maximizing response of an effectively cooperative industry would be to raise real prices – not lower them. One explanation of falling real prices is that the industry, rather than being characterized by cooperative conduct, actually behaves competitively. Another explanation is that there are not unsurmountable barriers to entry in refining and marketing. These explanations are not mutually exclusive. We believe that both are probably correct.

The profits of the companies in the petroleum industry set all time records in 1973. Two major sources of 1973 profitability for the petroleum industry were extraordinary events. These were the extent of the devaluation of the dollar and the Arab oil embargo. Exchange rates will continue to fluctuate and may become more generally flexible, but it is questionable whether foreign exchange earnings from adroit money management will soon again be as prominent a part of the petroleum industry earnings as they were in 1973. By forcing up prices to ration scarce supplies among competing users, the Arab oil embargo created substantial profits on inventories and improved operating margins. But once the system is fully adjusted to the new level of world prices, these profits will be dissipated. But it is important that they be allowed to be earned while they endure. This is because the profits are indicative of temporary shortages, and the way to cure shortages is to allocate more resources to the activity in question – in this case, almost the whole spectrum of petroleum industry activity. In general (despite grandiose talk of national petroleum companies in the United States and Canada and the existence of such companies elsewhere), the agents of society for resource allocation decisions are private business firms. These firms are attracted by high profits, even if they know that such profits are transitory. Thus, to eliminate quickly and effectively the shortages which are symptomatic of the energy crisis, it is essential that high profits are allowed to be realized in order that they serve as incentives for speedy resource allocation adjustments.

The 1973-74 profitability of firms in the US petroleum industry is a short-run measure of the performance of the industry. Current profits reflect the effect of the policy-induced energy crisis. A more relevant measure for evaluating the competitiveness of the industry is its record of long-run profit performance. Over the period of more than two decades from 1951 through 1971, the eight leading major firms in the industry were not exceptionally profitable. The eight as a group averaged slightly higher returns on stockholders' equity than an index of all manufacturing. But in any given year, several of the largest eight majors always earned less than the all manufacturing average. Over the whole 1951-71 period, approximately half of the eight largest majors on average earned less than the index for all manufacturing.

In Table 2, the profit rates of five of the eight major internationals is detailed, along with the average rate of return for manufacturing as a whole. It is difficult to evaluate these figures since the industries are so diverse in many respects, particularly risk. Moreover, accounting profits on book capital are not measures of economic profits. There is also the problem of how to evaluate the depreciation offset which the oil companies, but not manufacturing firms, receive. Before calculating net income for tax purposes, these oil firms can deduct 22 per cent of the value of crude oil sales. A simple example will indicate the effects of the depletion allowance on the accounting rate of return. Assume the company had sales of $1000, with an invested capital of $1000. (This is below the industry average of sales per dollar of invested capital.) Also assume that all sales were of crude oil, and the corporate profit tax rate is 50 per cent. After deducting the depletion allowance, the company has net income after taxes of $100; it earns 10 per cent on invested capital – below the manufacturing average. But depletion allowance (at 20 per cent) is $200. Therefore, after tax profit gross of depletion is $200, the rate of return is 20 per cent! This is but one adjustment which can be made to these accounting data. Another would be to use the market value of

TABLE 2

The five top American oil firms

	World sales ($ billions)					World return on invested capital, after tax and depletion[†]					USA manufacturing net return on equity
	Exxon	Mobil	Texaco	Gulf	SoCal	Exxon	Mobil	Texaco	Gulf	SoCal	Average
1964	10.8	4.5	3.6	3.2	2.3	12.2%	8.3%	14.4%	10.5%	11.1%	11.6%
1965	11.5	4.9	3.8	3.4	2.5	11.5	8.7	14.8	10.7	11.8	13.0
1966	12.2	5.3	4.4	3.8	2.7	11.6	9.3	14.9	11.5	11.0	13.4
1967	13.3	5.8	5.1	4.2	2.9	11.9	9.4	14.2	11.7	10.4	11.7
1968	14.1	6.2	5.5	4.6	3.2	11.8	9.8	13.4	11.3	10.3	12.1
1969	14.9	6.6	5.9	5.0	3.5	10.9	9.6	10.9	10.4	9.7	11.5
1970	16.6	7.3	6.3	5.4	3.7	10.8	9.5	10.9	8.9	9.2	9.3
1971	18.7	8.2	7.5	5.9	4.1	11.5	9.7	11.0	8.3	9.7	9.7
1972	20.3	9.2	8.7	6.2	4.5	10.9	9.6	10.2	6.6	9.6	na
*1973	28.5	12.7	11.8	na	6.5	14.0	11.7	12.1	na	11.4	na

* Estimate

† Net income/invested capital, annual average, except for 1973 where measure is for first nine months.
    Net income: income after taxes, before extraordinary items;
    Invested capital: sum of long-term debt, minority interest, preferred stock, deferred taxes and investment tax credit, and common
    equity, average for year.
na not available

SOURCE: *Business Week*, 2 Feb. 1974, p. 51. USA manufacturing average data from Federal Trade Commission, *Investigation of the Petroleum Industry*, Committee Print, Permanent Subcommittee on Investigation of Committee on Government Operations, US Senate (Washington: GPO 1973)

Edward W. Erickson and Leonard Waverman

assets, an adjustment which would relatively increase the rate of return of manufacturing firms.

The companies presented in Table 2 do not make all their profits from crude
oil sales. Actually, since they are fully integrated from crude production to gasoline marketing, it is impossible to tell where their profits are. Transfer pricing between subsidiaries does not provide a guide to internal profits. Some have argued
that all these profits are in crude production, to minimize profits in refining and
marketing so as to prevent entry. Others have argued that the profits are in refining to show producing countries the low rent available. Whatever the case, the
numbers in Table 2 do understate the true profits in the industry.

Even assuming that the true profits are 20 per cent higher than as depicted, the
us industry does not show great profitability. Actually, except for 1973, profits
in the 1960s were not much above profits in manufacturing and were declining.
Also, the 1950s were more profitable than the 1960s and the early 1960s were
more profitable than the late 1960s.

Another test is to compare the average profitability of the eight largest majors
to the profitability of firms generally regarded to have some market power. On
average, the eight largest majors are only about half as profitable as, for example,
such firms as International Business Machines, General Motors, and the prescription drug companies.

The profitability of the petroleum industry, as measured by the profits of the
eight major oil companies, is approximately what one would expect from a structurally competitive industry with some barriers to entry and generally increasing
competitive conduct. On average, the eight companies earn on shareholders' equity
a return probably about equal to the cost of equity capital. And despite their impressive recent profit performance, knowledgeable people in the financial community have not bid up the price of the majors' common shares in expectation
that these transitory profits indicate a permanent increase in earnings capacity.

THE CAUSE: THE UNITED STATES

The competitiveness of the petroleum industry is of more importance than simply idle curiosity to a few academic economists. It is a well known proposition
in economics that the efficiency of resource allocation is not necessarily improved
by removing a constraint that prevents prices from equalling long-run marginal
costs unless all other prices in the economy are also equal to marginal costs. Apparently this principle has also been incorporated into political wisdom as well.
One of the principal general causes of a divergence between price and long-run
marginal cost is the existence of market power – or non-competitiveness. In a
non-competitive situation, price exceeds long-run marginal cost. One of the prin-

cipal causes of the world energy crisis is the regulation-induced shortage of natural gas in the United States. The effect of the shortage of natural gas has been to shift natural gas demands to fuel oils. Because of the effective price ceiling, wellhead prices for natural gas are below long-run marginal costs of discovering and developing market clearing quantities of new natural gas reserves. This is well recognized. But one of the reasons why the US Congress has failed to deregulate the field market for natural gas is the erroneous belief that the suppliers of natural gas in particular, and the petroleum industry in general, are non-competitive and have monopoly market power.

If one accepts the thesis that imbalances in US energy supply and demand temporarily tightened up the world market for oil and made the consuming countries vulnerable to the supply interruptions and unilateral price increases which have characterized the recent situation, then what policies are most responsible? The chief responsibility lies on three:

failure to deregulate the wellhead price of natural gas;

price controls which impede both flexible use of refining capacity and petroleum exploration (by creating artificial shortages of drill pipe, etc.) and prevent the US oil market from clearing; and

the failure to rationalize US oil import policy resulting in costly uncertainty and delays in planning and implementing additions to US refinery and crude oil capacity.

A discussion of the general price controls policies of Nixon's phases I, II, III, and IV are beyond the scope of energy policy alone, but a brief comment is appropriate. If all but a few prices in an economic system are more or less effectively controlled, then the brunt of any adjustments must be borne by those prices which are relatively more free to move. A not insignificant share of the impetus for world spot market prices of $30 per ton for coal in the United States and $17 per barrel of oil in the Persian Gulf and Nigeria lies in the price control system. This was aggravated by an administrative mechanism which allowed high prices for imported oil to be passed on to US consumers, but which held US crude oil prices at controlled levels. The effects of wellhead ceiling prices on natural gas to shift demand to oil have already been discussed.

The failure to rationalize US oil import policy is more difficult to assess. In the late 1960s at the then prevailing prices for US crude oil, it was apparent that US production of crude oil from conventional sources would not keep pace with the expected growth in US demand. Imports of crude oil were tied to US production through the mandatory oil import quota which had been instituted in 1959 on grounds of national security. As a result of various provisions in the quota system, total oil imports approximated about 25 per cent of US crude oil production and 20 per cent of US consumption. As a result of the operation of the import

Edward W. Erickson and Leonard Waverman

control program, the US price of crude oil exceeded the world market price for crude oil landed in US ports by approximately 50 per cent – or about one dollar per barrel. Because of this situation, because of the impending imbalance in US supply and demand at the existing price level, and because the then existing quota arrangement was not sufficiently flexible to deal with the problem, the Cabinet Task Force on Oil Import Control was convened and a fundamental policy review undertaken. (The quite complicated details of the oil import control program, as it existed in 1969 and had developed prior to then, are discussed in *The Oil Import Question*, the report of the Cabinet Task Force.[3])

The majority of the Cabinet Task Force recommended replacing the quota system with a flexible tariff intended to be used to help minimize US energy costs while at the same time achieving national security objectives. The recommendation was not accepted. The general quota system was kept in place and no fundamental policy decision was made, but the basics of the situation continued to develop. The result was uncertainty about what would be done and when, a virtual cessation of new refinery construction in the United States, absorption of excess US domestic crude oil producing capacity, an increased US demand for imports of refined products, and a general tightening of world markets. All this was accompanied by some unusual US diplomacy with the Organization of Petroleum Exporting Countries. This diplomacy consisted of crying shortage; refusing to allow Venezuela most-favored-nation status under the US's Latin American 'Good Neighbor' policy; and suggesting that the price increases agreed to at OPEC's Teheran-Tripoli meeting were in consuming countries' interests. If a little tax is good, a bigger tax must be better.

Even with the advantage of hindsight, it is impossible to say what would have occurred in the world petroleum market if all the recommendations of the majority of the Cabinet Task Force and their corollaries had been adopted – that is to say, had the United States adopted a vigorous national energy policy of operating at home and abroad to minimize energy costs. In this regard it is useful to distinguish among the economics, the politics, and the theatre of events. The economics of the situation were clearly consistent with the view that it was advantageous for the United States to take greater advantage of lower-cost world oil supplies. But as the failure to move in that direction reveals, this was politically unacceptable. The failure to take decisive action set the stage for the dramatic price increases associated with the theatre of the Teheran and Tripoli conferences and the porous Arab oil embargo. It is possible that a policy approach which was an alternative to inaction might have averted some of these events. A plausible counter-argument is that adoption of the Cabinet Task Force majority recommendations would have made things worse today than they now are. That is possible, but probably they would not be much worse.

xx

A PRIMER ON EXPROPRIATION[4]

A nation quite naturally wishes to control its own industries, the petroleum industry being one of many. In most countries, however, this control has been difficult, since each stage in this industry requires large capital outlays, with exploratory ventures being particularly costly and risky. Oil occurs predominantly in underdeveloped countries which have a shortage of capital and which cannot afford to finance their own industries adequately from their own resources. Over the years, a recognizable pattern has evolved, with many of the developments having been pioneered in Venezuela. Initially, with little being known concerning the geology of a region, risks are high and governments must offer relatively high rewards and liberal terms in concessions in order to induce exploration and development by competent operators. Once large discoveries are made, potential investors tend to regard exploratory risks as being reduced, and new concessions will still find takers even with less attractive terms.

As a profitable industry is established in a country, two factors change the relative bargaining advantages of company versus country. First, the regulatory authorities require detailed reports and are thus able to appraise the promise of explored areas and the profitability of current operations. Second, the concession operator invests increasing sums in the country and thus becomes less flexible with regard to alternative sources of supply – its fixed assets are economic hostages. A basis is thus created which permits the producing country to appropriate an increasing share of the profits of oil operations. Up to a point, this approach is certainly consistent with the economic theory of free enterprise under competitive conditions, in that the economic 'rents' of high profits, which accrue to the exploitation of a low-cost resource (i.e., prolific oil fields) can be appropriated in full by the owner of that resource without affecting the rate of production from that resource. Unfortunately, however, the politics of industry control are not as self-regulating as the economics of competition. Changes in world market conditions, such as relative production and transportation costs, can reduce the competitive advantage of a given oil field and thus diminish the profitability of its exploitation. The governments of producing countries have shown greater awareness, in general, of the opportunities for increasing taxes, rentals, and royalties, than of the need for their reduction when market conditions at least temporarily deteriorate. It may become less costly for a company to reduce output or even temporarily cease production in a given area rather than persist in operating under adverse regulations. It is in such instances that the threat of expropriation arises.

The structure of the international oil industry is such, however, that in the past there were practical considerations which usually tempered a country's urge to

Edward W. Erickson and Leonard Waverman

nationalize the facilities of its oil companies. First, the largest petroleum deposits are usually far removed from the major consuming centers, so that transportation of oil across national borders is necessary. Thus, those who govern the producers do not govern the consumers. Second, the major international oil companies are fully integrated, from production through marketing. Third, since the late 1940s there has been a potential surplus of oil supply over oil demand at prevailing market prices. Thus a country which expropriated a major concessionaire might have a hard time marketing its oil, unless it were willing to sell at a rather low price – which in turn would tend to undermine world oil prices still further. Fourth, until 1970 the producing country cartel, OPEC, was not able to act in concert to force oil prices up toward the monopoly level. But after solidarity was achieved in 1970, prices were forced up by concerted action to keep output and production capacity expanding as rapidly as demand. This increased the threat of expropriation by reducing the penalties likely to be experienced by the producing country. Hence the countries felt increasingly free to experiment with more onerous regulation and taxation, and the company response was frequently reduced simply to making the best of a deteriorating situation. In a sense, for countries with established exporting industries, cartelization has become a substitute for nationalization, and the private companies, rather than being expropriated, have become tax collecting agents and service contractors by function, while retaining the formal status of independent companies.

This applies to countries with established exporting industries. Countries which have not yet attained that status still offer concessions and other inducements to outside investors. After all, a country must first obtain a petroleum industry before it can control it.

ADELMAN

The most encyclopedic analysis to date of the basics of the problem is that by M.A. Adelman in his book, *The World Petroleum Market*.[5] Adelman argues that even at the world price levels prevailing in 1970 prior to the recent massive price increases, there existed a potential excess supply of world petroleum. Because of this, Adelman has been subject to substantial criticism. Excess supply triggers price decreases. Prices have actually risen. But one has to distinguish between the weak and strong Adelman hypotheses. The strong hypotheses involve specific behavior by specific actors in the world petroleum market. As with any point estimates, they are likely to be wrong in detail. Because of the mass of specific detail in Adelman's analysis, it is tempting to focus on the strong hypotheses.

The weak hypotheses are of more interest and are apt to be of longer-run policy significance. The weak hypotheses focus on structural relationships, involving the fundamentals of excess supply and the difficulties of maintaining a stable international cartel. The actions of the participants in the Arab oil embargo are evidence of how quickly these effects can operate, even in the best of times. If Adelman is correct about costs, and if excess supply was a potential problem at 1970 prices, then it is an even greater potential problem at present prices. Two previous Adelman predictions are of interest here. On the basis of cost and demand data, he predicted a secular decline in the real price of world oil in the 1960s. On the basis of the realignments that occurred at Teheran and Tripoli, he in 1971 predicted substantial increases in the world price of oil. Both times he was correct.

What if Adelman is correct again? What if there is a surplus of oil? One of the most serious sources of potential friction in international policy, and discord in domestic policy within some countries, could be the machinations required to prop up an institutionalized world oil price that is far above the long-run marginal cost of finding and developing new reserves and is under serious pressure from incremental supplies. One suggestion for dealing with this problem is some form of international commodity agreement for oil. The history of international commodity agreements is not particularly encouraging. There are a number of scenarios through which the world might again arrive at a situation analogous to that which existed in the late 1960s - a decline in the real price of oil. Should such a circumstance come to pass - and until we see empirically supported analytical work which contradicts Adelman and is confirmed by supplier behavior, we believe such a circumstance is more probable than not - it is likely that the world will again fail to learn from its history. With appropriate changes of costume, casting, and choreography, the show will go on.

OUT ON AN OILY LIMB

It is our tentative judgment that, for the foreseeable future, dislocation rather than stability will characterize the world oil market. Rather than reflecting the inexorable pressure of demand upon supply, the source of instability is apt to be relentless pressure of supply upon demand. The historical variations will be the actions of supplier nations to keep the logical effects of that pressure from being realized, and the responses of consuming nations to those actions. The seasoning will be added by those nations who cannot decide whether they are suppliers or consumers.

The variations are unpredictable. The further one tries to see into the future, the more unpredictable the variations become. Changes in underlying source and use patterns will surely be reflected in energy supply and demand. But prediction of any specific changes will be in error. It was less than one hundred years ago that the first commercial electric generating station began supplying power.

Edward W. Erickson and Leonard Waverman

When the Standard Oil Trust was broken up in 1911, the principal use of the output of its refineries was for illuminating oil. An index of the likelihood of continued long-run technological change, modification in energy sources and uses, shifts in supply and demand, and pressure on real costs and prices is the fact that roughly 95 per cent of the scientists and engineers who ever lived are alive today. Extrapolation of exponential growth trends is a very unsatisfactory business. But if one is to extrapolate any trends, technological change must be included. The world is ultimately finite. The laws of thermodynamics are relevant. Economic activity does accelerate the rate at which entropy increases. The principles developed by Nicholas Georgescu-Roegen in *The Entropy Law and the Economic Process*[6] must be given more consideration by practical economists. And it is true that no perfect mechanism exists which allows future generations to vote in the market place of today's resource allocation decisions. But rather than arbitrarily abstaining from current consumption to preserve some of today's limited resources for future consumption, an alternative is to continue investing in technological change to make new and greater resources more available tomorrow for ourselves and our successors. Subject to the inevitable death of the sun, Adam Smith's invisible hand may also work intergenerationally.

Standing on an oily limb, months before publication, is not a very safe place to be. We feel that present world prices (e.g., Venezuelan tax reference prices of $14.50) are not in the long-run profit-maximizing interests of the oil exporters. We believe the supply of oil to be relatively price-elastic. At decontrolled wellhead prices in the US, tertiary recovery alone will add some 25 billion barrels to US domestic oil potential. Drilling activity in North America has reached the levels of the mid-1960s. Much new oil will be found inside North America and outside it – China, Sub-saharan Africa, Indonesia, Latin America, etc. Since the 'crisis' began in October 1973, Britain has found sufficient reserves of coal and oil to make that country an exporter by 1980. An embargo held much longer, a price of oil at its present level will set irreversible forces into play. These forces will be to find other sources of energy which are cheaper than $14.00 per barrel. Once nations have committed themselves to secure oil costing $10.00 per barrel, Middle East oil costing $.20 per barrel will be driven out of the markets. Everyone will lose. Nations will become committed to domestic oil shale (US), costly domestic pipelines (Canada), Russian LNG (Japan), and oil bought with armaments (Britain and France). Existing oil producers sitting on the cheapest energy imaginable will find few buyers. An nth best solution.

The eighteen papers presented in this book provide an encyclopedic wealth of information on past and future trends in exploration, production, and government policy. If they are read with care, these experts' opinions will convince the reader of the true nature of the energy question of the 1970s and 1980s – an international failure of policy, not a physical shortage of energy.

To end this introduction, we can do no better than to quote the *Economist* of 10 November 1973, p. 13, 'Most assumptions that the Arabs can go on holding the world to ransom are based on the commonest delusion of third-class political economy: the delusion that yesterday's attitudes, yesterday's market projections, yesterday's conditions of supply and substitution, yesterday's political trendinesses can be presumed to hold good for tomorrow, even if today's actions based on these delusions will by themselves change every one of them. But before these realisations strike home, while blackmail makes its headway against unnecessary panic, foolish mistakes can and will become embedded in official policies and popular thinking alike.'

NOTES

1 Exact figures are difficult to devise since crude oil is refined and reshipped as products. The US percentage of Mid East production could be 10 to 15 per cent, at this time, without an embargo.
2 Federal Trade Commission, *Investigation of the Petroleum Industry*, Committee Report of the Permanent Subcommittee on Investigations of the Committee on Government Operations (Washington: Government Printing Office, 1973)
3 Cabinet Task Force on Oil Import Control, *The Oil Import Question* (Washington: Government Printing Office, 1970)
4 This primer on expropriation has been borrowed from a draft from Henry Steele. No compensation is intended.
5 (Baltimore: Johns Hopkins, 1972)
6 (Cambridge, Mass.: Harvard University Press, 1971)

The energy question

M. A. ADELMAN

The fundamentals of Professor Adelman's point of view are very straightforward. First, increases in the world price of oil are not a result of increases in the real resource cost of oil in the Persian Gulf. Second, the current real resource cost of production of Persian Gulf oil is only a negligible fraction of the current price of oil. Third, even with zero new discoveries, potential reserve development in the Persian Gulf at approximately constant real resource cost would provide sufficient new oil to meet incremental world demand for the foreseeable future. Fourth, the current energy crisis does not represent a fundamental change in the basic relationship between man and nature, but is policy-induced. Fifth, this is not the first time that oil policy (national, multinational, world) has created more problems than it has solved. Sixth, the major ingredient of the world price of oil is monopoly rent. Seventh, the mo-

nopoly rent primarily accrues to the cartel of major oil exporting countries, *not* the international oil companies. Eighth, although it is not very productive to rant and rail about the evils of the international oil companies, one must understand their position in – and contribution to – the situation which we now call 'the energy crisis' in order to evaluate alternative policy proposals. Ninth, the dynamics of cartels makes them inherently unstable, but some cartels are more stable than others. Tenth, some people look at potential cartel instability with favor and some with horror, and all of the latter are neither citizens of producing countries nor executives of international oil companies.

The two most central pillars of the Adelman analysis are the cost estimates for the Persian Gulf which lead to his prediction of oversupply and his discussion of potential cartel behavior in the face of oversupply. All of the policy discussion flows from these two points. We know of no one who seriously disputes the order of magnitude of the Adelman real resource cost estimates for Persian Gulf incremental supply. Many people, however, explicitly or implicitly, challenge his interpretation of past, present, and possible future events in the context of cartel behavior with various producing-country, consuming-country, and multinational-company actors. We happen to believe that Adelman is correct, at least with regard to the past and present. But that does not solve the dilemma of choosing *and successfully implementing* a policy for the future.

If Adelman is right about costs and reserves, and if experience from the international oil market and other markets is relevant, there could be considerable downside risk in world oil prices in the latter part of this decade and in the 1980s. Is this good or bad? Multinational government policy could encourage price erosion, or it could shore up the market. People who shudder when they read Adelman's policy analysis ask, 'But what about the instability which would result from chaotic (i.e., declining prices) oil marketing conditions?' In reply, Adelman might respond, 'But what about the instability that is apt to result if we don't eliminate some of the monopoly rents by inducing lower prices?' One way to handle instability, as Adelman acknowledges, is through an international commodity agreement for oil. However, were the world to adopt such an arrangement, it would be confirmation of the Adelman hypothesis without accepting the Adelman policy prognosis. After all, an international commodity agreement is simply a means to administer a potential surplus at some approximation of the monopoly price.

Professor Adelman's contribution to these volumes should be especially compared to the chapters by Collado, Nye, Homet, and Grennes and Winokur. Moreover, this chapter is important background for all the other chapters in this volume. In addition, Professor Adelman provides significant perspective for the Kellogg, Roberts, and Barnett chapters, among others.

M. A. ADELMAN

The world oil market

For oil-importing countries, the two main components of the landed price of crude oil are transport service and the FOB price at the port of shipment. The two markets could hardly be more different, and there is much to be learned in the contrast.

TRANSPORT

Tanker operation is a purely competitive industry.[1] Shipowners and operators are many and the eight largest oil companies account for only 20 per cent of the world (non-US) fleet. During any given year, roughly one-fourth to one-third of the fleet is available for chartering at long or short term through a highly organized worldwide market with no protected enclaves (outside the United States, which we need to ignore). There are no strong economies of scale in ship operation. Many owners have only one ship – an oddity until one realizes that many firms perform services incidental to tanker shipping and take advantage of some particular opportunity to buy one or a very few ships. But although the industry is purely competitive it is imperfectly competitive because massive innovation, incompletely foreseen, has given large profits to the more alert, skilful, and lucky.

Forecasting is difficult because since 1963 there has been a chronic shortage of tankers. Shipbuilding capacity has tripled and is still expanding; shipyards have raised wages and scratched for labor. Ship prices have risen considerably. But tanker rates kept on declining through 1967, because new ships were so much larger and more efficient. Since May 1967 the market has been through violent turmoil. If we define equilibrium as a long-term rate equal to the short-term rate, the two have never been so far apart for so long. The long-term charter rate is appropriate for an investment decision in production at one end and refining at the other. More precisely, we need to identify the marginal ship for the run from the Persian Gulf (or Africa) to the United States east coast, assuming time enough to build the proper unloading facilities. (The US east coast will be used as a point of reference, but the argument applies to other markets as well.) I define the marginal ship as the smallest highest-cost vessel to be used regularly on a given run, one whose stock is being expanded by enough new orders to preclude scrapping. The neighborhood of the marginal ship was pretty clearly defined in 1969, when nothing at all was ordered in the range of 150,000–200,000 deadweight tons. Below 150,000 tons, ships are destined for specialized services, in relatively small ports. For long trunk line service, ships over 200,000 tons are required, the VLCCs (very large crude carrier).[2]

Since the run to the east coast from the Persian Gulf is farther than to either Northwest Europe or Japan, the marginal tanker will have a capacity of about 250,000 tons, assuming the necessary investment in unloading ports. Indeed, new orders for ships in the 250,000–300,000 ton class, nil in July 1969, in the next twenty-four months exceeded orders for the 200,000–250,000 class.

There are, of course, much larger tankers in operation today, and ships are actually being built of about 480,000 tons. Moreover, the Dutch government has in effect put some money on a wager that the optimal size to serve the port of Rotterdam will be in that range. If so, it would probably also be true of the US east coast. Nevertheless, it seems prudent to take actual commitments in the recent past as a practical or working maximum, and to assume that the growth in ship sizes has come permanently to a halt. At least we know the direction of error.

The recent rise in long-term rates was both cause and effect of about a 50 per cent rise in VLCC prices. But these reflected only short-run marginal costs. The yards were and are crammed with orders; they are working at top capacity on new designs and are chronically short of labor. Japan is speeding ahead in this field, despite the fear of eventual excess. The shipbuilding industry appears to be competitive, although the evidence is not as clear as for ship operation. If the governments of the shipbuilding countries were able to cartelize the shipbuilding industry – they have tried but not succeeded thus far – and raise prices, integration of shipping with shipbuilding, either by merger or by long-term contract, would probably follow and the result would be higher profits for vertically integrated groups at the expense of the non-integrated. Tanker rates would still be determined by investment cost at the margin plus operating costs. Hence a rough estimate of a dollar per barrel long-run charter real transport costs from the Persian Gulf to any destination appears to be not inconsistent with what can be discerned in the shipbuilding market. When supertankers are combined with superports, a barrel of oil anywhere in the world is a barrel everywhere. [Editors' note: For a detailed discussion of the world tanker market, see Chapter IV of *The World Petroleum Market.*]

CRUDE OIL – SUPPLY AND DEMAND

Our problem with crude oil is the exact contrary of that in transport. The market is not sufficiently competitive to be a good sensing mechanism, i.e. price does not register cost. We must measure it directly. In the late 1960s, the investment needed to establish an additional daily barrel of capacity in the four big Persian Gulf concessions was about $110. Some of the smaller sheikdoms may involve even lower cost. A price of just under six cents per barrel, if paid for the expected output of one initial barrel daily, declining at one per cent, over the next 25 years, and discounted at 20 per cent in view of low geological risk but high political risk, would have a present value of $110. Then six cents per barrel was the supply price or cost of capital. Operating costs in Iran in 1970 were 2.7 cents; there and also in Saudi Arabia and Kuwait labor requirements per unit of output have decreased greatly. However, we assume them to be 4 cents; total development cost was then about 10¢ per barrel.

This was the *current* long-run marginal cost in the recent past. In order to estimate *future* long-run marginal cost, we first need to estimate the volume of future output. For purposes of bounding the calculations reported here, we assume no natural gas or nuclear power, and the disappearance of two-thirds of non-US coal by the year 1980; it is further assumed that all of the 1969–80 increment to the consumption in the world market (i.e. outside North America) goes to the Persian Gulf. These assumptions throw the maximum likely weight on to that area. In order that the Persian Gulf be the supply source for incremental world consumption, two conditions must be met. First, the oil-producing countries there must be willing to produce at the implied rates. Second, the prices in the Persian Gulf must be sufficiently low to forestall development of incremental capacity elsewhere (for example, Indonesia, the American and Canadian Arctic and East Coast outer continental shelf, the North Sea, etc.). If we assume that one or both of these conditions is not met, higher Persian Gulf prices and a lower rate of increase of Persian Gulf output, the calculated Persian Gulf cost will be lower. Under our assumptions, Persian Gulf production increases not by the recent 11 per cent but by 13.5 per cent per year over the next ten years, after which it drops back to the worldwide energy growth rate of 4.5 per cent. Recent experience suggests these rates may be too high. To the extent that this is true, the

7

TABLE 1

Persian Gulf reserves and output, 1969-84 (in billions of barrels)
(in billions of barrels)

Year	Persian Gulf output	
	Per year	Cumulative
1969	4.5	–
1979	16.0	80.4
1984	20.0	87.5
		167.9
Persian Gulf reserves, end-1969		333
plus additions in known fields		+222
less cumulative production, 1970–84 inclusive		–168
Persian Gulf reserves, end-1984		387
Reserve-production ratio, end-1984		19.6
Annual growth rate: net reserves (per cent)		1.016

long-run marginal costs reported below are also too high. But under these extreme assumptions, over the 15 years beginning with 1970 we would have expected the following:

Under this scenario, end-of-1984 Persian Gulf reserves would be nearly 20 times production. But with assumed zero new discoveries this increase in reserves impounded from the much larger total of oil-in-place cannot be assumed available at constant cost. The increasing decline rate and the lower output per well both increase capital cost. Moreover, since we assume that there will be not only extension of old reservoirs but also new pools found in the old fields, we make allowance by including expenditures for geological-geophysical work and exploratory drilling, which were excluded from development costs. When conservative adjustments are made in these figures to reflect changes in capital and operating costs, the 1985 real long-run marginal cost of new oil is in round numbers about 20¢ per barrel, double the experience of the recent past. No allowance is made for new discoveries or for improved technology in oil development. [Editors' note: For a unified theory of oil operating-developing-finding costs and more detail on the Persian Gulf and elsewhere, see Chapters I and II of *The World Petroleum Market.*]

Obviously this is not an estimate of the most likely future cost but rather an overestimate, approximately what it would have cost in 1962-8 to produce from the big Persian Gulf fields had they been depleted to the point where the reserve-production ratio was down to about 20. In 1971, Persian Gulf production was six billion barrels and reserves were 367 billion barrels.

The deliberate bias in the procedure is seen by considering the corresponding estimates in an earlier publication.[3] A testable element of the projection was the assumed growth of Persian Gulf production at 10.4 per cent per year and assumed growth of proved reserves at about 1.4 per cent per year. Actually, production has grown somewhat more slowly, while reserves have grown at a rate of 11.5 per cent per year. This supports our 1966 treatment of the cost increase as high rather than probable. In fact, between 1960 and 1970, the investment needed per unit of new crude oil capacity fell by over 50 per cent, despite a rising general price level.

The basic theory is that development cost swallows up operating cost on the one side and finding cost on the other. The total increase in cost, in this case 10¢ per barrel, is called the Maximum Economic Finding Cost. In theory, since oil operators face a constant trade-off between higher development cost on the one side and discovery cost on the other, these should be equated at the margin. Hence MEFC should be an indirect measure or proxy for finding cost. Perhaps this is to carry a valid idea too far, suggesting a precision that does not yet exist. MEFC, the rise in development cost, remains merely a plausible limit, the penalty for doing nothing to find new oil. Severe as are the limitations of the method, it suffices to show that *the fears of long-run physical scarcity are unfounded*, at least for 15 years ahead. To look farther ahead is at best an exercise in method, at worst a vain presumption. The difference between a long-run physical shortage evidenced by sharply rising real resource costs and an economic shortage caused by a combination of poor planning and effective cartel action is significant in terms of long-run policy formation, but indiscernible in terms of short-run financial effects upon consuming countries.

At the center of our theory we put the investment process of creation of a ready shelf inventory, proved reserves, out of a much larger resource, oil-in-place.[4] This much larger but imperfectly known stock is replenished irregularly by discoveries. But over a long enough time horizon to where the present value of a good or bad guess is nearly zero, oil production costs are development costs, determined by an orthodox investment process. We see now that the traditional theory of 'exhaustible resources,' wherein, for example, a rise in interest rates makes future revenues less attractive, speeds up the rate of output, and lowers prices, covers only a very special case. In the mineral industries, greater scarcity of capital inhibits development investment, reduces output, and raises prices.

If this reasoning is sound it shuts the door on the irrelevant features of the problem. Over past years, since the end of the first Suez crisis in 1957, many have predicted that growing consumption would dry out the 'surplus' and naturally restore prices from bargain-basement to normal as a result of the pressure of demand upon costs. This remains the official truth in the capitalist, Communist, and Third Worlds, but it is a mistake. In a competitive situation, higher output tends to put up prices only by raising incremental cost, but even our generous or excessive allowance for increased cost is negligible in relation to prices (to be discussed below). Outside the United States, there has been no 'surplus,' in that current producing capacity was in good close relation to output. If by 'surplus' is meant the ability to expand output by drilling and connecting more wells at costs far below current prices, there has indeed been a surplus, but it will not disappear for many years to come. Cost in the Persian Gulf explains only a minor, almost negligible, fraction of price. Above all, it explains none of the recent explosive increases in price.

CRUDE OIL – MONOPOLY ELEMENTS

How sharp a contrast there is between the tanker market and the crude oil market. In tankers, the price of the service reflects the cost, but the cost is itself subject to great change and uncertainty, and the problem is to separate the transitory from the permanent. In crude oil, the cost is quite stable and even great percentage error would not have much importance, but competitive supply and demand, i.e. long-run incremental cost, have explained very little. A massive block to competition is registered by the price-cost gap. Of the approximately $1.70-$1.80 per barrel in the fall of 1971, the Persian Gulf governments already got about $1.50. Hence if we had been able to set to zero the monopoly element among the companies (assume that there are 100 or 1000 equal-sized competitors), the price would be decreased by only 10 to 20 cents per barrel. In the context of the 1971 example, however, if we removed the governmental element, the decrease is nearly $1.50. Today, of course, the comparison is even more dramatic. But picking a benchmark price in the current unsettled market is more difficult.

Private oligopoly in world oil is no longer important; were it not for the role of the companies as government agents it would be negligible. The main obstacle to competitive evolution is the per-barrel tax of the producing countries. Over the near term it acts like a cost. No oil company will commit itself to invest and deliver for anything less than the sum of costs plus taxes plus an allowance for contingencies. Hence, not only is the tax a floor to price, it is even effective at a distance.

A price forecast for the 1970s has nothing to do with supply and demand or the real scarcity value of crude oil. Hardly anything matters but the taxes levied by the producing countries. In late 1970, a plausible forecast was that they would in time shade taxes to permit the companies to shade prices. I consider this as still the long-run prospect for an unrestrained market, but the long run is now further away in calendar time, price erosion would start from a much higher level of prices and the likelihood of a market unrestrained by formal price maintenance agreements between producing and consuming nations is much less. The forces acting for and against long-run price erosion can be briefly set forth, before looking at the dramatic changes in 1973 which were wrought by fundamental changes in circumstances in January-February 1971.

The producing nations had already shaded taxes in isolated and peripheral instances. To maintain the price they must make and then enforce an agreement to limit output and allocate markets. There is no other way to remove the inducement to cut per-barrel tax to permit a lower price to increase sales and total tax revenues. One possibility would be a worldwide commodity agreement under the aegis of the United Nations Conference on Trade and Development (UNCTAD). World public opinion seems favorable to the plea of many less-developed countries that price ratios are 'unfair': the developed world is paying too little and charging too much. Such perennial opponents as the United States and France have been favorable to commodity agreements, and although I would not dare give odds on the chances of one in oil, they are not negligible. The likelihood of a commodity agreement increases as it becomes more desirable for producing countries to extract a formal ratification or guarantee of existing and expected prices from the *governments* of consuming countries.

The producing countries are making a successful output-sharing cartel more difficult and unlikely. They have brought in as many new concession operators as they can to take up new acreage, or acreage relinquished by other operators. They have set up national oil companies to compete with private ones, and acquired participation with the oil companies in the reserves of the established concessions. As a result, the number of competitors is increasing. The national companies have only cost as a price floor, without tax. Moreover, national prestige may become involved, and even where there is no profit in making a sale, it is possible that the national companies will still try to make it. National prestige, however, can cut both ways and may be a partial explanation of the exporting countries', particularly OAPEC's, ability to seem to hang together versus the developed world. But it is difficult to sort out any such effect from the effects of vulnerability caused by poor policy planning – particularly in the United States. Furthermore, the various governments have different attitudes about the time value of money. A small barren country can do little productive investment at home. After paying out some protection money in loans to other governments and in subsidies to nationalist movements, it invests in the European money market. All things considered then, a future dollar of tax revenues must be discounted at no more than 6 or 8 per cent because that is all it can earn, net, in the interim.

11

M.A. Adelman

Matters are very different in a country like Iran, which has a considerable population, arable land, and water. Its rate of growth has been seven per cent per year
in the past decade and more recently has speeded up to 10 per cent. The present
value of a dollar of future tax revenue must be discounted at well over 20 per cent
per year which it could earn if invested in public or private enterprise.

Although adroit and opportunistic behavior on the part of the producing countries has been the proximate cause of the recent surge in the world price of oil,
the ultimate obstacle to the competitive evolution of prices lies in the governments of the consuming countries. Among the developed nations, only the Scan-
dinavians (now excluding Norway) seem uncommitted to higher prices, while
Japan appears careful to keep its options open in both directions. Lower prices
for oil products have been assailed, especially in Europe, as ruthless economic
warfare by American companies whose 'vast financial resources' allow them to
ruin their rivals in any one spot – the whole bell-book-and-candle recited here
against 'conglomerates' and big business generally.

As high-cost European coal is eased out it is being replaced, especially in Britain,
by high-cost nuclear energy needing protection from oil. Various nations have direct producing interest in oil or gas, and are moving to acquire more. Solicitude
for an independent local refining industry leads to protection of local product
prices and indirectly of crude prices. There is a self-fulfilling prophecy at work.
Because they expect increasing oil prices, and cannot imagine the possibility of
competition in world oil, governments make or subsidize investments which will
be seen as grossly uneconomic if oil prices decline or fail to rise. Governments
cannot lose face; the more they invest and make oil cheap, the more they will
hold it dear. Waste of resources invested in high cost oil, coal, and nuclear power
leads to even more waste.

RECENT EVENTS AND CURRENT PROSPECTS

Over the decade of the 1960s, the net result of increased competition among the
increased number of international oil companies was a very slow price decline,
which I expected to continue. But in 1970-1, the producing nations twice raised
taxes, totalling about 50 cents per barrel, with another 10 cents for 1971-5; the
companies immediately raised prices by that amount 'and a bit more,' as some of
the companies stated, in order to improve price margins. By the end of 1973, the
'average' price for Persian Gulf crude oil (in an unspecified mixture of old and
new, short- and long-term contracts) was moving toward $4.00 per barrel, and
one spot market transaction was reported at a price in excess of $17.00.

The question is: why the abrupt and massive reversal of trend? It had happened
20 years earlier: in the 1950s world-market prices persistently rose following irre-

levant increases in the United States, to the accompaniment of European fears about an 'energy gap.' Now also, there are many statements that prices are up because demand exceeds supply, turning the market around, etc. As Adam Smith said of another protectionist argument: 'They who preached it were by no means such fools as they who believed it.' The irrelevance of supply-demand has already been pointed out, and the argument lost even its appearance of validity in late 1971 as consumption growth slowed down to nearly zero, but the few sellers held crude oil prices firm. The tax increase had been the signal which all sellers could follow in raising prices without any collusion, and a few sellers can hold the price so long as everyone waits for everyone else to make the first reduction. But the price increase over and above the tax boost was quite small and will probably be eroded. What is much more important is that the producing nations contrived the tax increase with the cooperation of the companies and of the United States government, which convened a special meeting of the OECD nations, accounting for nearly all world-market consumption, to get advance assurance that consuming countries would foot the bill and take no counter-measures. The United States had some solid reasons for wanting the settlement, which permitted higher company profits, benefiting our GNP and balance of payments. Whether on balance this intervention was a good idea need not be discussed here. The companies and the State Department spoke of the 'assurances' of a five year 'stability' in taxes and hence prices. How much of it they believed we cannot say. As Johnson told Boswell, such foolish talk as calling yourself a man's most humble servant was harmless, merely a form of speech, 'but you must not *think* foolishly.' I do not suppose the oil companies think foolishly, though as late as June 1971 one still heard talk about 'valuable assurances' of tax-price stability. The new demands and the embargo are sufficient comment on these assurances. Pretexts are unimportant. Reams of paper will be consumed in spelling out 'more.'

The 'agreements' of 1970-1 marked an irreversible change. The producing nations for the first time knew what previously was a likely but not sure bet: that the consuming countries were so divided and confused that they would yield to the threat of a concerted shutdown of output. The threats were forthcoming *after* the OECD meeting, and consumated in 1973. The producing nations are now limited only by the elasticity of demand for oil products, which is very low at current and prospective prices. Even at current prices, taxes could probably be raised much more without much immediate effect on the amount demanded (either in total, or from the Persian Gulf), and raised they will be.

Hence the crude oil price level in the latter part of this decade will probably exceed recent levels. It is less likely that the 1980s level will. [Editors' note: The first draft of this paper was written in 1971. At that time, Professor Adelman correctly predicted that 1975 prices would exceed 1971 prices.] For the higher prices above taxes will further stimulate discoveries, the higher taxes will widen the margin, tempting governments to shade. In addition, the development of incremental supplies elsewhere in the world may result in different countries sharing unequally in world market growth. In short, in the absence of an international commodity agreement for oil, or some other relatively stable vehicle through which consuming countries' preferences for higher prices can be administered, nothing has happened to change the analysis sketched above. The new factor, the cooperation of the producing nations, has had a large impact. But the Arab oil embargo has not been an unblemished tapestry of unity of action. And the longer-run consequences of the price increases which are the fruit of that cooperation may not all be in one direction.

To understand the recent events in the world oil market, one must understand the roles of the multinational companies and the leading position of the United States. To that task we now turn.

THE MULTINATIONAL OIL COMPANIES AS AGENTS OF THE PRODUCER COUNTRY MONOPOLY

The multinational oil companies have become, in the words of the board chairman of British Petroleum, the 'tax collecting agency' of the producing nations. In 1972, the companies operated the greatest monopoly in history and transferred about $15 billion from the consuming countries to their principals. If the arrangement continues, a conservative estimate for 1980 collection is over $55 billion per year. Much of that wealth will be available to disrupt the world monetary system and promote armed conflict. Oil supply is now much more insecure. Monopoly, the power to overcharge, is the power to withhold supply. Among nations, an embargo is an act of war, and an oil embargo ushered in the active phase of the Organization of Petroleum Exporting Countries (OPEC) cartel.

The oil companies are now the agents of a foreign power. They will be blamed for impairing the sovereignty of the consuming countries, and quite unjustly. They only did the will of the OPEC nations and of the consuming countries themselves, notably the United States. The consumers' 'strange and self-abuse' is the key to how the events of 1970-1 turned a slowly retreating into a rapidly advancing monopoly.

The most important player in the game is the American State Department. This agency is deplorably poorly informed in mineral resource economics, the oil industry, the history of oil crises and the participation therein of the Arabs with whom it is obsessed; in fact, State cannot even give an accurate account of its own recent doings. US policy cannot be justified by increased scarcity.

Prediction is unavoidable but risky. In 1963 I thought that, abstracting from inflation, a price of $1 per barrel at the Persian Gulf was not unlikely fairly soon. In terms of 1963 dollars it did go to 92 cents by early 1970. As predicted, supply remained excessive, and the companies could not control the market. But on the political side, the prediction went all wrong in 1970-1. Although I had warned that the producing countries might threaten a cut-off of supply, and urged insurance against it, I was mistaken to call it an unlikely event. Nor did I expect the consuming countries, especially the United States, to cooperate so zealously.[5] I may be equally wrong to expect that consuming countries will continue this way for most or all of the 1970s.

The unanimous opinion issuing from companies and governments in the capitalist, Communist, and Third Worlds is that the price reversal of 1970 and 1971 resulted from a surge in demand, or change from surplus to scarcity, from a buyers' to a sellers' market. The story has no resemblance to the facts. The 1970 increase in consumption over 1969 was somewhat below the 1960-70 average in all areas. The increase in 1971 over 1970, in Western Europe and Japan, was about half the decade average. In the first quarter of 1972, Western European consumption was only 1.5 per cent above the previous year. By mid-1972, excess producing capacity, a rarity in world oil (i.e. outside North America), was almost universal and had led to drastic government action, especially in Venezuela and Iraq. The industry was 'suffering from having provided the facilities for an increase in trade which did not materialize.' A drastic unforeseen slowdown in growth and unused capacity would make prices fall, not rise, in any competitive market.

Some powerful force has overridden demand and supply. This force did not enter before the middle of 1970, at the earliest. Up to that time the trend of prices had been downward, and long-term contracts had been at lower prices than short-term, indicating that the industry expected still lower prices in the future, even as far as 10 years ahead.[6]

If demand exceeds supply at current prices, sellers and buyers acting individually make new bargains at higher prices. When supply exceeds demand yet prices are raised, the conclaves, joint actions, and 'justifications' are strong evidence of collusion, not scarcity.

More precisely: in a competitive market, a surge in demand or shrinkage in supply raises price because it puts a strain on the productive apparatus. To produce additional output requires higher costs; unless compensated by higher prices, the additional output will not be supplied.

If there were increasing long-run scarcity at the Persian Gulf, discoveries falling behind consumption, the reservoirs would be exploited more intensively to offset decline, and to maintain and expand production. The world 'energy crisis' or 'energy shortage' is a fiction. But belief in the fiction is a fact. It makes people accept higher oil prices as imposed by nature, when they are really fixed by collusion. And sellers of all fuels, whatever their conflicts, can stand in harmony on the platform of high oil prices.

Twenty years ago, the Paley Commission made the classic statement of the problem: 'Exhaustion is not waking up to find the cupboard is bare but the need to devote constantly increasing efforts to acquiring each pound of materials from natural resources which are dwindling both in quality and quantity ... The essence of the materials problem is costs.'

Depletion of reserves at the Persian Gulf is only about 1.5 per cent a year. It is uneconomic to turn over an inventory so slowly. But Persian Gulf operators have not been free to expand output and displace higher cost production from other areas because this would wreck the world price structure. Therefore, it is meaningless to average production-reserve ratios for the whole world, as is too often done. A barrel of reserves found and developed elsewhere in the world is from five to seven times as important in terms of productive capacity as a barrel at the Persian Gulf. In other words, one could displace production from the entire Persian Gulf with reserves from one-fifth to one-seventh as large. And this is perhaps the only constructive aspect of the current drive for self-sufficiency in oil. This zero-discoveries model yields a much higher production-reserves per cent, hence a substantial increase in investment requirements and current operating costs per barrel. Today at the Persian Gulf, capital and operating costs are each about 5 cents per barrel; under our extreme assumptions, they are roughly double. The difference between 10 and 20 cents measures the value of discovering new fields: it takes the strain off the old.

No basis for fears of physical scarcity
The zero-discoveries model only estimates the worst that could happen; it is not a prediction of what will happen. When the procedure was applied in 1965, current and projected costs were higher than they are now; since many new discoveries have freshened the mix, not to speak of improvements in technology.

There is no more basis for fears of acute oil scarcity in the next 15 years than there was 15 years ago – and the fears were strong in 1957. The myth that rising imports (of the United States) will 'turn the market around' is only the latest version of the myth that rising imports of Europe and Japan would 'dry out the surplus in 1957-70.'[7]

More generally: supply and demand are registered in incremental cost, which is and long will be a negligible fraction of the current crude oil price of about $1.90 per barrel. Hence supply and demand are irrelevant to the current and expected price of crude oil. All that matters is whether the monopoly will flourish or fade.

In Europe and Japan, there was a mild and temporary shortage of refining capacity in early 1970. At the same time, a tanker shortage put rates at the highest level since shortly after the closing of the Suez Canal, and raised product prices.

In May 1970 the trans-Arabian pipeline was blocked by Syria to obtain higher payments for the transit rights, while the Libyan government began to impose production cutbacks on most of the companies operating there, to force them to agree to higher taxes. Although the direct effect of the cutback and closure was small, the effect on tanker rates was spectacular, and product prices and profits shot up.

The companies producing in Libya speedily agreed to a tax increase. The Persian Gulf producing countries then demanded and received the same increase, whereupon Libya demanded a further increase and the Persian Gulf countries followed suit. Finally, agreements were signed in Tehran in February 1971, increasing tax and royalty payments at the Persian Gulf as of June 1971 by about 47 cents per barrel, and rising to about 66 cents in 1975. North African and Nigerian increases were larger. In Venezuela the previous 1966 agreement was disregarded and higher taxes were simply legislated. These taxes are in form income taxes, in fact excise taxes, in cents per barrel. Like any other excise tax they are treated as a cost and become a floor to price. No oil company can commit for less than the sum of tax-plus-cost per barrel.[8]

Harmony between producing-country governments and multinational companies
The multinational companies producing oil were amenable to these tax increases because as was openly said on the morrow of Tehran, they used the occasion to increase their margins and return on investment in both crude and products. In Great Britain the object was stated: to cover the tax increase 'and leave some over,' and the February 1971 tax increase was matched by a product price increase perhaps half again as great. The best summary of the results was by a well-known financial analyst, Kenneth E. Hill, who called the agreements 'truly an unexpected boon for the worldwide industry.'

Mr Hill rightly emphasized product price increases, but arm's length crude prices also increased by more than the tax increases. When the producing countries made fresh demands later in 1971, an American investment advisory service (United Business Services) remarked that tax increases were actually favorable to oil company profits. And 1971 was easily the best year for company profits since 1963, although there was a profit slide off later in the year, as competition in products, though not yet in crude, again reasserted itself.

The price pattern is set for the 1970s. From time to time, either in pursuance or in violation of the Tehran-Tripoli 'agreements,' and enforced by embargo when convenient, the tax is increased, whereupon prices increase as much or more, but then tend to erode as the companies compete very slowly at the crude level and less slowly at the products level. Thus prices increase in steps, yet at any given moment there is usually a buyer's market, i.e. more is available than is demanded at the price, which is under downward pressure.

The companies' margin will therefore wax and wane, but they benefit by the new order. They cannot, even if they would, mediate between producing and consuming nations. As individual competitors, they are vulnerable to producing-nation threats to hit them one at a time. As a group, they can profit by a higher tax through raising prices in concert, for the higher tax is that clear signal to which they respond without communication. The Secretary General of OPEC, Dr Nadim Pachachi, said truly that there is no basic conflict between companies and producing nations. The then head of Shell, Sir David Barran, spoke of a 'marriage' of companies and producing governments. Most precise of all was Sir Eric Drake, the chairman of BP, who called the companies a 'tax collecting agency,' for both producing and consuming country governments. There is, however, a difference in kind between serving a government in its own country to collect revenue from its own citizens, and serving a government to collect revenue from other countries.

LEADING ROLE OF THE UNITED STATES

Without active support from the United States, OPEC might never have achieved much. When the first Libyan cutbacks were decreed, in May 1970, the United States could have easily convened the oil companies to work out an insurance scheme whereby any single company forced to shut down would have crude oil supplied by the others at tax-plus-cost from another source. (The stable was possibly locked a year after the horse was stolen.) Had that been done, all companies might have been shut down, and the Libyan government would have lost all production income. It would have been helpful but not necessary to freeze its deposits abroad. The OPEC nations were unprepared for conflict. Their unity would have been severely tested and probably destroyed. The revenue losses of Libya would have been gains to all other producing nations, and all would have realized the danger of trying to pressure the consuming countries. Any Libyan division or brigade commander could consider how he and friends might gain several billions of dollars a year, and other billions deposited abroad, by issuing the right marching orders.

Failure to oppose does not necessarily imply that the United States favored the result. But there was unambiguous action shortly thereafter. A month after the November agreements with Libya, a special OPEC meeting in Caracas first resolved on 'concrete and simultaneous action,' but this had not been explained or translated into a threat of cutoff even as late as 13 January, nor by 16 January 1971, when the companies submitted their proposals for higher and escalating taxes.[9]

Then came the turning point: the United States convened a meeting in Paris of the OECD nations (who account for most oil consumption) on 20 January 1971. There is no public record of the meeting, but – as will become clear below – there is no doubt that the American representatives and the oil companies assured the other governments that if they offered no resistance to higher oil prices they could at least count on five years' secure supply at stable or only slightly rising prices.

The OECD meeting could have kept silent, thereby keeping the OPEC nations guessing, and moderating their demands for fear of counteraction. Or they might have told the press they were sure the OPEC nations were too mature and statesmanlike to do anything drastic, because after all the OECD nations had some drastic options open to them too ... but why inflame opinion by talking about those things? Instead an OECD spokesman praised the companies' offer, and declined to estimate its cost to the consuming countries. He stated that the meeting had not discussed 'contingency arrangements for coping with an oil shortage.' This was an advance capitulation. The OPEC nations now had a signal to go full speed ahead because there would be no resistance.

Before 20 January 1971 an open threat by the OPEC nations would not have been credible, in view of the previous failure of even mild attempts at production regulation in 1965 and 1966. But after the capitulation, threats were credible and were made often. (This is clear from a careful reading of the press in January and February 1971.) They culminated in a resolution passed on 7 February 1971 by nine OPEC members, including Venezuela but not Indonesia, providing for an embargo after two weeks if their demands were not met. The Iranian finance minister, chief of the producing nations' team, said: 'There is no question of negotiations or resuming negotiations. It's just the acceptance of our terms.' The companies were resigned to this, but wanted assurances that what they accepted would not be changed for five years.

The United States had been active in the meantime. Our Under Secretary of State arrived in Tehran 17 January 1971, publicly stating his government's interest in 'stable and predictable' prices, which in context meant higher prices. He told the Shah of Iran the damage that would be done to Europe and Japan if oil supplies were cut off. Perhaps this is why the Shah soon thereafter made the first threat of a cutoff of supply. It is hard to imagine a more effective incitement to extreme action than to hear that this will do one's opponents great damage.

Resistance to the OPEC demands would have shattered the nascent cartel. As late as 24 January 1971, the Shah told the press: 'If the oil producing countries suffer even the slightest defeat, it would be the death-knell for OPEC, and from then on the countries would no longer have the courage to get together.'

When the Tehran agreement was announced, another State Department special press conference hailed it, referring many times to 'stability' and 'durability.' They 'expected the previously turbulent international oil situation to calm down following the new agreements.' They must really have believed this! Otherwise they would not have claimed credit for Mr Irwin or for Secretary Rogers, or induced President Nixon's office to announce that he too was pleased. They must have said this in Paris in January and again at an OECD meeting in May. We now live with the consequences.

State Department representative James Akins told a senate committee in February 1972: 'The approach we made in the Persian Gulf [was] primarily because of the threat to cut off oil production ... We informed the countries that we were disturbed by their threats, and these were withdrawn very shortly after our trip.' The public record outlined above shows that the threats of embargo began after the Under Secretary's arrival, culminated in OPEC Resolution XXII.131 on 7 February 1971, and were never withdrawn.

Scraps of paper
The oil companies knew better than to take the 'agreements' seriously; they had been there before. To be sure, one could cite many a statement by an oil executive about the 'valuable assurances of stability,' but this was ritual. The London *Economist*, always in close touch with the industry, expected any agreements to last only a few months, given the 'persistent bad faith.' The best summary was made by *Petroleum Intelligence Weekly*: 'If such agreements were worth anything the present crisis wouldn't exist.'

This was borne out in August of 1971. Devaluation of the dollar, the occasion for new demands, was of course an incident in the worldwide price inflation to which the Tehran and Tripoli agreements had adjusted by providing for periodic escalation. Moreover, Persian Gulf revenues were mostly not payable in dollars. The new element in the situation was not the increased dollar cost of imports to the producing countries, but the fact that prices in dollars increased, especially in Germany and Japan. This was another windfall gain to the companies, just as in early 1970. Again the producing countries were able to take most of that gain in the consuming countries because the multinational companies were the producers of oil as well as sellers of refined products.

The 'oil companies had hailed the agreements as guaranteeing a semblance of stability in oil prices ... they would seek to pass on the impact of any new cost [tax] increase.' The new demands, said the chairman of Jersey Standard (Esso, now Exxon), were a violation of the Tehran agreements, but 'the industry will solve these problems just as our differences with them were reconciled earlier this year and before,' i.e. higher taxes and higher prices. This was precisely correct both as to substance and as to ritual. The OPEC governments made their demands. The companies made an offer. The governments refused it and broke off the talks. The companies made a better offer, taxes were raised again, and crude oil prices with them.

Even before this deal, the producing nations had already made an additional demand, for so-called 'participation.' The companies said they were distressed that the agreements 'have not led to the long peace ... that they had anticipated.' They would resist the demands as a violation of the agreements. Whereupon the governments 'announced that they would take part in a "combined action" if they didn't receive "satisfaction,"' and the companies agreed to negotiate. In March, the Aramco companies, which account for nearly all output in Saudi Arabia, conceded participation 'in principle.'

'Participation,' recently negotiated by companies and various host governments, is a misnomer. 'Pseudo-participation' would be more apt. 'Participation' does not mean that the government actually produces or sells oil, or transfers it downstream for refining and sale. As we shall see later, selling oil is what Saudi Arabia wisely aims to avoid. 'Participation' is simply an ingenious way of further increasing the tax per barrel without touching either posted prices or nominal tax rates, thus apparently respecting the Tehran agreements. Once the tax increase is decided, everything can be cut to fit. The same oil is still sold or transferred by the same companies. On the terms discussed early in 1972, 'participation' meant about 9 cents more tax per barrel.[10] Those who at the time believed that this assured supply, stable prices, and a solution to the balance of payments problem would have believed anything.

There has been unparalleled turbulence since the State Department special conference. Venezuela dispensed with the elaborate sophistry of 'agreements,' and legislated: an additional tax increase in 1971 and again in early 1972, with another expected in early 1973; nationalization of natural gas; the requirement that companies deposit increasing sums of money lest they permit properties to run down before the national take-over in 1984; and the extension of this 'reversion' to all facilities rather than only producing facilities. Confronted with declining production because it was cheaper for the companies to lift additional output from the Persian Gulf, Venezuela set minimum production rates, with fines for insufficient output.

In Libya, the government followed the Persian Gulf countries in demanding and getting an increase on the same pretext of monetary adjustment; and also in demanding participation, whether 'participation' or the real thing is not yet clear. In December 1971, when Iran seized two islands near the mouth of the Persian Gulf, Libya seized the properties of British Petroleum in 'retaliation'; any stick is good enough to beat a dog.

The Algerian government took two-thirds of the output of the French companies, who were 'compensated' with what little remained after deducting newly calculated taxes.

In Iraq, the operating Iraq Petroleum Company cut back output sharply during 1972 for the same reason as everywhere else in the Mediterranean (where the main field delivers via pipeline) – costs plus taxes were lower at the Persian Gulf, where capacity was being quickly and cheaply expanded. Iraq demanded that production be restored, and that IPC make a long-term commitment to expand output by 10 per cent per year. The IPC counter-offer not being acceptable, Iraq made headlines by seizing the Kirkuk field 1 June 1972, then offered forthwith to sell at 'reduced and competitive prices,' for spot delivery or long-term contracts. This threat was aimed at the most sensitive point of the world oil industry: the permanent potential oversupply which in Iraq (and other countries) had already been made actual. Price-cutting is intolerable in a cartel; to avoid it, a flurry of complex negotiations began. A loan was soon made by other Arab OPEC members. 'Behind the Arab nations' action ... lies an offer by Iraq to sell its newly nationalized oil at a cut rate, which would have driven down the revenues received by the other countries for their oil.' This may also explain the gentlemanlike behavior of the expropriated IPC, which did not attempt to blacklist Iraq oil to be sold in non-Communist markets.

Onward and upward with taxes and prices
The genie was out of the bottle. The OPEC nations had a great success with the threat of embargo. They appear to be having even more success with the actuality. The turbulence will continue as taxes and prices are raised again and again. The producing nations are sure of oil company cooperation and consuming-country nonresistance. This is a necessary condition. There are two purely economic reasons why the situation cannot be stable. As the detailed outline of events illustrates, the difficulties in the world petroleum market have been brewing for a long time and the stage in the current act of the crisis was set in 1970 and 1971. The Arab-Israeli war was merely a pretext which perhaps at most determined the form of the most recent turn of the screw.

The crude oil price can go much higher before it reaches the monopoly equilibrium or point of greatest profit.

The average price in Europe of a barrel of oil products in 1969-70 was about $13 per barrel. It is higher today. If the new tax rates were substantially increased at the Persian Gulf, a straight pass-through into product prices would be a much smaller percentage increase. It is doubtful that such an increase would have any noticeable effect on the absolute level of oil consumption. Moreover, about half of the European price consists of taxes levied by the various consuming-country governments. The producing nations have long insisted that in justice they *ought* to receive some or most of this amount. Be that as it may, most or all of this tax *can* be transferred from consuming to producing nations, with help from consuming country governments who dislike unpopularity through higher fuel prices. The Italian government collaborated early in 1971.[11]

The current price of oil, however far above the competitive level, is still much less than alternatives. The producing nations are not a whit displeased by big expensive projects to produce oil or gas from coal or shale or tar sands, which are a constant reminder of what a bargain crude is, even at higher prices. Particularly outside the United States, nuclear power sets a high ceiling, coal a much higher ceiling. The price of British coal has long and well served sellers of fuel oil in Britain, who priced at or slightly below coal-equivalent. Small wonder that the head of Shell appealed in October 1971 for the maintenance of a British coal industry.

There has therefore been much discussion, mostly oral, of the goal for the Persian Gulf nations being the US price; or $5 per barrel, etc. These are attainable goals, and we must therefore expect attempts to reach them.

The producing nations cannot fix prices without using the multinational companies. All price-fixing cartels must either control output or detect and prevent individual price reductions, which would erode the price down toward the competitive level. The OPEC tax system accomplishes this simply and efficiently. Every important OPEC nation publishes its taxes per barrel; they are a public record, impossible to falsify much. Outright suppression would be a confession of cheating. Once the taxes are set by concerted company-government action, the price floor of taxes-plus-cost is safe, and the floor can be jacked up from time to time, as in early 1971, or early 1972, or by 'participation.'

It is essential for the cartel that the oil companies continue as crude oil marketers, paying the excise tax before selling the crude or refining to sell it as products. Were the producing nations the sellers of crude, paying the companies in cash or oil for their services, the cartel would crumble. The floor to price would then be not the tax-plus-cost, but only bare cost. The producing nations would need to set and obey production quotas. Otherwise, they would inevitably chisel and bring prices down by selling incremental amounts at discount prices. Each seller nation would be forced to chisel to retain markets because it could no longer be

23

assured of the collaboration of all the other sellers. Every cartel has in time been destroyed by one, then some members, chiseling and cheating; without the instrument of the multinational companies and the cooperation of the consuming countries, OPEC would be an ordinary cartel. And national companies have always been and still are price cutters.[12]

Chiseling will accelerate if national companies go 'downstream' into refining and marketing. One can transfer oil to downstream subsidiaries or partners at high fob prices, but with fictitious low tanker rates or generous delivery credits. The producing nation can put up most of the money or take a minority participation, or lend at less than market interest rates. One can arrange buy-back deals, barter deals, and exchanges of crude in one part of the world for availability elsewhere. The world oil cartel in the 1930s was eroded by this kind of piecemeal competition, and so will the new cartel of the 1970s if the individual producing nations become the sellers of oil. The arrangement between Iran and Ashland Oil may be the first step in this long, slow process.

The Saudi Arabian petroleum minister, Sheik Yamani, who designed 'participation,' warned in 1968 against nationalizing the oil companies, and making them 'buyers and brokers' of crude oil. This would, he argued truly, lead to 'collapse' of oil prices and benefit only the consuming countries. The experts retained by OPEC also warned in 1971 that 'participation' must not interfere with marketing of the oil through the companies. More recently, in 1971, Sheik Yamani warned that 'participation' had to provide the right kind of 'marketing operations.' In 1972 he added: 'We are concerned that prices in world markets do not fall down.'

OPEC has come not to expel but to exploit. And if the excess crude oil supply were not permanent, Sheik Yamani would have no cause for the 'concern' he rightly feels.

We may therefore conclude: the producing countries can raise prices and revenues further by jacking up the excise tax floor, in concert. Conversely, if and when the consuming countries want to be rid of the cartel, they can take their companies out of crude oil marketing. To avoid taxation, they can decommission the tax collecting agents who are their own creation. But this is not a step which any single country can unilaterally accomplish.

So far, the consuming countries have gone in precisely the opposite direction. As they develop high cost substitutes, and strive to get their respective companies, public or 'private,' into crude oil production and marketing, they will rivet the tax collection agency more firmly on their necks. It is time to ask why they do this, and whether the policy may change.

One can only guess at the unstated reasons why the United States has put OPEC in the driver's seat. First, American companies have a large producing interest in the world market. In 1971, American companies produced about 6.5 billion barrels outside the United States. For every cent of increase in prices above that in tax, there is an additional $65 million in profit.[13] Second, the higher energy costs will now be imposed on competitors in world markets; and in petrochemicals, higher raw material costs as well. Third, the United States has a large domestic oil-producing industry. The less the difference between domestic and world prices, the less the tension between producing and consuming regions.

Fourth, the United States desired to appease the producing nations, buying popularity with someone else's money and trying to mitigate the tension caused by the Arab-Israel strife, which, however, is irrelevant to oil. If the Arab-Israeli dispute were settled tomorrow, the producing nations would not slow down for one minute their drive for ever higher prices and taxes. The acknowledged leader of the Persian Gulf nations in early 1971 was Iran, which has in one important respect – the Trans-Israel Pipe Line – actually cooperated with Israel more than the United States, which in 1957 and 1968 discouraged the pipeline.[14]

The potential for a changing American interest
First, security has been greatly impaired for all importing countries by the cohesion of the OPEC nations which made an embargo feasible.

Second, the balance of payments impact will soon become unfavorable to us, as it is to all other importers.[15]

The fact will slowly be recognized that nearly all of the oil deficit could be abolished by getting American companies out of crude oil marketing, to produce on contract for the producing countries, who could then compete the price way down. The companies' profits (and contribution to the balance of payments) would not be much less, and in the long run they might be greater, as the experience in Venezuela proves: the companies producing there are at or over the loss line.

Larger American imports will, if anything, tend to put the world price down. The process was seen on a small scale after 1966, when quotas on (heavy) residual fuel imports were lifted. Imports increased considerably, and the price decreased. Moreover, concern over air pollution was growing rapidly, and alarm was felt over possible loss of markets for residual fuel oil. Hence the Venezuelan government made agreements with Esso and Shell granting them lower taxes on production of low-sulfur fuel oil. This bit of history was too rapidly forgotten.[16]

The declining price of fuel oil in the face of greater demand would be inexplicable in a competitive market, but is to be expected when the price is far above cost. It is exactly what happened in Europe to embarrass coal. The hope of greater profits on increased sales, and the knowledge that large buyers have now an incentive to roam the market and look for every chance of a better deal, means that one must reduce the price before one's rivals tie up the good customers. As

American quotas are relaxed, refiners who have a crude deficit will become exactly the kind of large-scale buyer whom Sheik Yamani rightly fears.

The prospect of world prices rising because of large-scale American imports has alarmed Europe and Asia, and the United States government has gladly fanned those fears. But they have no basis in theory or experience.

May the reader excuse our saying again what needs to be said often: larger consumption only raises price in a competitive market, by raising marginal cost. In so awesomely noncompetitive a market, cost is not relevant because price is 10 to 20 times cost. Supply and demand have nothing to do with the world price of oil: only the strength of the cartel matters.

OTHER CONSUMING COUNTRIES

Consuming governments are staying in the same groove that served them badly between 1957 and 1970, and worse afterward. Prices had risen in the 1950s because the oil companies were able to act in concert without overt collusion: they responded to a signal from the United States. Prices then jumped for a time when the Suez Canal was cut. The reaction was fear of shortage. One heard in 1957 what one hears now – 'True, reserves are ample, but in 15 years, say by 1972, they will mostly be gone! We must guard against the shortage, obtain concessions of our own, protect domestic energy industries against future scarcity, etc.' Thereby the consuming countries committed themselves to high oil prices.

The consuming countries were all the more ready to fear these imaginary demons because they had invested heavily in coal. The decline in fuel oil prices after 1957 was greeted with disbelief and resentment. Prices of oil assumed in government energy plans and forecasts were always much higher than actual market. In 1962 (and 1964) the EEC energy experts made a long-term forecast of heavy fuel oil at $18 per metric ton, when it was about $13. They were bitterly denounced for so low a forecast. Yet even in mid-1972, fuel oil in Western Europe was only $14.50, i.e., in 1962 prices $10.75 per ton. Seldom has so costly a mistake been so long and stubbornly maintained. Nationalized industries – and others which could be influenced or pressured – were and still are reserved to coal. Worse yet, the artificial European coal prices became a cost standard for building nuclear power plants; in Great Britain they are wildly uneconomic.

The costly insistence on self-sufficiency was mostly uninformed fear of the multinational oil companies. The more the companies lost control of the market and competed down the price of fuel oil, losing profits thereby, the more resentment at their 'ruthless economic warfare.' As late as 1972, a British economist wrote of the oil company 'design' to drive out coal. Fear of the multinational

26

firms leads consuming countries not only to protect coal but to seek 'their own' oil through government-owned or sponsored companies. Thereby the consuming-country government acquires a vested interest in high oil prices. Low oil prices, or the possibility thereof, become not an opportunity but a scandal, to be ignored as far as possible.

The fear of shortage in the 1970s as in the 1950s leads to attempts to obtain oil concessions. It may make sense to run risks in new areas where governments will keep taxes low. There is much oil which is profitable to find and develop at today's prices, even at costs 25 times that in the Persian Gulf. A non-Japanese can hardly object when Japan proposes to spend some $3 billion in the near future to find and develop new oil resources. If spent in new areas it will certainly add to the wealth of the world, and, perhaps, not be a loss to Japan. But there is nothing gained in seeking new concessions in the old areas, or buying into old concessions. Such a policy does not add any resources. The price paid for concession shares will discount the profits, which may not continue long. Perhaps worst of all, in committing itself to take oil from 'its' concessions, the consuming country loses all independence in buying, and is exploited worse than it could ever be by the multinational companies.

The French experience
The policy of seeking 'independence' has been carried farthest in France. In 1962, agreements were reached with newly independent Algeria, inaugurating a 'new type' of relationship, free from the burden of colonialism, etc. (One hears similar language today in Japan.) In early 1971, M. Fontaine described in *Le Monde* the dreary succession of broken promises, seizures, spoliation, and the like. Yet no more than the French government could he or his newspaper bring themselves to discard the policy; there were supposed political advantages, such as lessening Soviet influence in the Western Mediterranean. The logical result was the two-thirds confiscation in 1972 of what they had fondly thought to be 'their own' oil.

The head of ERAP, the wholly state-owned French company (as distinguished from Compagnie Française des Pétroles, only 35 per cent state-owned), summed up 10 years' experience and loss of the Algerian oil as 'une opération blanche.' Had the funds been invested at a steady rate and drawn a 7 per cent return, private or social (hospitals, schools, highways, etc.), it would have been worth one-third more in 1972. But that is only a small part of the real social cost. There has been substantial French aid to the Algerian economy and French oil prices have been among the highest in Europe. But the French insist on rose-colored glasses. A break-even operation is viewed as economic. High oil prices are aid to Algeria, loading French industry with heavy costs and taxes that reduce its export capability, are viewed as a help to the balance of payments.

M.A. Adelman

Four months after Algeria was written off, Iraq approached France as soon as they seized the Kirkuk field from Iraq Petroleum Company. Their experience had taught them who was an easy mark. In 1961, they had seized the whole IPC concession outside of fields actually producing, but although the expropriated area included the great undeveloped North Rumaila field nobody leased it. Then in 1967, after the Six-Day War, France obtained a large concession in Iraq for ERAP, 'ratified with great pomp in Baghdad (and hailed throughout the Middle East) as a great victory over Anglo-American imperialism.' The usually sober *Le Monde* was thrilled. Someone was needed 'who would not flinch' when IPC 'showed their teeth,' someone 'capable of braving the anger of the members of IPC.' Because of France, the 'Anglo-Americans [lose] any chance of expansion into the hitherto-unexplored parts of the country.' They have been outmaneuvered; they cannot block France from 'a place in the untouched zones of Iraq without provoking a grave political crisis.' This is their just reward because 'on the morrow of the last war they would not let France into the game in this region.'

Having used North Rumaila as bait to take in the French, Iraq dangled it before others, then decided to develop the field itself, with Russian assistance. There was great annoyance in France, where doubt was expressed that Iraq was capable of developing the field. But in April 1972, shipments began in the presence of Mr Kosygin, exclaiming 'Arab oil to the Arabs!' By early 1971, ERAP had found three fields worth developing, whereupon Iraq demanded higher payments than in the contract. ERAP was willing to give more, but not as much as demanded, and negotiations dragged on. Predictably, the French blamed the deadlock on the machinations of IPC, trying to block their intrusion into what *Le Monde* called 'the private hunting preserve of the Anglo-Saxons.'

In June 1972, when Iraq seized the Kirkuk field and threatened price cutting, they 'preserved French interests in Iraq.' Surely, they told newsmen, the French ought to be no more scrupulous in Iraq than the Americans, who had offered to do business with Algeria after the confiscation of French interests there. France, said *Le Monde*, feared a rejection of the Iraq offer 'would harm its prestige in the Near East and would be taken as a break with Gaullist policy in the region'; while acceptance would allow France to 'serve as a bridge between the West and the left wing regimes of the Arab world, a role whereby she, alone, can hope to counterbalance the growing Soviet influence.' (Does the Gaullist policy help in oil matters, or does France accept higher oil costs in order to keep the policy going? One wishes for something intelligible.) A few days later came a Soviet-Iraq agreement on economic cooperation. This was no break in policy; the Baghdad regime had lifted its ban on Communist political activity, and accepted two Communists in the government. But, of course, the greater the Soviet influence, the greater the need to counterbalance it, hence the more concessions would be made to the Baghdad regime in oil affairs.

When the strong man of the Iraqi cabinet, Vice Premier Saddam Hussein, visited Paris in June, he had a resounding success. The agreement with France gave CFP (the French partner in IPC) 'une position privilégiée,' which comes to this: CFP is obliged to lift its full share of Iraq oil for 10 years under the same conditions as before the nationalization: exactly that long-term commitment which it rejected as too expensive when it was a partner in IPC. Small wonder that CFP did not want this 'position privilégiée.' 'The reason is simple – the price is too high ...'

France also acquired the 'right' to buy additional crude – which Iraq had just offered to all the world at reduced prices. But France will buy not at reduced but at 'commercial prices,' i.e. higher than charged any knowledgeable arm's length buyer who has alternatives. Finally, France will extend about $80 million of long-term credits to Iraq. This, and future credits and grants, is an unacknowledged addition to the price of the oil.

Thus the French have again been had, most royally, and by their own strenuous effort. How are we to understand this rigid determination that France have 'its own' oil, whereby France is humiliated and cheated?

Two elements of an explanation are worth suggesting, because they are not peculiar to France. One is the romantic political aura surrounding oil, which lets all manner of nonsense sound plausible. 'Whatever touches on oil is at once adorned with romance. No other raw material stirs the imagination like this one, nor the taste for flowery language,' wrote Edgar Faure in 1938. Another key is to be found in such phrases as 'oil-hungry France' or 'France assured of oil needs,' etc. Similarly, in discussing Japan, Professor Brzezinski speaks repeatedly of 'access to raw materials'[17] as being so self-evident and serious a problem that it need not be explained. Yet the only example of effective withholding, the oil embargo of 1973, can actually be viewed as a result of the scramble for access. To pay for 'access,' through higher prices or otherwise, but to be denied oil, makes no sense, no matter how one views the future:

1 The price of crude oil, set by a world monopoly, is many times more than enough to make it worthwhile to expand output. Therefore, even if price declines and especially if it rises, there will always be more crude oil available than can be sold, as there is now and has always been.

2 Assume the contrary: that oil is becoming increasingly scarce in physical terms, and that the price will reach $5, $10, or whatever. At this price, the market is cleared, and just as with a monopolized market, anyone who can pay the price gets all he wants.

3 There is real fear, exploited but not created by the US government, that mas-

sive American oil and gas imports will somehow preclude buyers from other countries, especially if the producing nations take the advice to limit output. Let us assume they do so. Then lower-cost and more profitable companies will outbid their rivals for the limited supply. Japanese iron and steel companies, for example, are obviously much lower-cost than their American rivals. If so, at exchange rates which overvalue the dollar, high oil prices would have harmed this country more than others. One solution has been to devalue the dollar.

4 One often-expressed fear is that the American multinational companies will divert supplies to American customers in preference to non-American. But if there is some constraint such that both groups cannot be fully supplied, then the price must rise. To imagine American companies deliberately holding down the price, in order to precipitate a shortage, in order to be able to discriminate, is fantasy. They would not wish to do it, and their masters the producing nations would not allow it.

5 The OPEC nations may wish to deny oil to some particular country. This would be a single country selective embargo different from the embargo of 1973 which involved a concerted shutdown with differential stringencies applied to, for example, the Americans and the Dutch. But if some or even most of them do so, the capacity of others will be available, and at most there will be a reshuffling of customers. Yet let us now assume that all OPEC nations unite to boycott one country. They must also prevent diversion of supplies of crude oil and products from other consuming countries to the victim. Yet nobody has suggested why the OPEC nations should join in this profitless persecution. Moreover, non-OPEC oil is plentiful relative to a single consuming country's needs.

6 Even if all the foregoing is incorrect, and 'access' is a real problem, it is useless to try to obtain access through a company owned by the consuming nation, since real power is in the producing nation.

The obsession with a false problem of 'access to oil' wastes time and distracts attention from the real problem of security of supply. The old or new multinational companies can do nothing good or bad for security because they have no control of supply, no power to cut off anybody or to protect them from cutoff. Nobody owns oil at the wellhead or underground reserves any more except the governments who have the physical force above ground.

A LOOK AHEAD

As evidenced by the events of 1973, oil supply is threatened by one and only one danger: a concerted shutdown by the OPEC nations. No single nation can do any harm. The rhetorical question 'Would you like to see Saudi Arabia supply one-third of the oil?' is only marginally relevant. The fewer the sellers and the larger their market shares, the easier for them to collaborate and act as one. The central question is their union or disunion. If a single large seller breaks away, or a few minor ones, the cartel breaks down in a stampede for the exit. The cartel is only needed, only exists, to thwart the basic condition of massive potential excess capacity – ability to expand output at costs below prices – and prevent it from becoming actual.

Hence lower prices and secure supply are the two sides of the same coin: absence of monopoly, or impotence of disunion.

The monopoly may still have its finest hours before it, and prices should rise well into the decade. The fewer the sellers the better, and there will presently be fewer Persian Gulf states. Most of them have too few men, and stuffing them full of money makes them worth occupying. A decade ago, Iraq claimed Kuwait, and was only stopped by the threat of force: the British presence, now gone. Iraq will be all the more ready to occupy Kuwait if Iran occupies the Kirkuk area, site of the great oil field just expropriated. The local people are not Arabs but Kurds, Indo-European in language and Sunnite Moslem in religion, like the Iranians. If they behaved themselves the Iranian army might be hailed as liberators from the chronic bloody struggle with the Baghdad regime. A new pipeline to the Mediterranean could go through Iran and Turkey.

The important consuming countries even now in 1974 show no sign of understanding their plight. The situation is the same as in mid-1972 when the conventional wisdom held that 'European nations are believed to be concerned that another stalemate [on "participation"] could impair vitally needed oil supplies ... The companies are under considerable pressure to reach an agreement.'[18]

Also, the large consumer countries have export interests which will benefit by the higher oil prices because of oil nations' greater purchasing power. Export industries often have disproportionate political power, even if the real economic benefit to the nation, i.e. higher incomes to labor and capital than from the next best alternatives, are piddling compared to the outflow on oil.

Europe is rapidly becoming an important oil producer. Some European countries will become small net importers, some will be large net oil sellers. The head of Norsk Hydro oil operations recently noted Norway's 'economic interest in high prices.' He recognized that the OPEC gains 'were forced through by threats of a boycott.' Instead of maundering about 'political stability,' he defined it: 'first and foremost a political system under which agreements and terms of licenses are respected even if the circumstances may have changed ... [and under which] everyone ... feels secure that supply will be maintained in all circumstances.' It was an indirect but devastating comment on American policy.

The less-developed nations will suffer the most, with no offsets. For example, India today consumes about 150 million barrels per year, and is expected to use

M.A. Adelman

TABLE 2
Approximate OPEC revenues, 1972

Area	Estimated 1972 output (Bb)*	Per-barrel revenues†	Total revenues ($ billions)
Persian Gulf	6.50	1.42	9.2
Libya, Algeria	1.20	2.14	2.6
Nigeria	0.63	1.85	1.2
Venezuela	1.10	1.61	1.8
Indonesia	0.37	1.50	0.5
Total			15.3

* Output assumed at same rate as first quarter 1972
† *Petroleum Intelligence Weekly:* Persian Gulf, 14 February 1972; Libya,
Algeria, 15 May 1972; Nigeria, 3 May 1971, and 3 July 1972; Venezuela,
27 December 1971; Indonesia, rough guess

about 345 in 1980. The burden of monopoly pricing is direct (paying higher prices for imports) and indirect (being forced to find and produce higher-cost domestic oil). It amounts to a substantial sum per year, and is increasing rapidly. Yet at the 1972 UNCTAD meeting there was no breath of criticism of the oil-producing nations. Solidarity prevailed: things were felt to be going well 'on the oil front,' and, said *Le Monde*, the same ought to happen on other fronts.

This favorable public attitude also holds in the developed countries. A private monopoly which extracted billions per year from consumers would be denounced and probably destroyed; were they American, some executives would be in jail. An intergovernmental monopoly 10 times as big is viewed as a bit of redress by the Third World.

Now one may approve this double standard, or deplore it, or laugh to keep from crying, but it is a truth with consequences: no important resistance seems likely in the near term. In time, attitudes may change.

1 The fictitious 'world energy crisis' will gradually fade as it did after 1957, and the slow growth of understanding of oil prices will resume. This influence is minor but not negligible.

2 In 1972, the transfer from consuming to the OPEC nations was about $15 billion (see Table 2). If the tax only doubles (and the price is therefore about $3.35) and if output increases by 8 per cent per year, then the 1980 transfer will be over $56 billion per year. This is a very conservative forecast as compared with those of the Departments of State or Commerce as cited earlier. It now may be too low.

32

3 Some of the billions will be spent in ways some consuming countries find irksome or dangerous. The large amounts paid to Libya have already cost the NATO nations additional payments to Malta, for which Mr Mintoff could not have bargained without Libyan help.

Payments to the producing nations will increase over the years 1973-80. If these nations spend, say, three-fourths on goods and services from abroad and save 25 per cent by buying foreign assets, the additions to their holdings will be enormous. The oil companies see themselves as the decently paid investment managers for this fund; as Schumpeter said, 'This is the way the bourgeois mind works, always will work, even in sight of the hangman's rope.'

4 There will be monetary disorders when large holders speculate against a particular currency. Unlike the oil market, where the producing countries must act in concert or accomplish nothing, even a single nation with big enough foreign balances can do substantial damage to the world monetary system, or try to bring down a government it dislikes.

5 Security of supply has been severely impaired by the Paris capitulation and the great success of the embargo. 'Concerted action' has become a reality.

Security of supply – limited but genuine – can be had by stockpiling, combined with detailed plans for severe rationing supplemented by high excise taxes, to reduce oil consumption and thereby increase the effective size of the stockpile. The expense will be heavy (but had the consuming countries done this years ago, they would have made large savings).

The larger the reserves piled up by the OPEC nations, the greater their power to withhold oil. Hence the higher the price, and the greater the insecurity, the easier for the OPEC nations to make it still more expensive and insecure. The consuming countries can have cheapness and security only by a clean break with the past: get the multinational oil companies out of crude oil marketing; let them remain as producers under contract and as buyers of crude to transport, refine, and sell as products. The real owners, the producing nations, must then assume the role of sellers and they should be assisted in competing the price of crude oil down. The Yamani prescription will be as sound then as in 1968, or 1971, or 1972.

It is a simple and elegant maneuver to destroy the cartel by removing an essential part – the multinational company as crude oil marketers fixing the price on a firm excise tax floor. But this would only minimize conflict and confrontation; it is too late to avoid them. The producing countries, like many raw troops, have been welded by success into a real force, and the huge sums they receive and accumulate will be both the incentive and the means to fight, by embargo, monetary disruption, or even local wars. There will be non-negligible damage. To have put the power and the motive into the producers' hands was light-minded folly by the American government.

Moreover, clean breaks with past policy are rare. The honest confession of error is less likely than anger at the cartel's local agents, the multinational companies, and attempts to restrict and penalize them. Yet this misconception is exactly what has led to past mistakes. Bypassing the companies to make direct deals with producing nations can be helpful only when the objective is clearly seen: to mobilize national buying power, encourage domestic oil buyers to avoid established channels, and help compete prices down. Usually such deals sacrifice all buying independence in a vain attempt to get a good 'connection,' or placate a producing nation, and only raise costs.

The greatest difficulty in following the Yamani formula is the need for the leading consuming countries to act together. For example, the United States tax law might recognize, either by statute or judicial decision, that the 'income' taxes paid to OPEC nations were really excise taxes, hence not deductible from US income tax. Higher taxes coupled with the unceasing demands of the OPEC countries might well push one or more of these companies past patience or profit, and they would withdraw to become contractors or buyers, helping to undermine the cartel.

Yet today other large consuming countries would scramble to get one of their companies into the empty slot, and promise anything to the producing nation. Hence it would be literally worse than useless for the United States to take the first steps, without firm assurances from at least France, Germany, Italy, and Japan, that they would not try to replace the American company. These countries are still obsessed with vain notions of getting 'access' or 'security' through their own companies, and the suggestion that they refrain from taking their 'just share,' and ending their long-resented 'exclusion' from 'the game,' seems an obvious attempt to help the American companies keep their predominance. It is an old sad story. If one looks for the 'real motives,' one will never hear what is being said.

CONCLUSIONS

A settlement of quarrels among Arabs or with Israel promises nothing for security of supply because there is no logical relation between the two issues. The threat brought huge profits, and promises even greater profits; nothing that might happen in Middle East politics provides the slightest reason to withdraw the threat and give up the present or future gains. The consuming countries have been meek and tame because, as pointed out earlier, they are pulled two ways on prices, but they are worried about the threat of short-run physical scarcity and scared by the possible need of physical rationing. This will drive them to stockpile, which is expensive; a desire to lessen the burden will make them consider counteraction. Progress in this direction will be slow, and the need to exclude the United States (and perhaps also Great Britain and the Netherlands) from their councils will make it even slower.

Second, as the producing nations get directly involved in the market as sellers, with real cost not tax-plus-cost as the price floor, consuming-country governments will find it tempting to deal directly with producing nations at discriminatory low prices. Some governments' producing ventures in nuclear energy, oil, gas, etc. may in time turn out so badly as to be past disguising, and they may move to the simple objective of minimizing the real and foreign-exchange cost of energy. If one large country or a few small ones did so during the remainder of the 1970s, it would dovetail with the effort of one or more producing countries to gain more output even at lower prices.

A lower world price would have only a transitory effect on the profits of American companies, who sell the greater part of world-market oil. Governments have taken nearly all the oil production profits (over and above the incompressible minimum return on investment); henceforth it will fluctuate irregularly. This return is subject to considerable margin for error, and will lead to disagreeable confrontations and perhaps some expulsions. Price reductions will come from governments' share, not from the companies'.

The predictions made these days about cheap energy gone for good, higher prices on the way, etc. will in my opinion be as right and as wrong in the 1970s as in the 1950s. Unless consuming-country governments sponsor an oil analogue to the international coffee agreement, we must expect an overabundance of oil outside the United States, and a declining market price – even though it will be declining from a very high level. Governments will resist this strongly, perhaps violently. With strong conflicting forces thus building up, and exerted more than ever through political bodies, the result becomes too unstable to predict.

The multinational companies will probably survive the crisis. Yet there is a real danger that they will be forced out of crude oil production. This would be a grievous waste of resources and could precipitate a genuine shortage of crude oil.

What happens to oil in the 1970s depends altogether on the consuming countries. If they are as slow to learn as they have been, then the projection of $55 billion annual tribute paid the OPEC nations by 1980 will be surpassed. But they may also learn that transferring those billions is not only dangerous but unnecessary. Their energy economics would need to be updated at least to 1952, when the Paley Commission explained that shortage means only cost; they might then see that the 'world energy shortage' is a myth, that crude oil continues in oversupply, as the Venezuelans, the Iraqis, and the Saudi Arabs have recognized. And the consuming nations' strategic thinking would need to be updated at least to 1914, when Winston Churchill, who was then a young fox, not an old lion, explained to the House of Commons that access to oil is only a special case of monopoly; the power to withhold is the power to overcharge.[19]

APPENDIX: FROM THE TIME MACHINE

[The following document was retrieved from a trip in a Time Machine. Unfortunately, the letterhead and date are missing, and there is no identification of the writer or addressee, but the text is almost completely legible. – The Author] [Editors' note: A version of this document originally appeared in M.A. Adelman's book, *The World Petroleum Market*. We have edited it slightly, but the principles it illustrates are unchanged, and changeless.]

As you are aware, the US Federal Energy Agency has tentatively authorized increased oil imports into that country if long-term contracts can be negotiated on terms that are favorable relative to the cost of alternative sources. This could mean an increase of 3 million barrels daily over and above the current rate. Our country and others have therefore been approached by a number of American refiners, who are actively seeking the best terms on which they could buy very large amounts of crude oil under long-term contracts. It is obviously an attractive prospect, but has raised a problem which calls for immediate decision.

The Alpha Petroleum Corporation of New York and Houston has put in a firm bid for half a million barrels daily, delivery to begin on a smaller scale but escalating up to that figure over 30 months. Our own contractor company has estimated that they would need to drill 50 new wells, half of them in sites already chosen, and the other half either by closer drilling or in some pools discovered earlier but not altogether delimited. No exploratory drilling is needed.

Since the comprehensive contract revision of [illegible – probably a date] whereby the concession was formally changed to a service contract, our contractor has been paid his operating expenses plus enough to return him 20 per cent per year on a discounted-cash-flow basis. We have had his estimates audited, and can confirm that the per-barrel payment which would be due him on this new project would be a relatively small fraction of the weighted average price of our oil now being delivered under existing long-term contracts. The cost estimates are uncertain within limits, depending on some drilling estimates which cannot be altogether precise, but there can be no doubt that at current price levels costs will be an even smaller fraction of revenues than past experience would indicate. At the current long-term contract price for the stated grade of oil, which has recently hit a new high in terms of dollars per barrel for new contracts, the net return to our national treasury would be hundreds of millions – perhaps a billion – of dollars per year.

The problem is that Alpha is offering a price per barrel that is slightly less than the prices that we know have been contained in recent contracts executed here and elsewhere. Alpha alleges that they have received an offer below the going price, for oil of admittedly slightly higher quality, from [illegible]. The ambassador of that country has denied any such offer, and so has their minister of Petroleum. Our problem is whom to believe. In our opinion, Alpha is telling the truth. Their reputation is excellent, while the minister in question has not been candid with us in the past – you are familiar with the matter – and we consider him hostile to our government and nation. They would like us to let the good bids pass by. As you know, his government still works with a form of the old participation system where the oil-producing company still sells the oil and pays taxes, instead of the more modern contract system in force here, where title to the oil remains in the nation at all times until final sale, and the contractor is paid for the service of development and production. The difference between the prices we know they are receiving and current tax rate in their country is such that their operating company's costs, reckoned on the same basis as ours, cannot possibly be low enough to account for the discount they are reported to be offering. There must be a price shading agreement between their government and the company; the government has agreed to take a lower tax rate on this sale, in order to permit the company to quote the lower price. This agrees with the account which we have obtained from our usual and hitherto reliable source, whom you know.

The Alpha bid would bring us somewhat less per year than what we would have at the current price. But in seeking the incremental revenue associated with getting the price we think we are entitled to – instead of Alpha's offer – we seem to be endangering the whole deal, since it is our judgment that Alpha will get the offer from others. The small price reduction does not endanger the revenues we receive under existing contracts. Furthermore, if we close the deal quickly, we may be able to persuade Alpha to increase the amount to as much as a million barrels daily, since we have made some rather careful estimates of the requirements of their European and Japanese subsidiaries, and of the pattern of their production, much of it from more expensive sources. We know that Alpha's incremental North American supply is from oil shale, tar sands and synthetic sources with costs about equal to the current world price (after freight netbacks), but our real competition for this contract is [illegible] and the discount we believe that they are offering.

We therefore recommend: that Alpha be asked to pay only five per cent per barrel below the going market price, and if they persist in demanding a ten per cent per barrel discount to match others' offers, we then propose that the contract be for 750,000 barrels daily, if need be over a longer buildup period than

M.A. Adelman

30 months. But if necessary, we should take the original terms of 500,000 daily at a ten per cent discount.

NOTES

Except as stated, this paper draws on M.A. Adelman's *The World Petroleum Market* (Baltimore: Johns Hopkins for Resources for the Future, 1972) and M.A. Adelman, 'Is the oil shortage real? Oil companies as OPEC tax-collectors,' *Foreign Policy*, no. 9, January 1973, pp. 76-114

1 Zenon S. Zannetos, *The Theory of Oil Tankship Rates* (Cambridge: MIT Press, 1966); and *The World Petroleum Market*, chap. IV

2 The Suez Canal is no longer relevant, since it cannot be used by ships over 60,000 tons. This would entail too high a cost even with the saving in time. It is unlikely that the canal will ever be deepened or widened enough to take VLCCs.

3 M.A. Adelman, 'Oil Production Costs in Four Areas,' *Proceedings of the Council on Economics of A.I.M.E. 1966* (New York, AIME, 1966)

4 The most recent comparison was for the end of 1961, when Persian Gulf oil-in-place was four times the proved reserves. P.D. Torrey, C.L. Moore, and G.H. Weber, in *Proceedings Sixth World Petroleum Congress*, Sec. VIII, Paper 9. At that time, there were 45 fields identified; by the end of 1969, 20 more fields were producing, though their reserves are unknown. *Oil & Gas Journal*, 29 December 1969. The estimates made above, of the potential for more reserves in known fields, would seem to be conservative.

5 My publications summarized are: 'Les Prix Pétroliers à Long Terme,' Revue de l'Institut Français du Pétrole, December 1963; (trans.) 'Oil Prices in the Long Run,' *Journal of Business of the University of Chicago*, April 1964. Price evolution: see chap. VI, Appendix of *The World Petroleum Market, Resources for the Future*, 1972. Supply cut-off: Government Intervention in the Price Mechanism. Hearings before the Subcommittee on Antitrust and Monopoly of the Committee on the Judiciary, p. 17. US Senate, 91st Congress. 1st Session, 1969.

6 Growth rates and price trends: *The World Petroleum Market*, chap. VIII; BP Statistical Review of the World Petroleum Industry; Petroleum Press Service, June 1972, p. 222. Quotation from Presentation to a meeting of financial analysts in Tokyo on Friday, 12 May 1972, by F.S. McFadzean, Managing Director of Shell.

7 M.A. Adelman, *The Present and Future State of the World Oil Industry* (Japanese translation) (Petroleum Association of Japan, 1965), pp. 11-33,

and WPM, chap. II; also National Petroleum Council US Energy Outlook, vol. I (1971), pp. 41-53

8 Tax is calculated as follows: output multiplied by posted prices equals fictional 'receipts.' Production costs are subtracted, and however calculated they are very small. The difference is the fictional 'profit,' which goes usually 55 per cent to the nation. Thus the tax per barrel is completely independent of actual receipts, and only very slightly affected by costs, hence almost completely independent of profits. Therefore it is an almost pure excise tax.

9 Neither the *New York Times* nor the *Wall Street Journal*, in their stories on the subject (14, 17, 19 January 1971) had any reference to any retaliation or concerted action on the proposal.

10 The concession company and host government need to determine four items: (a) The government owes the concessionaire a certain sum per year to cover the amortized cost of the equity share. (b) The government loses the taxes it formerly received on the share it now 'owns.' (c) The concessionaire owes the government the 'price' of the oil which the government owns, and which it now 'sells' to the company. (d) The concessionaire owes the government its prorata share of the year's profits of the operating company. The subject of the negotiation is by what amount (c + d) shall exceed (a + b). The 9 cent estimate is from Petroleum Press Service, April 1972, p. 118.

11 Dr M.S. Al-Mahdi, chief of the Economic Department of OPEC, in a paper partly summarized in Middle East Economic Survey, 14 July 1972, p. 11, estimates the 1970 Western Europe average consumer price as $13.14, of which 57.3 per cent was tax. See also: *Direction des Carburants: Rapport Annuel* 1969. Italian collaboration: *Petroleum Intelligence Weekly*, 24 May 1971.

12 *Petroleum Press Service*, February 1972, pp. 53 and 64, notes that Algeria and Libya have shaved prices to move product.

13 See *The World Petroleum Market*, chap. VIII, note 32, for the calculation

14 *Wall Street Journal*, 20 February 1957 (the State Department thought a pipeline through Iraq would be preferable) and Platt's *Oilgram News Service*, 22 April 1968

15 Secretary of Commerce Peterson, in the *New York Times*, 20 June 1972, p. 51, estimates the American balance of payments deficit on oil account as $26 billion a year in 1980 if imports are 4.38 billion barrels. This implies $5.94 per barrel delivered, hence probably about the same $5 per barrel fob at which State aims.

16 See *The World Petroleum Market*, chap. VII

17 Zbigniew Brzezinski, *The Fragile Blossom: Crisis and Change in Japan* (1972),

pp. 46-7, 71. In justice to Professor Brzezinski, one should note that he slides quickly from 'access' to 'price' which is the only real problem.

18 A.P. dispatch in *International Herald Tribune*, 19-20 August 1972
19 See J.E. Hartshorn, *Oil Companies and Governments* (1967 ed.), pp. 255-60

PART ONE

The Actors

The oil-producing countries of the Middle East and North Africa are clearly the key to any short-run solution to the energy crisis. First, by raising prices through taxes based on 'posted prices,' then by actually cutting supplies to countries friendly with Israel, these procedures have clearly indicated a desire to gather monopoly rents, either in pure dollars or in other ways, from their oil reserves.

Crandall details the reserves and production in each of the many countries which are commonly called the Middle East. Both reserves and production have been increasing rapidly until very recently. Between the first quarter of 1972 and 1973 output in Saudi Arabia, Iran, Abu Dhabi, and Dubai rose by amounts ranging from 23 to 67 per cent. The trend in total oil reserves and production is strikingly upwards, destroying the myth of long-term scarcity of energy.

The formation of OPEC is analyzed as is its minor role until 1970. The great success of OPEC since 1970 is laid squarely at the feet of the multinational oil companies who allowed themselves to be whipsawed into price increases. When the time came for the oil company cartel to hold together, there was little incentive for it to do so. Crandall explains why this happened. The concluding remarks suggest that the divergence of interests among Middle East and North African countries, the nationalization of companies in Libya, and suggested action on the part of consuming countries, largely the United States, will lead to *decreased* prices for oil in the long run.

This paper should be read together with the papers by Mabro, Pearson, and Steele, all in this volume, and by Erickson & Spann in the North American volume. It was written in mid-October 1973.

MAUREEN S. CRANDALL

Oil in the Middle East and North Africa

To most people in the oil-consuming countries, the phrase 'energy crisis' evokes dire images of gasoline rationing and of lack of residential and commercial power. But the phrase brings to mind as well a fear that the major petroleum producers of the Middle East and North Africa may well have the economic and political ability to deny all oil supplies at will to Western Europe, the United States, and Japan.

The United States consumes more than one-third of the free world's annual output of petroleum and is the largest importer of oil and oil products. In 1972 it imported more than 4.7 million barrels a day (mbd), or close to 30 per cent of its consumption of 15.9 mbd (a barrel contains 42 US gallons). Just under half these imports came in the form of crude oil, the rest as products. Currently most US imports come from Canada and from other Western Hemisphere sources, but 15 per cent of them originate in the Middle East and North Africa. Japan uses only 10 per cent of the world's energy, but it imports 85 per cent of its demand, and satisfies 62 per cent of this demand from Middle Eastern and North African sources. Europe is also dependent upon these sources for over 80 per cent of its petroleum needs.

The United States has long been and still is the world's largest producer of crude oil. At 9.5 mbd of crude oil in 1972 (and 1.7 mbd of natural gas liquids), its output exceeded that of Saudi Arabia, which has the free world's largest reserves and produced 5.7 mbd in 1972. Predictions for 1973 suggest, however, that US output will fall by over 2 per cent,[1] while Saudi Arabian production of crude oil will rise above 7 mbd, perhaps as high as 8 mbd. Within the next few years, Saudi Arabia is expected to replace the US as the world's largest petroleum-producing nation.

Clearly the demand for energy in the developing countries will continue to rise over the foreseeable future. As less developed countries continue to grow and industrialize, their energy needs, particularly their petroleum demands, will grow at a rate much faster than the annual percentage increases in the demand of the developed nations. All buyers have been actively looking for additional oil reserves outside the Middle East and North Africa, but those areas will continue to be the center of petroleum output and sales for some time to come.

The oil nations of the Persian Gulf and North Africa are a diverse group in terms of the relative size of their deposits, their populations, their political alignments, their religious affiliations, and their states of economic development. What they have in common is oil, and an interest in the most profitable exploitation of those oil resources. It is this latter commonality of interest which was the basis for the founding of the Organization of Petroleum Exporting Countries, generally known as OPEC (see section 3).

Members of OPEC in North Africa and the Middle East are Libya and Algeria – the major producing countries in North Africa – and the Persian Gulf states of Iran, Iraq, Kuwait, Saudi Arabia, Qatar, and Abu Dhabi.[2] Originally characterized as an intergovernmental organization which 'has essentially reacted to changes that have taken place ... [with] little role in bringing them about,'[3] the events of 1971 and thereafter have shown OPEC's ability to win additional per-barrel tax payments and other arrangements much more favorable to its members than had been imagined at its inception in 1960.

The question for the future is what will be the role and the power of OPEC members if the demands for petroleum by consuming nations continue to be directed toward output from this region. It is the view of this author that OPEC is indeed a powerful group, but as production continues to expand in the Middle East and North Africa, downward pressure may be put on price if the consuming countries, particularly the United States, urge the international oil companies to take a strong stance in future negotiations.

1 THE MARKET FOR OIL

United States demand for petroleum products and crude oil for 1973 is expected to be at least 6 per cent above the level of 1972, and so to reach 17.5 mbd, while domestic US output is projected at just over 11 mbd, of which 9.2 mbd will be crude oil.[4] Imports of both crude and refined products will make up the difference, with 1973 imports of crude oil rising from 1972 levels by 31.5 per cent to 2.9 mbd and imports of refined products up by 28.9 per cent to 3.2 mbd.[5]

While imports of refined products clearly cover a variety of goods from heavy fuel oils to gasolines, it should be noted that crude oils themselves are by no means homogeneous goods. Crude oils may be distinguished by weight as measured in degrees of gravity, according to the standard American Petroleum Institute (API) scale. This scale, used all over the world, is linked to the specific gravity of water, which is equal to 1. For example, a heavy oil with a specific gravity of 0.904 is defined as 25° API. In general, light oils are those with API degree gravities of approximately 34° (specific gravity of 0.855) or more, whereas heavy oils have API gravities near 30° (specific gravity of 0.876) or lower. Relatively heavy oils are characterized by a high sulfur content, whereas light oils are generally low in sulfur but high in wax components. If delivered prices of both types of oil were identical in the United States, light oils would be preferred, since many users must comply with air pollution regulations limiting the amount of sulfur content in crude oil. Although the wax component must also be removed from low-sulfur oil, this process is much less costly than the methods used to desulfurize heavy crude oil in order to meet the air standards.

Predictions suggest that the present 6 mbd level of imports of both crude oil and products could rise to 12 mbd by 1980 and to 17 mbd by 1985.[6] As recently as 1970, the US Cabinet Task Force[7] estimated total US demand for 1980 at 18.5 mbd; it is now thought that this demand will be reached by the end of 1973, and by 1980 demand will be close to 25 mbd. Currently the US is importing primarily from Canada and Venezuela (1.1 mbd), but 15 per cent of US imports come from the Middle East and North Africa (0.97 mbd).[8] By 1980 or 1985 it is expected that imports will be required to satisfy 50 per cent of total US demand and that as much as two-thirds of these may come from the Middle East and North Africa, with the remainder coming from the Western Hemisphere. If accurate, these forecasts mean that the US in 1980 may be demanding about 25 mbd with half coming from what it regards as 'unstable' supplying areas – the Persian Gulf and North Africa.

The gap between the rate of growth in demand and domestic supply in the future is expected to be even greater for Western Europe and Japan, for these areas contain very small petroleum deposits. Although the estimates concerning future annual growth rates in demand for petroleum until 1985 or later vary for both the US and other areas of the world, most are predicting an annual rate of change in demand of above 6 or 7 per cent in the next 15 years, dropping to around 6 per cent thereafter until the end of the century as alternative sources of energy, such as nuclear power, become more widespread.

North Africa and the Middle East contain the largest known world oil reserves, totalling over 405 billion barrels (Bb) or about 60 per cent of the world's proved

TABLE 1

Reserves and production of major petroleum-producing countries

Country	Reserves (1/1/73) (Bb)	Production mbd					Selected forecasts mbd		
		1968	1969	1970	1971	1972	1973	1975	1980
Abu Dhabi	20.8	.500	.600	.695	.935	1.05	1.3		3.0–5.0
Bahrain	.375				.075	.072			
Dubai	2.0				.125	.130			
Iran	65.0	2.850	3.375	3.845	4.565	5.050	<6.0	8.0	8.0–10.0
Iraq	29.0	1.510	1.525	1.565	1.700	1.455			5.0–7.0
Kuwait	64.9	2.420	2.575	2.735	2.925	3.000	3.0	3.0	3.0–5.0
Neutral Zone	16.0	.425	.450	.505	.545	.565			
Oman	5.0	.235	.330	.330	.285	.280			
Qatar	7.0	.340	.355	.370	.430	.485	.6		1.8
Saudi Arabia	138.0	2.830	2.995	3.550	4.500	5.735	7.3	10.0	15.0–20.0
Libya	30.4	2.600	3.110	3.320	2.765	2.210			
Algeria	47.0*	.915	.955	1.040	.780	1.110			
United States	36.8	9.095	9.240	9.635	9.465	9.450	9.252	12.0	12.0
Canada	10.2	1.195	1.310	1.475	1.585	1.835			

*Revised (government figure)

SOURCE: Oil and Gas Journal, 25 December 1972, for reserve figures; BP Statistical Review of the World Oil Industry, 1972 for each year's output with the exceptions of outputs for Bahrain and Dubai, which come from Oil and Gas Journal; Wall Street Journal, New York Times, and James E. Akins, 'The Oil Crisis: This Time the Wolf Is Here,' Foreign Affairs, April 1973, pp. 462–90, for selected forecasts of future output.

reserves.[9] By comparison, proved reserves for the us have been placed at just over 36.3 billion barrels, giving it less than 6 per cent of the world's total. Comparisons of reserves, output, and prospective output are shown in Table 1.

More remarkable than the size of current and expected daily output is the speed with which countries in the Gulf, as well as Algeria and Libya, have expanded output in the last five years – on average, about 12 per cent a year. Predictions for 1980 are particularly speculative in the smaller Gulf states where output in several of them is just beginning and geophysical and seismic exploration is going on.

Oil reserves in this part of the world as well as elsewhere are known to be finite (whether or not the reserves have been discovered), for extraction of oil depreciates the asset in place. As more and more oil is produced, the costs of lifting additional barrels must eventually rise. Yet the fact remains that both current cost estimates and those projected for 1980 or beyond indicate that per-barrel costs in this region are nearly constant and among the lowest in the world. Rising economic costs of extracting oil in the Middle East are by no means imminent.

Costs of production are calculated as exploratory, development, and operating costs. Any per-barrel figure used as an estimate will vary with, for example, the expected size of the field, the scale and volume of lifted oil, and the decline rate.[10] Estimates of per-barrel production costs have been made by Adelman,[11] who suggests that the total cost per barrel in the late 1960s ranged from about us $0.07 in Iran and Iraq to $0.28 in Algeria. Adelman estimates the long-run supply price per barrel from 1970 to 1985 as no more than $0.20 per barrel in the Persian Gulf, and $0.54 and $0.57 for Libya and Algeria respectively. Each of those latter prices includes, in turn, a $0.34 and $0.37 per-barrel freight advantage for shipment to Europe over prices for Persian Gulf sources, given the closure of the Suez Canal.[12]

Thus the resource costs of lifting this oil are believed to be very low, yet this oil sells at many times cost. In early September 1973, Libya announced a price of $6 per barrel for its oil, not including transport charges. Clearly the largest component of the delivered price to Western European or North American consumers is the assessment made on each barrel by the governments of the producing countries. Freight charges are not, of course, inconsequential to Western Hemisphere markets; estimates of per-barrel transport charges are currently around $0.80 to $1.00 from the Persian Gulf to east coast ports in North America.[13]

The easy answer to the question of rising oil prices is that demand must have grown much more rapidly than supply. But we are not now speaking of a competitive market in crude oil; rather we are examining the production of oil by a cartel of opec nations, under conditions where price has long been so far above real cost as to make analysis of supply and demand relations nearly meaningless.

We cannot know what would be the price of oil if the market were more fragmented and more competitive than it is at present, for current prices would be in part determined by expected future prices. In terms of short-run equilibrium conditions in a competitive market, the price of oil would not necessarily equal the average cost of extracting it, but would rather equal the cost of lifting one more incremental barrel. The costs of lifting oil today would always include any loss in future revenues (when discounted back to the present) from choosing to lift and sell that barrel now rather than later. Any competitive seller is a price taker, but the members of OPEC do not behave according to the economist's model of competition and as such are not price takers.

OPEC is indeed a cartel of governments of the producing countries, and rising prices of oil reflect its control of the market rather than increasing scarcity of oil output, for which there is no supporting evidence.[14] If the cartel is able to maintain its cohesiveness, there is still considerable room for it to raise price, since the market demand for oil is not highly price-sensitive (although each single buyer within that market will look for the cheapest source). As long as the foreign demand for energy is not very price-sensitive, the cartel may be able to raise tax rates per barrel without lowering the total tax yield; perhaps it can even raise it.

Oil taxes are basically excise taxes, although calculated in a somewhat roundabout manner, and are made up of both a royalty charge and an income percentage levy. The basis for per-barrel taxes are what are known as 'posted prices,' which now bear no connection to real or transaction prices, but are simple tax reference prices.[15] The lengthy and sometimes acrimonious bargaining sessions between governments and operating companies have occurred over the level and rate of change of posted prices. In effect, posted prices may be at any level; from this amount a royalty charge, normally 12.5 per cent, and real production costs are deducted.[16] The balance is assessed at whatever is the prevailing income tax rate, usually in the range of 5–60 per cent. By way of example, we may use the following prices:

Posted price per barrel	$3.50
less: royalty (0.125)	.48
less: cost	.10
Operating 'profit'	2.92
Income tax at 0.50	1.46
Total royalty plus income taxes payable to host government	$1.94

Using the figures above, an increase of $0.50 in the posted price would raise the total tax paid by $0.26.

2 TRENDS AND SUPPLY
IN THE MIDDLE EAST AND NORTH AFRICA

Oil is currently produced by many companies in many lands. Privately held and publicly owned firms, as well as firms subscribed to by both private and public interests, are all actively extracting and exploring for oil. By far the largest volumes of oil have historically come, however, from the operations of the eight integrated or major international oil companies: Exxon, Mobil, Shell, SoCal, Texaco, Gulf, British Petroleum (BP) and Compagnie Française de Pétroles (CFP) (see Table 2).[17] In recent years the state-owned or national oil companies of the countries in the Middle East and North Africa distribute all refined products in their own countries and are expanding their refining, offshore-loading, and petrochemical complexes.

Saudi Arabia is the largest producer of oil in the Middle East, and its planned future output and policies are of particular interest to western consumers. Reserves are conservatively estimated at 138 billion barrels, but some sources place them at 157 billion barrels, and even this figure may be low. Output for 1972 was over 28 per cent larger than the comparable figure for 1971, and over the five-year period 1967 to 1972 output rose on the average of 17.2 per cent annually.

Crude oil production for export has been the backbone of the Saudi economy and of the government's budget since commercial production began in 1938. The Arabian American Oil Company (Aramco)[18] is the primary concessionaire and produces nearly all of the crude shipped out of Saudi Arabia. The company plans to increase both production and exports in the future and has already let contracts for close to 280 miles of new pipelines to carry oil from inland fields to its leading installation at the refinery and port facility of Ras Tanura on the Persian Gulf.[19] Ras Tanura is one of the world's largest crude-exporting facilities, handling more than 1.4 billion barrels in 1971.[20]

Saudi Arabian output is synonymous with Aramco production, and for years the Ghawar field in the south has been the largest producer (at over 2.7 mbd in early 1973).[21] Additional large onshore fields are the Abqaiq, Damman, and Khurais fields. In 1971, two other producing fields were discovered near Khurais, which may signal a major extension in the size of that field. To the north just below the border of the Neutral Zone is Sofaniya, the world's largest offshore field. Below Sofaniya is, among others, the Berri field, with both onshore and offshore

49

TABLE 2

Production of major companies by countries, 1972[1]
(thousand barrels per day)

	Exxon	Mobil	SoCal	Texaco	BP	Gulf	Shell	CFP	Others	Total
Iran	326	326	326	326	1867	326	653	279	617	5050
Iraq[2]	173	173			346		346	346	73	1455
Qatar	32	32			63		283	63	13	485
Abu Dhabi	83	83			400		168	283	36	1050
Kuwait					1500	1500				3000
Saudi Arabia[3]	1742	581	1742	1742						5807
Oman							238		42	280
Neutral Zone									565	565
Libya[4]	354	162	234		188				1275	2215
Algeria								255	855	1110

1 These figures are estimated by means of applying to each country's 1972 output (from *BP Statistical Review of the World Oil Industry*) the percentages of output each company lifted in each country in the first half of 1969. These extrapolations are based on Adelman's *The World Petroleum Market*, p. 80.

2 Estimates are for company output in the year 1972, but the actual figures might conceivably differ because of the Iraqi Petroleum Company's dispute with Iraq, settled only at mid-year 1972.

3 Including Bahrain

4 Because of Libya's expropriation of BP at the end of 1971, the figures reported for BP is Bunker Hunt's 50 per cent share of Sarir output. Texaco and SoCal operate in Libya jointly as Amoseas.

5 By the end of 1971, the state company, Sonatrach, controlled 77 per cent of Algerian output (see EIU, QER, *Algeria, Annual Supplement, 1972*, p. 9). The remaining 23 per cent may be attributed mainly to CFP and Getty.

deposits, which began production in 1970. Berri's expanded output will be carried to Ras Tanura by a new pipeline by the end of 1973. Several other fields discovered since 1967 are not yet in production.

While most of the oil-producing nations are primarily concerned with exporting crude oil, their governments are now encouraging the building of refinery and petrochemical facilities. This is as true in Saudi Arabia as elsewhere, with the complex at Ras Tanura exporting nearly 0.495 mbd of products, but these are still small compared with the 3.425 mbd of crude exports.[22] The complex contains as well a liquefied petroleum gas (LPG) plant, producing butane, propane, and natural gasoline.

The state-owned oil company of Saudi Arabia known as Petromin[23] has not been a producer of oil, but has entered into a number of joint-venture contracts as well as having acquired a 'participation' share in Aramco's operations.[24] Much of the seismic and geophysical work that the company has conducted recently has been in central and western Arabia along the Red Sea, covering both new areas and areas previously given up by Aramco. Petromin has a steel rolling mill, majority interests in drilling and survey companies and in refinery and fertilizer companies, where the latter produce anhydrous ammonia, urea, and sulfur.[25] Most of the Petromin's installations are at Jidda, the commercial capital of Saudi Arabia. Petromin's plans for the future include direct marketing of both crude oil and crude products internationally through its participation share of Aramco, as well as petrochemicals, desulfurization and recovery plants, and tankship operations.[26]

Adjacent to Saudi Arabia is Kuwait with oil reserves estimated at between 66 and 78 billion barrels. Saudi Arabia and Kuwait each have a one-half share of output from the Neutral Zone.[27] Recently there has been some doubt concerning the extent of Kuwait's reserves, and the country has engaged a US firm to make a new survey and estimate.[28] With commercial production begun in 1946, the country is well aware, regardless of the size of reserves, that the oil will not last forever and that the nation should be making contingency plans for that time.[29] It has already limited output to 3 mbd in an attempt to prolong the time of oil offtake.

The Kuwait Oil Company (KOC)[30] is the main producer and lifts the majority of its crude from the famous and rich Burgan field. Close by the Burgan field are two other producing fields, Magwa and Ahmadi. No new fields have been discovered in Kuwait in the last year, but production is also coming from the 1960s discoveries in northern Kuwait and in the area west of Burgan. Lengthy pipelines bring onshore oil to the export terminal at Mina al-Ahmadi, where, as at Ras Tanura, sea island offshore-loading facilities exist.[31]

51

The associated gas found with oil in Kuwait is used in large quantities for maintaining reservoir pressure, but much more is used for industrial purposes in Kuwait than in Saudi Arabia, where much of it is flared. Gas runs KOC's power plant in the Ahmadi complex of seawater distillation plant and refinery. Gas plants elsewhere process gas for condensates and LPGs.

The Kuwait National Petroleum Company (KNPC) is state-owned and like Petromin, is primarily a refiner and marketer of products locally. At home it runs a refinery of 0.150 mbd capacity and has interests in companies dealing in aviation fuel, petrochemicals, and chemical fertilizers. Abroad it has an interest in a Rhodesian refinery, and has set up marketing arms in Europe and the Far East. Recently it struck oil offshore, and this oil is to be produced commercially by joint venture with the Spanish company, Hispanoil. Back in 1967, terms for the joint venture provided that in the event of discovery, up to 25 per cent of Spain's import requirements would be reserved for oil from this source.

The national company's offshore operations have been hampered by continued border disputes with Iraq, disputes which have not been limited to water areas only. Iraq claims Kuwait islands near the head of the Gulf, and these disputes may be the basis for Kuwait's refusal of an Iraqi request for a loan at the end of 1972, which was later granted only as part of a deal for Iraqi cement. In recent years Kuwait's large oil revenues have permitted it to support generously other Arab governments, in amounts averaging $150 million annually since the Six-Day War with Israel in 1967.[32]

The area of the Neutral Zone, the peninsula of Qatar, and the island of Bahrain, are squeezed between Saudi Arabia and Kuwait along the west coast of the Gulf. The Arabian Oil Company (AOC), held by Japanese firms, is the main offshore producer in the Neutral Zone. AOC operates gas-oil separation plants and a refinery largely to provide for its own needs. Recently AOC announced plans for expansion of its offshore areas as well as plans to ship to the Caribbean. It is also considering exporting LNGs (liquefied natural gases) to Japan. Onshore interests of the Neutral Zone are held by Aminoil for Kuwait and by Getty for Saudi Arabia; output of both crude and products are shipped from terminals in both countries.

The reserves of both Qatar and Bahrain are not large and results from exploration have been disappointing. Recently, however, a Japanese group, as well as Shell, has discovered oil offshore from Qatar, which is expected to flow at over 0.200 mbd for the former, and at 0.120 mbd for the latter.[33] The national petroleum company in Qatar handles all local marketing and distribution of products, has built a small refinery, and plans a petrochemical complex. Bahrain output originates largely on land, with offshore acreage not productive. Large quantities of Aramco crude, however, are piped to Bahrain's 0.300 mbd refinery, and products are exported from the Sitra terminal. Natural gas is used for pressure injection and power generation to both the government and to new aluminum and desalination plants.[34]

At the head of the Gulf is Iraq, whose ill-concealed expansionist aims may in part be due to its forty miles of marshy coastline which do not permit the construction of modern terminal and offshore loading facilities. On 20 March 1973, Iraq seized the Kuwaiti islands now in dispute, allegedly as a means of forcing Kuwait to cede them to Iraq, for Iraq needs deepwater facilities beyond the size of those at the existing artificial island of Khor al-Amaya.[35] The land in the border area of the Shatt el-Arab estuary is in dispute with Iran.

Iraq's output actually declined from 1971 to 1972 by close to 20 per cent, dropping below the level of production in 1968–1970. While producers in all other countries were expanding their output, Iraq's behavior can only be explained by the lengthy dispute between the Iraqi government and the Iraq Petroleum Company (IPC), [36] culminating in the Iraqi government's seizure of the great Kirkuk field and two other northern fields in June 1972. Prior to seizure, IPC produced 99 per cent of all Iraqi crude. This dispute has a long history going back to 1960, when IPC refused to recognize Public Law 80 requiring it to confine its operations to the fields producing at that time. In effect, this law relieved IPC of more than 99 per cent of its original concession and especially of the large North Rumaila field. After the seizure in 1972, IPC recognized the law and moved to the southern Rumaila field areas of its Basrah Petroleum Company affiliate. It is predicted that production there can more than make up for lost output in the north, and that this output will be at extremely low cost.[37] Output from these southern areas reaches markets through the loading facilities of Khor al-Amaya.

The Iraq National Petroleum Company (INOC) now operates alone or with others in the North Rumaila field, shipping oil through the former IPC pipeline to Tripoli in Lebanon for export. As compensation for the nationalization, Iraq pays IPC in crude oil, but is also collecting past taxes and royalties.[38] The government has relieved another former IPC affiliate, Mosul Petroleum Company, of its concession and no compensation has been offered. If the IPC dispute is now finally settled, total output from Iraq can be expected to rise sharply, to as much as 5 or 7 mbd by 1975 to 1980.

The national oil company (INOC) has used the services of both French and Hungarian crews for seismic surveys and exploratory drilling. In recent years private exploratory activities had effectively reached a standstill because of the disagreement between IPC and the government. An Italian group is studying the possibilities for another pipeline to the Mediterranean through Turkey.

53

Maureen S. Crandall

INOC subsidiaries operate five small refineries and plan a sixth and larger one. Sulfur recovery and gas (from the Kirkuk fields) plants are also operating. Plans are being made for expanded facilities at Basrah to include production of fertilizer, ammonia, sulfuric acid, and various other products.[39] INOC has signed contracts for oil purchases with Yugoslavia, Morocco, Spain, Turkey, and France. The contract with France followed Iraq's seizure of the Kirkuk field. The terms now require CFP to lift as much oil volume for the next ten years as its percentage ownership in IPC before the nationalization. After the Kirkuk seizure, Iraq had threatened to sell expanded output to the world at lower prices, but now CFP had agreed to buy at higher prices in the future. In addition, the agreement calls for France to extend long-term aid to Iraq. Iraq has also signed technical and financial agreements with Russia to develop the North Rumaila field.

Iran is the second largest producer of petroleum in the Gulf area and the only non-Arab producer of the littoral oil states. Commercial production began in 1912, and Iran has increased production and exports rapidly in recent years, oil revenues being the foundation of the Shah's development plans. Oil output virtually halted, however, from 1951 to 1954 following the National Iranian Oil Company's (NIOC) nationalization of what is now BP. A new consortium of companies formed in 1954, made up of American firms and CFP, now produces 92 per cent of Iranian output. About 85 per cent of total output is exported, both by consortium members and by NIOC, with the remainder generally going to the refineries at Abadan on the Shatt el-Arab and at Teheran.[40] Iran's facilities at the Kharg Island export terminal and its refinery complex at Abadan with crude capacity of 0.430 mbd (together with catalytic reformers and cracking processing plants) are among the largest in the world.

Iranian fields produce both light and heavy oils. Associated gases are being processed, both as dry gas and as LPGs, and exported. A natural gas pipeline to Russia was completed in 1970. NIOC remains, however, a producer of not more than 1 per cent of Iranian crude oil, and has been primarily engaged in the marketing and distribution of products. It and its subsidiaries have engaged in numerous joint ventures, but few have struck oil in commercial quantities. NIOC supplies products to Afghanistan, crude to India, LNGs to Japan, and sells petrochemicals abroad from the complex at Abadan. Joint petrochemical ventures are now being planned with both US and Japanese firms. In July 1973, NIOC concluded an agreement with Ashland Oil of the US which guarantees Ashland long-term oil supplies in return for interest in Ashland's refinery and marketing operations in the US and in September 1973 NIOC's subsidiary, National Iranian Gas, and Transco Energy Company of the US, signed a 22-year agreement to produce

54

and export natural gas to the eastern US.[41] NIOC and Belgium have also agreed on a marketing company, and French and Philippine refineries are proposed, as well as an additional refinery at home at Tabriz.

Across the entrance to the Gulf, called the Strait of Hormuz, lie the Union of Arab Emirates, of whom Abu Dhabi and Dubai are the primary oil producers.[42] Commercial production began in Abu Dhabi in 1962, and in Dubai in 1969. Most Abu Dhabi production originates offshore, but onshore concessions are actively sought by European, American, and Japanese consortia. The government's Abu Dhabi National Petroleum Company (ADNPC) participates with both the onshore and offshore private producing companies, and in February 1973 sold to Japan almost all of its expected crude participation share of oil over the next eight years (730 million barrels). In December 1972 Japan purchased a 45 per cent interest from BP in the Abu Dhabi Marine Areas offshore company for $780 million.[43] An additional onshore field is expected to begin production in 1974, with output of 0.450 mbd, while reservoir pressure maintenance is being used in the offshore areas so as to increase output there to 0.800 mbd by 1975 and 1.25 mbd or more by 1980.[44] Projects for storage tanks, increased drilling facilities, and LNG exports are currently under way.

1970 was the first full year of production from Dubai, and output is rising rapidly from two offshore fields. Extension and further exploration are planned for 1973 and 1974. Dubai's prosperity in the past has been due less to oil development and revenues than to its having been a large trading and gold smuggling center for illegal gold imports into Pakistan and India. Prosperity from future oil revenues is now expected to play a greater role than in the past.

The remaining sheikhdoms of the Union have little oil and many of their concessionaires have relinquished their areas. Boundary definitions are still at issue in many cases and this makes the award of concessions difficult. Iran seized Abu Musa and two other islands claimed by Sharjah in the Strait of Hormuz just prior to the British departure; Occidental held a concession from Sharjah in the area and a moratorium on its drilling activities was imposed. This dispute was settled with a treaty involving joint management of the island and its revenues. Most recently a major new oil field, Mubarek, nine miles off the island of Abu Musa, has been discovered.[45]

Adjacent to the Union of Arab Emirates lies Oman which began petroleum production in 1969. Its output has grown at a rapid rate since that time, and active offshore exploratory drilling by a Sun Oil consortium is now under way. Oman's future is somewhat clouded by the rebellion in the southern province of Dhofar (1972 oil production fell below that of 1971).

Libya and Algeria are both now major North African producers of petroleum, although Libya only began production in 1961. For political reasons, most of Libya's operating companies producing both crude oil and oil products have been nationalized or will soon have granted the government participatory shares of 51 per cent. Libyan output is distinct from Persian Gulf output in that it is primarily a low-sulfur light oil of approximately 40°. The Libyan National Company, LINOCO, is a producer of crude from the Umm Farud field. Output from all fields has been restricted in recent years in order to force the companies to agree to higher posted prices. Given the political climate, drilling fell off substantially until the government required by edict that oil companies set aside a certain percentage of profits for exploration. Here as elsewhere the national company is primarily engaged in marketing and industrializing; it entered an agreement with Occidental in 1970 to build a methanol plant as part of a petrochemical installation at Benghazi on the Mediterranean coast. Japanese firms are interested in obtaining exploration rights from the government, but so far no agreements have been reached. The majority of Libya's crude goes to Western Europe.

Algerian oil is also light and relatively sulfur-free. After prolonged disagreement with the French operating companies and falling output, the national company Sonatrach[46] emerged after the nationalization measures of 1971 as the country's main producing company and now controls over three-quarters of crude output. Other producers are CFP and ERAP[47] as well as Getty Oil. Sonatrach's pipelines carry both oil and natural gas to the ports of Algiers and Skikda. Current estimates of natural gas supplies give Algeria one-tenth of the world's reserves. Algerian gas is 'non-associated' (with oil production or wet gas). Pipelines bring the gas over 300 miles to liquefaction plants now operating at Arzew and Skikda, and more pipelines are planned. The biggest gas export plans, if approved by both Algeria and the US, call for El Paso Gas to buy 20 billion cubic meters per year of LNG beginning in 1975 for a period of 25 years.

With the Algerian nationalization measures of 1971 and subsequent withdrawal of French oil interests, many people were doubtful that Sonatrach would have the marketing outlets for its oil and gas supplies, but it has been selling oil to American independents and to West Germany, and arranging gas contracts with Spain and with Eascogas of the United States.[48] Sonatrach and the state oil company of Brazil, Petrobras, are now jointly engaged in exploration and development projects, and other oil companies are negotiating similar contracts.

Exploration by Sonatrach has largely taken the form of seismic and geophysical surveys. While the company has made some discoveries of oil, only part of the results have been disclosed: two new fields tested at only 0.003 mbd.[49] With Soviet assistance, Sonatrach is studying the feasibility of a water injection program, the Russians having estimated that such injection could raise output substantially.

3 OPEC AS A POLITICAL FORCE:
PAST AND PRESENT

The Organization of Petroleum Exporting Countries is now a major political and economic force in the international petroleum market. It has always been so since its formation in 1960, but only in recent years have the member governments been able to act together as a cartel and successfully raise tax revenues to each participant.

In September 1960 Iran, Iraq, Kuwait, Saudi Arabia, and Venezuela joined to form OPEC in protest against the reduction in posted prices initiated by Esso and BP and thus the concomitant decline in the tax income to these countries. OPEC's responsibility was to prevent such reductions from happening again, and to raise or at least stabilize government revenues from petroleum production. By 1973 OPEC had grown substantially, and included Qatar, Algeria, Libya, Egypt, Nigeria, Indonesia, and Abu Dhabi. Recently, OPEC representatives have secured very favorable agreements on both posted prices and participation plans from companies operating within their borders.

OPEC accomplished very little during its first two years. Its secretary instructed that all member countries be paid taxes and royalties calculated on posted prices prevailing before August 1960, but to no avail. With the surplus in world oil production at this time, market prices were below posted prices, and no producing company chose to volunteer higher tax payments to governments.

During the period 1962 to 1965, protracted discussions between OPEC and the companies were held concerning royalties and market allowances. On these issues OPEC was ultimately successful, but failed once more in its attempt to raise posted prices. Discounts from posted prices for marketing expenses of crude oil were eliminated. Uniform per-barrel royalty rates of 12.5 per cent were agreed upon, and such royalties were deducted as costs before the assessment of income taxes (usually 50 per cent). Prior to this time companies credited their royalty payments against their income tax liability. The new arrangement resulted, of course, in more tax income to member governments.

By 1968 OPEC and operating companies had agreed to eliminate by 1975 all discounts from posted prices based on gravity. This elimination again raised the income tax payable to member governments by as much as $0.07 per barrel.[50] More importantly, the June 1968 meeting of OPEC resulted in the adoption of a resolution which voiced the rights of governments to participate in ownership and to change the terms of existing concessions or contracts under a new doctrine of 'changing circumstances.'

One may trace the origins of the change in power in OPEC to the separate pact between the government of Libya and its concessionaires in the middle 1960s.

Maureen S. Crandall

The agreements in Libya during the fifties had linked tax payments to realized rather than posted prices, and had permitted depletion allowances which were not present in contracts at the Gulf. In 1961, Libyan taxes were linked to posted prices, and the depletion allowances were abolished. Under threat of 'compulsory legislation,' Libyan companies agreed in 1965 to additional terms including higher per-barrel taxes. While the 1965 decree was never cited during the negotiations in 1970 and 1971, it contained provisions for limiting or prohibiting both the export and the production of oil. Libya has since used these terms on several occasions, without citing them, over the last three years.

By 1970 under the leadership of Libya, OPEC began playing for higher stakes. The Libyan military and nationalist regime of Colonel Muammar Qaddafi had overthrown the monarchy in the fall of 1969. Suez was still closed after the Six-Day War with Israel, the tanker market was in disarray, the pipeline from Arabia to the Mediterranean was cut in Syria, and Libyan light crude with its low sulfur content was becoming more desirable in pollution-conscious West Germany, Italy, and the United States.

At the beginning of 1970 Libya began negotiations for increased posted prices from its operating companies. With no progress in six months, the Revolutionary Command Council ordered all twenty operating companies in June to cut back daily output in order to force them to accept higher prices and thus taxes. Occidental Petroleum was particularly singled out and forced to reduce output by more than 50 per cent. By September 1970, agreement was reached, first with Occidental, for higher posted prices and income tax rates up to 55 per cent from 50 per cent. Occidental was allowed to increase output to 0.700 mbd again and to attempt to meet its earlier sales obligations. It is argued that Libya knew its concessionaires were particularly vulnerable to output restrictions, since most of them were independents like Occidental, without substantial alternative sources of crude when their Libyan operations were restricted. Had other companies operating elsewhere provided Occidental with crude oil at that time, neither Libya nor other OPEC countries might have secured higher posted prices.

In response to Libyan successes, 'leap-frogging' began as the countries of the Persian Gulf began demanding similar increases in both posted prices and income tax rates. When others achieved settlements similar to those in Libya, Libya reopened negotiations demanding more, only to find the Gulf countries imitating these demands a second time. The final settlements in 1971, known as the Teheran-Tripoli agreements, were to run to 1975 and provided for higher posted prices in all producing countries, an annual increment to offset inflation, and a freight premium for Libya due to its location west of Suez.

Algeria, however, was not party to these bargaining rounds, being in bitter dispute with France over similar questions. Algeria was then trying for posted prices

58

even higher than those in Libya, and when negotiations finally broke down in February 1971, Algeria seized 51 per cent of the French companies ERAP and CFP. Then the terms of the dispute changed to the amount of compensation to be offered. Less than two weeks after the signing of the Teheran-Tripoli agreements, the Algerian government raised the posted prices for Algerian oil to the level agreed at the Tripoli meeting.

With Gulf-posted prices at $2.23 per barrel at that time, the Teheran-Tripoli agreements were believed to have raised per-barrel payments at the Gulf from $0.86 in 1970 to $1.24 in 1971, with provision for rises in payments to $1.50 by 1975 had no dollar devaluations occurred. Posted prices in Algeria were set at $3.60 and in Libya at $3.45, with per-barrel tax payments in both countries estimated at between $1.70 and $1.80.[51]

But after the first of the two dollar devaluations in August 1971, OPEC reopened the Teheran-Tripoli agreements, citing the doctrine of changing circumstances. In January 1972 posted prices rose by 8.49 per cent, equivalent to the decline in the value of the dollar. In April 1973 posted prices in the Gulf varied between $2.50 and $2.80 per barrel depending on gravity; in Libya and Algeria at that time they were above $4.00.[52] The agreement reached at the end of May to reflect the devaluation of February 1973 raised posted prices over 11 per cent and linked them to an index of exchange rates of eleven major countries. Each month these rates are to be examined, and posted prices will be readjusted if the index moves by more than 1 per cent in either an upward or downward direction.[53]

Before OPEC had gained the rewards of Teheran-Tripoli, Saudi Arabia, Libya, and Kuwait formed the Organization of Arab Petroleum Exporting Countries (OAPEC) in 1968. Since that time Iraq, Syria, Egypt, Qater, Bahrain, Abu Dhabi and Algeria have joined (Dubai joined but later withdrew when OPEC decided to build drydock facilities at Bahrain rather than at Dubai).[54] OAPEC's goal is to achieve even closer cooperation on oil policy than can be done through OPEC, provided OAPEC's policies do not conflict with those of OPEC. OAPEC's achievements are few, and it rests in the shadow of OPEC. Most recently, however, OAPEC formed the Arab Maritime Company for Oil Transport (AMCOT), with headquarters in Kuwait, whose goal is to pay Arabs rather than others to carry Arab oil.

On 1 January 1973, the first of OPEC's new 'participation' agreements went into effect. Member government 'participation' means partial ownership of private companies. Each agreement must specify how the participation share is to be purchased and at what price by the government, the government's profits on operations, and the price at which the government may sell its oil back to the operating company. The producing government will gain income only if the new terms are more profitable than the tax receipts based on the share the government now owns.

Saudi Arabia's oil minister, Sheikh Ahmad Zaki Yamani, was instrumental in negotiating participation agreements in Saudi Arabia and for other countries in the Gulf. So far, such agreements are in effect in Saudi Arabia, Kuwait, Abu Dhabi, and Qatar; Iraq is expected to arrange similar terms. While the companies did not receive full compensation for their loss of production rights, compensation has been promised on the basis of updated rather than net book value. The current arrangements provide for national ownership of 25 per cent of oil and gas production and associated facilities, but not of refineries or of transportation equipment. After 1 January 1978 the ownership share is to rise (provided the governments have paid for the initial share) to 25 per cent in 1979, 40 per cent in 1980, 45 per cent in 1981, and 51 per cent in 1982.[55] Governments will share in all decisions and expenses. In the early period the companies will buy back oil from the government (called bridging) to meet their previous sales commitments; it is these negotiated prices which are more favorable to the governments currently than their previous tax receipts. 'Phase-in' oil and its price was also an issue in the settlement; 'phase-in' oil is 'certain maximum quantities of oil that the governments can require the companies to buy if they have any difficulty in disposing of it themselves over a period ending no earlier than 1991.'[56] All buy-back prices are higher than previous tax-paid costs and the difference is estimated at between $0.09 and $0.18 per barrel.[57]

Yamani of Saudi Arabia has said he prefers participation to nationalization, for in the latter case each country by expanding output to increase sales and revenues would be engaged in price competition with every other country, and prices for oil would drop dramatically. Participation uses the international companies to increase governmental revenues but does not bring about disintegration of the current price level. News in June 1973 from Saudi Arabia showed that the state oil agency, Petromin, which now owns a 25 per cent share of Aramco, has made arrangements to dispose of its crude oil over the next three years at what were in June thought to be all-time high prices: 70 million barrels for each of the next three years, at $2.30 (for heavy oil) to $2.71 (for light oil) per barrel, or prices which are 93 per cent of current posted prices.[58]

Participation arrangements are not in force in all of the producing nations in this part of the world. Iran has struck out on a different course. The twenty-five year concession of the consortium in Iran was due to expire in 1979, but the Shah announced in the beginning of 1973 that the companies had their choice of having their assets and producing operations taken over immediately or of continuing to operate until 1979, at which time the further renewals provided for in the 1954 agreement will be denied and the consortium will purchase oil from Iran like any other buyer. The incentive to agree to the former proposal was a more favorable set of purchasing prices over a known horizon than those prices involved in the alternative offer. The companies have chosen the first offer, and expect to have ' "secure" purchase contracts for oil at preferential discounted prices for 20 to 25 years.'[59] The national company NIOC will operate and finance all oil operations, and try to secure greater recovery of associated gases for marketing, gases which are now frequently flared and wasted.[60] The Shah has announced that output *must* be expanded to 8 mbd by 1978. In what he hopes will continue to be a sellers' market, he expects this take-over and outlet for his country's oil to be at least as profitable as the participation agreements elsewhere in the Gulf.

At the end of April 1973, Libya demanded 100 per cent control, or 51 per cent nationalization, of all oil operations within the country, with compensation to be based on net book value rather than on updated book value. These terms amount to nationalization with almost no compensation. Two months later Libya expropriated Bunker Hunt's 50 per cent share in the rich Sarir field, allegedly for overproduction. The government had expropriated the BP 50 per cent interest in that field a year and a half earlier as political retaliation for Britain's failure to prevent Iran from seizing the island of Abu Musa on the eve of Britain's withdrawal from the area. In August 1973 the government announced its acquisition of 51 per cent of the independent Oasis group of companies (Continental, Marathon, and Amerada-Shell) and of Occidental; and less than a month later, on the fourth anniversary of his accession to power, Colonel Qaddafi announced that the Libyan government had nationalized 51 per cent of the Libyan operations of all producers, both majors and independents. Compensation terms, if any, have yet to be elucidated. The producers plan to join BP and Bunker Hunt in resisting the government by suing buyers of Libyan crude oil (clearly identifiable by its wax components). BP and Bunker Hunt have already filed several suits, but both maintain that most buyers are boycotting Libyan sources of crude. Libya, however, says it has had no difficulty in selling output from the Sarir field, and has raised price per barrel to $6. If Libya succeeds in its take-over of the operating companies by these moves, it will have secured better terms than did the Gulf countries, and the door may open to revisions in the participation agreements there.

Algeria has in effect taken its cue from Libya, and has already assumed control fully, or of at least 51 per cent, of most of oil- and gas-producing companies. After the nationalization measures of February 1971, Sonatrach became the main producing company of both oil and gas, although CFP and ERAP continue to operate. As of 1 October 1973 Sonatrach is selling oil at $5 per barrel, and that figure may shortly be revised upward.

In September 1972 Saudi Arabia proposed through its oil minister Yamani a 'special relationship' with the United States. What Saudi Arabia would like to secure is a guaranteed market for its oil by convincing the US of its need for a guaranteed future supply of oil. But the special relationship proposal goes further: Saudi Arabia suggests that its imports into the US not be limited by quota or any other exclusionary tariff or device, and in return Saudi Arabia would make substantial investments in the United States primarily in both refining and distribution operations. The State Department has said that it would welcome such foreign investment in the US, but that the US does not choose to offer any other producer a special position in its market. The US prefers producing countries to compete for a share of its market, rather than making the country especially dependent on one foreign source of oil and thus losing its ability to bargain for a more favorable price elsewhere.

4 OPEC AND THE FUTURE

Oil production in the Middle East and North Africa has risen dramatically in recent years. Those who believe that oil is in real terms so scarce or in such short supply as to have pushed prices up to consumers are clearly wrong. Oil production will continue to expand markedly, as small producers such as Dubai and Abu Dhabi tap new sources, and Iranian, Iraqi, and Saudi Arabian outputs expand. Saudi Arabia's proposal for a special relationship with the US and Iran's arrangement with Ashland Oil are both evidence of producing countries' desires to have long-term sales contracts at price and quantity levels agreed upon now which may indeed be higher and more favorable to governments than the unknown prices of the future.

The real question is how OPEC members have continued to resist competitive urges in recent years. For a group of producers to act successfully as a cartel, they must be able either to allocate markets and to enforce these market shares, or they must fix a market price and have a means of quickly detecting price shading and of punishing any member who attempts to use price competition to increase his sales at the expense of those of his colleagues. OPEC members have never been successful in agreeing to production quotas or market-sharing arrangements, but have instead chosen the alternative route. Since per-barrel tax payments are a matter of public record, no producer is able to sell at lower prices without being detected quickly. The benefits of a reduction in price by one supplier would quickly be negated as rivals responded to the price shading with reductions of their own. Such a disintegration in the price structure would, of course, be ruinous to all producers. Thus, the system of tax payments based on posted prices has served to keep prices up and prevent price chiseling by any one member of the cartel.

Indeed the international companies have been OPEC's tax collectors,[61] providing rising revenues without spoiling the price structure and without involving the governments in transport, refining, and marketing facilities elsewhere in the world. All that participation plans add is an extra means for the governments to increase their revenues without inviting the tumbling of the price structure which 100 per cent nationalization would bring about. For in the latter instance, real cost would be the floor to price, not cost-plus-tax, and public records of tax-paid costs would no longer be available. Price competition for oil sales would ensue, with each producing government attempting to sell its oil before other producers gained its markets.

Why, then, does it appear by hindsight that producing companies were so ready to acquiesce to the demands made upon them for higher posted prices in 1971? Had Occidental and other independents in Libya stood firm rather than agreeing to the Libyan demands, Libya would undoubtedly have reduced their outputs still further in the short run. But had other companies agreed to supply Occidental with crude oil from their sources, Occidental's hand would have been strengthened, even enough perhaps to have forced Libya to back down; Libya would have found that its attempt to secure higher revenues had backfired, as its concessionaires could meet their sales commitments by other means. In the face of the Libyan government's recent actions, the industry has now agreed to make available alternative crude supplies to Libyan independents in order to increase their resistance.

But even more important to the explanation of the victories of Libya and the Gulf nations are the United States tax laws. Up to a certain point, higher per-barrel taxes paid are in effect costless to US firms, for US tax laws permit dollar-for-dollar credits of foreign taxes against US domestic tax liabilities. Higher foreign taxes will only become costly for American companies under present law if those taxes amount to more than their other taxes due to the US Treasury. One way of stiffening American companies' resistance to higher per-barrel assessments would, of course, be to revise the law so as to eliminate these tax credits. Under such circumstances, oil companies operating abroad would be forced to absorb some positive fraction of foreign assessments, and they could surely be expected to resist as strongly as possible any treatment by foreign governments which substantially raises their costs.

What might have happened had operating companies throughout the Gulf and North Africa refused to agree to the new posted prices in the course of the several rounds of negotiations in 1971? They probably would have faced expropriation, but then the governments would have been forced to shoulder directly the refining and marketing responsibilities of crude production, and they were unprepared to do so at that time. Sheikh Yamani has said in the past that indeed such an outcome is not what the producing countries desire, for he knows that this will bring about price competition in oil at the Gulf with falling prices for all producers: 'Nationalization would be a disaster ... because it would undermine the price structure. ... After nationalization ... , the pressure on individual companies to enter into price competition to increase the volume of their sales would be very much greater. ... A situation of this sort could have only one outcome: a dramatic collapse of the price structure ... (W)e like the majors because they provide the buffer element between us and the consumers which is indispensable for the maintenance of world prices.'[62] For without the ready market contacts of the major companies, each country would have had to compete for buyers, and would need to cover only cost per barrel, not cost-plus-tax per barrel, of output.

Why, then, the haste of France through CFP in Iraq and of a Japanese group in Abu Dhabi to engage in exclusive contracts at higher-than-market prices over lengthy periods of time?[63] Would not each have been better advised to act as competitive buyer, surveying all alternative sources of supply for the best price-quantity package rather than putting itself at the mercy of one country's whims and politics? The answer must be yes, yet the fact that such arrangements as those of CFP and the Japanese group have been made suggests the gripping fear of consuming countries that, unless they carve out for themselves a particular geographic production area, they will be cut off from all oil supply. Yet by choosing 'access' to oil at above-market prices and by avoiding competitive shopping, Japan and France have already conceded a substantial part of their independence as buyers.[64]

It is my belief that the key to the demise of the cartel lies in the behavior of Iran and of the Mediterranean producers Libya and Algeria. By choosing nationalization rather than participation, these countries should soon no longer be able to use the international oil companies as a means of preventing price competition. Iran plans to push output to 8 mbd from a current level of 5 mbd, and it is soon to take over operations of its concessionaires. Since domestic development plans in Iran are heavily keyed to rising oil revenues in the future, Iran can be expected to engage in price competition to sell its expanding oil output. Without the public record of tax-paid costs, this price chiseling can take place easily and attract purchasers to Iranian sources of supply.

It already appears that posted prices and tax payments in Algeria and Libya are far above those prevailing elsewhere. If Iran behaves as expected, and as desulfurization methods and facilities grow, both Libyan and Algerian oils will no longer be able to command their current premia, for cheaper, heavier oils will be purchased elsewhere and then processed to remove sulphur. Libya and Algeria have come close to acquiring 100 per cent control, or nationalization, of all operations, and thus the tax-paid costs of neither their oil nor that of Iran will appear on public record. For Algeria to engage in price competition, however, the willingness of the French to buy at high and non-competitive prices must diminish. If prices do indeed decline in the future through competition, Kuwait may yet come to regret its decision to limit output to 3 mbd; its attempt to prolong oil offtake may indeed be successful but costly if future prices are lower than present ones.

How will the producing countries use their revenues if they do not spend them on domestic development? For a long time these funds have been placed in assets in Western Europe and the United States, as oil nations have sought to earn the highest competitive return on their funds. It is now the expectation that producing nations will try to integrate into downstream operations in the developed countries, acquiring refining and distribution outlets in the United States and elsewhere. This route seems a natural path, connected as it is to the expanding production of crude oil and serving as a guaranteed outlet for such crude supplies. All the indications are that most of the countries of the Gulf are actively establishing interests in marketing and refining facilities outside their own borders.[65]

Yet if this forward integration occurs, another weakness, the fatal one, is likely to appear in the structure of the cartel. For in these circumstances, there will be no method for any member to detect rapidly other members' sales prices of refined and finished products; the door will be wide open for price competition. A key to the maintenance of the cartel, in both crude and refined products, is few transactions at readily observable prices. With competition, there will be a multiplicity of transactions and prices will not be easily observable by the former members of the cartel. Producing nations will then be earning no more than a competitive return on their investments in refining and marketing facilities.

The 1971 OPEC agreements were supposed to have been in force until 1975. But by October 1973 it was clear that what had been widely heralded in 1971 as a long-term stable agreement was to be revised. At the time of the OPEC meetings in October, oil economics and oil politics were vastly complicated by the outbreak of another war between Israel and Arab countries. OPEC members, led by Sheikh Yamani, and international oil company representatives discussed oil issues for two days before adjourning without settlement. The points under discussion included OPEC's desire to revise upward the inflation clause of the 1971 agreement, which had provided for a 2.5 per cent annual increase in price plus five cents a barrel, as well as its desire to raise posted prices by at least 50 per cent. Private discussions continued, nonetheless, against the backdrop of the war. OAPEC members then convened in Kuwait to consider how petroleum policy could be used against Israel and countries sympathetic to Israel.

On 17 October 1973, Kuwait announced that it would contribute $350 million to the Arab war effort, but that it did not expect to stop oil output, for such a policy might encourage the US and other oil-consuming nations to 'actions that could lead to a prolonged war.'[66] On the following day, OAPEC mem-

Maureen S. Crandall

bers announced that petroleum output from Arab states would be cut immediately by 5 per cent, and would be cut every month thereafter by (at least) 5 per cent 'until an Israeli withdrawal is completed and until the restoration of the legal rights of the Palestinian question.'[67] No method of enforcing this output reduction has been stated. [Editor's Note: Iran, not a member of OAPEC, increased production. Rumors suggest that Iraq has not cut its supplies by the amounts announced by OAPEC.]

At the same time, OAPEC countries and Iran in addition announced unilateral increases in prices based on the 'market' price of $3.65 per barrel for Arabian light crude oil. (The international oil companies have yet to respond at the time of writing.) Until this change, posted and market (or transaction) prices had been for a number of months about equal at $3 a barrel, but October's announcement set a new 'market' price of $3.65 as well as a new means of calculating posted prices (for tax reference purposes). Posted prices will now be set at 140 per cent of the new 'market' prices, or at $5.11 based on the $3.65 price for Arabian light crude oil. From the international companies' point of view, their costs will rise about $1.25 per barrel.[68]

Neither Libya nor Algeria has announced what their new prices will be, but they are widely expected to follow suit.[69] While Iran was party to the price announcement, it did not agree with the Arab decision to cut back production and has no plans to do so. This is the chance for non-Arab producers to expand their share of the world market. The Arabs themselves have assured France continued supplies of oil despite the planned cutbacks, presumably in appreciation for France's foreign policy toward Arab states. But if France and any other countries considered to be friendly to Arab nations continue to receive oil from Arab producers, the Arabs are in effect engaging in a selective embargo. This type of embargo has failed in the past and will fail again, as oil will ultimately be transshipped – admittedly an inefficient and costly allocative process – to the national markets where it is in greatest demand, regardless of whether these consuming nations are sympathetic to the Arab cause. [Editor's Note: The Arab countries of the Middle East have reduced shipments to all consumers, recognizing that transshipment is a real possibility.]

If the international oil companies do not choose to agree to the new price terms, the producing governments have announced that oil will be sold (at reduced rates of output at the Gulf, except for Iran) at prices keyed to the new 'market' price of $3.65 for Arabian light crude.[70] No specific mention has been made of nationalization of assets of those companies who might not choose to comply with the new posted prices, but it is highly likely that nationalization would result. Then producing governments would have to shoulder the direct responsibilities of setting the price and selling oil, crude or refined, which they have already indicated that they are prepared to do at a price of $3.65, not $5.11. Producing governments would in effect be required to hire the companies to extract the oil, guaranteeing them no less than their next best alternative return. With costs equal only to real costs rather than cost-plus-tax per barrel, and each government looking to expand its *share* of the market (even if some governments reduce their *level* of output), prices to consuming nations will begin to decline.

In conclusion, there is as yet no world shortage of crude oil, and production has risen rapidly between the first quarter of 1972 and 1973; for example, output rose in Saudi Arabia, Iran, Abu Dhabi, and Dubai by amounts ranging from 23 to 67 per cent.[71] Today's levels of prices for both crude and refined oils are due to the success of OPEC members in winning higher taxes and to short-run pressures on refining capacity. While it is very difficult to project operating levels in the Persian Gulf and North Africa over the next ten to fifteen years, from fields discovered but not yet producing, or from additional reserves yet to be discovered, all indications are that rising output from this geographic area will continue to be a major source of world oil. The battles against rising tax payments assessed by the OPEC cartel will be fought strongly or weakly now and in the future. If OPEC demands are resisted, the international major companies will be only hired contractors for oil production in a world market where each producing country searches to sell its oil at any price above real cost plus contractor's fees. Thus, the cartel will be ended, as each selling nation is forced to compete by means of price to attract buyers.

If the battle is lost, posted prices will rise to that level at which extraction of oil from more expensive sources, such as oil shale, or the generation of energy from non-oil inputs, becomes economically feasible.[72]

NOTES

1 United States Department of the Interior, Bureau of Mines, Mineral Industry Surveys, *Petroleum Forecast Monthly,* March 1973, p. 4
2 The full membership of OPEC includes petroleum producing countries elsewhere in the world, such as Venezuela, Indonesia, and Nigeria.
3 Edith T. Penrose, *The Growth of Firms, Middle East Oil, and Other Essays* (London 1971), p. 237
4 *Petroleum Forecast Monthly,* March 1973, p. 4
5 Ibid.
6 James E. Akins, 'The Oil Crisis: This Time the Wolf Is Here,' *Foreign Affairs,* April 1973, pp. 462-90, and US Senate, Committee on Interior and Insular Affairs, Hearings, *Oil and Gas Imports Issues, Part 3,* 10, 11, and 22 Jan.

1973, testimony of Willis Armstrong, Assistant of Economic Affairs, Department of State, p. 830

7 Cabinet Task Force on Oil Import Control, *The Oil Import Question: A Report on the Relationship of Oil Imports to the National Security* (Washington, DC, 1970)

8 *New York Times,* 28 May 1973. Most figures for reserves, consumption, and output are taken from *Oil and Gas Journal,* Worldwide Oil Issue 1972, and *BP Statistical Review of the World Oil Industry,* 1972.

9 'Proven reserves are generally taken to be the volume of oil remaining in the ground which geological and engineering information indicate with reasonable certainty to be recoverable in the future from known resevoirs under existing economic and operating conditions' (*BP Statistical Review,* 1972, p. 4). The API definition of proved reserves is a very strict concept and measure, and is not directly transferable to foreign reserve measurements which are generally less strict. M.A. Adelman suggests in his 'Long Run Cost Trends: Persian Gulf and United States' (Richard J. Schanz, Jr., ed., *Balancing Supply and Demand for Energy in the United States* (Denver 1972), pp. 39–72) that the reserves reported in the Middle East and North Africa may in fact be in the neighborhood of 20 to 33 per cent greater than the comparable API calculations. In any event, the relative size of those reserves is clear, and Saudi Arabian reserves as well as those of other countries in the area are constantly being revised upward.

10 For any reservoir, the decline rate represents the rate at which output falls owing to declines in underground reservoir pressure as oil is extracted.

11 M.A. Adelman, 'Crude Oil Production Costs,' *Petroleum Press Services,* May 1966, p. 178, and *The World Petroleum Market* (Baltimore 1972), p. 76

12 *The World Petroleum Market,* p. 76. The freight-advantage estimates are based on the proximity of Libya and Algeria to European markets as well as their position west of the closed Suez Canal.

13 There appears to be no such thing in recent times as a stable market price for tankship services. With the majority of tankship capacity on long-term charter, the spot rate reflects current changes in both demand and supply. Yet the tendency toward very large crude carriers (VLOCs) of 205,000–285,000 dwt (in 1972 making up almost 25 per cent of tankship capacity), together with the five-fold increase in tankers even larger than this over the past five years, leads most students to believe that transport charges should show no marked upward movement.

14 'Supply and demand are as irrevelant to the future price as to the past. A price set by supply equalling demand means a price in the neighborhood of incremental cost, which in crude oil is chiefly the return on the new invest-

ment. In prudence, the worst possible supply situation has been imagined – that of zero discoveries; even so, the price equating demand and supply is still only a negligible fraction of the actual price. Hence the reader can safely put out of his mind any forecasting of supply and demand conditions over the next 10 to 15 years' (Adelman, *The World Petroleum Market*, p. 253). See also 'The Phony Oil Crisis: A Survey,' *The Economist*, 7 July 1973, pp. 1–38

15 Posted prices take their name from the days when companies posted the prices at which they were prepared to buy crude at the wellhead, and thus when posted prices were representative of market prices. With the expansion of crude production in the late 1950s, market prices began to decline, however, and exporting countries were reluctant to see their tax revenues decline as well.

16 Deductions have in the past included additional small sums for gravity and marketing allowances and some other discounts.

17 CFP is owned jointly by the French government and private interests.

18 Aramco is owned jointly by Mobil, SoCal, Exxon, and Texaco.

19 Economist Intelligence Unit, Quarterly Economic Review, *Oil in the Middle East*, no 1, 1973, p. 6

20 Ibid., *Annual Supplement, 1972*, p. 5

21 Ibid., no 2, 1973, p. 7

22 Ibid., *Annual Supplement, 1972*, p. 5

23 General Petroleum and Mineral Organization

24 See section III on participation.

25 Petromin's refinery has a capacity of 12,000 bd, whereas Aramco's at Ras Tanura refines 415,000 bd.

26 *Oil in the Middle East, Annual Supplement, 1972*, p. 6

27 Prior to December 1969, when Saudi Arabia and Kuwait agreed on the governance of the Neutral Zone, this area had been under the protection of Great Britain.

28 Some sources rumor them as low as 25 billion barrels (see *Middle East Monitor*, 1 May 1972).

29 Kuwait now places 12.5 per cent of annual revenues in a reserve fund to be used when oil production is terminated.

30 KOC is owned equally by Gulf and BP.

31 These facilities can accommodate tankers up to 300,000 dwt, not 500,000 dwt as at Ras Tanura.

32 United States Department of Interior, Bureau of Mines, *1970 Minerals Yearbook*, vol. III, *Area Reports: International* (Washington, DC 1972), p. 495

33 *Oil in the Middle East, Annual Supplement, 1972*, p. 17

34 Ibid., p. 17

35 This facility replaced the coastal terminal of Fao in 1962.

36 IPC was owned by BP, Shell, CFP, Exxon, Mobil, and the Gulbenkian estate.

37 *Middle East Monitor,* 15 March 1973, and *Oil in the Middle East,* no 2, 1973, p. 2. With the outbreak of war in the Middle East in 1973, Iraq nationalized the 23.75 per cent holdings of Exxon and Mobil in the Basrah Petroleum Company.

38 *Petroleum Press Service,* April 1973, p. 124

39 *Oil in the Middle East, Annual Supplement, 1972,* p. 14

40 Ibid., p. 7

41 *Oil and Gas Journal,* 2 July 1973, p. 21; *New York Times,* 28 Sept. 1973, p. 1

42 The UAE came into existence with the departure of the British in 1971. The union or federation is composed of the sheikhdoms of Abu Dhabi, Dubai, Sharja, Ajman, Fujaira, Umm al-Qaiwain, and Ras al-Khaima.

43 *Oil in the Middle East,* no 1, 1973, p. 11

44 Ibid.

45 *Oil and Gas Journal,* 11 June 1973, p. 59

46 Société Nationale pour la Recherche, la Production, la Transport, la Transformation et la Commercialisation des Hydrocarbures

47 Entreprise de Recherches et d'Activités Pétrolières, the French national oil company

48 This latter agreement calls for the annual purchase of 6 billion cubic meters of gas from 1975 to 1978 (EIU, QER, *Algeria, Annual Supplement, 1972,* p. 12).

49 *1970 Minerals Yearbook,* vol. III, p. 73

50 Adelman, *The World Petroleum Market,* p. 209

51 John Hamer, 'Persian Gulf Oil,' *Editorial Research Reports,* 28 March 1973, p. 235

52 *Petroleum Press Service,* June 1973, p. 238

53 Middle East states are also considering a new reserve currency, tied to the price of gold at the date of issue, so as to protect themselves from future devaluations.

54 Dubai is proceeding to build its own drydock facility.

55 *Petroleum Press Service,* February 1973, p. 44

56 Ibid., p. 46

57 Ibid.

58 *Oil and Gas Journal,* 4 June 1973, p. 42

59 *Middle East Monitor,* 15 March 1973, p. 2

60 *Oil and Gas Journal,* 4 June 1973, p. 40; see also footnote 4 above

61 The arguments in this section concerning tax-paid costs, real costs, and cartel

behavior draw heavily from the work of M.A. Adelman as stated in his *The World Petroleum Market,* in his 'Is the Oil Shortage Real?' *Foreign Policy,* Winter 1973, pp. 69–107, and in his unpublished paper, 'The Impact of the Tehran-Tripoli Agreements on US Oil Policy and Prices.' Adelman's views and the position stated here are not without controversy.

62 Ahmad Zaki Yamani, 'Participation versus Nationalization,' *Continuity and Change in the World Oil Industry,* Zuhayr M. Mikdashi, Sherrill Cleland, and Ian Seymour, eds. (Beirut 1970), pp. 215, 218, 222

63 The Japanese contract for Abu Dhabi oil 'was so much over the going market price that it brought a scolding from MITI' (the Japanese Ministry of International Trade and Industry), *The Economist,* 17 July 1973, p. 12. See also *Oil in the Middle East,* no 2, 1973, p. 11, on the high prices paid by the Japanese.

64 Adelman places the additional cost per barrel to the Japanese at $0.60 ('The Impact of the Tehran-Tripoli Agreements on US Oil Policy and Prices,' p. 5); it is his view that France and Japan have greatly erred by conceding their independence as purchasers.

65 For a recent example, the Saudi Arabians are discussing with Canadian officials facilities including a refinery and deepwater port to be constructed on the lower St Lawrence River (*Wall Street Journal,* 22 June 1973, p. 6).

66 *New York Times,* 18 Oct. 1973, p. 16. Since 1967, Kuwait had been giving $150 million annually to the Arab cause.

67 *Wall Street Journal,* 18 Oct. 1973, p. 3. From the point of view of the US, such a cutback means a monthly drop of about 0.050 mbd, a decline which is not expected to inflict serious harm upon the US.

68 Ibid.

69 *New York Times,* 18 Oct. 1973. p. 81

70 *Wall Street Journal,* 18 Oct. 1973, p. 3

71 *Oil in the Middle East,* no 2, 1973, pp. 5–6

72 An Arab oil representative is quoted in the *New York Times* of 18 October 1973 (p. 18) as saying, 'We are helping you find new energy sources more quickly.'

There are three aspects to any discussion of the energy crisis – the short term (now), the medium term (next ten or so years), and the long term. Professor Mabro discusses each of these in turn, stressing the medium term as the one which is most interesting and amenable to political action.

Mabro suggests that the embargo would have had much more effect (more is hard to imagine) had it come five years hence when the US would be importing 30 per cent of its oil from the Middle East. The present embargos can only have a minor impact on the US, but a more profound one on Europe and Japan. The salient event is that the power of Saudi Arabia is emerging over and above the power of OPEC. Only the Saudis have the power to disrupt world oil markets by refusing to commit new supplies; all other countries would have to cut back supplies. The incremental medium-term world oil supplies will likely come from Saudi Arabia. Therefore, Saudi Arabia faces a dilemma. Should it restrict output, thus increasing the economic power of rivals such as Iran and hastening the development of substitutes for oil, decreasing the value of oil reserves? Should Saudi Arabia expand production to increase its reserves of foreign currencies? Given some move to settle the Arab-Israeli conflict, it is likely that the Saudis could be convinced to expand production. First, based on past experiences, the Saudi Arabians have acted responsibly in the oil market. Second, a policy package could interest them. After all, world economic prosperity and world political stability is crucial for economic development and political stability in Arab oil lands.

Mabro's policy package consists of technical aid for development; concrete proposals for refining capacity as a basis for industrialization, inviting the Arabs to participate in the Group of Ten discussions on world monetary and currency reform; subsidies for underdeveloped nations; new international debt and equity instruments for Arab investment.

This proposal is remarkably similar to the proposals made in the Collado and the Homet chapters. It is quite startling to find an American diplomat, an oil company executive, and an Oxford scholar all approaching the same policy conclusions.

ROBERT MABRO

Political and financial aspects
of the oil game

THREE ASPECTS OF THE ENERGY CRISIS

It may be helpful to distinguish from the outset three different issues which current discussions on the so-called energy crisis often fail to separate clearly. The
first may be termed the long-term problem, the second the present-day, and the
third the medium-term problem. The long-term issue relates to the exhaustion
of a finite natural resource. It is essentially, though not exclusively, a geophysical
problem which need not detain us for very long here. Estimates of ultimate oil
reserves are to some extent uncertain and prediction of the date at which physical exhaustion will constitute a serious threat are difficult to make. These predictions involve economic assumptions generally marred by a lack of exact knowledge. We do not have sufficient information, for example, on the quantitative
impact of higher oil prices on the volume and pattern of demand, on the stimulus they may provide to the search for new oil fields, to technical progress in
methods of exploration and production in difficult locations or in consumers
equipment or the invention of substitutes. What knowledge we have is based on
incomplete geological data. Whatever the case may be, it is certain that a physical
as opposed to economic or other types of shortage will not be felt before the end
of this century. Ample time is available for adapting production and consumption
structures to the new requirements of the twenty-first century. The redeeming
feature of long-term problems, if we believe in the inventiveness of the human
mind and in the significance of time in removing constraints, is precisely their
long-term nature.

Robert Mabro

The present-day oil supply problem largely arises from the decision of major
Arab oil producers to restrict output and impose an embargo on shipments to
the United States of America and Holland, a decision taken after the outbreak
of hostilities in October 1973 between Egypt, Syria, and Israel. I hesitate to refer
to this issue as a short-term problem partly because its fundamental cause is the
old and seemingly intractable Middle-East conflict, partly because predictions on
the duration of the embargo are difficult to make. Arab-Israeli wars have been responsible in the past for some interuptions in oil supplies – in 1956/7, when the
Suez Canal was damaged and closed to navigation; in 1967 when some producers
imposed a short-lived and rather unsuccessful embargo, and a few years later
when a pipeline was sabotaged in Syria. As a peaceful and permanent peace in
the Middle East may be difficult to achieve (it may entail in any case long and
protracted negotiations if not new outbreaks of hostilities), Arab countries may
continue to restrict output for a relatively long time. They may, of course, be
persuaded to lift the restrictions in the near future either because of the damage
inflicted on friendly states in Europe, or in a gesture of goodwill after early successes in Arab-Israeli negotiations, or for a host of other reasons. But the temptation to resume the embargo will remain strong as long as the Middle-East conflict
is not satisfactorily settled. The use of the oil weapon may become a recurrent
feature of international relations in the years to come.

The present-day problem is essentially – but here again, not exclusively – political. Politics provide the main motivation but the effectiveness of the oil weapon
depends on specific economic conditions and its use entails economic consequences. Arab governments have had the political motivations for a relatively
long time, but until very recently did not carry the degree of monopoly power
required. It may indeed be argued that the timing of the Fourth Arab-Israeli war
was not optimal for an efficient use of the oil weapon. The dependence of the
United States of America, the main target, on oil from Arab sources although
continually growing is not yet significant. The USA was expected to suffer from
localized energy shortages during the winter of 1973/4 because of inadequate refining facilities and other factors; and the Arab boycott will no doubt aggravate
the situation. Small restrictions in output may have disproportionate effects in
conditions of tight supply. But the impact of the oil weapon on the USA may be
mitigated by small economies in consumption, increases in domestic output and
by changes in the allocation of non-Arab oil to different markets through the distributive operations of international oil companies. Given the volume of United
States imports from Arab sources, the problem seems to be tractable at least in
the next few months. The oil weapon could have been more immediately effec-

tive in 1976 or 1977 when US dependence on Arab imports may approach a peak. Its significance at later dates is more uncertain because the energy situation may begin to change in the USA in response to an investment drive for self-sufficiency. The opportunities for an efficient use of the oil weapon against the US seem therefore restricted to a specific period of four or five years and the choice of the appropriate time is further constrained by political factors. A favorable conjunction of all the enabling conditions is necessarily a rare event. The period, however, is sufficiently long to cause legitimate concern about the damage that the oil weapon could inflict on the world economy.

It is too early to assess the consequences of the oil weapon on consuming countries. Producers are not likely to suffer in the short-run because price increases more than compensate for output reductions. The Persian Gulf members of OPEC announced on 16 October 1973 new posted prices which raised government take per barrel by some 70 per cent; governments are also benefiting to some extent from higher market prices as direct sellers of 'participation' oil. As output reductions do not seem to exceed 25 per cent, their revenues (barring further cuts in production unmatched by a rise in price) will increase by at least 48 per cent. It is often alleged, however, that oil producers in the Middle East and North Africa stand to suffer in the medium- and long-term from their present policies which may hasten the search for and invention of substitutes. But the problem is more complex than this simple proposition tends to suggest. The inducement to search for substitutes relates to more permanent and powerful causes than the present embargo: fears about rapid exhaustion of known oil reserves, fears that Middle Eastern countries will adopt conservation policies for economic reasons and restrict output in the medium-term in the face of a growth in demand, and fears that a prolonged state of political instability in the Middle East will repeatedly disrupt oil supplies. The embargo is irrelevant to the first concern. It could increase fears about the medium-term because the embargo enabled Arab governments to test the strength of their monopoly position and may have enhanced their willingness to exercise it in the future for economic motives. Fears about politically motivated restrictions on oil supply have of course materialized with the embargo. Paradoxically the present recourse to the oil weapon, to the extent that it precipitates a peace settlement in the Middle East, may eventually contribute to removing these fears. And there are other considerations. The inducement to search for substitutes has been hitherto inhibited by (a) the price of oil which, despite recent rises, is on average still relatively low, (b) the sheer size of the resources required to effect significant substitution, and (c) the strength of the environmentalist and conservation lobby, particularly in the USA. The question is whether the impact of the present embargo on both governments and public opinion will be sufficiently great to override the cost argument and remove the political obstacles placed by environmentalist and other sectional interests. Further, substitution of one source of energy by another is a long and complicated affair. The present embargo, for all we know, may well be short-lived. It may initiate a process of substitution but a change in the political climate or in Arab policies could remove, soon after, the incentive to sustain at the same rate the considerable investment required. Finally, moderate substitution need not have adverse effects on the long-term economic interests of certain Arab countries. A lower rate of growth of future demand for Middle East oil than forecast at present may indeed be beneficial. It could enable them to conserve oil for the days when its contribution to their own development will be greater than at present with less risk of antagonizing powerful but frustrated consumers. Moderate substitution – which is all we can expect in the next ten years – even if it lowered the price of oil in the ground may not reduce its social value to the economies concerned. All considered, the present embargo does not necessarily entail dire consequences on Arab oil producers. Our argument is that the effects are ambivalent and that the complexity of the issue precludes at this stage any firm statement on their aggregate impact.

We have distinguished a long-term problem from present-day disturbances. The third aspect of the oil supply crisis, which will be the subject of the remainder of this paper, relates to the medium-term. It involves economic and political issues, some of which are more amenable to speculation than analysis. The problem, as we shall see later, is not exclusively monopoly power. There are complications.

The three aspects of the oil crisis distinguished here are related. The long-term energy problem has been skilfully exploited in recent years by various lobbies and the media, especially in the USA, for a variety of motives. The State Department, worried by the prospects of American import dependence for a strategic commodity, played a significant role in a campaign designed to promote a vast energy program. Oil companies have an obvious interest in propagating the belief that petroleum is in tight supply and OPEC can only derive benefits from such a belief. There is no doubt that a climate of opinion was created which may have influenced recent bargaining rounds between companies and producer countries as well as the attitudes of Arab governments in the present-day situation. On the other hand, an early awareness of the long-term problem by influencing the timing and the rate of substitution may alter to some extent the energy situation in the medium-term. Finally, the present-day difficulties could extend to the medium-term if political mediation between Israel and the Arabs fail to produce a satisfactory settlement. But they may also help by forcing the hitherto passive governments of the major consumer countries to take a close look at the whole energy situation. The medium-term problem, as we shall repeatedly stress, may be solved by new and imaginative forms of cooperation between producer and consumer countries.

The medium term refers to a period of time which extends to 1980 and perhaps 1985. Certain characteristics of supply and demand define the setting and hence the problem. First, world demand for oil is not only considerable but is expected to grow at a fairly high rate. Forecasts differ widely on the predicted figure – some suggest a rate of growth of 7 or 8 per cent, others 10 to 12 per cent – but they all agree on the qualitative point of rapid growth. Past performance, say the annual average rates of 1967/72, suggest the following figures: USA and Canada, around 5.4 per cent, Western Europe, 9.0 per cent, Japan, 14 per cent, non-communist world, 7.8 per cent, world, 8 per cent. It seems that the income elasticity of oil is high and that a sustained rate of economic growth in the world of say 4 per cent may well entail average annual increases in the demand for oil of the order of 7 to 9 per cent.

Second, substitution of other forms of energy for oil involves relatively long gestation periods in research and development. The impact of a vast energy program even if immediately launched by the USA, Europe, and Japan may not have significant effects for six or seven years. We cannot expect a major shift of the demand curve for oil in the near future in this country. Reference to substitution poses the question of price elasticities. The uses of oil are diverse; strictly speaking, there is a demand curve for every use, and price elasticities are likely to differ significantly between the various curves as well as between different price ranges in any given schedule. Although there is room for immediate substitution in certain uses, it is generally thought that price elasticities of many oil demand schedules are fairly low in the short run.

Third, the supply curve of oil may shift as a result of major discoveries especially outside OPEC countries. These depend on the rate of exploration which is strongly influenced by economic (mainly prices and rates of return) considerations, the state of geological knowledge, and on chance factors. The supply curve may shift sooner than expected if it is true that North Sea oil reserves are much more significant than currently acknowledged and if the long-deferred exploitation of Alaskan fields is accelerated. But here again lead-in periods, although shorter than for non-oil substitutes, may be significant.

Fourth, there is a high degree of geographical concentration in the present distribution of known (taken here to mean published proven) oil reserves. The Middle East at the end of 1972 was supposed to possess some 62 per cent of known reserves in the non-communist world and North Africa, perhaps another 10 per cent. The degree of concentration is lower in production as the Middle East accounted in 1972 for some 41 per cent of total output in the non-communist world and North Africa for about 9 per cent, but concentration is expected to increase significantly. The area with the largest reserves will be called upon to satisfy the bulk of incremental demand in the medium term.

These main features are indeed those of a monopoly situation. The problem and its implications, however serious and worrying for consumer countries, would be relatively simple to analyze if it were shorn of all other elements. The reality is more complex as certain features qualify our description while others tend to accentuate the nature of the monopoly problem.

A *The market structure*
In a simple monopoly situation, a single producer faces all consumers and dominates the market. Middle Eastern and North American oil producers are many, and until the recent participation agreements had virtually no direct access to the markets. (National oil companies have existed for some time in many oil-producing countries, but oil crude transactions were relatively minor.) The very number of producers seems to weaken the monopoly model. Paradoxically, the intermediation of a few multinational and vertically integrated oil companies between producers and consumers enabled producers to behave since the late 1960s as if they constituted a cartel. But the description of OPEC as a cartel is misleading. The characteristic of a true cartel is an ability to control output, and the organization never succeeded in adopting a production program with prorationing between members. There was no need for such a program because of the peculiar structure of the oil industry which provides a more convenient instrument: the posted price or, if one prefers, the tax level on oil output. Agreement on production quotas involve the partners of a would-be cartel in difficult negotiations between themselves and expose their conflict of interests. Price bargaining takes place between rivals – governments and companies. Tax agreements between rivals proved easier to reach than production agreements between partners. The main, though not the only, reason is that oil companies have little incentive to resist government demands for higher dues, especially when these demands are made in periods of temporary supply difficulties. They can always shift the burden of higher taxes to the final consumer (because of their oligopolistic power in the product market) or to the US Treasury (thanks to the provision of American fiscal legislation). Once a new tax agreement is reached between one or a group of oil-producing countries and the companies, other governments will ask and obtain similar treatment. The main difference with a cartel or a pure monopoly is that higher prices could be obtained without necessary restrictions on output.

78

The situation as depicted above seems to have prevailed until 1972 or 1973. Important changes are now taking place. First, Saudi Arabia is assuming the role of the crucial oil producer for the coming seven to ten years. The distribution of oil reserves and productive capacity in the Middle East and North Africa is such that a large proportion of the huge incremental demand of the non-communist world has to come from Saudi Arabia. The ultimate monopoly power, which hitherto could only be exercised through agreements between producers, is being increasingly vested in Saudi Arabia. True, all significant producers carry some monopoly power in conditions of tight supply: Iran and some lesser members of OPEC also matter in this respect. The difference between Saudi Arabia and other countries is that it will be increasingly able to cause serious disruption by altering the *rate of growth* of output. To achieve similar results, any of the other producers would have to curtail significantly the *level* of production.

Second, participation agreements are beginning to expose oil-producing countries to the market. Consumers would have benefited from this development had it taken place earlier in a more competitive market. This is essentially the Adelman thesis which criticizes oil companies for protecting producer countries from the risks of price competition. But the Adelman thesis seems to have lost part of its significance: some countries, with or without the intermediation of companies, are now in a position to exercise monopolistic power. Despite this major proviso, I feel that exposure to the market is to be welcomed. As producers are many, some competitive forces will tend to operate at certain times. These pressures, however weak, influence to some extent the behavior of potential monopolists.

Third, an actual exercise of monopoly power is now taking place for the first time. Sooner or later, all those engaged in the present-day crisis will learn a number of lessons. Their impact on future policies depend on the final outcome of the embargo, but the effects, whatever their nature, are likely to be significant. The lessons, at this stage, are manifold: (a) certain countries have the power to inflict economic damage to both friends and foes by withholding oil supplies; (b) agreement on a common strategy is impossible to achieve, save by a few producers, even when the political objective of the strategy is shared by a larger group; (c) oil-producing countries which do not participate in the common embargo action derive enormous economic benefits from it.

I think that the experience so far involves positive elements of considerable significance. Saudi Arabia and fellow states, having achieved recognition of their power and hence of a certain international identity, can now play with even greater confidence and maturity than hitherto the responsible role which the world community expects from them. It must be recognized here that Saudi Arabia and other Amirates of the Gulf have, despite widespread suggestions to the contrary in certain Western circles, always behaved responsibly. Saudi Arabia

79

Robert Mabro

did not attempt to limit the rate of growth of oil production before the Fourth Arab-Israeli War; in fact the average level of output during January–September 1973 was some 35 per cent higher than in 1972. The embargo of October 1973 could have been averted if US diplomacy had taken King Faisal's warnings more seriously. My point, however, is that the present exercise of power, by weakening the opposition of political extremists to King Faisal, instilling a sense of national pride in the country and reinforcing the domestic position of the regime, may enhance the king's freedom and ability to pursue a policy of cooperation with the Western world in the future. All that hinges, of course, on the successful settlement of the Arab-Israeli conflict.

The experience that agreement between producers is difficult to attain will no doubt have some restraining influence on the exercise of monopoly power. True, Saudi Arabia or Iran acting alone could create serious problems for consumers. But no government likes to stand alone when its actions precipitate an international crisis.

Finally, the consideration that output restrictions implemented by one country can produce greater economic benefits to others may also become a moderating factor. This is particularly important for Saudi Arabia and Iran. Saudi Arabia will keep an eye on the growing power of Iran in the Persian Gulf and would not always want to contribute by its own policies to the building up of this power. The intricacies of regional politics are not often taken into account by analysts, but they matter too.

B *The surplus-earning problem*
Although some characteristics of the Middle-Eastern situation seem to qualify our earlier description, others add new and difficult complications. Middle Eastern and North African countries do not form a homogeneous group either politically or economically. Some, like Iran, Iraq, and Algeria have large populations and are endowed with non-oil resources. They need most of the foreign exchange earnings which may accrue to them for current and capital expenditures on their economic development. Others, like Kuwait, the small amirates of the Gulf, and to a lesser extent Libya and Saudi Arabia have relatively small populations and few proven resources outside oil. Some of these countries had difficulty in spending all their foreign exchange earnings and are building bank reserves. The volume of these holdings is not at present excessively large but they are expected to accumulate, as output grows and prices rise, to the level of $100 to $200 billion by 1980.

The dilemma of these countries is fairly simple: to deplete their mineral wealth for the sake of building up liquid foreign exchange reserves now or to leave oil in the ground at the risk of triggering a process of substitution which may lower its future price. The accumulation of foreign exchange reserves is not very attractive because of management and political problems relating to their investment abroad, the continual loss in their real value as a result of world inflation, and the real or imagined fears of instability in the international monetary system. Oil conservation policies also pose problems. If applied by a large producer like Saudi Arabia they will result in higher prices, serious problems of international relations with powerful consumer countries, and, perhaps, economic losses in the long term. Paradoxically, conservation policies, if politically feasible, need not affect very significantly the accumulation of foreign exchange reserves as price rises may compensate to some extent for losses arising from restrictions in output.

Every producer country faces a problem of optimum oil extraction over time. This is always a complex issue, but the present context brings in additional difficulties: the interdependence of producers' decisions in markets with high degrees of concentration; the conflict between consumers immediate objectives and producers long-term aims; the appraisal of evolving *rapports de force* between partners; the evaluation of the social return of oil revenues to the producer countries at different dates which is related to but not identical with oil prices. In an ideal world, the relationship between present and future prices would arbitrate between keeping oil in the ground and investing in alternative assets. Neither the structure of the industry, nor that of capital markets, nor the political environment approach the conditions of the ideal world.

We have said enough to suggest that the issues of oil supply from the Middle East and North Africa could not be reduced to a pure cartel or to a pure monopoly problem.

POLICY PROPOSALS

A solution of the medium-term problem involves a reconciliation between the world requirement for continual increases in oil output from the Middle East and North Africa and producers' preferences. There are reasons for hope because these conflicts, whether real or apparent, tend to conceal a more fundamental community of interest. The economic prosperity and the political stability of the world are crucial to the prosperity and stability of Middle Eastern oil producers. We all belong to the same world, a simple truth which, despite certain appearances to the contrary, the West tends to forget more frequently than rulers and governments in the Middle East.

A prerequisite to any solution is a peaceful settlement of the Arab-Israeli conflict. There is no suggestion of sacrificing Israel's existence or security in some sordid deal. The suggestion is that a settlement, with strong outside guarantees, is to the best interest of all concerned: Arabs, Israelis, and the rest of the world.

81

Political guarantees by the Big Powers for *all* Middle Eastern states (their boundaries and national integrity), whether in the Levant or in the Gulf, may also help.

But these are necessary rather than sufficient conditions. The West should prepare for a significant diplomatic initiative, soon after the beginning of the Geneva conference (December 1973). Britain or Canada or France could take the lead. The initiative may take any of several forms but should result in a rapprochement between major oil consumer countries – including representatives of the third world – and oil producers. (Initiatives which produce a consumer cartel are certain to exacerbate the conflict.) It is relatively easy to devise a list of proposals, say an agenda for a conference between governments, which could ease the medium-term supply problem to the mutual advantage of all parties concerned. A policy package could include the following. First, specific technical assistance to the desert oil-economies. The aim is to enhance their absorptive capacity and help their long-run development. Second, serious feasibility studies of investment in refining and petrochemicals for producer countries. The notion that oil should serve as a base for industrialization rather than as a source of external rents has considerable appeal. Political concessions may be called for in this area as the objections to refining *in situ* are not purely economic. Third, Saudi Arabia and Kuwait should be invited to participate in all discussions relating to the management or reform of the international monetary system. I am thinking of the Group of Ten. Their stake in the system, if they were to hold large surpluses of foreign exchange, is so large as to justify such a move. Fourth, a two-tier price system or some form of subsidy to less-developed countries may be discussed. Fifth, new international financial instruments, either indexed bonds or units of an international trust holding equities and real estate throughout the world, or both, could be devised as an alternative to holding reserves in cash. Either asset presupposes the creation of specialized institutions by treaty whose role is to provide financial and political guarantees to both investors (producer governments and others) and host countries (those in which the investment are made). Many other suggestions could be added to the list.

The incentive to produce more at an early date relates to the contribution of today's earnings to the economic development of the oil-producing country. The policies suggested may not suit perfectly all parties involved. Concessions will have to be made. A recognition that the economic and political interests of consumers and producers are interdependent and the creation of a climate of mutual understanding will facilitate these concessions. There are some grounds for optimism.

The USSR is viewed rather enigmatically by most people when it comes to energy. One knows of the vast Siberian reserves of oil and gas; one reads about the huge pipelines being constructed across vast distances. Yet how does one evaluate the desire of private capitalist Western firms not only to purchase oil and gas but also to lend the Soviets the roubles to develop these fields? If we feel that supply is insecure when it comes from 'friendly' lands, how about the security of Russian supplies?

Wright advances a number of hypotheses which can explain Soviet exports and interest in deals with American capitalists. Rather than a socialist conspiracy to undermine the West, Wright sees the Russians as acting as eminently sensible capitalists, buttressing OPEC nations, raising the world price of oil, and increasing the foreign exchange the USSR can earn from oil and gas sales. Wright sees the Russians continuing to export outside Communist Europe as long as the price is right. Afraid of investing in high-cost energy (sending LNG 3000 miles to the US) and being left holding the vapors, the Russians insist that if Americans really want the stuff, they can hold the bag too. In short, the Russians are quite willing to export oil and gas to Western nations, but the Russians will be sure to get the best terms imaginable.

As interesting sidepieces, read the papers on the Middle East by Crandall and Mabro, and on the US by Erickson & Spann.

ARTHUR W. WRIGHT

The Soviet Union in world energy markets

In virtually every sphere of world affairs, the USSR is a pre-eminent power not to be ignored, and energy is no exception. The Soviet economy produces and uses enormous quantities of every important form of primary energy – oil, natural gas, coal, and hydropower (see Table 1) – and is in the forefront of nuclear energy development. The USSR is presently a major world exporter of oil and to a lesser extent coal; exports of natural gas and electric power have been added to the list and promise to increase substantially (see Table 2). What Soviet leaders can and do decide on in the energy field will obviously have a significant impact on the world energy question.

Like the infamous 'energy crisis,' the Soviet role in world energy markets has become the subject of various assertions and theories, many of them involving sinister motives and dire warnings. My purpose in this chapter is to show that economic analysis can help remove much of the emotion and pettifoggery which presently surround the subject of Soviet energy prospects. I shall argue that the best explanation of most Soviet energy decisions is that the people making them are rational economic men: they make a decision, as Jacob Viner once put it, 'for the difference it will make' in economic wellbeing, as that is determined in their own political system. Where mistakes are made, they learn from them. Where 'political' ends figure in energy decisions, Soviet decision-makers are well aware of the opportunity costs incurred and appear ready to give up the political ends if the economic opportunity costs go too high.

The basic ingredients of the analysis in this chapter are the familiar economist's tools of supply and demand. Using these tools, I shall examine the past development, current situation, and the outlook for the rest of the 1970s of Soviet

TABLE 1

Soviet production of major forms of primary energy, selected years, 1940–71

Year	Coal (millions of metric tons)				Crude oil (millions of metric tons)	Natural gas (millions of cubic meters)	Hydroelectric power	
	total	anthracite	bituminous	'brown coal'			capacity (thousands of kw)	production (millions of kwh)
1940	165.9	35.7	104.3	25.9	31.1	3.2	1,587	5,113
1945	149.3	16.9	82.5	49.9	19.4	3.3	1,252	4,841
1950	261.1	40.2	145.0	75.9	37.9	5.8	3,218	12,691
1955	389.99	57.8	218.8	113.3	70.8	9.0	5,996	23,165
1960	509.6	74.1	300.8	134.7	147.9	45.3	14,781	50,913
1965	577.7	76.5	351.4	149.9	242.9	127.7	22,244	81,434
1970	624.1	75.8	400.6	147.7	353.0	197.9	31,368	124,377
1971	640.9	75.8	411.7	153.3	377.1	212.4	33,448	126,099

NOTE: 1 metric ton = 2,204.6 lbs. (slightly more than 7 US (42-gallon) barrels on average); 1 cubic meter = 35.316 cubic feet.

SOURCE: Tsentral'noe Statisticheskoi Upravlenie SSSR (Central Statistical Administration of the USSR), *Narodnoe khoziaistvo SSSR, 1922–1972 gg: iubileinyi statististicheskii ezhegodnik (National Economy of the USSR, 1922–1972: Jubilee Statistical Annual)* (Moscow 1972), pp. 158, 163, 164

TABLE 2

Major Soviet exports and imports of fuels, selected years, 1938–1971
(million metric tons)

	Exports			Imports	
Year	bituminous and anthracite coal	crude oil	refined oil products	bituminous and anthracite coal	crude oil and refined oil products
1938	0.4	0.2	1.2		0.1
1950	1.1	0.3	0.8	9	2.6
1960	12.3	17.8	15.4	5	4.4
1965	22.4	43.4	21.0	7	1.9
1970	24.5	66.8	29.0	7	4.6
1971	24.9	74.8	30.3	8	6.6

SOURCE: as for Table 1, pp. 493–4

energy production and use. Three derivative issues which merit attention are the role of Soviet relations with her East European Communist neighbors; the role of Soviet relations with the United States, Japan, and other non-Communist powers; and the position of the USSR in the Middle East, especially among the major oil-producing countries.

1 SOVIET ENERGY DEVELOPMENT THROUGH 1960

The Soviet government inherited well-developed oil and coal fields from its tsarist predecessor. The oil fields, located in Azerbaidzhan (Baku) along the western coast of the Caspian Sea and in the North Caucasus (Grozny), were developed under the tsars with large amounts of West European equity capital. Production from those fields made pre-Bolshevik Russia the world's leading oil-producing and exporting nation in the first two decades of this century. The development of the coal fields, by far the largest of which was located in the Don River basin (Donbas) in the Ukraine, was spurred by the industrial growth which occurred under the tsars beginning in the late nineteenth century. The tsarist legacy of oil and coal fields was tied in with European Russia, where most of the industry was located; although romantics had long dreamed of harnessing the mineral riches of Siberia – the vast northern area of Asiatic Russia – very little development had taken place there by 1917, the year in which the Bolsheviks took power.

The first decade or so of the Soviet regime was a time of reconstruction from war and of laying plans for the future. Looking ahead to the rapid build-up of iron and steel output, Soviet leaders undertook extensive geological work on coal in the 1920s; additions to current productive capacity, however, were few. In oil, which became embroiled in international disputes over Soviet nationalization policies,[1] it was all the Soviets could do just to restore the Baku and Grozny oil fields to their pre-Soviet capacities; very little geological work was done there or in other potential oil-bearing regions.

The all-out industrialization campaign, which began in 1928, included massive programs to expand Donbas coal capacity and to bring large new coal deposits into production. While considerable fanfare attended the construction of large hydropower projects, coal was viewed as the key source of energy in the ambitious Soviet plans for industrial growth – for railway steam traction, for industrial boilers, for commercial and residential space heating in the mushrooming industrial centers, and for the burgeoning electric power network ('Communism is Soviet power and electrification,' the motto ran). In addition, high-grade bituminous coal converted into coke was a crucial input into the high-priority iron and steel industry.

Oil was not totally neglected in the first three five-year plans (1928-32, 1933-37, and 1938-42): oil exports helped finance imports of machinery and other industrial inputs in the early 1930s and to supplement coal as a source of domestic fuel. New reserves did not, however, suffice to sustain the growing export and domestic demands, and by the late 1930s oil production peaked and eventually turned downward. It is interesting to note that the depletion of the Baku and Grozny oil fields apparently did not evoke panic in Moscow; for example, one finds no references from the period warning that the USSR was 'running out of oil.' The best explanation seems to be that Soviet leaders had more important things on their minds – not the least of them being the approaching world war.

Following the Second World War, the rapid industrialization policy of the 1930s was resumed. In energy, that meant the continued priority expansion of electric-generating and coal-producing capacity. The share of coal in total Soviet primary energy production (measured in units of homogeneous thermal content) actually rose after the war, reaching a peak of about two-thirds in the early 1950s. The experience of the war had, however, changed the thinking of Soviet leaders on oil.

First, military strategy and tactics had become heavily dependent on oil, in both combat and logistical operations. Second, the German invasion, which penetrated deep into European Russia, had led perforce to massive and irreversible industrial development in the Ural Mountains and to the east: both strategically and economically, further industrial growth in the eastern regions of the USSR now made compellingly good sense. The eastward thrust of Soviet industrialization led to the opening up of a huge oil- and gas-producing region in the Urals-

Volga triangle, beginning in the early 1950s. In the mid-1960s, a second major oil and gas region, across the Urals in western Siberia, was opened up. As will be seen later, the Siberian petroleum discoveries, whose full implications still remain to be worked out, are at the very center of the current Soviet energy situation and prospects for the future.

Moscow's post-war interest in oil initially took the form of renewed geological work in the traditional oil fields, particularly Baku. Some attention was also given to promising prospects in the Urals-Volga triangle, where minor finds had been made just prior to the Second World War; but the principal hopes were placed on the work in the Baku region. By the early 1950s, however, two circumstances brought about a shift of emphasis between the two areas.

First, the considerable investment in the traditional oil fields yielded disappointingly few new reserves. Second, several unexpectedly attractive finds in the Urals-Volga region led Soviet planners to step up geological activity there. By 1953, the Urals-Volga oil fields had replaced Baku as the focal point of Soviet petroleum development. Moreover, the economic scale of the Urals-Volga fields – that is, the production levels which could be attained at or below the costs of alternative fuel sources – was large enough to bring about a shift in long-term Soviet plans for primary energy.[2]

The Soviet strategy for primary energy after 1953 consisted of the following components.

a / Urals-Volga oil production rose almost ten times between 1950 and 1960 (from about 11 million metric tons (mmt) to 109.4 mmt annually), accounting for almost 90 per cent of the fourfold increase in total Soviet oil output over that period.

b / Somewhat later than oil but no less vigorously, natural gas output was sharply expanded, rising from a tiny amount in 1950-55 (an annual average of about 7.5 billion cubic meters (Bcm) to 45.3 Bcm in 1960. During 1957 and 1958, annual rates of growth of 52.6 and 46.1 per cent, respectively, were achieved. A portion of this growth came from the gathering of gas associated with oil in the Urals-Volga region; far more, however, was from major new natural gas deposits discovered and developed in the Ukraine, the North Caucasus, the Baku area, and (later) in Soviet Central Asia.

c / Coal output expansion plans were revised downward, and the intended regional distribution and product composition were modified. Growth in Donbas output leveled off in the late 1950s, while newer producing areas were expanded in the Urals, Kazakhstan, and eastern Siberia. Output of coking coal continued to grow, keeping pace with the high-priority iron and steel industry. Strip-mining received increased emphasis, especially in conjunction with the development of new thermal electric-generating capacity east of the Ural Mountains.

d / Publicity kept outrunning actual results in hydropower, but the Soviets did make impressive strides in harnessing their major river systems to produce electric power. Some people (including Nikita Khrushchev, first secretary of the party and premier) believed those strides were *too* impressive – that is, excessive investible resources were tied up in the dams and equipment, which often operated at only part-capacity for years because of insufficient demand.[3] In defense of the hydropower projects, it can be argued that scale economics justify building ahead of demand, and that the hydropower capacity may make sense when one considers the peak-load problem, the increased use of large grids for sharing electric power, and recent Soviet achievements in reducing the cost of long-distance electricity transmission.[4]

The direct result of the new long-term strategy for primary energy after 1953 was an abrupt shift in the proportions of the Soviet fuel balance. The share of coal in total fuel output (in thermal equivalents) dropped from the peak of two-thirds in the early 1950s to less than half by 1962; that share has continued to decline ever since. Oil and natural gas more than made up the difference, as the shares of local (i.e., low-quality) fuels such as peat and wood also declined.

Also associated with the shift in fuel strategy was a marked increase in Soviet oil exports. From only 1.1 mmt (0.3 crude oil and 0.8 products) in 1950, those exports rose to 33.2 mmt (17.8 crude oil and 15.4 products) in 1960. They continued to rise until the late 1960s, and may well increase again in the 1970s – but that is getting ahead of the story.

A proper understanding of Soviet oil export behavior requires discussion of two related issues: Soviet ties to the Communist nations of Eastern Europe, and Soviet sales of oil outside the Communist bloc. These two issues will also figure in our subsequent discussion of the current situation and future prospects. I shall discuss each issue in turn.

2 THE SOVIET UNION AND COMMUNIST EASTERN EUROPE

Taken most broadly, this subject merits, and has received, whole volumes of analysis and discussion. The essential point for my narrower purpose is that the USSR has important long-term political goals with respect to Eastern Europe, for reasons related to national security and international power relationships. Two major mechanisms for promoting those goals are of relevance here: rapid industrialization of the Communist East European countries, and the operation of a customs union known as the Council of Mutual Economic Assistance, commonly abbreviated as CMEA or Comecon.

The pursuit of rapid industrialization in Eastern Europe after the last World War carried with it, of course, rapidly rising demands for energy. In the countries which in 1945 were relatively undeveloped - e.g., Romania, Bulgaria, and Yugoslavia[5] - the postwar growth in demand for the modern fuels (oil, gas, and high-grade coal) was especially rapid, as traditional fuel sources were replaced along with the increased use of energy from growth alone. By the mid to late 1950s, East European energy demands had reached the point where continued heavy reliance on high-cost indigenous sources would have seriously constrained further growth.

As in other customs unions, Comecon has been a vehicle for increasing economic co-operation among the member nations by the use of trade preferences within the union and of uniform trade restrictions towards the rest of the world. In many cases, of course, the customs union members pay a price - in the form of foregone import and export opportunities - by belonging; however, the benefits (including political ones) received may be quite valuable. Within Comecon, the Soviet Union emerged in the mid to late 1950s as the major supplier of oil to the bloc. It is noteworthy that in the early 1950s Eastern Europe was a net *exporter* of oil and oil products to the USSR (chiefly from Romania); by 1960 the situation was reversed, and East European net imports of Soviet oil rose steadily thereafter.[6]

A principal element in the swift rise of Soviet oil exports to Eastern Europe was the construction of the Friendship pipeline from the USSR into Eastern Europe; the recipient countries participated in the financing and construction of this pipeline. Both the large size of the exports and the construction of a major international pipeline to carry a large proportion of them indicate that the Soviets made a deliberate decision to expand their productive capacity in oil (and in natural gas, to release oil for export) beyond their own domestic consumption targets, in order to supply their allies in Eastern Europe. The notion, frequently encountered in the early 1960s, that the exports were from a Soviet surplus - with the implication that oil exports would decline as domestic Soviet demand grew - is not consistent with the evidence so far as exports to Eastern Europe are concerned.

3 SOVIET OIL EXPORTS TO NON-COMMUNIST COUNTRIES

Exports to Eastern Europe did not, however, account for all of Soviet oil sales abroad. Such major non-Communist - even anti-Communist - powers as West Germany and Italy became important customers for Soviet oil soon after the export sales began to expand rapidly. These sales to the 'free world' were the subject of a minor scare, largely promoted by the major international oil companies, in the early 1960s. The Soviets were alleged to be trying to disrupt orderly world oil markets, to create mischief for capitalist companies, to foster dependence on Soviet oil which could then be turned to political advantage – and, yes, to be dumping surpluses which would later dry up.

A careful look at the evidence, however, failed to bear out the alleged causes of concern. A better – and simpler – explanation was that Moscow wanted to export oil to the West to earn foreign exchange with which to buy foreign goods on world markets. Consistent with this interpretation is the fact that Soviet oil exports as a percentage of total oil production rose persistently from 1950 until well into the 1960s – and this at a time when they were also expanding production rapidly each year.[7] Furthermore, Soviet deals with capitalist countries never were such as to cause serious price breaks. At worst (for the international oil companies), the Russian oil added some competition to the world oil market, but only at prices which were attractive enough in Moscow to warrant the continued rapid development of oil and gas production. In effect, the companies had the choice of letting the Soviets in on their good thing, or driving prices down to levels which would induce them to stay out of the world market.

Thus the best explanation of Soviet oil export behavior in the 1950s and 1960s is that the USSR – the world's leading socialist country – was using oil in world trade in classical capitalist style. This practice was developed and utilized years before Brezhnev's triumphal visit to Washington in 1973 and that other display of socialist market acuity in the celebrated grain deals of 1972.

4 THE CURRENT SITUATION
AND FUTURE PROSPECTS FOR SOVIET ENERGY

Background
Since 1960, the Soviet energy strategy adopted in 1953 has been followed through in detail. Massive production capacity has been developed in the Urals-Volga oil and gas region; however, because new output increases must come from higher-cost prospects, expansion there has slowed considerably. Hydropower and strip-mined coal output have continued to increase, but again at a slower pace than in the hectic 1950s. In the mid 1960s, vast new petroleum deposits were discovered in western Siberia at Surgut and Samotlor (oil) and in the far north at Nadym (natural gas). Both distance from consumption centers (or ports) and difficult accessibility because of near-Arctic conditions, however, make these new deposits higher-cost than were those in the Urals-Volga region at a comparable stage of development.[8]

As mentioned earlier, Soviet oil exports peaked in the late 1960s and have largely leveled off since then. The deceleration of exports can be traced to the continued rise of internal demand and to the higher costs of new energy sources. Within Comecon, the East European countries have begun re-examining their heavy reliance on Soviet oil (at prevailing prices), and the Soviets for their part have been re-examining the attractiveness of further long-term export commitments to Eastern Europe (at those same prices).[9]

An important recent development in the world oil market which will have a strong effect on Soviet (and most other major industrial nations') energy decisions is the formation in 1971 of a cartel among the members of the Organization of Petroleum Exporting Countries. (Only the United States and the USSR among the major oil-producing nations are not members of OPEC.) The cartel presents the Russians with both attractive opportunities and problems – on balance, more of the former than the latter. The chief opportunity is higher world prices for oil and natural gas than would exist if the world petroleum market were competitive. As shown above, Soviet energy decisions, including those on exports, are sensitive to price: the higher the price, the more will be supplied, and conversely with respect to demand. There is no reason to expect Soviet behavior in this regard to change in the foreseeable future.

With the above general discussion as background, I turn now to three specific topics having to do with the current and likely future situations in Soviet energy: Soviet ties with Eastern Europe, Soviet sales of petroleum to non-Communist countries, and the role of the USSR in the Middle East, where the principal members of OPEC are located.

Energy in Soviet-East European trade
In Eastern Europe, while both the scale and the terms of economic relations within Comecon are under review (as mentioned earlier), the basic relationship remains strong. The available evidence suggests that the USSR has decided at least to contain within 'tolerable' limits, if not to prevent outright, the shift of East European energy imports to the world market. The Friendship oil pipeline has been expanded in size. A projected network of natural gas pipelines will bring increasing quantities of Ukrainian natural gas into Eastern Europe. And the Comecon electric power grid, named Peace, will continue to grow in size and density. None of these projects, especially the first two, would be worthwhile if there were any doubt of the continued expansion of Soviet energy exports to Eastern Europe. The likely range of variation in their magnitude is positive, but small.

As to the *terms* on which the energy imports will be obtained by the East Europeans, the Soviets are likely to continue to charge prices roughly in correspondence with what their oil and gas could fetch on the world market. It is probable that the East Europeans will be requested to continue their participation in joint ventures to develop Soviet oil and gas deposits (as well as other kinds of industry and minerals); such participation will make it more difficult than ever to estimate the actual transaction terms between the USSR and the East European countries with any degree of accuracy.

Soviet oil and gas exported to Eastern Europe will not, of course, be available to customers in the world market. However, except for a general increase in over-all world energy costs as a result of the trade preferences within a customs union, the *net* effect on world energy markets of the USSR's providing most of Eastern Europe's oil and gas imports will not be very great. It is doubtful that the Russians would use any extra sales outside Comecon to try to drive down world prices, which will in any case be dominated by the actions of OPEC; and if the East Europeans did not get their energy imports from the Soviets, they would have to seek them in the world market.

Soviet energy exports to non-Communist countries
The scare of the early 1960s over Soviet oil exports outside the bloc has largely disappeared; perhaps it has even been replaced by euphoria (to listen to Occidental Petroleum's Dr. Armand Hammer).[10] Today the representatives of Japanese, American, West German, and sundry other capitalist countries' private firms are tripping over one another in Moscow, trying to negotiate deals for Soviet oil, natural gas, and liquefied natural gas. The Soviet negotiators are warmly receptive; however, judging from the length of the bargaining periods, the air of intrigue which surrounds the negotiations, and the terms of the deals so far announced, the Soviets are not giving much away. In virtually every case, a precondition even of preliminary talks is the principle of joint-participation hard-currency loans, or at least direct credit.[11]

Why all this interest in Soviet petroleum goods? Oil piped 3000 miles to the Soviet Pacific coast; natural gas piped 2230 miles to the Pacific coast or over 3000 miles to Hokkaido, Japan; LNG manufactured from gas piped over 2000 miles and then transported to the US in tankers costing $80-100 million apiece – in short, *costly* petroleum goods? The answer, of course, is that the prices implied in such cost figures are not unattractive beside the prices OPEC looks like getting for Middle East oil. Were it not for the price increases already realized and expected to come in the world oil market, it is highly doubtful that the capitalists would be in Moscow at all – at least not negotiating energy deals.

Looking at the Soviet side, there has been considerable talk in the Western press of how the Russians 'need' Western capital in order to develop their fuel riches, and of how the construction lags and capital shortages of the Soviet planned economy have led to problems only the financial and engineering resources of capitalist business can resolve.[12] Such talk is reminiscent of an earlier day when press reports repeatedly told of how the Soviet economy was on its last legs and likely to collapse at any time. For their part, the Russians do not discourage such talk (they may even add to it by pretending to harken back to the romance of the untapped 'riches of Siberia'), but not because they believe it. One is tempted to remind outside observers again of the operations of the Soviet *naïfs* in the American grain market.

Far from 'needing' Western capital to develop their fuel resources, the Soviet Union is fully capable of expanding fuel output for domestic and export purposes – *if* the price is right. At the present time, that price for export markets includes some sharing of the risk that inflated world energy prices will plummet, leaving the Soviets with a lot of capital sunk in expensive energy assets; hence the emphasis on joint participation. The bulk of previous Soviet oil export trade with non-Communist countries has been conducted on a straight commercial basis; there are no signs of a change in attitude.[13]

The role of the USSR in the Middle East
The Soviet role in the Middle East is a prime candidate for a new scare campaign. Rumblings to the effect that Moscow is trying to 'pin down' Western oil supplies have already been heard.[14] (Why Japanese and American businessmen should then be negotiating in Moscow for Soviet oil and gas as insurance against being 'pinned down' has not been explained.) It is worth looking at the available evidence to see what exactly Soviet interests in the area appear to be and how Soviet leaders may be expected to act to achieve them.

The first point to note is that the USSR obviously has strong strategic and diplomatic interests in the Middle East – the eastern Mediterranean, Suez, the Persian Gulf, etc. A glance at a map will reveal one source of those interests – sheer military security – which has nothing to do with the presence of vast quantities of oil. Given these strong interests, of course, and the presence of the large international oil companies in many of the countries in the region, it is to be expected that Moscow would welcome the chance to weaken the companies and their attendant Western influence – provided, of course, seizing that chance did not seriously jeopardize the attainment of some other goal, such as a détente with the United States. (The Russians anyhow may not have to work very hard to weaken oil-company influence in the Middle East; several of the sovereign governments in the area have them on the run already.)

A second point to take note of is that, while the Soviets may be interested in purchasing some Middle Eastern oil or gas to supplement their own production, they are not likely to do it on any significant scale for other than reasons of cost-savings – for example, to supply southern areas of the USSR which are closer to

Arthur W. Wright

the Middle Eastern oil fields than to Soviet sources.[15] Further, Moscow is not likely to count on substantial price favors from the OPEC countries, most of whom exhibit a clear command of the principles of operating a successful cartel.

A third point is that the Soviet Union may be expected from time to time to dabble in Middle Eastern oil on a non-commercial basis for short-run tactical reasons. An example is the response to the Iraqi nationalization of the Iraq Petroleum Company in 1972, when the Soviets bought Iraqi oil produced on the IPC properties. The impact of such dabbling on world energy markets, however, will be small.

A final point about Soviet actions in the Middle East is that they will be governed by an interest in supporting OPEC in forcing up and maintaining world oil prices at monopoly levels. That is to say, the Russians have more to gain from the high prices as exporters of oil and gas than they stand to lose as purchasers of Middle Eastern or other foreign oil.

Taken together, the above four points may spell trouble for the US and other Western interests. However, the trouble will be no worse than is regularly generated by Soviet moves on other fronts, and certainly no cause for panic.

5 SUMMARY AND CONCLUSIONS

I have argued in this chapter that the Soviet role in the world 'energy question' can best be understood in terms of simple economic analysis. Soviet energy decision-makers are sensitive to costs and returns. The USSR is an ambitious industrial power, still bent on overtaking the United States and the other advanced industrial nations in total and *per capita* output. Energy demand in the Soviet Union can therefore be expected to continue to grow at a brisk pace. The USSR has a large and growing energy production capacity with which it will be able economically to supply a high proportion of its internal demand; however, some imports (e.g., of Middle Eastern oil and gas) are likely where they are cheaper than indigenous sources. The Soviets will continue to export oil, gas, and electric power to their East European Communist neighbors, probably in growing amounts as the economies of those neighbors continue to develop. Soviet oil and gas exports will also continue to come on the world market, in varying quantities depending on the prices they can command compared to the costs of developing and producing additional output.

Thus the USSR will in fact be a significant actor on the world energy stage, as was suggested at the outset of the chapter. As a major fuel exporter and also an importer, and as a world power with strong strategic interests in the Middle East with its major oil-producing nations, the USSR will have a keen interest in world energy market conditions. There is every reason to expect the Russians to watch

96

out carefully for their own interests; among other things, that will mean driving hard bargains for their own fuel exports and supporting OPEC's efforts to raise and maintain monopoly-level world oil prices. They will, of course, be no different in such behavior from any other rational country (or from private companies).

NOTES

1 See Philip S. Gillette, 'American Capital in the Contest for Soviet Oil, 1920-1923,' *Soviet Studies* XXIV, no. 4 (April 1973), pp. 477-90.
2 The details of this shift, as well as sources and discussion of much else in the present chapter down through 1965, can be found in Part Two of my unpublished PhD dissertation, 'The Theory and Practice of Soviet Investment Planning (with Special Reference to the Mineral Fuel Industries)' (Massachusetts Institute of Technology 1969). A scholarly paper on the switch from coal to oil and gas, based on the Urals-Volga discoveries, is in preparation. On the Soviet petroleum industry generally, the basic reference is Robert W. Campbell, *The Economics of Soviet Oil and Gas* (Baltimore: Johns Hopkins Press for Resources for the Future 1968). The timing of the Soviet switch to petroleum has been criticized as being too late; both Campbell and I would hold, however, that (except for common errors in human judgment about the future) it occurred at about the right time, in about the right manner, given Soviet goals and information about alternatives.
3 Khrushchev chose the opening of the Kuibyshev hydro station in 1958 as the occasion for his skeptical remarks. Long lags of demand behind new hydro capacity are occasionally a problem even today; see the *New York Times,* 16 Nov. 1972, pp. 69ff.
4 I am indebted to Francis M. Leversedge for pointing out the first two qualifying factors to me.
5 Yugoslavia is included in Eastern Europe in the present analysis, even though she was expelled from the European Communist bloc in 1948 and has had alternately warm and cold relations with the USSR since then. The Yugoslav economy is closely tied to the other East European economies, because obvious relative cost factors have continually overridden short-term political differences.
6 See Jaroslav G. Polach, 'The Development of Energy in Eastern Europe,' in US Congress, Joint Economic Committee, *Economic Development in Countries of Eastern Europe* (Washington 1970), pp. 393ff. Polach's paper is a valuable source of information on East European energy, and I have drawn upon it at several points in the present chapter. It is sometimes charged (e.g., in Polach, pp. 400, 402) that the USSR 'discriminates' as a monopolist against Eastern

Arthur W. Wright

Europe in foreign trade. That is, goods sold to Eastern Europe allegedly carry higher prices than the same goods sold outside the bloc, and goods bought from Eastern Europe move at prices lower than the Russians pay for comparable non-bloc goods. However, the present state of the debate in the literature seems to be that the null hypothesis of 'no discrimination' cannot be rejected on the basis of the available evidence. In energy, Polach concedes (p. 402) that Soviet pricing of natural gas exports to Eastern Europe 'is not out of line with practices followed in Western Europe where the price ... is aligned to the nearest competitive fuel.' Such pricing practices are not, of course, evidence of monopoly price discrimination.

7 See my dissertation, Table 10. The general subject of Soviet oil exports is discussed there on pp. 271ff.

8 To move the Siberian oil and gas to domestic and export markets will require several thousand miles of large-diameter (48-inch) pipelines over permafrost terrain – conditions similar to those encountered in the Alaskan North Slope field. It is noteworthy that, unlike the Alaskan case in the US, the Soviet government has not had to contend with the organized and persistent opposition of environmentalists in planning those pipelines.

9 In the late 1960s and early 1970s, there were numerous rumors, 'agreements in principle,' and minor actual bargains struck between East European countries and members of OPEC. See Polach, *Economic Developments*, pp. 399-400, and *New York Times*, 21 Jan. 1972, p. 69.

10 '[Dr. Hammer] indicated that he discussed [the] "political decisions" upon which the [Yakutsk gas] pipeline deal depends during a recent two-hour Kremlin conference – in Russian – with Mr. Brezhnev, whom he described as "a man of great humanism and vast warmth and understanding, enormously intelligent and sophisticated in the ways of the world."' *New York Times*, 21 May 1973, p. 52.

11 The continuing saga of the Moscow negotiations has been well reported in the *New York Times* and the *Wall Street Journal*. On the Japanese quest for Siberian oil, see *NYT*, 25 Nov. 1972, p. 41, and *WSJ*, 27 Nov. 1972, p. 15. On Japanese hopes for importing natural gas by undersea pipeline, see *NYT*, *ibid.*; similar West German plans *via* overland pipeline are detailed in *NYT*, 11 April 1972, p. 55. There are two different ventures afoot to import LNG, manufactured from natural gas in the USSR, into the US: the Texas Eastern Transmission–Tenneco–Brown & Root proposal to ship LNG from Murmansk (on the Soviet western coast of the Arctic Ocean) to the US east coast (*WSJ*, 15 June 1972, p. 42; *NYT*, 9 Jan. 1973, pp. 49ff; *WSJ*, 2 July 1973, p. 14); and the Occidental Petroleum–El Paso Natural Gas proposal (jointly with Japanese interests) to ship Yakutsk gas, liquefied near Vladivostok, to the

US West Coast (*NYT*, 30 Oct. 1972, pp. 47ff, 9 June 1973, pp. 41ff; *WSJ*, 11 June 1973, p. 7).

12 For discussions of a Soviet 'energy pinch' and how it was supposed to have spurred Mr Brezhnev's visit to Washington, see *NYT*, 24 March 1973, pp. 43ff, *WSJ*, 10 April 1973, p. 42, and *NYT*, 8 June 1973, pp. 51ff. Curiously, the same newspapers, and even the same reporters, can be found dismissing notions of such a pinch; see, for instance, *NYT*, 28 March 1973, pp. 63ff.

13 Western press reports of Soviet-Western deals and negotiations stress the Russians' reputation for living up to their contractual obligations (e.g., *WSJ*, 22 Aug. 1973, p. 30). A further indication of Soviet willingness to trade energy goods if the price is right is a recent story about Soviet plans to export uranium if an expected 'shortage' appears on world markets in the late 1970s; see *NYT*, 3 May 1973, pp. 63ff.

14 See William D. Smith, 'What is Moscow's Motive? Economic Gain, or Blackmail Suggested,' *NYT*, 11 June 1972, sec. 3, p. 3; also, an article by Drew Middleton in *NYT*, 20 April 1973, p. 8.

15 The Russians have also acted as middlemen for Middle Eastern oil sales on the world market (*NYT*, 21 Jan. 1972, p. 69).

The recent beginnings of negotiations and trade with China lead to the possibility of Chinese energy reserves being shipped to Western consumers. Rawski provides new and valuable data on Chinese reserves and production. He suggests that, while China is at present still a coal-based economy, the transition to oil will be relatively easy because of the vast probable reserves both on the mainland and on the unexplored continental shelves. Rawski develops seven scenarios as to the possible rates of development of Chinese energy. Growth rates of production for coal, oil, and gas to 1985 at rates substantially below past achievements will enable a 10 per cent industrial growth rate. If output of oil and gas grows in excess of 15 per cent annually, large energy surpluses will appear by 1980 even if industrial output grows faster than 10 per cent a year. Since only 1 per cent of the Chinese land mass and none of its offshore areas have been explored for oil and gas, very large growth rates may well occur in energy production. An annual growth rate in oil and gas production of 25 per cent would result in an annual surplus in 1980 of 18,000 trillion BTUs and in 1985 of 62,000 trillion BTUs (3 billion barrels in 1980, 10 in 1985).

For Japan, the picture is quite opposite. Japan now imports 85 per cent of its energy needs, with 84 per cent of its petroleum (62 per cent of total energy consumption) coming from Middle Eastern countries. Despite an accelerated nuclear program, this re-liance will not decrease in coming years. Japan's demand for imported energy is likely to grow at rates above the world average. In order to diversify its oil imports to improve their security, Japan is likely to attempt to import Soviet and Chinese oil and gas. The Japanese government has set a target that, by 1985, 30 per cent of oil imports should flow from fields developed with Japanese participation. In this regard, Japanese firms have offered to collaborate with China and Russia in developing their reserves.

This paper should be read along with Wright on the Soviet Union and with Crandall and Mabro on the Middle East.

THOMAS G. RAWSKI

China and Japan in the world energy economy

China and Japan occupy important positions on the world energy scene because of the large size, rapid growth, and potential for future expansion of their production and consumption of commercial energy. Japan and China, each of which used approximately 12×10^{15} BTU [British thermal units] of energy in 1971, are currently the world's third and fourth largest energy consumers, surpassed only by the United States and the Soviet Union. China, with no significant trade in energy, is among the world's largest producers, while Japan leads all nations in energy imports. Basic data on energy consumption and trade for the two countries appears in Table 1.[1] Chinese and Japanese energy consumption is not only large, but has grown for over two decades at a rapid pace unmatched by other large nations. Since 1955 the share of China and Japan in world energy consumption has risen steadily from 5.6 to 12.4 per cent.[2] However, per capita consumption is still low, particularly in China. While China shows little interest in attaining the personal consumption levels of the industrial west, even a modest per capita energy goal such as the US level of 1900 would require prodigious multiplication of energy supplies. The desire to emulate American consumption patterns will continue to exert upward pressure on Japan's per capita energy use, which now approximates West European levels.

THE PRESENT ENERGY POSITION

China
China possesses substantial energy reserves, which have sufficed to support two decades of rapid though erratic economic growth and transformation while eli-

TABLE 1

Basic energy statistics for China and Japan, 1952-71*

Year	Apparent energy consumption				Energy consumption		Shares of major sources (%)				Share of imports in total consumption (%)
	Coal (million tons)	Crude oil (million barrels)	Natural gas (billion cu.m.)	Hydro power (billion kwh)	total 10^{12} BTU	per capita 10^6 BTU[c]	Coal	Crude	Gas	Hydro	
CHINA[d]											
1952	65	3.8	0.06	1.3	1,964	3.3	84.2	2.3	0.1	1.4	–
1955	97	8.9	0.11	2.4	2,885	4.5	85.5	3.9	0.2	1.7	–
1965	219	40.0	11.3	16.5	6,732	9.3	82.3	3.5	6.4	3.1	–
1971	324	189.2	52.1	29.8	11,893	14.9	68.9	9.2	16.6	2.2	–
JAPAN											
1955	47	75.1	0.3	48.5	2,223	24.9	49.2	20.2	0.4	21.2	24.0
1960	66	235.4	1.0	58.5	3,720	39.8	41.5	37.7	1.0	15.3	44.2
1965	73	640.7	2.0	76.4	6,572	66.9	27.3	58.4	1.2	11.3	66.2
1970	92	1478.3	2.8	84.6[a]	12,319	118.8	20.7	70.8	0.9	6.7[a]	83.5
1971	80	na	2.8	94.8[b]	12,722	121.2	17.5	73.5	0.9	7.3[b]	84.9

na not available

– less than 0.5%

*Metric tons and the American billion are used throughout this paper.

a includes 4.6 billion kwh produced by nuclear generating plants.

b includes 8.0 billion kwh produced by nuclear generating plants.

c Population data: for Japan, from *Japan Statistical Yearbook 1971* (Tokyo 1972), pp. 10-11; for China, we assume the following mid-year populations, in millions: 1952, 596; 1955, 638; 1965, 725; 1971, 800.

d owing to disruption caused by the Great Leap Forward, no reliable data are available for 1960.

SOURCES: Taken or calculated from Rawski, 'The Role of China in the World Energy Situation' (unpublished paper prepared for the Brookings Institution, June 1973) and *Sōgō enerugii tōkei – Shōwa 47 nendo [Overall Energy Statistics, 1972]* (Tokyo 1972), pp. 161-72.

minating reliance on Soviet oil. Aggregate product rose at an estimated annual rate slightly above 5 per cent during 1952-71, while industry's share in total product grew from 13 per cent to 45 per cent and its share of energy consumption rose from 31 to 69 per cent during the same period.[3]

Additional energy output has come primarily from coal, which still dominates China's energy economy, accounting for over two-thirds of 1971 energy consumption, a figure unequalled by any major world region.[4] Despite rapid growth of oil and gas production, coal also accounted for 51.3 per cent of incremental energy supplies between 1965 and 1971.

China's coal reserves are sufficient to provide for the indefinite future. The most frequently cited figures of 1-1.5 trillion tons, approximately equal to US reserves, are based on Chinese statements of the mid-1950s which should be revised upwards to take account of extensive and reportedly successful prospecting since 1957.[5] Even if present (1971) output of 325 million tons grows at 8 per cent annually, 1985 output will fall short of 1 billion tons, less than 0.1 per cent of a low reserve estimate.

Despite the continued dominance of coal, China has begun the transition to a fuel economy based on oil and gas which occurred during the 1950s and 1960s in Japan. Coal's share in total energy supplies fell sharply after 1965, while the share of oil and gas jumped from 10 per cent to over 25 per cent between 1965 and 1971.

Recent developments, including the discovery and tapping of new oil fields in Heilungkiang (at Ta-ch'ing), Shantung (Sheng-li), and Ch'inghai (in the Tsidam basin) provinces, contradict the previous belief that China lacks petroleum reserves. Although there is no authoritative account of China's reserves, A.A. Meyerhoff offers a figure of 19.6 billion bbl for 'ultimate' reserves which he describes as 'probably ... very conservative.' Meyerhoff comments that Ho Ko-jen's estimate of 51 billion bbl of natural and 136 billion bbl of synthetic (shale and coal) oil 'appears to be more realistic.'[6] Since all observers agree that large areas of the Chinese mainland remain unexplored, it seems clear that oil reserves will suffice to meet future needs of China's economy.[7]

These reserve estimates exclude possible seabed deposits. A team of UN geologists has described the unexplored continental shelf between Taiwan and Japan, much of which is claimed by the People's Republic, as possibly 'one of the most prolific oil reservoirs in the world.' They also report that the Yellow Sea floor contains addition favorable formations, some of which are clearly subject to Chinese sovereignty.[8]

Little is known about China's natural gas industry. Major deposits occur in the northwest and southwest regions, especially in Szechwan province. There are also reports of gas fields near Shanghai, China's leading industrial metropolis.[9] Recent

103

estimates place gas reserves (in the northwest and southwest only) at 500-600 billion cubic meters, or less than 10 per cent of US reserves.[10] But recent gas discoveries in twenty-seven counties and cities of coastal Chekiang province, less than 200 miles from Shanghai, illustrate the limited geologic work upon which all reserve estimates are founded.[11]

China's hydropower resources, estimated at 535 million kilowatts, are among the world's largest. Installed capacity is estimated at only 7.4 million kilowatts (for 1971/72) or about 1.4 per cent of potential capacity.[12] In comparison with the US and Japan, where installed capacity amounts to 25-50 per cent of estimated potential, China's hydroelectric capabilities remain largely unexploited.[13]

Although I have found no reference to present or proposed construction of nuclear power plants, Chinese delegations to Japan and Canada have recently expressed interest in nuclear power stations.[14] Chinese achievements in military applications of nuclear energy suggest a capacity to undertake civilian projects as well. While the present state of reserves and production of radioactive materials is unknown, it appears that China possesses the resources to support a large nuclear power industry.[15]

As is shown below, China's energy industry can satisfy the requirements of future economic growth, and may become a major source of foreign exchange. At present, the chief concern of China's domestic energy planners appears to be an imbalance between the regional distribution of reserves, output, and demand. Prior to recent discoveries, China's energy reserves were concentrated in the northwest region, with half of estimated coal deposits situated in rugged Shansi province (southwest of Peking) and all major crude oil fields located in a corridor running some 1500 miles northwest from Lanchow, itself 700 aerial miles from Peking. Demand for energy, in contrast, is concentrated in the coastal industrial areas of northeast and central China, while energy production comes largely from the north and northeast regions.

Japan

Japan's current energy position is sufficiently familiar to require only a brief account. Among industrial nations, Japan is uniquely dependent on imported energy products. Conversion from coal to oil as the prime energy source has raised Japan's reliance upon energy imports to the present level of 84.9 per cent of all forms of commercial energy, with further increases expected in the future.

Japanese discomfort with the current energy position is heightened by the extent of dependence on Middle Eastern oil, which currently accounts for 84 per cent of Japan's petroleum supplies and 62 per cent of total energy consumption.[16] Concern over possible instability in the oil supply of this region is magnified by the absence of alternative energy supplies of comparable size and by the low level of domestic fuel stocks. Security along the sea route from the Arabian Gulf, particularly in the Malacca Strait, is another source of uncertainty for Japan.

Domestically, Japan's energy policy problems are similar to those now encountered in other industrial nations. These difficulties are particularly serious because of the single-minded determination with which Japan has pursued industrial growth in recent decades, and because of the geographic concentration of the Japanese economy, which generates approximately five times the aggregate product per square mile as does that of the United States.[17]

Japan is now enmeshed in a dilemma created by the simultaneous desire of her increasingly affluent citizens for improved environmental conditions and for such energy-consuming novelties as private automobiles and air conditioners which exacerbate existing problems of pollution and congestion. As a result, conflicts arise in many sectors of the economy. Thermal power plants, for example, are bombarded with contradictory demands, being expected to meet growing consumption requirements while cutting emissions, avoiding construction in residential or recreational areas, economizing on consumption of low sulfur oil, and refraining from excessive price increases. The inability of government, long accustomed to automatic favoritism toward industry, to respond promptly and effectively to changing public attitudes toward resource allocation is one important cause of the political unease which is much discussed in Japan today.

FUTURE SUPPLY AND DEMAND FOR ENERGY

China
In view of the current dominance of industry in national energy consumption, projection of future requirements depends mainly on the assumed behavior of industrial output and unit energy requirements. China's industrial output has risen at an average annual rate of 11.9-12.7 per cent from 1952 to 1971: over 19 per cent from 1952 to 1957, 9.0-10.8 per cent from 1957 to 1965, and 9.9 per cent from 1965 to 1971.[18] On general economic grounds, there is reason to expect similar growth rates in the future.[19] Since industry has grown to occupy nearly one-half of aggregate product, its future growth will strongly influence the pace of overall economic expansion. As shown in Table 2, aggregate growth is likely to exceed the 1952-71 rate of 5 per cent per year even if annual industrial growth declines to 8 per cent. Retention of previous industrial growth rates will cause marked acceleration of overall growth.

Chinese energy requirements for 1975, 1980, and 1985 are projected in Table 3 using varying rates of industrial growth. Industrial energy requirements are derived by assuming no change from the estimated 1971 unit energy coefficient of

105

TABLE 2

Projected growth of Chinese net domestic product
under alternative a sectoral growth rates, 1971-85
(average annual growth rates)

Non-industrial growth rate	Industrial growth rate		
	8%	10%	12%
1%	4.9%	6.2%	7.7%
2%	5.2	6.5	7.9
3%	5.6	6.9	8.2
4%	6.0	7.2	8.5

NOTE: calculations assume that industry accounted for
44.6 per cent of 1971 net domestic product.

TABLE 3

Chinese energy requirements under alternative assumptions
concerning industrial growth, 1971-85 (trillion BTU)

Year	Non-industrial requirements	Aggregate energy requirements if industry's growth rate is		
		8%	10%	12%
1971	3665	11,893	11,893	11,893
1975	4377	15,570	16,422	17,323
1980	5624	22,073	25,024	28,441
1985	7463	31,632	38,708	47,673
Average annual growth rate 1971-85		7.2%	8.8%	10.4%

SOURCE: Rawski, 'The Role of China,' p. 39

33,694 BTU per yuan of gross output.[20] Future non-industrial energy demand is
projected from the 1971 figures as follows: annual growth of energy consumption between 1971 and 1985 is assumed to be 8 per cent for transportation, 15
per cent for agriculture, and 3 per cent for household use.[21]

The resulting demand forecasts indicate that China can continue a 5 per cent
pace of economic growth even if energy output fails to maintain its past rate of
growth. As shown in Table 1, domestic energy consumption has risen 9.9 per

cent per year since 1952; because of import replacement, energy production grew slightly faster. Yet Table 3 shows that a growth rate as low as 7.2 per cent annually for energy products can support an 8 per cent industrial growth rate, which in turn implies (Table 2) that overall growth will exceed 5 per cent unless the non-industrial sectors come to a standstill.

Continuation of past growth rates for energy output will cause supplies to outrun domestic requirements at recent rates of economic growth. However, maintenance of recent industrial growth rates, implying overall economic acceleration, will cause energy consumption to rise at approximately the same pace experienced since 1952.

To investigate China's ability to meet these energy requirements from domestic sources, we examine a range of future output possibilities bounded from below by assumptions which seem unduly pessimistic (Profile 1, Table 4) and from above by assumptions which imply continuation of previous output growth rates for major energy sources (Profile 3b).[22] Profile 1 incorporates extremely conservative assumptions about future energy output. The 1971-85 growth rates for coal (4 per cent a year) and for oil and gas (15 per cent a year) are well below past achievements (Table 1).

Profiles 2a-d bring out the implications of higher growth rates for either coal or oil and gas, China's major energy sources. Since the share of coal in total energy output is large but declining, while that of oil and gas is small and rising, marginal increases in the growth rate of coal output contribute most to raising energy output in the short term, while incremental growth of oil and gas output is more significant for longrun energy prospects.

Profiles 3a-b illustrate the result of allowing both coal and oil and gas output to increase at rates higher than those underlying Profile 1. In Profile 3a, growth rates for coal and for oil and gas are raised from 4 and 15 per cent to 6 and 20 per cent respectively. Profile 3b assumes growth rates of 8 per cent and 25 per cent for coal and for oil and gas.

There can be little doubt that Profile 1, which assumes a sudden decline in the growth rate of energy output, underestimates China's capacity to expand energy production even with no increase in the presently low level of technological imports. China can certainly raise coal output faster than 4 per cent annually with no foreign contribution. Although delivery costs might increase, the resulting burden is one which the economy could easily bear in order to ensure satisfactory economic growth. Similarly, there is no reason to expect a major reduction in the rate at which oil and gas production can grow without sharply raising import requirements.[23]

Once this view is accepted, the conclusions of our survey are clear. The basic results appear in Table 4, in which energy balances (domestic output minus re-

TABLE 4

China's energy balance, 1975–85, under various assumptions concerning growth of industrial and of energy output: domestic production minus energy requirements (trillion BTU)

Profile	1	2a	2b	2c	2d	3a	3b
8% growth for industry							
1975	251	1,157	2,172	1,015	1,823	1,921	3,744
1980	1579	6,409	20,877	3,773	6,325	8,783	17,805
1985	6011	23,209	52,340	10,158	15,913	27,356	62,242
10% growth for industry							
1975	-601	305	1,320	163	971	1,069	2,892
1980	-1372	3,458	17,926	822	3,374	5,832	14,584
1985	-1065	16,133	45,264	3,082	8,837	20,280	55,166
12% growth for industry							
1975	-1502	-596	-400	-1,557	-749	-651	1,172
1980	-6755	-596	14,509	-2,595	-43	2,415	11,437
1985	-10030	41	36,299	-5,883	-128	11,315	46,201
Underlying annual output growth rates for (%)							
Coal	4	4	4	6	8	6	8
Oil & gas	15	20	25	15	15	20	25

NOTE: − indicates a deficit of energy output over projected requirements

SOURCE: Rawski, 'The Role of China'

quirements) are calculated for 1975, 1980, and 1985 under a variety of assumptions concerning future growth rates of industrial output and energy production.[24]

Barring highly improbable simultaneous declines in output growth of all major energy sources, domestic production will provide sufficient energy to support a 10 per cent industrial growth rate to 1985 and beyond. This means that China will not require energy imports. If output of oil and gas grows in excess of 15 per cent annually (Profiles 2a-b, 3a-b), large energy surpluses will appear by the 1980s unless industrial output grows faster than 10 per cent per year.

If oil and gas maintain past annual growth rates of 25 per cent or higher (Profiles 2b, 3b), the surpluses generated after 1980 will be extremely large, even if the assumed rate of industrial growth is raised to 12 per cent. Under any probable rate of industrial growth, expansion of oil and gas output in excess of 25 per cent annually will permit China to become a major exporter of oil and/or gas during the 1980s.[25]

Finally, of the output profiles shown in Table 4, only Profile 3b is consistent with industrial growth in excess of 12 per cent annually. Sharp acceleration of China's economic growth will create energy requirements calling for maintenance of previous performance levels in the energy sector.

Japan

Japan faces the prospect of steadily rising energy imports. Despite offshore drilling in the seas surrounding Japan, which has already yielded some commercial deposits, and plans to construct a network of nuclear power plants, which require imported fuel, Japan has no alternative to continued dependence on foreign sources for the bulk of her energy.[26]

Official and private Japanese organizations as well as international bodies and foreign scholars have completed a number of studies of future Japanese energy requirements.[27] The results of some of these projections appear in Table 5. Although these studies reach somewhat differing conclusions, the basic results are similar. In accordance with the recently issued 'Economic and Social Plan,' the growth rate of real national product, which averaged 11 per cent annually during the 1960s, is expected to decline to about 9 per cent in the 1970s and 6 per cent during the subsequent decade.[28] Overall energy demand, which grew slightly faster than national product during the 1960s, is expected to grow in step with total product.[29]

In accord with the reduced emphasis on industrial expansion, the energy share of mining and manufacturing is to decline, with the metallurgical sector suffering the largest relative drop. The shares allotted to transport, commerce, household, and other non-industrial uses are to rise. The supply shares of major energy sources will not undergo large shifts, although the importance of nuclear power

TABLE 5

Some projections of Japanese energy requirements, 1975, 1980, 1985

Year	Physical units (percentage shares in parentheses)					Aggregate energy consumption 10^{12} BTU	Required primary energy sources
	Coal (million tons)	Crude oil (million barrels)	Natural gas (billion cu.m.)	Hydro power (billion kwh)	Nuclear power (billion kwh)		
SOURCE A							
1975	(18.1)	(73.0)	–	(4.5)	(2.2)	17,400	18,668
1980	–	–	–	–	–	37,033-40,827	39,672-43,469
1985	(16.7-16.8)	(67.8-69.1)	–	(2.5-2.3)	(9.9-9.1)	–	–
SOURCE B							
1975	83	2025	2.5	87	42	–	–
1980	96	2887	2.5	95	200	–	–
1985	107	3887	2.5	126	453	–	–
	(9.6)	(72.2)	(0.2)	(3.8)	(13.8)		
SOURCE C							
1975	119.3	2254[a]	2.9	86.7	41.6	–	19,856
1985	225.0-246.1	4479-4989[a]	10.7-10.8	100.9-103.8	406.6	–	42,204-46,243

– not given in source

a including imports of 'oil products'

SOURCES:

A *Tsūshō sangyō daijin*, pp. 14, 25

B 'Japan's Energy Prospects,' *Petroleum Press Service*, June 1972, p. 203

C Fiscal year projections from ibid., Sept. 1970, p. 341

and liquid natural gas will rise at the expense of coal. The dominant role of pet-roleum is expected to continue, with oil to account for 65-75 per cent of Japan's energy supplies through 1985.[30]

To summarize, we have found that the share of China and Japan in world energy consumption will continue to grow. One study has concluded that world energy consumption should increase at slightly over 5 per cent annually during the 1970s, with a 4.5 per cent annual rate projected thereafter.[31] If Japan's energy consumption keeps pace with anticipated changes in national product, rising by 9 per cent annually during the 1970s and by 6.0 per cent thereafter, and if Chinese energy consumption is projected at a conservative rate of 7.2 per cent per year, the two countries' share of world consumption will reach 15.7 per cent in 1980 and 17.3 per cent in 1985.[32]

While Japan will be obliged to import growing quantities of energy products during coming decades, we have seen that China is likely to experience an energy surplus which may be large. For some years, China has exported small quantities of petroleum to North Vietnam and North Korea, apparently for political rather than economic reasons. In view of the findings in Table 4, the recent beginning of crude oil exports to Japan, amounting to 1 million tons in 1973 and a planned 1974 level of 3 million tons, raises the possibility that these small flows foresha-dow China's emergence as a significant oil exporting nation.[33] It is to this possi-bility and other issues of national energy policy in China and Japan which we now turn.

ENERGY POLICIES

China: policies of a potential energy exporter
Although Table 4 incorporates strong elements of arbitrary assumption and of possible data errors, its evidence of export potential is consistently strong. If China's industrial growth rate falls below 10 per cent, a surplus equivalent to 75 mmt of crude oil by 1980 and over 200 mmt by 1985 will appear under most energy output assumptions. If oil and gas output continue to rise at over 20 per cent annually, large surpluses are likely even with a 12 per cent rate of in-dustrial growth.

To conclude that China will probably develop a substantial energy export potential, however, is not to predict large energy exports. At $3.80 per barrel, 100 million metric tons of crude oil would yield $2.8 billion, more revenue than China earned from her total 1972 exports.[34] China would not undertake such large exports in the absence of similarly large requirements for added imports.

The Chinese government at present seems committed to raising the rate of economic growth. As diplomacy creates opportunities to tap markets formerly closed to China, Chinese leaders seem to favor increased participation in world trade, and look to selective purchase of advanced western capital goods and technologies as a stimulus for China's economic modernization. Continuation of these attitudes creates a strong likelihood that China will seek to expand energy exports, particularly if agricultural imports are not reduced. This prediction should be qualified by noting the existence within China of political and economic thinking inimical to domestic and international specialization which might challenge the desirability of increased capital goods imports or even of rapid growth itself. If such views become prominent in Peking, the rationale for energy exports would be weakened. Assuming that current policies prevail, however, it does not seem unrealistic to predict that Chinese exports of crude oil, presumably to Japan, could reach 100 mmt per year by 1985, and might rise considerably higher.

As a potential energy exporter, China may be expected to offer moral and political support for the positions taken by individual producing countries and by OPEC in the world energy arena. This stance fits nicely with China's self-image as a champion of the Third World, which includes most energy exporters, in opposition to the interests of the Soviet Union and the advanced non-Communist industrial states.

High energy prices are thus politically as well as economically advantageous to the Chinese. China will continue to demand high prices for her own energy exports (at $3.80 bbl, Ta-ch'ing crude commands one of the world's top export prices). At the same time, China should support OPEC demands for higher prices, and will back the efforts of producing countries to raise their share of the energy dollar at the expense of the consuming nations and the international oil companies. [Editors' note: August 1973 prices]

A second facet of China's international energy posture arises from her continuing conflict with the Soviet Union. Some observers speculate that China's sales of crude oil to Japan are an attempt to sabotage Russo-Japanese cooperation in Siberian energy development. Although this seems unlikely, it is possible that Chinese energy policies will be affected by the future course of Sino-Soviet relations.

Finally, China has a strong interest in asserting control over the oil and gas fields now believed to lie beneath the Yellow Sea and the East China Sea. China's stance on offshore mineral rights is complicated by the issue of sovereignty over Taiwan, which in turn is linked with disputes among China, Taiwan, Japan, and Okinawa over the uninhabited Tiao-yu-t'ai or Senkaku Islands located near potential undersea oil deposits.[35]

As with her support of OPEC, China's advocacy of unilateral determination of offshore mineral rights has political as well as economic aspects. China's stand on maritime rights was forthrightly put by Chuang Yen, China's chief representative to the UN Seabed Committee:[36] 'Each country has the right to determine its territorial sea limits ... We consider that it is in the exercise of the sovereignty of a state to reasonably define ... the scope of their jurisdiction over economic resources beyond their territorial seas, using the names of exclusive economic zone, continental shelf, patrimonial sea or fishing zone, etc. Neighboring countries situated in a common sea should equitably allot their limits of jurisdiction through consultations.'

China thus rejects a uniform twelve- or twenty-mile territorial limit, and supports the wider fishing zones claimed by Peru, Ecuador, and other Latin American nations. At the same time, she shows no intention of unilaterally appropriating disputed resources: while attacking encroachment by outsiders, statements such as Chuang's seem to indicate willingness to negotiate with Japan, South Korea, and possibly even Taiwan (although here the issues go far beyond seabed sovereignty) over equitable division of disputed mineral wealth. China remains adamant, however, on the issue of exploitation of marine resources by non-contiguous states and their corporate representatives. In the speech cited above, Chuang stated: 'At present the ... superpowers are dispatching many so-called survey ships, fishing fleets, etc., all over the world to barge into the coastal seas of other countries at will, freely gather intelligence and plunder their marine resources. This is out-and-out piracy.'

We may therefore conclude that in addition to supporting the price demands of energy exporters, China will defend the right of resource-rich nations, including herself, to control and administer seabed mineral deposits without consulting international bodies, and to exclude international oil companies and non-contiguous states from sharing in these resources.

Japan: policies of a major energy importer
The goal of Japan's energy policy is to obtain assured supplies of energy at minimum cost. Because of Japan's unique dependence on imports, the security objective must take precedence over cost considerations. Of all the energy importers, Japan is least able to join in any action which entails risking even a brief interruption of Middle East petroleum shipments. Similarly, Japan has the strongest reasons to pursue close diplomatic and economic ties with the oil exporters.

To improve the security of her future energy imports, Japan must diversify her sources of supply: in 1971, 84 per cent of oil imports came from the Middle East, with 42.4 per cent, or 26 per cent of total national energy consumption, from one country, Iran.[37] This objective underlies the eager response to Chinese and Soviet offers to begin energy sales to Japan.

Japanese interest in Chinese oil is shown by the formation of a joint enterprise by four firms, Idemitsu Kosan, Maruzen, Kyodo, and Daikyowa, to import a trif-

Thomas G. Rawski

ling initial shipment of 200,000 tons of Ta-ch'ing crude.[38] The Japanese have repeatedly pressed for an increase in the size of future shipments, and have asked Peking to consider exporting natural gas as well as crude oil to Japan.[39]

The Soviet Union is also likely to join the list of Japan's energy suppliers. Several projects are currently under discussion, including suggestions that Japan and the United States provide financing for exploration and development of natural gas deposits near Yakutsk, oil deposits at Tyumen, and oil and gas fields in Sakhalin. In return for financial contributions and supplies of pipe and processing equipment, Japan and the US would receive large shipments of gas or oil: annual flows of ten billion cubic meters of liquefied natural gas and 10-40 million metric tons of crude oil to each participant have been mentioned in connection with the former two projects.[40]

Agreement on each of these projects awaits compilation of detailed geologic surveys and negotiation of the size and terms of foreign participation. Despite the uncertainty surrounding these proposals, it would appear that, taken together with the likelihood that China will expand her energy sales to Japan and the possibility of new seabed fields on the Chinese continental shelf, they indicate that the coming decade will bring a major expansion of energy shipments from the two Communist giants to Japan. We therefore conclude that present projections which envision only minor Japanese energy purchases from the Communist bloc exaggerate Japan's probable dependence on the Middle East for incremental energy supplies during the 1980s.

The Japanese government has set a 1985 target of 30 per cent of oil imports to be secured from sources developed with Japanese participation, and hopes eventually to raise this figure to 50 per cent.[41] In addition to joint ventures with the USSR, Japanese oil firms receive official encouragement for their present worldwide campaign of petroleum investments.[42] While some outsiders scoff at the low capitalization and technical level of these firms, Japan's oil industry has entered a process of consolidation and expansion which has generated internationally respected enterprises in other industries, and could do so in the petroleum sector as well.[43]

Even if, as we have suggested, Japanese reliance on Middle East oil is likely to decline, at least at the margin, Japan will certainly continue to import large and growing quantities of oil from the Middle East. To safeguard this vital energy source, Japan not only eschews actions which might antagonize Arab oil exporters, but seeks to draw the exporting nations into a network of mutually advantageous diplomatic and economic interchange which neither side will be anxious to disrupt. This approach, which includes active participation in the industrialization of the exporting countries, is what Japanese officials mean when they assert that oil is not merely a commercial commodity.[44]

114

Japan's view of proposed cooperation among the industrial energy importing states is shaped by concern for the security and cost of her own energy supplies. Japan will gladly share in cooperative ventures which are not inimical to the oil exporters: multinational resource development, emergency oil swap arrangements, joint investment in nuclear fuel production, and international research in such areas as sulfur removal, tanker design, and energy conservation fall into this category.[45]

Japan is not likely, however, to join with other consuming countries in a common effort to negotiate with OPEC or with individual producing countries. As a result of a series of recent US actions harmful or insulting to Japan and because of Japanese suspicions that the United States is not unwilling to use energy negotiations as a means of raising Japan's relative manufacturing costs, Japan will be extremely hesitant to yield its limited bargaining power to a collective which would inevitably be dominated by American interests.[46]

CONCLUSION

This brief survey has shown that China and Japan are likely to increase their international standing as energy consumers and, in China's case, as a producer as well. Although both China and Japan will probably adopt or espouse energy policies which create conflict with the United States and other western energy importers, their ultimate contribution, through investment in energy production, exploration, and research, should help to expand future energy supplies for all nations.

NOTES

1 The Chinese data in this paper were assembled primarily on the basis of official Chinese claims. The rationale for this procedure, together with references to other discussions of Chinese data, appear in T.G. Rawski, 'Recent Trends in the Chinese Economy,' *China Quarterly,* vol. 53 (1973), pp. 1-34, and 'Chinese Industrial Production, 1952-1971,' *Review of Economics and Statistics,* vol. 55, no. 2 (1973), pp. 169-81.

2 World consumption data from S.H. Schurr et al., *Middle Eastern Oil and the Western World* (New York 1971), p. 172, and *U.N. Statistical Yearbook 1971* (New York 1972), Table 137, converted from coal equivalents to BTU at 28.528 million BTU per metric ton. The 12.4 per cent figure is derived from 1971 data for China and 1970 data for Japan and the world.

3 Rawski, 'Recent Trends,' and 'The Role of China in the World Energy Situation' (unpublished paper prepared for the Brookings Institution, June 1973).

Thomas G. Rawski

'Industry' is broadly defined to include mining, manufacturing, and utilities.
4 Among the world's major regions, only one other area, Eastern Europe, derived over half its energy from coal in 1968. See S.H. Schurr, ed., *Energy,
Economic Growth, and the Environment* (Baltimore 1972), p. 187
5 Reserve estimates from Y.L. Wu, *Economic Development and the Use of
Energy Resources in Communist China* (New York 1963), p. 35 and J. Ashton, in US Congress, Joint Economic Committee, *An Economic Profile of
Mainland China* (Washington 1967), p. 302. Recent exploration has focused
on provinces south of the Yangtze River.
6 A.A. Meyerhoff, 'Developments in Mainland China, 1949-1968,' American
Association of Petroleum Geologists, *Bulletin*, vol. 54, no. 8 (1970), p. 1577.
For Ho's figures, see K.J. Ho, 'Peiping's Petroleum Industry,' *Issues and
Studies*, Aug. 1968, pp. 22-35.
7 The American Petroleum Institute estimates year-end 1972 US 'published
proved' oil reserves (presumably a less inclusive concept than Meyerhoff's
'ultimate' reserves) at 43.1 billion bbl. Cited in *BP Statistical Review of the
World Oil Industry* (1972), p. 4.
8 J.M. Wageman, *et al.*, 'Structural Framework of East China Sea and Yellow
Sea,' American Association of Petroleum Geologists *Bulletin*, vol. 54, no. 9
(1970), pp. 1611-43
9 *Asahi*, 10 May 1973, p. 1; *Ta-lu tien-li kung-yeh kai-lan* [*General Survey of
the Power Industry in Mainland China*] (Taipei 1968), pp. 21-2
10 Reserve estimates from Meyerhoff and Ho
11 US Department of State, *Survey of the China Mainland Press, 1971-2*, pp.
164-5 translates a brief statement on the Chekiang discoveries.
12 Potential estimate from Ashton, *Economic Profile*, p. 301; installed capacity
estimate from Rawski, 'The Role of China,' pp. 27, 74-5
13 US data from S.H. Schurr *et al.*, *Energy in the American Economy, 1850-
1975* (Baltimore 1960), p. 447; Japanese data from Hoshino Seiya, *Nippon
no enerugii mondai* [*Japan's Energy Problem*] (Tokyo 1964), p. 53
14 *Current Scene*, March 1973, p. 7; US Department of State, *Foreign Broadcast Information Service*, vol. IV, 3 Nov. 1972, p. C-10
15 Reports of Chinese mining of radioactive materials appear in *Ta-lu tien-li
kung-yeh kai-lan*, pp. 22-4; Y.L. Wu, ed., *China: A Handbook* (New York
1973), p. 77; C.M. Hsieh, *Atlas of China* (New York 1973).
16 Data from 1971 calculated from *Sōgō enerugii tōkei – Shōwa 47 nendo*
[*Overall Energy Statistics, 1972*] (Tokyo 1972), pp. 161-72 and Ushijima
Toshiaki, *OPEC Shin sekiyū teikoku no tanjō* [OPEC: *Birth of a New Oil
Empire*] (Tokyo 1972), pp. 14-15.
17 Calculated from 1969 GDP data in current prices (¥ 260 = $1) and total land

116

areas. Since mountain and volcanic lands comprise 61 per cent of Japan's land area (*Japan Statistical Yearbook 1971* [Tokyo 1972], p. 6), a comparison based on inhabited land would show even greater geographic concentration of economic activity in Japan.

18 Rawski, 'Chinese Industrial Production,' Table 1
19 Rawski, 'Recent Trends'
20 Rawski, 'The Role of China,' p. 40
21 Estimated energy requirements are quite insensitive to deviations from these assumptions. A change of one percentage point in the assumed industrial growth rate shifts estimated 1985 energy requirements by about 4000 trillion BTU, while a similar shift in the same direction for transport, agriculture, and households combined changes estimated requirements by only 1000 trillion BTU. The nuclear weapons sector is ignored in these projections because its energy consumption has no significant impact on China's overall energy balance.
22 All profiles assume the following annual rates of output growth (in BTU) for the minor energy sources: 2 per cent for fuel wood and 10 per cent for hydroelectric power. No allowance is made for possible nuclear generation of electricity.
23 Recent reports that crude oil production is outstripping refinery capacity (*Current Scene,* March 1973, p. 6) reflect the temporary disruption of investment projects associated with the Cultural Revolution (1966-8) and do not indicate inability to construct sufficient refining facilities to accommodate growing demand. Offshore oil drilling is another area in which outsiders may underestimate Chinese abilities. Although foreign observers believe that exploitation of China's seabed resources will necessitate some form of technical assistance from major oil companies, Chinese purchase and lease of drilling equipment (*Business Week,* 23 Sept. 1972; *Asahi,* 29 July 1973, p. 8), close inspection of offshore rigs by Chinese visitors (eg to Canada, Toronto *Globe and Mail,* 23 April 1973), eyewitness reports that the Sheng-li field has moved offshore (ibid.), and strong rebuffs to would-be collaborators (eg by Chou En-lai: BBC *Daily Broadcast Report* FE 4199, A3-A6) all suggest the possibility that China plans to develop offshore oil without foreign participation.
24 Rawski, 'The Role of China,' offers a more elaborate analysis in which additional possibilities are considered, including changes in unit energy requirements for industry and in the underlying output estimates for coal and natural gas. These do not alter the major qualitative conclusions described in the text.
25 To place the surpluses of Table 4 in perspective, we may note that 4000 trillion BTU is roughly equivalent to 100 Mmt of crude oil. The Middle East

Thomas G. Rawski

exported 377 mmt of crude in 1965, equivalent to about 15,000 trillion BTU (Schurr, *Middle Eastern Oil*, p. 180).

26 Reports of offshore activities appeared in *Asahi*, 29 July 1973, p. 8 and *Petroleum Press Service*, April 1972, p. 150. For accounts of present and proposed nuclear power stations, see Tsūshō sangyō daijin kambō chōsa ka, ed., *Nippon no enerugii mondai* [*Japan's Energy Problem*] (Tokyo 1972), pp. 132-3 and *Japan Times*, 21 July 1973, p. 3.

27 Additional English-language studies of future energy requirements are cited in Schurr, *Middle Eastern Oil*, pp. 162, 164. Nippon Enerugii Keizai Kenkyūjo [Institute of Energy Economics] in Tokyo has also compiled a number of unpublished reports in English.

28 *Economic Information File: Japan, 1973 edition* (Tokyo 1973), p. 24

29 Schurr, *Middle Eastern Oil*, p. 172, assumes an energy-GNP elasticity of 1.05 for 1965-80; Tsūshō sangyō daijin, p. 14, assumes elasticities of 0.98 for 1969-75 and 0.94-0.92 for 1976-85.

30 Ibid., p. 25

31 Schurr, *Energy, Economic Growth*, p. 203

32 World energy consumption derived from 1970 data (see note 2) and growth rate projections in ibid., pp. 202-6. Chinese and Japanese consumption calculated from Table 1 and the rates mentioned in the text.

33 *Asahi*, 29 July 1973, p. 8

34 China now receives $3.80 per barrel from Japan for low-sulfur Ta-ch'ing crude (*Washington Post*, 21 May 1973, A-24). China's evenly balanced two-way trade amounted to $4.6 billion in 1972 (*Current Scene*, March 1973, p. 7).

35 One of many descriptions of Chinese claims to the disputed areas is the following item from New China News Agency on 14 March 1962: 'The seabed resources ... around these islands [Taiwan, Tiao-yu-t'ai, and others are listed] and of the shallow seas adjacent to other parts of China belong completely to China and it is absolutely impermissible for any foreign aggressor to poke his fingers into them.'

36 *Peking Review*, 30 March 1973, pp. 9-12

37 Data on imports from Ushijima, pp. 14, 15

38 *Canada-Japan Trade Council Newsletter*, Feb. 1973, p. 6

39 *Asahi*, 10 May 1973, p. 1

40 *Japan Times*, 18 July 1973, p. 10; 26 July 1973, p. 12

41 Ushijima, *OPEC*, p. 193

42 Ibid., pp. 194-5, lists a total of 435 petroleum projects in which Japanese interests are currently involved.

43 Tsūshō sangyō daijin, *Nippon no enerugii mondai*, pp. 82-5, lists Japanese

118

investments in overseas oil ventures (including contributions to joint ventures) totalling ¥ 84 billion as of 1 January 1972. This sum is equivalent to about $324 million, well below the comparable figure for any of the major international oil companies shown in the same source.

44 See 'Japan Plans its Own "Oil Diplomacy" in the Middle East,' *Petroleum Intelligence Weekly*, 14 May 1973, pp. 5-6. The *Japan Times* of 25 (p. 11) and 26 (p. 12), 1973 reports on potential Japanese investments in steel- and automobile-making facilities in Saudi Arabia.

45 For recent discussions of oil swapping and plans for US-Japanese joint investment in a uranium enriching plant, see *Asahi*, 18 July 1973, p. 9; *Japan Times*, 24 July 1973, p. 10; and the Tanaka-Nixon communiqué printed in ibid., 3 Aug. 1973, p. 5

46 Recent US actions apparently intended to harm or embarrass Japan include dollar devaluation and resumption of Sino-American contact without prior consultation; numerous threats and actions to limit Japanese exports, among them the economically unwarranted quotas on US textile imports; unilateral suspension of Japanese imports of US soybeans and other farm products; and such petty harassment as the sudden replacement of cabinet members by subordinates at ministerial meetings. In the energy field, *Economist*, 7 July 1973, pp. 15-19, cites suspicions that easy US acceptance of higher oil prices in 1970-1 was motivated by a desire to undercut the competitive position of Japanese industry. In addition, the Japanese press has been quick to repeat suggestions that the United States has used its patron-client relations with the Thieu government of South Vietnam to secure offshore drilling concessions for American firms (*Asahi*, 29 July 1973, p. 8).

Sub-Saharan Africa is a significant exporter of oil today and according to Pearson will be an even more significant exporter of oil and gas in the near future. Between January 1969 and January 1973, the *known* reserves in this region climbed from 5 billion barrels of oil to 22.8 billion barrels and from 10 Tcf of natural gas to 48 Tcf. Nigeria has 70 per cent of these oil reserves and 85 per cent of these gas reserves and is already the world's sixth leading producer. Pearson suggests that these reserve estimates are highly conservative, and it is highly likely that these reserves will increase sharply in the future. In the four-year period which saw a 450 per cent increase in petroleum reserves, production in Nigeria increased 350 per cent. The 1972 production-to-reserve ratio in Nigeria was 23 to 1. Nigeria also exports 97 per cent of its production. Indications are clear that exports will increase from Nigeria. Gas and oil are also being discovered in Angola, Gabon, and the Congo (Brazzaville). Production from these areas is minimal and can be expected to increase markedly.

Sub-Saharan Africa represents an area where near- to middle-term exports can be expected to rise rapidly.

This paper, with its excellent discussion of the government policies and tax decisions, should be read along with Crandall's and Mabro's papers on the Middle East, Steele's paper on Latin America, and Erickson & Spann on US oil. Together these three papers provide valuable insights on the formation and power of OPEC and the probability that the cartel will remain in force, given the different motivations of the various government authorities.

SCOTT R. PEARSON

Petroleum and natural gas
in sub-Saharan Africa

Two decades ago, petroleum and natural gas were not known to exist in sub-Saharan Africa.[1] Indeed, in 1953, a noted British geographer wrote:[2] 'Apart from the fields along the shores of the Gulf of Suez in Egypt and a small yield from three tiny fields in Algeria and four in Morocco, Africa has no oil. The conditions favoring the accumulation of oil in quantity, in folds among sedimentary rocks on the margins of great sedimentary basins, do not exist in Africa.' Beginning with the initial discoveries of oil and gas in Angola in 1955 and in Nigeria and Gabon in 1956, this analysis has been shown to be increasingly incorrect. By mid-1973, tropical Africa was producing approximately 2.3 million barrels per day (bd) of crude petroleum, and Nigeria alone was the sixth largest exporter of crude in the world. Petroleum output in Africa has grown rapidly, more than doubling in the last three years, and it is expected to increase perhaps 50 per cent above its current level by the early 1980s. Very little natural gas is now utilized, but plans are being made to tap the significant amounts of gas being flared as well as the large non-associated gas discoveries.

The purposes of this chapter are threefold: first, to analyze the major physical and economic influences affecting oil and gas production in sub-Saharan Africa; second, to review trends in ownership, exploration, reserves, production, taxation, costs, and government policies in the principal African producing countries; and, third, to provide an indication of future trends and hence of the likely position of sub-Saharan Africa as a net supplier of oil and gas to the world energy market. Principal attention is given to Nigeria, reflecting its predominant position as the producer of 85 per cent of tropical Africa's recent output of petroleum. Secondary attention is paid to the other oil producers of sub-Saharan Africa –

TABLE 1
Petroleum companies operating in Nigeria July 1973

Participating companies	Equity share (per cent)	Affiliation
Nigerian Agip Oil	33.3	subsidiary of the Italian State Company, ENI
Phillips Oil (Nigeria)	33.3	subsidiary of Phillips Petroleum Company of United States
NNOC	33.3	Nigerian National Oil Company
Deminex	44	subsidiary of German oil consortium
NNOC	51	*
Niger Petroleum Company	5	Nigerian independent
Gulf Oil (Nigeria)	100	subsidiary of Gulf Oil Company of United States
Japan Petroleum (Nigeria)	49	Japanese consortium
NNOC	51	*
Japan Petroleum (Nigeria)	40	*
NNOC	51	*
Niger Oil Resources	9	Nigerian independent
Mobil Producing Nigeria	100	subsidiary of Mobil Oil Corporation of United States
Mobil Producing Nigeria	50	*
Tenneco Oil (Nigeria)	37.5	subsidiary of Tenneco Incorporated of United States
Sun DX Nigeria	12.5	subsidiary of Sun Oil Company of United States
Occidental Petroleum (Nigeria)	49	subsidiary of Occidental Petroleum Company of United States
NNOC	51	*
Pan Ocean Oil (Nigeria)	na	subsidiary of Pan Ocean of United States
Delta Oil	na	Nigerian independent

Company	%	Notes
Safrap (Nigeria)	65	subsidiary of French Elf Erap group
NNOC	35	*
Shell (Nigeria)	32.5	subsidiary of Royal Dutch Shell of United Kingdom and Netherlands
British Petroleum (Nigeria)	32.5	British Petroleum Oil Company of United Kingdom
NNOC	35	*
Henry Stephens and Sons	49	Nigerian independent
NNOC	51	*
Texaco Overseas Petroleum (Nigeria)	50	subsidiary of Texaco of United States
Chevron Oil (Nigeria)	50	subsidiary of Standard Oil of California of United States

* listed elsewhere

na not available

SOURCE: *Annual Review of 1972 – Nigeria*, March 1973, as quoted in R.K. Meyer and S.R. Pearson, 'Contributions of Petroleum to Nigerian Economic Development,' in *Commodity Exports and African Economic Development*, Scott R. Pearson and John Cownie *et al.* (Lexington, Mass., forthcoming 1974), p. 5a.

Scott R. Pearson

Gabon, Angola, including Cabinda, and Congo (Brazzaville) – all of which are located southeast of Nigeria, bordering the Atlantic Ocean.

THE DEVELOPMENT OF PETROLEUM PRODUCTION IN NIGERIA[3]

Ownership, exploration, and reserves[4]

Nigeria Bitumen Corporation, a German company, initiated the search for petroleum in Nigeria in 1908 and drilled fourteen dry holes before giving up at the outset of World War I. No further interest was shown in the then British colony until 1937 when Royal Dutch/Shell and British Petroleum formed an equal partnership, with Shell acting as operating partner, and received exclusive exploration rights in Nigeria. For three years Shell-BP undertook preliminary geological reconnaissance, interrupting operations in 1941 with the intensification of World War II. Following the war, Shell-BP spent five years carrying out geological surveys before drilling its first wildcat well in 1951. During the first half of the 1950s, the company concentrated its efforts without success in the Cretaceous area to the north of the delta of the Niger River. After shifting to the delta itself, Shell-BP struck oil at Oloibiri in 1956.

Exploration activity was intensified thereafter, and several other companies showing increased interest in Nigeria, shifted to the southwestern coast in the late 1950s, but failed to find oil in either area. Shell-BP was required by law to release a portion of its original acreage; Tenneco, Gulf, Agip, Safrap and later Phillips obtained onshore prospecting leases in areas formerly held by Shell-BP.

In 1961 Nigeria divided its offshore continental shelf into twelve blocks of about 1000 square miles each and leased four of these blocks to Shell-BP, two to Gulf, two to Mobil, and two to Texaco/Chevron (which made Nigeria's first offshore discovery in 1963); Gulf obtained one of the remaining offshore blocks in 1964 and Union took up the other in 1967. By agreement, these companies had to relinquish half of each of their offshore blocks in 1968, and this acreage was leased in 1971 to an entirely new group of companies.

Each of the new offshore concessionaires is a 49 per cent minority partner with the Nigerian National Oil Corporation (NNOC), which was established in May 1971 to participate in all phases of the petroleum industry's operations. Companies engaged in these offshore joint ventures with NNOC include Occidental, Japan Petroleum, Deminex/Niger Petroleum, and Henry Stephens and Sons. The affiliation and equity share of these and all other firms currently operating in Nigeria are presented in Table 1.

As indicated in Table 1, by mid-1973 NNOC had taken equity participation in nine of the fourteen companies active in Nigeria. Upon its incorporation NNOC

124

obtained an immediate 35 per cent interest in Safrap, a French company; NNOC's
share will rise to 50 per cent if production should increase to 400,000 bd.[5] NNOC
also exercised the government's option to assume a $33\frac{1}{3}$ per cent share in the
Agip/Phillips operation, an arrangement which had been allowed for in the mid-
1960s by mutual agreement between the two companies and the government. In
both of these instances, NNOC is paying for its equity through revenues from future petroleum production.

Following prolonged negotiations, NNOC acquired a 35 per cent equity share in
Shell-BP in June 1973. The government's share is scheduled to remain at this level
until 1982 and then to jump in one step to 51 per cent. Shell-BP, the giant of the
petroleum industry in Nigeria from the beginning, has an updated book value
which is probably in excess of $1.5 billion. In spite of the large amounts involved,
the government has agreed to pay for its 35 per cent share in four installments
over a two-year period.

The agreement with Shell-BP could well be a precursor to similar arrangements
with the five companies that are not in partnership with NNOC. Gulf and Mobil,
the second and third largest producing companies in Nigeria, have each offered a
20 per cent participation for NNOC, but no final agreements had been announced
by mid-1973.[6]

Significantly, the Nigerian government has vested all future concessions for production of petroleum and natural gas in NNOC. Moreover, as existing mining licenses
expire, beginning in the early 1990s, surrendered concessions will also revert to
NNOC. As a result, no new oil and gas concessions are expected to be granted to
any company or individual. As occurred in the recent offshore arrangements, however, NNOC might well choose to accept minority partners in joint ventures; alternatively, NNOC is free to institute management contracts with foreign companies.
Whatever path NNOC selects, it is clear that the era of foreign concessions, fully
owned and managed by international oil corporations, is drawing rapidly to a close.

Exploration activity accelerated rapidly as the number of companies operating
in Nigeria grew. After Shell-BP's initial strike, exploration first centered in the
Niger delta, and virtually all of Shell-BP's production has been located in this
area. Offshore exploration began in the early 1960s and has been carried on intensively, especially by Gulf and Mobil, whose production has originated entirely
from offshore fields. In addition, several companies have returned successfully to
the onshore Cretaceous areas where Shell-BP had earlier come up dry. In spite of
the fact that Nigerian fields have not been large by Middle Eastern standards –
the most productive well, a recent offshore discovery by Occidental, proved at
about 18,000 bd – the success ratio of drilling has been high. To date over 40 per
cent of wildcat wells have resulted in commercial discoveries, and more than 80
per cent of appraisal and development wells have been successful.

TABLE 2

Estimated reserves of petroleum and natural gas in sub-Saharan Africa 1969–73
(Petroleum in millions of barrels; natural gas in billions of cubic feet)

	1 Jan. 1969		1 Jan. 1970		1 Jan. 1971		1 Jan. 1972		1 Jan. 1973	
	petroleum	natural gas	petroleum	natural gas	petroleum	natural gas	petroleum	natural gas	petroleum	natural gas
Angola, including Cabinda	500	625	645	625	500	1,000	803	1,500	1,200	1,000
Congo (Brazzaville)	7		6		4		3,300		5,000	
Gabon	465	4,500	500	5,000	700	7,000	750	6,500	1,100	7,000
Nigeria	4,000	3,900	5,000	5,000	9,300	6,000	11,680	40,000	15,000	40,000
Other	21[a]	1,000[b]	21[c]	1,500[d]	3[e]	500[f]	502[g]		501[h]	
Total sub-Saharan Africa	4,993	10,025	6,172	12,125	10,507	14,500	17,035	48,000	22,801	48,000

a Dahomey 20; Zaire 1
b Mozambique 1000
c Dahomey 20; Zaire 1
d Mozambique 1000; Republic of South Africa 500
e Dahomey 1; Zaire 1; Ghana 1
f Republic of South Africa 500
g Dahomey 1; Zaire 500; Ghana 1
h Dahomey 1; Zaire 500

SOURCE: *The Oil and Gas Journal*, 30 Dec. 1968, p. 103; 29 Dec. 1969, p. 95; 28 Dec. 1970, p. 93; 27 Dec. 1971, p. 73; 25 Dec. 1972, p. 83.

Data on estimated reserves of petroleum and natural gas in Nigeria are contained in Table 2 (data for the other countries in the table are discussed in the following section). Estimates of petroleum reserves have risen from four billion barrels in 1969 to fifteen billion barrels in 1973, an amount which would permit production at the May 1973 rate of 1.95 million bd until 1994. These estimates are highly conservative, however, and at best they provide only a lower limit on future availabilities. Estimates of natural gas reserves in Nigeria were substantially increased recently, from 3900 billion cubic feet in 1969 to 40,000 billion cubic feet in 1973.

Production, exports, and local consumption[7]
Table 3 contains data on the volume of production, exports, and local refining of crude petroleum in Nigeria. As the table illustrates, petroleum output and exports grew at a rather modest rate from 1958, when Shell-BP first began to produce, through 1963. From 1964 until mid-1967 crude output increased rapidly. When the Nigerian Civil War broke out in July 1967, oil production was severely curtailed, though it began to recover before the conflict ended in January 1970. Following the conclusion of the war, the output of oil expanded at an unusually rapid rate; much of this expansion was based on the delayed development of prewar discoveries. More recently, the rate of increase has slowed, reflecting the recovery of production to the level which the industry probably would have reached in the absence of the interruptions caused by the war.

For the first seven years, 1958–64, Shell-BP was the sole producing company in Nigeria. Gulf began production in 1965 and Safrap in 1966. Because Gulf produced from fields located offshore in the Midwestern State, its activities were largely unaffected by the civil war. In spite of the fact that Shell-BP had production in the midwest as well as in the three war-torn eastern states, at that time its only offtake and export facilities were in the east; Safrap was also using Shell-BP's facilities, and hence both of these companies were forced to discontinue production. Shell-BP was able to resume production at a reduced scale in October 1968. Its production crews literally followed on the heels of the federal Nigerian troops, as they regained oil-rich Rivers State, and therefore Shell-BP began to produce at substantial levels even before the war was over. But Safrap, probably because of the Nigerian government's displeasure over French support of the Biafran regime, was not allowed to produce again until May 1971, following the conclusion of its participation agreement with NNOC.

Shell-BP has always been the most important producer of crude in Nigeria (save for the war-affected year, 1968). Its predominance has recently diminished somewhat, as other companies have expanded at faster rates, but in 1972 Shell-BP still accounted for 66 per cent of Nigerian petroleum production. The remainder of

Scott R. Pearson

TABLE 3

Production, exports, and refinery use of petroleum in Nigeria 1958-72
(thousands of barrels per day)

	Production[a]	Exports	Refinery use[b]
1958	5	5	
1959	11	11	
1960	17	17	
1961	46	46	
1962	68	68	
1963	76	76	
1964	120	120	
1965	270	266	4
1966	415	383	32
1967	317	300	17
1968	142	142	0
1969	540	540	0
1970	1084	1064	20
1971	1531	1490	41
1972	1817	1772	45

a For the years 1958-64 all production is Shell-BP; 1965: Shell-BP 243,
Gulf 27; 1966: Shell-BP 352, Gulf 51, Safrap 12; 1967: Shell-BP 243,
Gulf 55, Safrap 19; 1968: Shell-BP 44, Gulf 98; 1969: Shell-BP 352,
Gulf 188; 1970: Shell-BP 807, Gulf 217, Mobil 51, Agip/Phillips 5,
Texaco/Chevron 4; 1971: Shell-BP 1108, Gulf 277, Safrap 25, Mobil
72, Agip/Phillips 39, Texaco/Chevron 10; 1972: Shell-BP 1208, Gulf
325, Safrap 55, Mobil 167, Agip/Phillips 52, Texaco/Chevron 10.
b The refinery began operations in October 1965, shut down in July
1967 with the outbreak of the Civil War, and resumed operations in
May 1970.

SOURCE: Data on production and exports for 1958-68 from S.R.
Pearson, *Petroleum and the Nigerian Economy*, p. 56, and for 1969-72
from *Monthly Petroleum Report*, Ministry of Mines and Power, Lagos,
as quoted in R.K. Meyer and S.R. Pearson, 'Contributions of Petroleum
to Nigerian Economic Development,' in *Commodity Exports and African Economic Development*, Scott R. Pearson and John Cownie, *et al.*
(Lexington, Mass., forthcoming 1974), p. 9a; refinery use is calculated
as a residual.

crude output in that year was produced by five other companies – Gulf (18 per
cent), Mobil (9 per cent), Safrap/NNOC (3 per cent), Agip/Phillips/NNOC (3 per
cent), and Texaco/Chevron (1 per cent).[8] Two companies, Gulf and Mobil, produce entirely offshore, while all other production has been onshore; hence slightly

128

TABLE 4

Destination of crude oil exports from Nigeria 1970, 1971, 1972

	Volume (thousands of barrels per day)			Percentages of total exports		
	1970	1971	1972	1970	1971	1972
EUROPE	710	1019	1094	69	68	62
United Kingdom	238	271	313	23	18	18
France	121	269	296	12	18	17
Netherlands	186	197	229	18	13	13
Other	165	282	256	16	19	14
WESTERN HEMISPHERE	308	432	574	29	29	32
USA	130	295	426	12	20	24
Caribbean refineries	97	69	87	9	5	5
Canada	33	27	29	3	2	2
Brazil	37	30	23	4	2	1
Other	12	11	9	1	1	1
AFRICA	31	25	30	3	2	2
FAR EAST	1	14	76	*	1	4
Japan	*	14	74	*	1	4
Other	1	*	2	*	*	*
TOTAL	1051	1490	1774	101	100	100

* less than 500 bd
Discrepancies in totals accounted for by rounding of individual averages.

SOURCE: *Monthly Petroleum Report,* Ministry of Mines and Power, Lagos.

more than one-fourth of total output has recently been produced offshore.[9] Of the eight non-producing companies in Nigeria, only Occidental/NNOC and Japan Petroleum/NNOC had announced commercial petroleum discoveries by mid-1973.

Most of Nigeria's oil production is exported; in 1972, exports made up 97 per cent of total output. The destination of exports during 1970-72 is presented in Table 4. The United States emerged in 1971 as the leading single market for Nigerian crude and consumed nearly one-fourth of the fast growing total in 1972. Europe is still Nigeria's principal market, however, and three members of the European Community – the United Kingdom, France, and the Netherlands – together purchased almost half of the 1972 export total. Japan took 4 per cent of Nigerian exports in 1972 and may become an increasingly important buyer of Nigerian oil, especially if the Japanese consortium attains commercial success in

129

its offshore venture. The other countries of Africa constitute a very limited market for Nigeria's crude petroleum, accounting for only 2 per cent of export sales in 1972.

The small portion of crude output which is not exported is processed locally. The Nigerian Petroleum Refining Company (NPRC) owns and operates Nigeria's only refinery at Alesa-Eleme near Port Harcourt in Rivers State. NPRC is a joint venture among the Nigerian government (which originally held a 50 per cent share and now has a 60 per cent share), British Petroleum (originally 25 per cent, now 20 per cent), and Royal Dutch/Shell (originally 25 per cent, now 20 per cent). The refinery went on stream in 1965, closed down when the war began in mid-1967, and reopened in May 1970 after being repaired.

The current capacity of the refinery, 60,000 bd, has been more than adequate to supply Nigerian needs for most petroleum products producible from Nigerian crude (exceptions include bitumen, asphalt, lubricating oil, and aviation gasoline). In 1972 refinery throughput was 45,000 bd of crude. Limited quantities of refined products are exported to neighboring African countries. In addition, the refinery produces high pour fuel oil which is not in much demand in Nigeria and is thus exported to Europe and the United States. A second refinery is being planned to meet future increases in local consumption of petroleum products; the new refinery may have a capacity of about 60,000 bd and be sited at Warri in the Midwestern State.[10]

Brief mention can be made of the production and use of natural gas in Nigeria. Relatively little gas is consumed domestically, and none is exported. Although the petroleum industry has been selling gas to gas-fired power stations and industrial establishments since 1963 (with interruptions during the war), the amounts consumed remain small. In 1972 over 1.6 billion cubic feet per day (cfd) of natural gas were produced in association with crude oil, but more than 98 per cent of this amount was flared at the wellhead; only 0.7 per cent was used by the oil industry itself, and 0.9 per cent was sold to industrial consumers.

Payments to the Nigerian government[11]

The terms governing the amounts of payments made by the petroleum companies to the Nigerian government have undergone several major revisions in the past seven years, generally in step with similar changes in the other less developed countries which are major producers of petroleum. The basic leasing structure - very low concession bonuses, $12\frac{1}{2}$ per cent royalties, 50 per cent profits taxes - through which the Nigerian government originally extracted its share of the economic rent generated in petroleum production was established in the Petroleum Profits Tax Ordinance of 1959. (Although exact taxation arrangements are specific to each individual company, the major provisions apply uniformly to all companies.) Under this law, royalties and profits taxes for each producing company were calculated on the basis of realized prices (internal company transfer prices). In calculating profits taxes, chargeable profits were found by subtracting operating expenses and useable capital allowances (depreciation) from gross proceeds. A company's total tax obligation to the Nigerian government could not exceed 50 per cent of its chargeable profits, because royalties, rentals, and other minor taxes were treated as offsets against the profits taxes.

The first change in these financial arrangements took place in 1966 when the Nigerian government cut nearly in half the rates at which the petroleum companies could depreciate their capitalized investment. In the following year a much more important alteration occurred. Decree 1 of 1967 required that the companies post prices on which profits taxes and royalties would be calculated and that royalties be treated at expenses rather than as offsets against profits taxes. Accordingly, in November 1967 Shell-BP announced a posted price of $2.17 per barrel (for API 34° crude) which resulted in an effective tax reference price of approximately $1.95 per barrel after allowing for deductions for harbor dues and port charges, a gravity allowance, a percentage allowance, and a marketing allowance. The other producing companies later posted effectively the same price, reflecting the 'most-favored-company' clauses in each company's covenant with the government which guarantee that no one company will receive better treatment than any other.

These covenants also contain 'most-favored-nation' clauses which in effect assure that Nigeria can bargain for and presumably obtain treatment equal to that agreed to by the companies with respect to their operations in any other African or Middle Eastern country. As a result, in September 1970 the Nigerian government negotiated an increase in the posted price of $0.25 per barrel, emulating a similar change in Libya to which companies operating in both countries had acquiesced; consequently the base posting rose to $2.42 per barrel and the effective tax reference price to $2.18 per barrel.

Although not then a member of the Organization of Petroleum Exporting Countries (OPEC), Nigeria followed the Teheran and Tripoli settlements of early 1971 with considerable interest. The 'most-favored-nation' clauses afforded Nigeria all the bargaining power it needed, and in April 1971 the Nigerian government negotiated a settlement that was even more favorable to it than those reached by the governments of the Persian Gulf countries and of Libya. The base posting was increased by $0.36 per barrel to $2.78 per barrel, the previous allowable deductions from this base were eliminated, and a complex set of premia (for closure of the Suez Canal, freight differentials, and low sulfur content) and annual escalations was instituted. The net effect was to raise the tax reference price from its previous level of $2.18 per barrel to a new level of $3.21 per

Scott R. Pearson

TABLE 5

Prices, costs, and payments to government of the petroleum industry in Nigeria 1970–2
(US $ per barrel)

	Jan. 1970– Aug. 1970	Sept. 1970– Mar. 1971	Mar. 1971– Feb. 1972	Feb. 1972– Dec. 1972
Posted price	2.17	2.42	2.78	3.02
Tax reference price	1.95	2.18	3.21	3.42
Realization price	1.95	2.08	2.79	2.99
Production costs	.46	.46	.46	.46
Payments to government	.86	.99	1.70	1.90
Residual retained by companies (interest, return of capital, profits, economic rent)	.63	.63	.63	.63

SOURCES: *Petroleum Press Service* and *Petroleum Intelligence Weekly,* various issues;
author's estimates.

barrel. In addition, the rate of taxation of chargeable profits was increased from
50 to 55 per cent, the rate of generation of capital allowances was reduced by
about 30 per cent, and the lag in the timing of payments was shortened from
about six months to less than three months.[12] This new set of financial arrangements, negotiated to cover a five-year period, was altered in February 1972 to
compensate for the devaluation of the US dollar; the base posted price was raised
to $3.02 per barrel, resulting in a new tax reference price of $3.42 per barrel.

The results of this series of changes in taxation terms are summarized in Table
5. The estimation of realization prices in the table is based on the assumption
that production costs are constant and the share accruing to the industry is fixed.
Accompanying increases in per barrel revenues received by the Nigerian government are as follows: during the first eight months of 1970, government take was
about $0.86 per barrel; the changes in September 1970 brought about an increase
to nearly $1.00 per barrel; a major increase – to roughly $1.70 per barrel – resulted from the April 1971 alterations; finally, the February 1972 increase in the
base posting was responsible for a further rise in government revenues to about
$1.90 per barrel.[13]

These abrupt increases in taxes paid per barrel, coupled with rapidly expanding
output, have caused the petroleum industry's payments to the Nigerian government to grow dramatically in the past three years. The historical trend of these
payments in aggregate is portrayed in Table 6 below. Taxes and royalties on profits are the most important kinds of payments, accounting for nearly all of recent

TABLE 6

Cost structure of the petroleum industry in Nigeria 1963-71

	1963	1964	1965	1966	1967	1968	1969	1970	1971
Industry expenditures (million £N)									
Gross output[a]	20.7	32.8	69.1	100.6	80.6	36.9	139.4	280.4	523.9
Local purchases of goods and services	7.2	10.3	18.5	27.9	21.9	11.2	22.8	36.1	51.1
Local wages and salaries	2.0	2.3	2.7	2.7	2.5	1.8	2.8	4.4	6.0
Payments to government[b]	5.0	12.3	13.3	18.7	27.0	15.8	60.5	126.8	306.3
Harbor dues and port charges	0.6	1.0	2.0	2.7	2.4	0.4	3.3	7.9	4.3
Imports of goods and services	10.6	24.0	35.7	58.0	51.2	48.4	60.8	74.7	83.1
Residual (interest, return of capital, profits, economic rent)	-4.7	-17.0	-3.3	-9.5	-24.5	-40.7	-10.8	30.5	73.1
Factor shares based on total expenditures									
Gross output[a]	1.000	1.000	.999	.999	1.000	1.000	.999	1.000	1.000
Local purchases of goods and services	.346	.315	.268	.277	.277	.304	.163	.129	.098
Local wages and salaries	.097	.070	.039	.027	.031	.051	.020	.016	.011
Payments to government[b]	.242	.375	.193	.186	.335	.428	.434	.452	.584
Harbor dues and port charges	.030	.030	.029	.026	.030	.011	.023	.028	.008
Imports of goods and services	.513	.731	.517	.636	.636	1.312	.436	.266	.159
Residual (interest, return of capital, profits, economic rent)	-.228	-.520	-.047	-.094	-.304	-1.103	-.077	.109	.140

a 1963–8 figures include local sales of natural gas.

b 1963–8 figures are actual payments to government for each calendar year; 1969–71 figures are author's estimates based on generation of payments to government per barrel of output, rather than on accruals.

c Residual is calculated as total proceeds less imports of goods and services less gross total expenditures in Nigerian currency.

SOURCES: Data for 1963–8 from S.R. Pearson, *Petroleum and the Nigerian Economy*, p. 61 and for 1969–71 from unpublished sources and author's estimates, as quoted in R.K. Meyer and S.R. Pearson, 'Contributions of Petroleum to Nigerian Economic Development,' in *Commodity Exports and African Economic Development*, Scott R. Pearson and John Cownie et al. (Lexington, Mass., forthcoming 1974), p. 11a.

Scott R. Pearson

government revenues from petroleum, with profits taxes alone contributing about three-fourths of recent totals. These revenues, which until recently were of modest proportions, have increased to the point where they now make up well over half of total government revenue in Nigeria.

Costs of production [14]
The sole published estimate of the long-run (1970-85) supply price of Nigerian crude is $0.46 per barrel.[15] On the basis of this estimate, oil production in Nigeria is on average somewhat more costly than in Libya and perhaps three times as expensive as in most Middle Eastern countries.

Table 6 contains annual data on the petroleum industry's structure of costs and on the share of each major expenditure item in gross output. The trends portrayed in the table reflect both the relative youth of the oil industry in Nigeria, causing several companies to have abnormally large costs in comparison to earnings, and the disruptive influence of the Nigerian Civil War, resulting in severely reduced earnings and some cutback of expenditures in the 1967-9 period.

In spite of these anomalies, the dominant characteristics of the oil industry's structure of costs are clear in Table 6. First, the share of payments to government in gross output has risen rapidly, reflecting the changes in fiscal terms and the exhaustion of accumulated capital allowances; in 1963 taxes amounted to only 25 per cent of the value of output, but by 1971 this proportion had increased to almost 60 per cent. Second, expenditures on local goods and services and local payments of wages and salaries show the exact opposite trend; in 1963 these two items together accounted for about 45 per cent of gross output, but by 1971 they took only slightly more than 10 per cent. Third, imports of goods and services similarly declined as a proportion of gross output, from over 50 per cent in 1963 to only 16 per cent in 1971. Finally, the residual share accruing to the foreign-owned companies (interest, return of capital, profits, and retained economic rent), which was negative until 1970, rose to 14 per cent of gross output in 1971. These trends – proportionate increases in payments to government and in foreign earnings and decreases in both local and imported costs – reflect the increasing maturation of the industry in Nigeria, the ending of the civil war, and the alterations in financial arrangements.[16]

Policies of the Nigerian government [17]
Nigeria became a member of OPEC in July 1971, following a long courtship by some of the other OPEC countries. As noted in the earlier discussion of taxation terms, Nigeria relied on the 'most-favored-nation' clauses in the company covenants, not on collective OPEC pressure, to obtain its favorable settlement in April 1971. In effect, Nigeria was then in a position akin to a non-unionized worker

receiving a wage hike which had been brought about by unionized workers. From the point of view of bargaining power with the petroleum corporations operating in Nigeria, therefore, there was little immediate need for Nigeria to seek OPEC membership. Nigeria could have waited for the OPEC countries to bargain for and receive more favorable tax terms and then collected equally favorable changes via the 'most-favored-nation' provision.

Several other considerations pointed in the direction of membership, however. As a member of OPEC, Nigeria is better able to originate, influence, and aid implementation of the organization's policies and thereby help itself and other less developed oil exporting countries to obtain increasing shares of the enormous amounts of economic rents associated with petroleum production. In addition, by becoming a member of OPEC, Nigeria can allow for the possibility that OPEC may sometime be faced with having to divide exports of petroleum among member countries in order to buttress the existing cost-price structure; in such a situation Nigeria may be better off dealing from strength as a member. Finally, Nigerian leaders no doubt felt that the country should accept its responsibilities as one of the world's leading petroleum exporters (and as the largest nation in tropical Africa) and join the organization established to promote the interests of low income oil producers. Whether Nigeria's decision to join was importantly influenced by the marked success of OPEC countries in the 1970-1 settlements is a matter of some debate, though the timing of Nigeria's joining is suggestive of some cause and effect in this regard.

The three major policy issues affecting the petroleum companies operating in Nigeria – taxation, participation, and conservation – are all, at least in part, interwoven with one central question: how should the sizeable amounts of economic rent generated in oil production be divided between the Nigerian government and the foreign-owned oil corporations, and what should be the future timing of these flows of scarcity rents? Because of this interdependence, each of these policy issues impinges directly or indirectly on one or both of the others.

The major elements in the evolution of the Nigerian government's policies on taxation of oil and gas production have already been outlined. Prior to 1967, the international petroleum corporations had a financial incentive to invest in Nigeria because of the favorable tax terms relative to most major exporting areas. The fiscal changes in that year put Nigeria on a more or less equal footing with other producers as far as tax terms were concerned, but Nigeria still had substantial advantages over most of its major competitors in terms of tax-paid cost per barrel laid down in Europe or in the United States. These differentials evaporated with the 1970-1 settlements, because the absolute increase in tax cost of Nigerian crude exceeded that of other major producers. As a result, further policy changes to increase the effective tax rate on Nigerian oil either will occur in concert with those in other major sources of supply or else could place Nigeria's future competitive position in jeopardy.

The recent move toward participation of the Nigerian government through its statutory corporation, NNOC, has also been chronicled in detail above. The intention of the government to assume a substantial equity position in all petroleum ventures in Nigeria seems clear, and it is undoubtedly only a matter of time before NNOC will purchase at least a 35 per cent share of the five companies in which it is not already a partner. As it has done in virtually all government-company negotiations, the government dealt first with Shell-BP (following the arrangements for participation earlier concluded with firms having special circumstances – Safrap and Agip/Phillips, and all of the new offshore companies). Given the reduced scope for increases in the effective tax rate, the Nigerian government apparently feels that it can extract an increasing portion of the economic rent from oil by assuming part ownership, especially if that ownership can be obtained on favorable terms. Whether the government should (from an economic viewpoint) invest in oil production depends, of course, on rates of return in its alternative investment opportunities. It seems doubtful, however, that there are many alternatives in Nigeria with a higher payoff than oil production.

Conservation policy often encompasses any or all of three related concepts: legislating practices to ensure that total recovery from oil and gas fields is not decreased by unusually rapid extraction; timing the future flow of production in order to spread out the benefits from a nonrenewable asset; and protecting the environment from damage during exploration, development, and production. Little outward concern has been expressed by the Nigerian government about unusual environmental damage or about any over-exploitation of producing fields. Greater attention rests with the issue of whether or not to conserve Nigeria's petroleum resources for future exploitation, but to date there have been no indications that the government intends to limit production of oil. Indeed, the emphasis has been very much in the opposite direction. In light of Nigeria's large population (60-70 million) and great development needs and the lack of information on the extent of petroleum resources in Nigeria, a conservation policy aimed at limiting output seems both unlikely and inappropriate.

THE DEVELOPMENT OF PETROLEUM PRODUCTION IN OTHER SUB-SAHARAN AFRICAN COUNTRIES

Gabon[18]
The exploration for oil and gas in Gabon began in the 1930s when the country was a French colony and part of French Equatorial Africa. In 1956 the first

Sub-Saharan Africa

TABLE 7

Production of petroleum in Angola, Gabon, and Congo (Brazzaville) 1956–72
(thousands of barrels per day)

	Angola[b]	Gabon	Congo (Brazzaville)
1956	*		
1957	*	3	
1958	1	10	
1959	1	15	
1960	1	16	1
1961	2	15	2
1962	9	16	3
1963	16	18	2
1964	18	21	1
1965	13	25	1
1966	13	29	1
1967	11	68	1
1968	19	90	1
1969	10	101	*
1970	14	108	*
1971	115	115	*
1972[a]	137	134	7

* less than 500 bd
a preliminary
b including Cabinda

SOURCES: Date for 1956–62 from E.L. De Golgyer and L.W. MacNaughton, *Twentieth Century Petroleum Statistics 1972* (Dallas 15 June 1972), p. 10. Data for 1963–72 from *International Petroleum Encyclopedia 1973* (Tulsa, Oklahoma 1973), pp. 263–5.

commercial discovery of oil was made onshore in the Port Gentil area by the predecessor company to the current principal concessionaire, Société Elf des Pétroles d'Afrique Equatoriale (Elf-Spafe), a company controlled by the government of France through Elf-Erap. Elf-Spafe is in partnership with Shell Gabon in all areas which are currently in production. Many other companies, including Texaco/Chevron and Gulf, hold exploration rights, both onshore and offshore.

As shown in Table 7, production and export of crude began in 1957 and rose gradually for a decade, reaching 68,000 bd in 1967. In the past five years, output has grown more rapidly as a result of the development of fields discovered by Elf-Spafe in 1968 and of more recent offshore discoveries. Output in 1972 of 134,000

137

bd was nearly double the 1967 level, and by May 1973 oil production had increased to 172,000 bd. Approximately 40 per cent of output in 1972 was produced offshore, and this share is increasing since most recent fields are located offshore.

Estimates of reserves of petroleum have increased from 500 million barrels in 1970 to 1100 million barrels in 1973 (see Table 2) reflecting both these newer discoveries and the delineation of older fields. During the same period estimates of natural gas reserves have risen much less rapidly, from 5000 billion cubic feet in 1970 to 7000 billion cubic feet in 1973. By comparison, the level of gas production in 1972 was 3.2 billion cubic feet.[19]

Gabon refines about 17,000 bd of crude and exports the remainder of its production. The refinery, which went on stream in November 1967, is jointly owned by the Equatorial African Customs Union (UDEAC) (including 5 per cent shares by Gabon, Congo (Brazzaville), Cameroon, Central African Republic, and Chad), and by Compagnie Française des Petroles, Elf, Mobil, Texaco, Petrofina, British Petroleum, Shell Gabon, and ENI. In 1970 the destination of crude exports from Gabon was 14,000 bd to other African countries, 39,000 bd to Western Europe (mainly France), and 39,000 bd to refineries in the Netherlands Antilles and Trinidad.[20]

In April 1971 the government of Gabon signed a new convention with Elf-Spafe, which also applies to Shell Gabon, replacing the fiscal terms of a 1949 convention.[21] Under this arrangement, government revenues from petroleum doubled to about $11 million, based on the 1971 rate of output of 115,000 bd. The new convention is valid through 1989, and the specific fiscal terms may be revised every five years by mutual agreement. Current terms are much more favorable to producing companies than those in OPEC countries: the profits tax rate is 38 per cent (up from 23 per cent under the earlier convention); the royalty rate is 12 per cent (up from 9 per cent); and capitalized exploration expenses are amortized at a 20 per cent annual rate (down from the previous rate of 100 per cent).

Angola[22]

The first commercial discovery of petroleum in sub-Saharan Africa was made in Angola in 1955. As indicated in Table 7, production began in 1956, but was very limited for 15 years, never exceeding 18,000 bd before 1971. Oil output in the large, southern portion of this Portuguese territory remains small, attaining a level of 13,000 bd in May 1973. All of this production is onshore, and most is by Petrangol, a company owned by the Portuguese government and by Petrofina of Belgium, the operating partner; the remainder is by Petrangol/Angol/Texaco, also headed by Petrofina.

The rapid recent expansion of oil production in Angola is due principally to offshore output from Cabinda, a tiny enclave which is located north of the Congo River and is geographically separated from Angola proper by a narrow stretch of Zaire. All production in Cabinda is entirely by Cabinda Gulf Oil Corporation which began exploration activities in the mid-1950s and first struck oil in 1966. Exporting started in 1968, increased slowly at first, and then spurted during the early 1970s, reaching 132,000 bd in May 1973. As a result, oil production for Angola, including Cabinda, moved from low levels in the 1960s to an average of 137,000 bd for 1972 and to 145,000 bd in May 1973.

Estimated reserves in Angola, including Cabinda, have risen from 500 million barrels of oil and 625 billion cubic feet of natural gas in 1969 to 1200 million barrels of petroleum and 1000 billion cubic feet of gas in 1973 (see Table 2). Production of gas, by comparison, was 38.4 billion cubic feet in 1972.

Angola has a 13,200 bd refinery at Luanda which uses local crude and is operated by Petrangol. The capacity of this refinery is due to double in 1973. A second refinery of 13,000 bd capacity is planned for construction at Lobito-Benguela in 1975.

Congo (Brazzaville)[23]

The first oil discovery in the People's Republic of Congo was made in 1957, when the country was still a French colony and part of French Equatorial Africa. The onshore Pointe Indienne field was put on production in 1960, reached its annual average peak at 3000 bd in 1962, and is still producing small amounts of crude. In 1969 a sizeable offshore discovery, the Emeraude field, was made by France's Elf-Congo and Italy's Agip. Production from this field began in 1972, averaging 7000 bd in that year, and then increased to 43,000 bd in May 1973. This field plus another large offshore find by Agip has caused a tremendous jump in estimated reserves of petroleum from 4 million barrels in 1971 to 5000 million barrels in 1973 (see Table 2). The 1973 estimate is one-third of the comparable figure for Nigeria, and more than four times that of any other tropical African country. Estimates of reserves of natural gas are not available; gas production was 5 billion cubic feet in 1972.

Zaire[24]

Two oil discoveries, one offshore and one onshore, have been made in Zaire, formerly known as the Belgian Congo and Congo (Kinshasa). By mid-1973 word was still awaited as to the potential for commercial production. The offshore strike was made in 1971 by the Gulf/Teikoku/Solico group which holds Zaire's entire offshore concession. A group including Petrofina, Shell, and Mobil made the onshore discovery in 1972 in the province of Bas Zaire. Estimated petroleum

Scott R. Pearson

reserves in Zaire are 500 million barrels (see Table 2). No information is available on reserves of natural gas. Zaire's Kinlao-Muanda refinery is owned by the government and by ENI and has a capacity of 16,200 bd.

Isolated discoveries in other sub-Saharan African countries
Single offshore petroleum discoveries have been made in two West African countries, Dahomey (1968) and Ghana (1970); reserves were initially estimated at 20 million barrels for the Dahomeyan well and 1 million barrels for the Ghanaian discovery, though these estimates have since been reduced (see Table 2). Isolated natural gas wells have been discovered in three other African countries – Mozambique (1965), South Africa (1969), and Ethiopia (1972); estimated reserves, originally 1000 billion cubic feet for Mozambique, 500 billion cubic feet for South Africa, and unannounced for Ethiopia, have since been lowered for the first two countries (see Table 2). The South African strike led to a considerable amount of exploration between 1969 and 1971, and the offshore search resumed again in 1973 following two dormant years.[25] Apart from these isolated discoveries and the more substantial finds in the five countries discussed separately above, oil and gas have not been found in sub-Saharan Africa. The list of the other African countries in which unsuccessful wildcat wells have been drilled includes Cameroon, Equitorial Guinea, Kenya, Liberia, Malagasy Republic, Mauritania, Senegal, Southwest Africa, Spanish Sahara, and Togo.[26]

OUTLOOK FOR THE FUTURE

The purpose of this section is to provide a speculative look at the likely future position of sub-Saharan Africa in the international markets for petroleum and natural gas. In view of the hazards implicit in such an undertaking, no attempt is made to forecast annual net exports from Africa. Existing information permits no more than a presentation of broad trends and rough orders of magnitude of African production, consumption, and net supplies of oil and gas during the next decade.

As presented in Table 2, estimated reserves of petroleum in sub-Saharan Africa at the beginning of 1973 were approximately 22,800 million barrels. These reserves would support production almost to the end of the century at the May 1973 rate of 2,308,000 bd.[27] The estimated oil reserves in 1973 were more than five times the African estimate for 1969. While it is highly unlikely that the future growth of oil reserves will even approach this rate of increase, the changing reserve picture does point up the conservative nature of production estimates based on current reserves. The amounts of petroleum likely to be produced in

140

sub-Saharan Africa are almost surely far greater than recent estimates of reserves, but it would be fanciful to attempt to guess the extent of final production.[28]

Much the same thing can be concluded with respect to natural gas in sub-Saharan Africa. Estimates of gas reserves, as reported in Table 2, have increased from slightly more than 10,000 billion cubic feet in 1969 to 48,000 billion cubic feet at the beginning of 1973, principally as a result of additions in Nigeria in 1971. These reserves would allow over 500 years of production at the May 1973 rate of 7.9 billion cubic feet per month.[29]

A recent forecast of world oil production for 1973 places the total for sub-Saharan Africa at 4.2 per cent of the amount forecast for the world and 5.1 per cent of the projection for the non-Communist world.[30] During the next several years, oil production in sub-Saharan Africa is likely to continue to expand quite rapidly, though at rates substantially less than those achieved in the early 1970s. In Nigeria the capacity of production and export facilities has recently been expanded to allow output of 2.5 million bd. This level could be reached in the next three or four years, assuming no unforeseen changes in government or company policy. Output might then continue to increase until a rate of three million bd is achieved, perhaps in the early 1980s, before levelling off. Similar, or possibly even faster rates of expansion can be expected to occur on average in the other producing countries in tropical Africa. Hence it is not unreasonable to guess that the production of crude oil in tropical Africa may be 50 per cent greater than its recent level, or about 3.5 million bd, by the early 1980s.

Corresponding guesses for gas production are even more hazardous, because current output is small and most associated gas is flared. Plans are underway in Nigeria to construct large new facilities to produce liquefied natural gas (LNG) and liquefied petroleum gas (LPG), mostly for export, beginning in the late 1970s. If these plans materialize, Nigeria could provide important quantities of gas products, since the planned LNG and LPG industries would consume about 1.5 billion cubic feet per day of natural gas.[31]

The likely role of sub-Saharan Africa as a supplier of oil and gas resources to the world market can be delineated by comparing these projected trends in output with guesses about future African consumption in order to find net exports as a residual. Natural gas can be treated summarily; almost all of any LNG or LPG production will be a net export since African consumption is likely to be limited.

Data on petroleum consumption in sub-Saharan Africa are presented in Table 8. During the ten-year period covered in the table, 1963-72, the average annual rate of increase of petroleum consumption was about 7.0 per cent for all of sub-Saharan Africa and approximately 4.5 per cent for the region less South Africa. In 1972 total petroleum consumption in Africa was 581,000 bd, of which

TABLE 8

Petroleum consumption (1963–72) and refining capacity (1973) in sub-Saharan Africa (thousands of barrels per day)

	1963	1964	1965	1966	1967	1968	1969	1970	1971	1972[a]	Refining capacity 1973
Angola	8	10	11	12	11	14	12	14	13	14	16
Ethiopia	3	3	3	6	8	10	9	9	13	13	15
Ghana	12	13	12	10	12	16	14	16	17	19	27
Kenya	17	19	19	21	19	18	28	30	30	31	48
Liberia	2	5	5	5	7	5	5	7	11	12	13
Malagassy	3	3	3	4	4	9	7	7	9	9	15
Mozambique	5	8	6	8	9	10	12	15	14	14	17
Nigeria	22	24	25	28	26	23	27	30	35	35	60[b]
Rhodesia	7	9	15	na	na	na	na	na	na	na	10
Sierra Leone	7	8	8	4	5	3	6	6	7	7	20
Sudan	11	11	11	12	12	18	30	30	17	30	17
Tanzania	7	7	7	9	10	10	11	13	14	15	16
Zaire	10	7	9	11	12	10	10	11	13	14	16
Others	85	98	93	108	103	125	112	88	99	103	41
SUB-TOTAL	219	225	227	238	238	271	283	276	292	321	327
South Africa	100	129	127	125	154	166	182	202	229	260	243
TOTAL	319	354	354	363	392	437	465	478	521	581	570

a   preliminary
b   not operating
na not available

SOURCE: *International Petroleum Encyclopedia 1973* (Tulsa, Oklahoma 1973), p. 271.

260,000 bd occurred in South Africa. Since crude output was 2,095,000 bd (see Tables 3 and 7), the region was a net supplier of 1,514,000 bd of crude to the rest of the world.

If the rate of growth of 7.0 per cent were maintained in the future, petroleum consumption in sub-Saharan Africa would reach one million bd in the early 1980s. At that time, if the countries of tropical Africa were to produce at the rate of 3.5 million bd estimated above, they would provide 2.5 million bd for consumption outside of Africa. Although the rate of growth implicit in the production forecast (about 5 per cent) is less than that guessed for consumption (7 per cent), net exports of petroleum can be expected to increase in absolute amounts because production is much larger than consumption in the base year. For example, net exports in 1973 might be 1,742,000 bd (production of 2,364,000 bd, the level given in the forecast mentioned above, less consumption of 622,000 bd, an amount 7 per cent above the actual level in 1972). Based on the assumptions stated above, estimates for 1974 would be production of 2,482,000 bd, consumption of 666,000 bd, and thus net exports of 1,816,000 bd. The amount available for export outside of Africa would thus increase by 74,000 bd, in spite of the higher assumed rate of growth of consumption relative to that assumed for production. For the foreseeable future, therefore, the strong likelihood is that sub-Saharan Africa will be a major supplier of petroleum and probably of natural gas to consuming countries in other parts of the world.

NOTES

The author is very grateful to Ronald K. Meyer for permission to use materials contained in a jointly authored study of the Nigerian petroleum industry, for comments on an earlier draft of this paper, and for statistical assistance, and to Alan Logan for providing valuable information.

1 Sub-Saharan Africa is defined here to include all of the African continent less Egypt, Libya, Tunisia, Algeria, and Morocco. The terms Africa or African in this study refer to sub-Saharan Africa.

2 L. Dudley Stamp, *Africa: A Study in Tropical Development* (New York 1953), p. 53

3 This section is based largely on Scott R. Pearson, *Petroleum and the Nigerian Economy* (Stanford 1970) and Ronald K. Meyer and Scott R. Pearson, 'Contributions of Petroleum to Nigerian Economic Development,' in *Commodity Exports and African Economic Development,* Scott R. Pearson and John Cownie *et al.* (Lexington, Mass., forthcoming 1974). More detailed information and complete footnote citations are contained in this book and chapter, respectively.

Scott R. Pearson

4 Information in this subsection is drawn from Pearson, *Petroleum and the Nigerian Economy*, pp. 13-18, and from Meyer and Pearson, 'Contributions of Petroleum to Nigerian Economic Development,' pp. 2-5

5 'A Dowry for a New Oil Corporation,' *Petroleum Press Service*, June 1971, p. 228

6 'What's Happening in Those Oil Talks?' *African Development*, March 1973, p. N19

7 Information in this subsection is drawn from Pearson, *Petroleum and the Nigerian Economy*, pp. 55-6, and from Meyer and Pearson, 'Contributions of Petroleum to Nigerian Economic Development,' pp. 8-11, 20-2

8 These production shares were not unlike the recent distribution of concessions held by the six producing companies: Shell-BP (17,000 square miles); Gulf (5000); Agip/Phillips/NNOC (2000); Mobil (1000); Safrap/NNOC (1000); and Texaco/Chevron (1000).

9 A complete listing of all oil fields in Nigeria (and in the other producing countries of tropical Africa), including data on recent production levels and on cumulative total output, is contained in *The Oil and Gas Journal*, 25 Dec. 1972, pp. 116-18.

10 *Petroleum Press Service*, Oct. 1972, p. 362

11 Information in this subsection relies heavily on Pearson, *Petroleum and the Nigerian Economy*, pp. 22-30, 176-88, and on Meyer and Pearson, 'Contributions of Petroleum to Nigerian Economic Development,' pp. 6-8, 11-13.

12 *Petroleum Press Service*, May 1971, p. 163

13 'Nigeria Revenues Jump with New Oil Currency Pacts,' *Petroleum Intelligence Weekly*, 3 July 1972, p. 7

14 Information in this subsection is drawn mainly from Meyer and Pearson, 'Contributions of Petroleum to Nigerian Economic Development,' pp. 11-13.

15 Morris A. Adelman, *The World Petroleum Market* (Baltimore 1972), p. 76

16 For an analysis of the contributions of the petroleum industry to Nigerian income, see Meyer and Pearson, 'Contributions of Petroleum to Nigerian Economic Development,' pp. 13-24.

17 The discussion in this subsection is based in part on Pearson, *Petroleum and the Nigerian Economy*, pp. 153-66, and on Meyer and Pearson, 'Contributions of Petroleum to Nigerian Economic Development,' pp. 26-30.

18 Information in this subsection is drawn largely from 'Gabon,' *International Petroleum Encyclopedia 1973* (Tulsa, Oklahoma 1973), p. 63, and from 'New Gabon Field to Hit 60,000 b/d by 1974,' *The Oil and Gas Journal*, 16 April 1973, p. 141.

19 This figure for gas production and those provided below for Angola and

Congo (Brazzaville) are from 'Worldwide Gas Production,' *The Oil and Gas Journal,* 19 Feb. 1973.

20 United Nations Statistical Papers, *World Energy Supplies, 1961-1970,* Series J, no 15, pp. 114-20

21 'Gabon: New Fiscal Terms,' *Petroleum Press Service,* June 1971, p. 228

22 Information in this subsection is principally from 'Angola,' *International Petroleum Encyclopedia 1973,* pp. 62-3, and 'Angola,' *Geological Survey Professional Paper 817,* 1973, p. 8

23 Information in this subsection is mainly from 'Congo (Brazzaville),' *International Petroleum Encyclopedia 1973,* p. 70

24 Information in this subsection is based on 'Zaire,' *International Petroleum Encyclopedia 1973,* p. 70

25 'South Africa,' *International Petroleum Encyclopedia 1973,* p. 71

26 'Non-Communist Well Completions,' *International Petroleum Encyclopedia 1973,* p. 208

27 Of this total, Nigeria produced 1,948,000 bd, Gabon, 172,000, Cabinda, 132,000, Angola proper, 13,000, and Congo (Brazzaville), 43,000. 'Worldwide Crude Production,' *The Oil and Gas Journal,* 16 July 1973, p. 162

28 One expert on Africa, speaking in terms of the entire continent, is of the opinion that 'Large additional oil and gas finds are particularly likely.' See William Hance, 'Africa's Minerals: What the Future Offers,' *Africa Report,* June 1971, p. 33.

29 Of this total, Nigeria produced 5.7 billion cubic feet, Angola, 1.9, Congo (Brazzaville), 0.2, and Gabon, 0.1. 'Worldwide Gas Production,' *The Oil and Gas Journal,* 16 July 1973, p. 162.

30 The African total was 2,364,000 bd, of which Nigeria was projected at 2,000,000 bd, Gabon, 190,000, Cabinda, 132,000, Angola proper, 12,000, and Congo (Brazzaville), 30,000. Larry Auldridge, 'Surging World Oil Flow to Hit 56 Million b/d in '73,' *The Oil and Gas Journal,* 18 June 1973, pp. 27-8.

31 Meyer and Pearson, 'Contributions of Petroleum to Nigerian Economic Development,' pp. 21-2

Of the twenty-nine countries in Latin America, two have been major producers and exporters of oil: Mexico in the 1930s and Venezuela in the 1960s. In recent years, Venezuelan production and exports have increased more slowly than world totals, but Venezuela is still the third largest exporter to the US and the largest exporter to Canada.

Consumption of energy is low in Latin America, but growing quickly. Major consumers are Argentina, Mexico, and Brazil, the latter importing 73 per cent of its oil needs. Self-sufficiency is not widely achieved in Latin America, and significant imports of oil come from the Middle East and North Africa, Venezuelan crude being relatively costly in the southern regions of Latin America. Recent discoveries of oil have been in countries which are not major producers – Ecuador and Argentina. The total potential oil reserves of this area look small, however; Venezuela has been thoroughly explored and geological conditions are not favorable in most of the Latin American regions.

Professor Steele details the history of energy exploration and exploitation in Latin America. Government policies in each major country are analyzed, and the preponderant use of government companies explained. Venezuela was a charter member of OPEC and has been in the forefront of raising posted prices. Venezuela, with a far lower reserve-to-production ratio than any other OPEC country, was willing to trade off decreases in production rates for increases in oil prices. Having small reserves of high-cost, high-sulfur oil, the Venezuelan oil industry prospered only because of American oil quotas. With free competition in the American market (and a competitive world oil industry), Venezuela would likely not have sold much to the US or Canada.

Increasing prices of Middle East oil and Arab embargoes have made Latin American crude very valuable today, and Venezuela is taking advantage of the world situation and maximizing production. Tomorrow, high-cost high-sulfur oil may not be in as great demand.

HENRY STEELE

The Latin American petroleum industry

For purposes of this article, Latin America is defined to include Central America, the Caribbean Islands, and South America. In regard to trade patterns, however, the relevant division is into two areas: (1) the northern region, including the South American countries of Venezuela, Colombia, and the island of Trinidad; and (2) the southern region, comprising the remainder of South America. The northern region is a large net exporter, while the southern region has a major net import balance.

In the north, exports from Venezuela, Colombia, and Trinidad either go directly from the fields to North American, South American, African, or western European markets, or else are shipped to Caribbean area refineries, from which refined fuels are then shipped to the same general market areas. The southern region obtains its imports in large measure from the northern region, but also imports significant amounts from the Middle East, Africa, and eastern Europe. Table 2 shows that in 1970 the composition, by destination of shipment, for northern region exports was: United States, 52 per cent; Europe, 20 per cent; Canada, 15 per cent; southern Latin America, 10 per cent; Africa, two per cent; and Japan, one per cent. The southern region obtained 43 per cent of its oil from the northern region, 19 per cent from the Middle East, 14 per cent from Russia and eastern Europe, 14 per cent from Africa, and 9 per cent from the United States and Europe combined. The southern region does not import all its needs from the northern area since it can often buy oil more cheaply from Africa and the Middle East. A combination of lower wellhead prices and low shipping rates by tanker made it possible through 1971 for these Eastern Hemisphere exporters to undersell Venezuelan crude oil. The Venezuelans, in turn, were more anxious

TABLE 1

Crude oil production, consumption, imports, exports, refineries, reserves, refinery capacity, and petrochemical plants – Latin America by regions, 1972. Natural gas: production and reserves, 1972

Northern Region	Crude oil production (000 bd)	Crude oil consumption (000 bd)	Net oil imports (000 bd)	Net oil exports (000 bd)	Estimated oil reserves (billion bbl)	Refineries Number 1-1-73
Mexico	445	540	95		4.50	6
Bahamas		52	52			2
Barbados		11	11			1
Bermuda		11	11			
Costa Rica		9	9			1
Cuba	4	90	86		.01	4
Dominican Republic		19	19			
Guatemala		20	20		.01	2
Haiti		4	4			
Honduras		11	11			1
British Honduras		1	1			
Jamaica		33	33			1
Nicaragua		10	10			1
Panama		90	90			1
Puerto Rico		190	190			3
El Salvador		10	10			1
Trinidad and Tobago	151	57		94	2.00	3
Netherlands Antilles		106	106			2
Subtotal	600	1264	758	94	6.52	29
Southern Region						
Argentina	435	485	50		4.90	16
Bolivia	43	13		30	.20	5
Brazil	166	620	454		1.00	12
Chile	33	115	82		.13	3
Colombia	198	134		64	2.50	6
Ecuador	69	27		42	6.00	3
The Guianas		23	23			
Paraguay		6	6			1
Peru	68	107	39		.75	5
Uruguay		44	44			1
Venezuela	3219	240		2979	13.70	12
Subtotal	4231	1814	698	3115	29.18	64
Total Latin America	4831	3078	1456	3209	35.70	93
Total net exports				1753		

SOURCES: Natural gas: *International Petroleum Encyclopedia*, 1973, pp. 486-93. Other data: *World Petroleum Report*, 1973, pp. 11, 14, 15

Throughput capacity (000 bd)	Refinery capacity minus 1972 oil consumption (000 bd)	Natural gas production 10^9 ft^3/yr	Estimated gas reserves 10^{12} ft^3	Petrochemical plants			
				Operating in 1972	New projects in 1973		
					New plants	Expansions	Total
592	52	687	11.5	32	4	6	10
268	216						
3	-8						
	-11						
8	-1			1			
82	-8				1		1
	-19						
25	5						
	-4						
14	3						
	-1						
36	3						
22	12			1			
75	-15						
221	31			14		1	1
13	3			1	1		1
426	369	125	7.5	2			
800	694			2			
2585	1321	812	19.0	53	6	7	13
630	145	230	8.8	21	4	9	13
24	11	110	5.0		1		1
783	163	40	1.0	32	6	4	10
127	12	290	5.0	2	3	1	4
136	2	120	2.4	12	1	3	4
36	9	4	.5				
	-23						
10	4						
99	-8	1	3.0	3	1		1
40	-4			1			
1330	1090	1668	34.6	7	6	1	7
3215	1401	2463	60.3	78	22	18	40
5800	2722	3275	79.3	131	28	25	53

to sell their oil in the United States since at that time US prices were above world prices.

SUMMARY OF PETROLEUM INDUSTRY STATISTICAL DATA FOR LATIN AMERICA

Table 1 presents 1972 statistics on the petroleum industry in each of the Latin American countries. It is evident that the petroleum industry possesses different characteristics in different countries. All countries consume petroleum products, to be sure, but only eleven produce any oil, and only five of these produce more oil than they consume. Venezuela is the only country of major standing in the world petroleum trade, producing 66.6 per cent of Latin American oil while consuming only about 8 per cent. It is, however, noteworthy that Venezuelan production and exports have increased much less rapidly than world totals, with the consequence that Venezuela, which was for many years the largest oil exporter and the third largest producer, has dropped to third largest exporter and fifth largest producer.

Table 1 indicates that total Latin American oil production in 1972 was 4.83 million barrels per day, while consumption was 3.08 million, providing a daily export surplus of 1.75 million barrels. This is down 18 per cent from the 1971 surplus of 2.14 million barrels per day. Estimated crude oil reserves as of the end of 1972 were 35.7 billion barrels, which gives the region a ratio of 20.2 to one between total reserves and annual production. While about 67 per cent of the oil is produced in Venezuela, the remainder is divided among a number of countries: 9 per cent each in Mexico and Argentina, 4 per cent in Colombia, 3 per cent each in Brazil and Trinidad-Tobago, and the remaining 5 per cent shared by Peru, Chile, Bolivia, Ecuador, and Cuba.

The largest consuming countries are Brazil, Mexico, and Argentina, which together account for about 50 per cent of total consumption. While Venezuela, Puerto Rico, Colombia, and the Netherlands Antilles are also relatively large consumers, their totals include not only final consumption but also refinery use for fueling the large refinery activities in these areas. Chile and Peru complete the list of those consuming more than one hundred thousand barrels per day. Chile's moderate oil consumption is due to its lesser degree of dependence upon petroleum fuels than the typical Latin American country, which does not possess Chile's supplies of low-cost coal and hydroelectric power.

Self-sufficiency in oil supplies is a general goal in most countries, but it is not widely achieved in Latin America. Among major consumers, Argentina and Mexico have attained a ratio of 85 to 90 per cent, while Brazil, with its meager petroleum resource base, must import about 73 per cent of its oil needs, and is by far

TABLE 2

Latin American petroleum exports and imports, by geographic location of sources and destinations, 1970

Areas receiving exports	Exports from Caribbean area		Exports from rest of Latin America		Source of imports	Imports into Latin America, excluding Caribbean area	
	Thousand barrels per day	% of total exports	Thousand barrels per day	% of total exports		Thousand barrels per day	% of total imports
USA	1680	52	80	88	USA	50	6
Canada	480	15			Caribbean area	335	43
Other Western Hemisphere	335	10	5	6	Other Latin America	5	1
Western Europe	640	20	5	6	Western Europe	25	3
Africa	50	2			Middle East	150	19
Japan	45	1			North Africa	25	3
					West Africa	90	11
					USSR & Eastern Europe	105	14
Total	3230	100	90	100	Total	785	100

SOURCE: *British Petroleum Statistical Review of the World Oil Industry – 1970*

the largest oil importer in Latin America. Although some oil was found in Guatemala in 1972, no oil is currently produced in Central America, and while consumption there is relatively low in absolute terms, the rate of increase is the highest in Latin America.

With the exclusion of the Netherlands Antilles, where demand is for refinery input for re-export, and of Puerto Rico, which is a part of the United States oil-industry complex, the total import needs of the northern region are only 367 thousand barrels per day. The further elimination of Cuba, which does not participate in the world petroleum market but engages in barter transactions for Russian oil, would reduce net commercial-basis imports to 277 thousand barrels per day.

In the southern region, only Uruguay, Paraguay, and the Guianas are completely dependent upon imports. Until 1972, Colombia was the second largest oil exporter in Latin America, but in 1972 it was replaced by Trinidad. Even so, Trinidad's exports of 94,000 b/d make it a poor runner-up to Venezuela's 1.33 million b/d. Ecuador's production increased sixteenfold between 1970 and 1972, providing it with an export surplus of 42,000 b/d. Bolivian production is only 43,000 b/d, but since its domestic consumption is lower than that of any South American country except Paraguay, an export level of 30,000 b/d was achieved. Peru in 1972 was producing only about two-thirds of its own oil needs, although prospects for greatly increased output in the future will eventually permit Peru to market an export surplus. Chile currently produces only 29 per cent of its own oil needs, but here too there are at least some prospects for substantial future increases in output.

With regard to oil reserves, Table 1 shows that Venezuela, with two-thirds of Latin American production, has only 38 per cent of reserves. Recent discoveries in Ecuador bring its reserves up to 6 billion barrels, or 17 per cent of the Latin American total, even though in 1972 Ecuador produced only about 1.5 per cent of the total oil output. Eighty-two per cent of Latin American reserves are in South America, with Northern region reserves being limited to Mexico's 4.5 billion barrels (13 per cent of the Latin American total) and 2 billion barrels in Trinidad which, while it is a Caribbean country, is geologically a part of Venezuela.

In the remainder of South America, Argentina has 4.9 billion barrels, Colombia 2.5 billion, Brazil one billion, and Peru, Bolivia, and Chile have only 1.03 billion barrels among them. Apart from Venezuela, Ecuador, and eastern Mexico, the petroleum endowment of Latin America is unusually poor. By way of contrast, it is estimated in 1971 that Middle Eastern reserves were at least 324 billion barrels, with 85 billion in Russia and Asia, 60 billion in the United States and

Canada, and 47 billion in Africa. Europe is the only continental area more scant-
ily endowed than Latin America, and recent large oil and gas discoveries in the
North Sea have more than tripled European reserves. Hence, apart from Venezuela, the Latin American regions do not have a comparative advantage in petroleum resource endowment.

Table 1 also shows data on gas production and reserves. Gas reserves are overall well correlated with oil reserves, with the notable exceptions of Trinidad,
Bolivia, Chile, and Peru which have an unusually high ratio of gas to oil reserves,
and Ecuador, where this ratio is unusually low. Total gas reserves are estimated
at 79.3 trillion cubic feet, with over three-fourths of the total in South America.
Venezuela's 34.6 trillion cubic feet accounts for about 43 per cent of total reserves, while its gas output is about 51 per cent of total Latin American production. Second in total reserves is Mexico, with 11.5 trillion cubic feet, followed
by Argentina's 8.8 trillion, Trinidad-Tobago's 7.5 trillion, and five trillion each
in Bolivia and Chile. The gas industry in Latin America, apart from Venezuela
and Mexico, is relatively underdeveloped, and plans are underway to expand gas
production in Chile, Trinidad, Bolivia, and other areas. The ratio of reserves to
production is almost 25 to one, indicative of a less-than-intensive degree of development.

Turning now to the refinery and petrochemical plant data of Table 1, it
appears that in 1972 there were 29 refineries in the northern region and 64 in
the southern. Throughput capacity, however, was more equally divided: 2.59
million barrels per day versus 3.22 million in the two areas. The two refineries
in the Netherlands Antilles are among the world's largest, and those in Mexico
and the other Caribbean countries are also relatively large. In South America,
only the Venezuelan refineries are of comparable average size. In the exporting
countries, refining capacity is uniformly greater than domestic consumption.
While Venezuela exports most of its petroleum as crude oil, much of this oil is
shipped to Caribbean-area refineries where it is refined and the products shipped
to other markets in Europe and the Western Hemisphere. This is registered in the
circumstance that for the Caribbean countries, excluding Cuba, consumption is
634,000 b/d while refinery capacity is 1.911 million b/d.

While the petroleum exporters may have refinery capacity greatly in excess of
domestic consumption needs, the other countries with refineries possess refinery
capacities equal to from 85 to 125 per cent of consumption levels. Hence, apart
from those few small countries which have no refineries, there would appear to
be no serious shortage of refining capacity anywhere in Latin America.

In 1972 there were 131 petrochemical plants operating in Latin America, 78
of which were in South America. Expansion of capacity was proceeding at a

brisk pace; during 1973, 28 new plants were under construction and 25 existing plants were being expanded.

OUTLINE OF FUTURE PROSPECTS FOR LATIN AMERICAN PETROLEUM OPERATIONS

The future of the Latin American petroleum industry depends largely upon the discovery of new reserves and the development of additional productive capacity. It seems obvious that new reserves and productive capacity must be developed if the area is to keep pace with its rapidly increasing internal consumption demands and still maintain its position as a major exporting area. But while consumption is certain to increase, growth in reserves and production is less certain. Venezuela has dominated the area in the past, but there are several factors, discussed below, which suggest that Venezuela's role in the world oil market will tend to decline. New discoveries will no doubt continue to be made in Venezuela, but if the country's output is maintained at current levels, reserves will probably decrease. The major new prospects in the rest of Latin America appear to be in offshore areas, particularly seaward of the coasts of Ecuador, Colombia, Peru, Brazil, Argentina, and Chile. Oil prospecting in the interior of the continent has been negative in Brazil, but very promising in Ecuador and Peru. These recent finds, coupled with some discoveries in Bolivia in the recent past, indicate that new onshore areas in South America may prove very productive.

In projecting the future of Latin American petroleum, however, much depends upon Venezuela. Although Venezuelan developments are discussed at greater length in the next section, the major reasons for some pessimism in this regard can be cited here. First, except for some offshore areas, Venezuela has been rather thoroughly explored over a long period of time, and there is little chance that many new giant fields will be found in the future. Second, since 1959 the policy of the government has been to reduce the nation's degree of dependence upon oil for conservation and public policy reasons. While other oil-exporting countries have increased their output greatly since 1959, Venezuela has been content with more modest growth goals, and has in fact experienced little growth in exports. Third, Venezuelan oil is becoming increasingly overpriced in world markets in view of its high sulfur content and the high costs of desulfurization to meet air pollution control standards, and as a result of declining freight rates which have reduced its transport cost advantage relative to Middle Eastern oil. Fourth, the trend of tax and regulatory policy over the last fifteen to twenty-five years has been such as to discourage development of the oil and gas by foreign capital, while the national oil company has shown little sign of developing such capability on its own.

154

DETAILED CONSIDERATION
OF DEVELOPMENTS IN INDIVIDUAL COUNTRIES

Northern region of Latin America
Mexico The history of oil production in Mexico in modern times is interesting. In 1884, a law was passed which transferred title to minerals from the state to the surface land owner, thus stimulating private exploration. American, British, and Dutch groups began operations in the latter part of the nineteenth century, and within the next ten to twenty years, the four major petroleum provinces of Mexico had been discovered and partially developed. All of these provinces are on the east coast, very close to the Gulf of Mexico.[1]

These fields were developed rapidly during and after the First World War, and production in Mexico reached its peak in 1921. As in the United States, the largest fields were the first to be found, and production practices at that time were wasteful in both countries, leading to an early decline in output even in the largest fields. Other factors contributing to the rapid decline in Mexican output between 1921 and 1931 included the increasing maturity of the industry, and the incidence of political unrest. The resource base of the Mexican oil industry had in all likelihood been broadly outlined by the mid-1920s, at least with regard to onshore fields of the type capable of discovery with the methods then in use, so that by 1930 the industry was past its peak. Political factors steadily reduced incentives to invest after the end of the First World War. The revolutionary uprisings of the 1910s culminated in the new constitution of 1917 which transferred minerals ownership back to the state – a step that fostered a decline in exploratory activity. Not only was land access difficult and uncertain, but by the 1920s a surplus of oil had been built up in world markets, and there were more promising new prospects elsewhere in Latin America.

In 1938 the Mexican oil industry was nationalized, and a government monopoly company, Petroleos Mexicanos, or Pemex, was created to operate the seized properties. Since then, authorities are in agreement that Pemex has on the whole made the best of sometimes rather difficult circumstances. Although Mexican production had been over half a million barrels per day in 1921, by 1938 output had shrunk to 128,000 b/d, with 118,000 b/d of refinery output and domestic consumption of only 60,000 b/d.[2] For a period in the 1920s, Mexico was the world's largest oil exporter and second largest producer, and even in 1938 exports were a major factor in the industry. Because of the hostility which persisted for some time after expropriation, however, exports declined for some time. Attempts were then made to cultivate the internal market. Consumers were subsidized by setting prices at low levels, and the market grew rapidly. Table 3 indicates a growth from 64,000 b/d in 1940 to 139,000 in 1950 and 298,000

155

TABLE 3

Crude oil production, consumption, net imports and exports, refining capacity, and refining capacity relative to consumption, for Latin America, 1940-72 by selected years

	Crude oil production (000 bd)							Crude oil consumption (000 bd)						
Major producing countries	1940	1950	1955	1960	1965	1970	1972	1940	1950	1955	1960	1965	1970	1972
Argentina	56	64	84	172	269	393	435	90	155	192	244	381	423	485
Bolivia	1	2	7	10	9	16	43	1	2	4	6	9	10	13
Brazil		1	55	81	94	161	166	26	86	176	274	328	508	620
Chile		2	7	20	35	35	33	14	21	34	48	60	88	115
Colombia	70	93	111	153	201	214	198	10	20	40	54	69	96	134
Ecuador	6	7	10	8	8	4	69	2	4	6	11	17	21	27
Mexico	120	199	250	271	323	430	445	64	139	180	298	341	503	540
Peru	33	41	47	53	63	72	68	9	24	40	50	76	97	107
Trinidad and Tobago	61	57	68	116	134	140	151	14	22	36	47	98	54	57
Venezuela	507	1498	2157	2846	3473	3708	3219	28	56	112	155	178	200	240
Other major countries														
Netherlands Antilles								46	109	148	152	144	73	106
Panama (+ Canal Zone)								9	14	20	24	70	139	145
Cuba					4	3	4	14	38	58	83	95	90	90
Puerto Rico								5	14	24	58	99	156	190
Uruguay								13	18	20	31	35	38	44

Refining areas not included above*

Barbados
Costa Rica
El Salvador
Guatemala
Honduras
Jamaica
Nicaragua
Paraguay

SOURCES: 1940-70: *International Petroleum Encyclopedia*, 1973, pp. 486-93; 1970: *World Petroleum Report*, 1973, pp. 11-15

* Consumption data not available for these countries individually

TABLE 3 *continued*

Crude oil production, consumption, net imports and exports, refining capacity, and refining capacity relative to consumption, for Latin America, 1940–72 by selected years

	Net crude oil exports (+) or imports (−) (000 bd)							Refinery capacity (000 bd)						
Major producing countries	1940	1950	1955	1960	1965	1970	1972	1940	1950	1955	1960	1965	1970	1972
Argentina	-34	-91	-108	-72	-112	-30	-50	103	152	186	238	393	502	630
Bolivia	0	0	3	4	0	6	30	1	7	12	12	12	21	24
Brazil	-26	-85	-121	-193	-234	-347	-454	4	12	106	156	335	575	783
Chile	-14	-19	-27	-28	-25	-53	-82	1	4	20	24	54	115	127
Colombia	60	73	71	99	132	118	64	15	24	40	51	94	140	136
Ecuador	4	3	4	-3	-9	-17	42	2	5	5	7	16	37	36
Mexico	56	60	70	-27	-18	-73	-95	98	160	244	357	461	515	592
Peru	24	17	7	3	-13	-25	-39	22	35	48	49	56	104	99
Trinidad and Tobago	47	35	32	69	36	86	94	49	104	115	182	345	417	426
Venezuela	479	1442	2045	2691	3295	3508	2979	55	254	528	886	1087	1324	1330
Other major countries														
Netherlands Antilles	-46	-109	-148	-152	-144	-73	-106	495	617	640	680	670	795	800
Panama (+ Canal Zone)	-9	-14	-20	-24	-70	-139	-145					55	140	75
Cuba	-14	-38	-58	-83	-91	-87	-86	4	7	8	87	87	93	82
Puerto Rico	-5	-14	-24	-58	-99	-156	-190				84	155	155	221
Uruguay	-13	-18	-20	-31	-35	-38	-44	5	16	28	28	51	40	40
Refining areas not included above*														
Barbados														3
Costa Rica													8	8
El Salvador												13	14	13
Guatemala											4		21	25
Honduras													10	14
Jamaica												26	28	36
Nicaragua												6	21	22
Paraguay													5	10

SOURCES: 1940–70: *International Petroleum Encyclopedia*, 1973, pp. 486–93; 1970: *World Petroleum Report*, 1973, pp. 11-15

* Consumption data not available for these countries individually

TABLE 3 *continued*

Crude oil production, consumption, net imports and exports, refining capacity, and refining capacity relative to consumption, for Latin America, 1940-72 by selected years

	Refinery capacity minus crude oil consumption (000 bd)						
	1940	1950	1955	1960	1965	1970	1972
Major producing countries							
Argentina	13	-3	-6	-6	12	79	145
Bolivia	0	5	8	6	3	11	11
Brazil	-22	-74	-70	-118	7	67	163
Chile	-13	-17	-14	-24	-6	-27	-12
Colombia	5	4	0	-3	25	44	2
Ecuador	0	1	-1	-4	-1	16	9
Mexico	34	21	64	59	120	12	52
Peru	13	11	8	-1	-20	7	-8
Trinidad and Tobago	35	82	79	135	247	363	369
Venezuela	27	198	416	731	909	1124	1090
Other major countries							
Netherlands Antilles	449	508	492	528	526	722	694
Panama (+ Canal Zone)	-9	-14	-20	-24	-15	1	-70
Cuba	-10	-31	-50	4	-8	3	-8
Puerto Rico	-5	-14	-24	-26	-56	-1	-31
Uruguay	-8	-2	-8	-3	-16	2	-4

Refining areas not included above*

Barbados
Costa Rica
El Salvador
Guatemala
Honduras
Jamaica
Nicaragua
Paraguay

SOURCES: 1940-70: *International Petroleum Encyclopedia*, 1973, pp. 486-93; 1970: *World Petroleum Report*, 1973, pp. 11-15

in 1960. In the late 1940s Pemex increased its exploration efforts with good success, although production never grew as rapidly as consumption. The export surplus existing in 1938 had disappeared by the late 1950s. Throughout the 1950s and 1960s, however, Mexico continued to export some oil to the United States despite the inadequacy of domestic production to satisfy internal demand. It was profitable for Mexico at that time to buy cheap imported oil at low world prices and sell some of its own production to the US market at the higher protected American price, in accordance with intergovernmental agreements.

In 1959 the Mexican government raised domestic prices and reduced the degree to which Pemex had to subsidize Mexican fuel buyers. For a number of years, however, the government had provided certain indirect subsidies to Pemex itself, such as the postponement of tax payments, and these subsidies persisted after the price increase of 1959. Since 1960, Mexican consumption had outdistanced the ability of Pemex to find and produce oil, to the extent that the country is only about 82 per cent self-sufficient at present. With a ratio of over 20 to one between reserves and production, it is likely that more intensive development of existing reserves is possible. In recent years, some success has been encountered in offshore exploration in the Gulf of Mexico and gas discoveries have been noteworthy. The industry is handicapped, however, by the geographic dispersion of production and consumption centers, with major consuming points being located at great distances from most production points, separated not only by many miles but by mountains and deserts.

The only exceptions allowed to complete the Pemex monopoly of all operations since 1938 have been some permits granted to private firms in the manufacturing of intermediate and end products in the petrochemical industry.[3] It seems likely that the most that Pemex can hope for in the future is to keep pace with domestic consumption, with very little chance that Mexico will ever regain its former position as a significant oil exporter.

Trinidad and Tobago The oil industry in Trinidad has been greatly stimulated by large oil and gas discoveries in offshore waters since 1970. Oil has been produced since 1908, but until the 1960s it was a continuing struggle to keep production at adequate levels since production was from old fields that needed high-cost additional recovery projects to stimulate output.

Trinidad has long been rather unusual in its status as not only a significant oil producer (by Caribbean standards) but also a major refiner and exporter of petroleum products. Table 3 shows that by 1969, refinery capacity exceeded domestic demand by 369,000 b/d. But in the 1960s, the oil industry of Trinidad was in rather serious straits. Production of oil was then a high-cost operation, and most oil was being imported – not only from Colombia and Venezuela, but increasingly from Libya and the Persian Gulf. Refined products were exported primarily to European and West African markets. But with more refineries being built in Europe and Africa, and with the 1960s surplus of Middle Eastern oil depressing prices realized on sales to Trinidad's traditional buyers, the former relative cost advantage of the local refining industry was lost, and the primary factor in maintaining operations was the fact that Trinidad's facilities lay in the established channels of trade used by the major integrated international oil companies.

Beginning around 1970, however, major discoveries were made in offshore areas, and by 1972 new oil amounting to 2 billion barrels of reserves had been estimated to be found and capable of recovery. Discovery of this new and lower-cost oil also changed the legal climate. Before 1970, land and mineral rights might be held either publicly or privately, more or less as in the United States.[4] By 1972, however, the national government was participating much more actively in the oil industry. Trinidad and Tobago had joined OPEC, domestic marketing operations had been purchased from British Petroleum and a national petroleum company established to run these facilities, and plans were under way to create a state-owned integrated oil company.

The large new offshore fields have not yet been fully developed, and the current output rate of 151,000 b/d could be doubled in a few years. Large gas reserves of about 7.5 trillion cubic feet have also been found, and the government has taken a 51 per cent interest in a joint venture with two US companies to produce liquefied natural gas and ship it to the Chicago area.[5]

Guatemala Guatemala has long been of interest to geologists because of the presence of possible oil-bearing formations in much of the country. Exploration began on a rather large scale after 1945, but the level of effort fluctuated because of lack of commercial discoveries, the high cost of jungle operations, and changes in mineral laws. In 1949, previously workable concession laws were repealed and foreign companies were expelled. In 1955, the law was amended to permit foreign operations, although mineral ownership remained with the state. State participation of 30 per cent is required for all companies, with a split of 50-50 on all oil profits before foreign taxes.[6] Many wells were drilled following 1955, but not until 1972 was oil in commercial quantities actually found. This discovery, the first in Central America, was made by a Canadian group, and by 1973 a conservative estimate reserves of some 10 million barrels had been made, although no oil had yet been marketed.[7]

Netherlands Antilles The Netherlands Antilles are important because they house two of the world's largest refineries: Jersey's 440,000 b/d unit on Aruba, and Shell's 360,000 b/d plant on Curaçao, which is scheduled to be increased to

435,000 b/d by the end of 1973.[8] Traditionally these refineries have relied upon relatively high-sulfur Venezuelan crude oil, and have exported refined products to Europe and Africa. Given the increased demand for low-sulfur-content fuels, these refineries have recently invested heavily in desulfurization facilities. In mid-1973, plans were being made for the construction of another refinery at Aruba, with initial capacity of 50,000 to 70,000 b/d and a contemplated expansion to an ultimate output of 200,000 b/d.

Table 3 shows that as early as 1940 these two refineries had a capacity of almost half a million barrels per day. The political and legal climate has always been such as to encourage investment, with the area being associated with the European Economic Community under an arrangement which allows duty-free imports into EEC nations of up to 40,000 b/d. Since 1954, when the area obtained full autonomy within the Dutch realm, industry has been encouraged by a program that includes the absence of any restrictions on foreign investment and ownership, guarantees against expropriation, the absence of import duties and profit taxes, and many other inducements to investment.

Cuba Oil exploration in Cuba began before 1900, but not until 1954, with the discovery of oil in Camaguey province, did a real exploration boom occur. Shallow fields had been found previously, but total production never exceeded 800 barrels per day, and declined after 1946. No discoveries of any importance were made after 1954, however, and exploration was dormant even before the seizure of oil properties after the revolution of 1959. Among the properties acquired by seizure, however, were four refineries with a capacity of 82,000 b/d. Since 1959, Cuba has obtained all its oil imports from Russia in barter trading for sugar. Russian efforts to find new Cuban oil began immediately after the revolution, but have not been notably productive. Although verifiable statistics are lacking, it appears that production today is between 2500 and 4000 b/d. Reserves are perhaps ten million barrels.[9]

Other Northern Latin American countries
The remainder of the northern region countries have neither production nor reserves. Many of them, however, have refinery capacities roughly equal to their consumption levels, and the Bahamas resemble the Netherlands Antilles and Trinidad in that these islands house large refineries oriented toward exporting. The larger of the two Bahamas refineries, owned by Chevron Oil and New England Petroleum, had a 1972 capacity of 250,000 b/d, but current expansion should double output by the end of 1973. Furthermore, the first deep-water terminal to serve the US east coast, a $35 million installation capable of handling 400,000 b/d of oil, is scheduled for completion in 1974.[10]

Barbados has one small refinery with a capacity of 3000 b/d, and the island consumes about 11,000 b/d. Although the legal and tax climate is favorable, and although sporadic exploration efforts have occurred since about 1950, no oil worth producing has ever been found.

In the British and French West Indies there is no oil production, as yet no refinery output, and very limited petroleum products consumption. In Costa Rica, exploration began as early as the 1880s, and renewed efforts were made in the 1950s, but without success. No petroleum law exists, but concessions made in the 1950s called for 50-50 profit sharing, with no depletion allowance. Costa Rica has one refinery with a capacity of 8000 b/d and its 1972 oil consumption was 9000 b/d.[11]

Oil development in the Dominican Republic has been hampered by political unrest and by lack of exploratory success. Although no marketed commercial production has ever taken place, some oil has been discovered, as early as 1905. In 1939 a test well produced a total of 40,000 barrels, and after further exploration a concession was awarded to a US based group in 1957. But this property was relinquished in 1963 after a number of dry holes had been drilled, and no significant developments have taken place since then. As of 1972, consumption was 19,000 b/d and no refineries were operating, although a 30,000 b/d plant owned jointly by Shell and the Dominican government was opened in 1973.[12]

Oil experience in Haiti broadly parallels that of the Dominican Republic. Exploration efforts in the late 1940s and early 1950s proved unsuccessful, but in 1973 a very large concession, largely offshore, was awarded to two small American firms. There are no refineries, and consumption is only 4000 b/d. An oil transfer terminal is currently being built at Fort Liberté, with an initial capacity of 750,000 b/d and an ultimate capacity of over a million barrels per day. Completion is anticipated some time in 1974.[13]

Oil exploration has never been very active in Honduras, although many surveys have been made in the past, and some drilling has taken place intermittently, particularly in the 1960s. Currently some offshore activity exists, although no success has yet been registered. Consumption in 1972 was 11,000 b/d and there was one refinery with a capacity of 14,000 b/d. British Honduras has Latin America's lowest consumption rate, only about a thousand barrels a day, with no production or refining. There has been little oil activity of any kind.

Exploration in Jamaica, although periodic, has never been successful. Consumption in 1972 was 33,000 b/d and the Jersey refinery at Kingston had a capacity of 36,000 b/d, all supplied from Venezuela. In 1972 plans were made with an Italian group to build a 250,000 b/d refinery to serve the US east coast market.[14]

In Nicaragua exploratory activity has increased in recent years, although no positive results have been obtained so far. Since 1965, exploration and drilling on a considerable scale has been undertaken, particularly in offshore areas, by several major companies. Consumption in 1972 was 10,000 b/d and the Esso refinery in Managua had a capacity of 22,000 b/d. Early in 1973 plans were being discussed for building a 250,000 b/d refinery at Monkey Point, to be completed by late 1975.[15]

In Panama, oil has been sought since about 1900, but with very little success and no commercial production. Consumption in 1972 was 90,000 b/d and the single refinery with its capacity of 75,000 b/d was then the largest in continental Central America. In 1972 Texaco purchased the controlling interest in this refinery and announced plans to increase capacity by 30,000 b/d.[16]

Relatively little oil and gas exploration has been conducted in Puerto Rico. The first well was drilled in 1960, but no oil has been found. Chiefly because of the special incentives created by the administration of the US oil-import program in the 1960s, Puerto Rico has become an important refining and petrochemicals center, although tax incentives and the presence of low-wage labor have been major contributing factors. Consumption in 1972 was 190,000 b/d and three refineries had a combined capacity of 221,000 b/d. As of 1973 a fourth refinery of some 57,000 b/d capacity was planned by Crown Petroleum.[17]

Geologically, El Salvador is regarded as the least promising of all the Central American countries with regard to oil prospecting, and it does not appear that any drilling has ever taken place. Consumption in 1972 was 10,000 b/d and the single refinery, owned by Esso and Shell, has a capacity of 13,000 b/d.

Southern region of Latin America
Argentina Oil production began in 1907 in Argentina with the discovery of the Rivadavia field in the far south. The Argentine government made this discovery, and the government oil company has long played a major role in the country's petroleum industry. Private companies began exploration in 1910, first finding oil in 1916. Governmental oil operations were consolidated in 1922 under the aegis of a state agency, Yacimientos Petroliferos Fiscales, known as YPF. The private companies, chiefly Esso and Shell, together with some domestic Argentine companies, continued to operate as such until 1964. Government policies, however, limited these firms to acreages held as of the early 1920s, and since the mid-1930s have restricted their expansion in other ways. Private oil output thus declined for a number of years, with some temporary reversal after 1958 when the Frondizi regime made a number of service contracts with private companies, allowing them to use their own funds to find and develop oil which they would then sell to YPF for a sort of per-barrel contract fee.[18]

Although Argentina had always preferred to produce its oil through YPF, it was not until 1958 that monopoly control was conferred upon the state company. Self-sufficiency had long been a national goal, but was not achieved since YPF had never been given enough capital to do the job on its own, while private firms were confined to their existing concession areas after 1922. Hence Argentina fell further and further behind its goal as the economy developed and demand increased. Argentine development itself, however, was hampered by fuel shortages, and under the chaotic and inflationary regime of Perón the high cost of fuel imports was merely one burden among many. After Perón's ouster in 1955, the Frondizi government concluded the 1958 service contract agreements with several private companies. Exploration and development activities expanded and oil output tripled between 1958 and 1963, bringing Argentina up to some 70 per cent of self-sufficiency. The chief increase was in YPF output, achieved with the aid of its drilling contractors. Reserves also tripled, but this was due almost entirely to increased development of known fields rather than to discovery of new ones.[19]

Frondizi was overthrown in 1962, and the service contracts which he had awarded were looked upon with disfavor by the new regime. Payments to the private contractors were allowed to become delinquent during 1962-3, and the agreements were annuled at the end of 1963. Arrangements were undertaken to pay the balances due, although they were not concluded until 1966, and the payments were to be stretched out over a period of up to nine years.[20]

Consumption increased rapidly in the 1960s, and imports increased apace. Again the government reversed its policy, announcing in October 1966 that private firms were to be encouraged, the YPF monopoly of marketing and importing was to be eliminated, and competitive pricing of oil was to be allowed. These reforms were at best shortlived, and in some instances were never implemented. Nevertheless, in August 1967 three large offshore blocks were opened up to private bidding, and in 1968 awards were made to Sinclair, Phillips, and Tenneco, while YPF took over those tracts for which no bids were received. Onshore concessions were obtained by such firms as Esso and Sinclair, and new service contracts were granted. Private investment also took place on a large scale in petrochemicals.[21]

During 1968-70 output grew by almost 10 per cent per year, and kept ahead of consumption growth. But in 1971 steps were taken to weaken the position of the private firms. YPF was restored to its import monopoly status, and was given the power to limit the allotment of oil to private refineries, thus effectively stopping new investment on their part. YPF was also given tracts upon which bids were to have been received, and the state company embarked on a vigorous program to enlarge its domestic sales at the expense of private rivals. Early in 1972

YPF announced an expanded exploration program under which service contracts were to be awarded subject to more onerous terms than had hitherto been exacted. Negotiations for large US investments in Argentine petrochemical plants broke down after several years of discussion, and YPF and other government agencies began to invest more heavily in petrochemicals.[22]

Eight companies initially indicated interest in the new service contracts, but when it became clear that the terms were prohibitive, their bids were cancelled. YPF then announced that it would do all exploration on its own. Contributing to the private companies' pessimism was the pending enactment of a new minerals law which would have given YPF a monopoly all through the oil and gas industry, prohibiting any expansion of private firms. Passage of the law was postponed because of the fear of driving out the private companies entirely, a prospect which – given the chronic shortage of capital to finance YPF – could not be faced without misgiving. Shell and Esso refineries were, nevertheless, reduced to operating at less than 50 per cent of capacity because of YPF allocations of imports away from private firms.[23]

Table 1 shows that in 1972 Argentine production was 435,000 b/d while consumption was 485,000 b/d and refinery capacity stood at 630,000 b/d. Hence the country had not fully achieved self-sufficiency, although it had come rather close. Success in achieving this goal in the long run is problematical, given the disinclination of the government to allocate sufficient capital to YPF, and the inconsistent policy changes in regard to foreign investment.

Bolivia The pattern of oil development in Bolivia has many parallels with that of Argentina, but on a much smaller scale and with even more abrupt changes of policy. Major exploration began in 1921 when concessions were obtained by Jersey, and commercial production began in 1931. In 1936 Bolivia expropriated Jersey, paying compensation equal to about one-fourth of the value of the seized properties. These properties were then transferred to a state monopoly company, Yaciementos Petroliferos Fiscales Bolivianos, or YPFB. YPFB found some new oil, and built pipelines and refineries and eventually achieved self-sufficiency – a not too difficult task in the slow-growing low-income Bolivian economy with its limited consumption.[24]

In the early 1950s Bolivia wanted to increase output in order to earn more foreign currency, but was short of capital to finance YPFB. Beginning in 1952, Bolivia offered concessions to selected foreign companies, and in 1956 it drew up a new oil law which permitted large-scale development by outsiders. Fourteen firms undertook extensive exploration, but only Gulf made major discoveries, and most of the other companies left after four or five years. YPFB continued to develop its own assigned areas in Bolivia, but was hampered by government policies which required subsidizing internal consumption through low prices and free deliveries to governmental users. YPFB retained a monopoly on refining and marketing, but since the bulk of output was sold domestically this was not a very profitable activity.[25]

Gulf's concessions called for the payment of an 11 per cent royalty, a 19 per cent exploration tax, and a 30 per cent tax on gross profits. By 1964 Gulf had found fields capable of production of some 30,000 b/d, more than three times domestic demand. Production was held up until pipelines were built. In 1969 Bolivia nationalized the Gulf properties, including the oil pipeline and a gas pipeline under construction for the marketing of large gas deposits also found by Gulf. In the resulting dispute over the marketing of the seized Gulf production, a 50 per cent drop took place between 1969 and 1970.[26] After the Gulf nationalization, other companies ceased Bolivian operations, and the country found itself faced with decreasing oil reserves at a time when it had acquired pipelines and was trying to stimulate export sales. Accordingly, in 1972 Bolivia again reversed its position and began trying to induce the companies to return. The new law of 1972 contemplates the offering of service contracts under the terms of which 30 per cent of the oil is given to the state and provincial governments, and the remainder is shared with YPFB, with payments exempt from taxes and made on a per-barrel basis. Response to this plan has been extremely cautious.

In 1972 the oil produced was being exported in part to Brazil, while a major gas pipeline had been completed to Argentina. Bolivian gas reserves, obtained from the Gulf discoveries, were estimated at 5 trillion cubic feet, and further gas exports are planned.[27] In 1972 Bolivian production was 43,000 b/d, with consumption of 13,000 b/d and refinery capacity of 24,000 b/d. Neither the production nor the consumption of oil seems likely to increase very rapidly in the future, although gas exports may expand considerably.

Brazil Despite its enormous geographic extent, and the wide expanse of sedimentary basins favorable to the occurrence of petroleum, Brazil appears to be poorly endowed with oil and gas. Oil production has always been a state monopoly in Brazil with early exploration being conducted between 1938 and 1954 by the Brazilian National Petroleum Council. The first discovery was in Bahia state in 1939.[28] In 1953 a state monopoly company, Petroleos Brasileros, or Petrobras, was formed to conduct all Brazilian oil operations except for some rather small existing private refineries. In 1954 Brazil hired Walter Link, the head of Jersey's geology staff, to conduct an intensive six-year $300 million survey of Brazil's petroleum resource base. This was the largest and most expensive oil exploration venture ever conducted in a single country by a single agency, and the result was virtually complete failure. Some new oil was found, but not in appreciable amounts, and reserves were actually lower in 1960 than in 1954 because of rapidly increasing consumption. Furthermore, almost all of the oil produced in Brazil by 1960 came from the Bahia fields. Link concluded in his final report that no oil worth finding could be discovered in new areas, and he urged instead the more intensive development of known regions. This recommendation has been generally followed, and the increase in Brazilian output since 1960 has been due largely to exploration for new pools in old fields, and new fields in the close vicinity of old fields.[29]

In the late 1960s, exploration efforts shifted toward offshore regions, and three moderately large new fields were found, thus bringing Brazil's total reserves up to about one billion barrels – about 12 barrels per capita. In 1972 and 1973 Petrobras decided once again to launch a major exploration drive to see if enough oil for self-sufficiency could ever be found. So far no major new discoveries have been registered. In 1972 production was 166,000 b/d, consumption 620,000 b/d, and refinery capacity 783,000 b/d. Although Brazil has now achieved some surplus refining capacity and has engaged in exporting of refined products, it is currently forced to import more than 70 per cent of its oil needs. Petrobras is not only the largest importer in Latin America but is one of the largest single oil-buying agencies in the world.

Petrobras has a complete monopoly over every phase of petroleum except refining, transportation, and marketing. Over 90 per cent of refining capacity is held by the state company. Six private refineries were in existence at the time Petrobras was established, and were allowed to continue operations, although under regulation their expansion was discouraged, and by 1971 only three of them remained in business. The only privately owned transport facilities consisted of some tankers, the owners of which were not permitted to expand their tonnages. Petrobras receives large public subsidies of indeterminate value through its various privileges of monopoly status, tax immunities, tariff protection, and foreign exchange allocation priorities.[30]

The long-run outlook for oil and gas in Brazil would appear severely limited because of the lack of adequate resources. Major hopes for increased reserves must by default be placed in offshore exploration. Brazil, however, has huge deposits of oil shale which have been developed on a limited basis, but which may form the ultimate basis for the Brazilian energy economy – particularly if world oil prices continue their precipitous increase of the early 1970s.

Chile Oil exploration in Chile began in 1900, but no drilling took place until 1945. A few private concessions were issued in the first quarter of the twentieth century, but in 1926 a law was passed which gave the state monopoly powers in all phases of oil-industry operations. Since 1950 the state monopoly company has been known as Empresa Nacional del Petroleo, or ENAP.

Henry Steele

Chile's first exploratory well was drilled in the extreme southern part of the country in 1945, and was a successful oil producer. Although ENAP conducted additional exploration efforts in other parts of the country, this area has remained the only producing region. More intensive development of the field resulted in production increases through the early 1960s, but after 1965 production began to decline due to the natural depletion of the deposits.[31] In 1972, production was 33,000 b/d, consumption 115,000 b/d, and refinery capacity 127,000 b/d. Chile, as previously mentioned, is less dependent upon oil than most Latin American countries because of its deposits of low-cost coal and its hydroelectric power sites. Nevertheless, oil demands have increased rapidly in Chile, and with the decline in domestic output, imports have increased even more rapidly.

Chilean petroleum marketing is controlled by a private domestic company, with about half of the market, and by Shell and Esso, each with about one quarter of the market. In 1971-2 there was a move to nationalize marketing, but it was not implemented. The political and economic disorders attendant upon the confusion of the last years of the Allende regime seriously disrupted marketing activities, but state exploration efforts were carried out as planned. Unfortunately, the results of the stepped-up exploratory program of 1972-3 have been uniformly disappointing. Chile is now importing some oil from Bolivia, and it appears that import demands will increase in the future. There is a vast area for exploration offshore from the Chilean coast, but nothing yet has been found. Chile's gas endowments appear to be richer than its oil reserves, with five trillion cubic feet estimated as of 1972. In that year, gas production was 290 billion cubic feet, second only to Venezuela in South America. Plans are currently being made for the construction of a liquefied natural-gas plant in extreme southern Chile, with a capacity of 2 million metric tons per year.[32]

Colombia Oil exploration in Colombia began before 1900, but production did not occur until 1921. The economics of Colombian exploration have always been relatively unfavorable. Since the oil fields are located far inland, in terrain characterized by both mountains and jungles, the cost of all operations is high. Most of the oil has been found in the north, relatively close to Venezuela. Texaco has bee the major operator, producing roughly 40 per cent of the oil, followed by Chevron, Shell, BP, and the national company Ecopetrol, which have from 10 to 13 per cent of the market each. Roughly a dozen smaller independent companies are exploring for oil at any given time, but few have any significant production. Jersey is a small factor in production, but operates two of the country's major refineries. The state company, Empresa Columbiana de Petroleos (Ecopetrol) operates chiefly from declining and relinquished fields, and in partnership with other companies for secondary recovery and further exploration.[33]

In 1955 Colombia attempted to encourage a higher rate of exploration by increasing incentives, and the desired result was achieved. But a few years later the interpretation of these incentives became more restrictive, and exploration not surprisingly declined. After 1966 renewed interest developed in providing higher incentives, and some additional exploration followed. Further interest was created in expanding exploration in 1971 and 1972 when the prospect of declining production became more evident, and by 1972 Colombia was offering not only concessions under the old laws, but service contracts under newer laws. Applications were numerous, and a substantial number were approved. The resulting new exploration covered areas not previously drilled, including the eastern plains and several extensive offshore regions. It must be reported, however, that to date the results of this increased exploratory activity have been rather meager.[34]

Since most of the major fields in Colombia have been producing for from 20 to 50 years, production has inevitably declined. Total output has fallen about 10 per cent since 1970, and further declines are in prospect. As in many other countries, these declines have been accompanied by increasing internal consumption, and the Colombian industry's export surplus has gone down sharply, from 132,000 b/d in 1965 to only 64,000 b/d in 1972. As of 1972 production was 198,000 b/d, consumption 134,000 b/d, and refinery capacity 136,000 b/d. Unless major new fields are found and developed, Colombia anticipates the time when oil imports will be required. It is believed by many that major new fields will be found both onshore and offshore since the geology is favorable, particularly in the Gulf of Venezuela, which Colombia shares with its eastern neighbor. But new discoveries will have to proceed at a more rapid pace than in the past if export levels are even to be maintained.

Colombian government-industry relationships are reasonably good, and the situation has been characterized with the observation that both the country and the oil firms have waited long and patiently for greater things from Colombian oil.[35] Colombian taxes take 45 to 50 per cent of oil profits, but a law passed in 1961 permitted taxes to be raised above 50 per cent at the government's discretion, by increasing rents and royalties, reducing allowable depletion rates, reducing concession areas and required accelerated relinquishments of concession lands under certain circumstances. The provisions of the tax law are very complex, but in general it appears that the higher tax rates are imposed only on the more profitable production, and lower rates prevail for higher-cost output. Colombia has not achieved per barrel tax revenues equal to those of Venezuela, but there is the realization that its oil has not provided companies with the bonanzas resulting from producing conditions in some Venezuelan fields.[36]

Estimated crude oil reserves in 1972 were 2.5 billion barrels. This indicates the presence of a significant remaining resource base. Natural gas reserves of 2.4 trillion cubic feet were also notable by South American standards, and the country's ratio of gas reserves to production was about 20 to one.

Ecuador Oil exploration in Ecuador predates 1910, with production beginning in 1917. Until the early 1970s, the only output came from small and rapidly declining coastal fields. Since the 1920s, however, there had been persistent interest in the interior to Ecuador, in the Amazon basin jungles and along the Colombian border. Shell and Esso conducted exploration operations in this area for years, but finally gave up because of the inhospitable terrain and the resulting high cost of operations. In 1964 Texaco and Gulf were awarded concessions in the same general area, and in 1967 they registered a major discovery with their first well. Further large discoveries followed rapidly, and the companies built pipelines to transport the oil to export markets. Additional concessions were soon granted, and new companies such as Cayman and Texas Petroleum found new oil in the same jungle areas. With the completion of the pipeline, Ecuadorian production soared, from 4000 b/d in 1971 to over 250,000 b/d in 1973. Output of from 400,000 to 500,000 b/d is predicted for 1975, depending upon the rate at which new pipelines can be completed.[37] Oil reserves in 1972 were estimated at 6 billion barrels, and are expected to grow. It is clear that in the near future Ecuador will narrow the gap between Venezuela and the rest of the South American oil-exporting countries.

These discoveries rapidly changed the government's philosophy on oil matters. Before the oil boom, Ecuador was the only country in South America without a national petroleum company. The Anglo-Ecuadorian oil company produced about 90 per cent of the oil, but was required to sell oil locally at prices below the world market level. In July 1965 a decree was promulgated which favored new oil investment by revising taxes and improving operating conditions.[38] After the major discoveries of 1967 were registered, however, things changed considerably. In 1971, after much discussion, a new hydrocarbons law was passed which increased royalties and reduced the size of concession blocks. A national oil company, Corporacion Estatal Petrolera Ecuatoriana (CEPE) was established and authorized to operate in all phases of the industry. The minister of natural resources was quoted as stating that 'existing legal commitments would be respected but some modifications obviously were necessary to make them conform with the new regulations.'[39] In 1972, CEPE began operations by taking over three small coastal properties from companies whose contracts had expired, with total output of only 581 b/d. Future plans were more ambitious, featuring the proposed take-over of a participation share in the Texaco-Gulf fields. Also planned is the construction of a large state-owned refinery, and the possible take-over of the three existing refineries now owned by Gulf and Anglo-Ecuadorian Oil. Late in 1972, there was a move to cancel promising offshore concessions and transfer them to CEPE. Taxes were revised to increase Ecuador's share in oil income to 80 per cent, and in 1973 Ecuador joined OPEC.[40]

From all indications, much additional oil and gas remains to be found in both the onshore and offshore areas of Ecuador, and immediate prospects here are brighter than in any other Latin American region. The chief negative factor is the possibility that the Ecuadorian regime may overreach itself by adopting policies which make it possible for only the lowest-cost oil to be produced, thus discouraging exploration for any but the richest deposits.

The Guianas No oil production has ever occurred in the Guianas, and exploration efforts have been moderate. The onshore areas are not regarded as good prospects, although there has been more activity offshore in recent years. There are no refineries, and local consumption in 1972 was 23,000 b/d.

Paraguay Oil exploration in Paraguay began in 1946, and many wells have been drilled without success. Efforts have nevertheless continued over the years, since the geology of northwestern Paraguay is regarded as favorable for the occurrence of large fields, and the attitude of the government has been favorable to foreign private investment. The main obstacle is the forbidding nature of the jungle terrain. The lack of roads and water, and the presence of hostile Moro Indians, make exploration very costly. (In recent years, one of the most active sites for exploration is a thorn-bush area known locally as the 'Green Hell.')[41] In 1972 Paraguay consumed only 6000 b/d of oil products, and there was one refinery with a capacity of 10,000 b/d.

Peru Peru has the oldest petroleum industry on the South American continent. Until the late 1960s, however, its long-established industry was rather stagnant. Despite intensive exploration, no major new fields had been found for more than 20 years, and production rates began to decline after 1970. As internal consumption increased, subsidized by low prices, the traditional export surplus disappeared and increasing imports were needed after 1960. In 1952 a new and liberal oil law was passed, but the response was only moderate. The 1952 law placed a 50 per cent tax rate on oil income from the established lower-cost coastal fields, with a lower rate for the higher-cost fields in the inland jungles. A depletion allowance of 15 per cent applied to coastal areas, and 25 per cent to inland fields.[42]

Of the exploration efforts following the 1952 law, successes were limited mainly to the discovery of fields of moderate size offshore and in the interior. In the late

1960s, however, the major discoveries in the interior of Ecuador stimulated much interest in adjoining areas in Peru, where the geology was similar. Leasing was impeded by the expropriation of a Jersey subsidiary which was the country's largest producer. Its properties, together with several others, were taken over by the state oil company, Petroleos del Peru, or Petroperu. By 1971, however, the desire to explore in the Peuvian Amazon jungles exceeded the fears of expropriation, and a genuine exploration boom was launched. The signing of a 'model contract' with Occidental Oil in 1971 induced many other firms to seek similar agreements. This contract called for the concessionaire to pay all costs and share production with Petroperu equally, but to pay no taxes. If production reached 100,000 b/d, a pipeline would be laid which would revert to Peru in 15 years. These terms were considered favorable, and soon such US companies as Tenneco, Union Oil, Phillips, Shell, Sun, and Anco, as well as a number of British, French, German, Japanese, and Spanish companies, were at work. The discovery of oil by Petroperu in this area in November 1971 was especially impressive, since this was the highest flow rate well in Peru's history. Optimism among explorers soared, with estimates being made that by 1985 Peru might be producing as much as a million barrels a day.[43] Petroperu announced plans to build a 250,000 b/d pipeline across the Andes to the Pacific coast in order to market the new oil production. As of late 1973, however, there were no firm data available on the volumes of oil actually discovered during the current exploration boom.

In 1972 Peruvian oil production was only 68,000 b/d and consumption was 107,000 b/d, with five refineries in operation possessing a total capacity of 99,000 b/d. Total oil reserves then proved were estimated at only 750 million barrels, but gas reserves of 3 trillion cubic feet were regarded as confirmed. Future developments in Peru may result in reserves greater than those of Ecuador, basing an estimate on comparative volumes of promising formations, but there is as yet no conclusive evidence to confirm this optimistic prediction.

Uruguay Oil operations in Uruguay have always been monopolized by a state company, Administration Nacional de Combustiles, Alcohol y Portland, or ANCAP. ANCAP has made several surveys, the first in 1922, and has done some exploration and drilling, but without success.[44] In the early 1970s the government wished to offer offshore tracts for bids by foreign companies, but inability to work out the details of such service contracts prevented the undertaking of this exploration as originally planned. As of 1972, consumption was 44,000 b/d, and there was one refinery with a capacity of 40,000 b/d.

Venezuela The first oil concession in Venezuela was granted in 1878, although significant commercial production did not occur until 1913. The major fields in

TABLE 4

The Venezuelan oil industry, 1920–73: production, consumption, reserves, drilling, and refinery statistics

Year	Production (Mbd)	Proved reserves (billion bbl)	Wells drilled			Drilling results			Refinery throughput (Mbd)	Refinery capacity (Mbd)	Domestic demand
			Exploratory	Development	Total	Oil	Gas	Dry			
1920	1										
1925	55										
1930	371										
1935	407										
1940	502										
1945	886									133	
1950	1498	8.7	188	415	603	536	4	63		258	
1951	1705	9.1	358	815	1173	1054	11	108		258	
1952	1804	9.2	413	914	1327	1181	14	132		360	
1953	1765	10.2	437	514	951	780	13	158		444	
1954	1895	10.9	441	396	837	682	11	144	441	521	
1955	2157	12.4	473	661	1134	984	13	137	544	521	
1956	2457	14.0	590	859	1449	1267	11	171	624	669	
1957	2779	15.6	533	1188	1721	1574	9	138	688	673	
1958	2605	16.8	598	586	1184	972	13	199	732	883	
1959	2771	17.0	341	351	692	547	8	137	824	946	
1960	2846	17.4	276	168	444	342	1	101	882	1004	
1961	2920	16.9	279	198	477	372	2	103	928	1037	
1962	3200	16.8	197	339	536	455		81	1025	1073	55,296
1963	3248	17.0	169	329	498	425		73	1042	1127	57,160
1964	3395	17.2	179	442	621	560		61	1092	1182	60,646
1965	3505	17.2	181	513	694	592		102	1175	1200	64,170
1966	3400	16.9	90	304	394	349		45	1174	1212	65,574
1967	3575	15.9	75	243	318	276		42	1166	1338	66,857
1968	3640	15.7	100	338	438	400		38	1186	1349	70,888
1969	3639	14.9	102	387	489	446		43	1156	1324	70,303
1970	3708	15.1	183	440	623	540	1	83	1188	1343	73,930
1971	3549	14.8	166	438	604	502	1	101	1149	1341	76,927
1972*	3219	13.9	169	357	526	412	1	113	1136	1330	79,429

SOURCE: *Petroleo y otros datos estadísticos*, 1971 Venezuelan Ministry of Mines and Hydrocarbons, Caracas, Venezuela, 1972. 1972 data from *World Petroleum Report*, 1973, pp. 103–4

* Preliminary

173

Lake Maracaibo were found in the early and middle 1920s, and large fields in the interior were found in the late 1930s. The rate of development of Venezuelan petroleum has been determined primarily by two factors: the nature of world demand, and the evolution of the nation's oil policy.

It is evident from Table 4 that production grew spectacularly in the 1920s, increasing from 1000 b/d in 1920 to 55,000 in 1925 and 371,000 in 1930. In the early 1930s it had become the second largest oil producer in the world, and the largest exporter. Under the dictator Gomez, who ruled until 1935, oil concessions were available on easy terms. In the 1920s and 1930s, oil revenues received by the government were about 13 per cent of the value of the oil.[45] During the Second World War, output declined as the threat of German submarines reduced tanker shipments. This reduction in output cut Venezuelan tax revenues, and in 1943 the government first began to impose an income tax on oil earnings. At the time, the income tax was small and, in conjunction with a higher royalty payment, was designed to achieve a roughly equal division of oil-industry net profits between the companies and the country, on an industry-wide basis. In 1948 the tax law was amended to make the total tax burden for each company equal to the company's net profits after taxes, through the addition of a special tax surcharge. Thus the principle of 50-50 profit sharing was firmly established in Venezuela by 1948.

After 1944 production again began to grow rapidly, and the ratio of reserves to production started to decline. New concessions were offered in 1956 and 1957, and the three companies which had traditionally controlled Venezuelan production – Jersey with about 45 per cent, Shell with about 30 per cent, and Gulf with about 15 per cent – were joined by a dozen or more major independents and smaller integrated companies. Significant new reserves were found in these concession areas, and both production and reserves increased during the next eight to ten years. In 1958 a new government took over, and the tax rates were increased so that the government's share in profits rose from 52 per cent in 1957 to 65 per cent in 1958 and 69 per cent in 1959. This tax increase put Venezuelan oil at a cost disadvantage relative to most oil produced for export elsewhere in the world, and companies in Venezuela tended to cut back on expansion plans and even to disinvest. Other motives, however, were present which added to the desire to slacken the pace of Venezuelan output. Rapid development of oil in the Middle East had created a supply surplus, and the US government in 1959 imposed import controls, thus restricting demand in Venezuela's major market.

In 1960 Venezuela established a national oil company, Corporacion Venezolano del Petroleo (CVP) to undertake various operations. CVP has not, however, been as active as most other state oil companies, and much of its activity has centered around domestic marketing, which in Venezuela, as in many other Latin American countries, is not very profitable since internal consumption is subsidized through prices controlled at levels below the world market.

Until 1966 tax liabilities were based on oil prices actually received by the companies, and not on posted prices, as in the Middle East. After 1958, however, it became increasingly necessary for Venezuelan oil sellers to 'discount' their oil, since competition had sharpened with an increase in the number of smaller sellers, the decline in demand resulting from US import controls, and the reduction in oil tanker rates which offset Venezuela's proximity advantage to Western Europe in comparison with the Persian Gulf shipping distances. In 1966 tax laws were revised so that not only was the tax rate increased (from 47 to 52 per cent), but profits were based on arbitrary 'tax reference prices' which were set independently of actual prices, and past tax liabilities were increased by $560 million for the period 1958-65 on the assumption that prices in the past should have been higher. The government's share in profits increased to about 72 per cent as a result of this tax change.

As early as 1945 Venezuela had decided against issuing any new concessions. In 1943 a compromise was reached whereby tax rates were raised in exchange for a 40-year extension of concessions, through 1983. The only concessions issued after 1943 were those permitted by the Jimenez regime in 1956-7. This failure to allow access to new areas was a major factor in the decline of reserves, and since 1965 there has been a continuing attempt to formulate service contract arrangements under which the companies would provide specified services for CVP. In 1968 bids were submitted to explore tracts in south Lake Maracaibo on such terms, but not until 1971 were the awards made – to Mobil, Shell, and Occidental. Eighty per cent of these areas were to be relinquished at the close of the exploration period. The government estimated that the area might contain 3.25 billion barrels of oil, but drilling results to date have not found oil.

In March 1971 Venezuela increased tax reference prices by about 60 cents per barrel, and nationalized the natural-gas industry. A further tax reference price increase of 26 cents per barrel occurred in December. In July 1971 a new law required increased supervision of the companies, and limited the control of the companies over their own properties before expiration of the concessions, claiming in addition all assets related to the concessions, although not physically located upon them, such as refineries and office buildings.[46] As Persian Gulf oil prices increased during 1970-3, Venezuelan prices increased in a parallel manner, with tax reference prices taking an amazing 56 per cent leap in October 1973 to an average level of $7.24 per barrel.

Venezuela was one of the charter members of OPEC in 1960. OPEC, as an international cartel of oil-exporting countries, aimed at achieving monopoly prices for oil, even at the possible expense of some decline in the rate of production increase.

Venezuela, more than any other exporting country, was prepared in 1960 to trade off lower output growth for higher prices, since its ratio of reserves to production was much lower than that of the other members, and it had for some time been concerned over possible resource base depletion. Until the cartel managed to achieve monopoly power after 1970, it is hard to see precisely how Venezuela's own interests were advanced by its membership in OPEC, except of course to the extent that anything that increased the cost of Middle East oil made Venezuelan oil more nearly competitive.

The net impact of all these policy actions by Venezuela has been to reduce its role in the world oil industry. Having smaller reserves of higher-cost (and often lower-quality) oil than are elsewhere available in exporting areas, its attempts to increase its per barrel revenues led to a shrinkage in reserves and to declines in output when production was increasing rapidly in every other exporting country during 1971-2 and earlier periods. A reduction in the rate of increase was not entirely unwelcome, since as early as 1959 the desire had been expressed that Venezuela should sell fewer additional barrels of oil, but should sell all of its oil at higher prices. But the actual decline in output, for example between 1965 and 1972, was certainly not desired. Reference to Table 4 shows that oil production increased rapidly during the mid-1950s, with output hitting a temporary peak in 1957. Venezuelan oil was then in high demand in Europe as a replacement for the Middle East oil temporarily unavailable during the 1956-7 Suez crisis. But while production almost doubled between 1950 and 1957, there was only a 22 per cent increase during the next seven years, and output in 1972 was actually about 10 per cent lower than in 1965.

Changes in proven reserves were even more disquieting. Reserves increased apace with production until about the end of 1960, but then fell and in 1972 stood at their lowest level since 1955. Drilling also declined, and its character changed. With no new concessions to explore, wells drilled dropped from a maximum of 1721 in 1957 (when concessions were last awarded) to a low of 318 in 1967, and then increased to 623 in 1970, falling to 526 in 1972. Even more significant, however, is the sharp decline in exploratory wells drilled: from 598 in 1958 to 75 in 1967, with a recovery to 169 in 1972. This series is perhaps somewhat misleading since it includes outpost wells (long lateral extensions to pools in known fields) together with true exploratory wildcat wells (aimed at the discovery of entirely new fields in undrilled areas). The number of new-field wildcat wells drilled fell all the way to zero in 1970; one was drilled in 1971, and while 14 were drilled in 1972, only two found oil. A further indication of declining prospects is the incidence of dry holes, up from 8 per cent in 1957 to 22 per cent in 1972.

Table 4 also shows that, while refinery capacity increased through 1970, it has declined slightly since that time, and that refinery throughput in 1972 was lower than in any year since 1964.

As long as the OPEC cartel remains successful in its endeavors to obtain monopoly prices for oil in a sellers' market, Venezuela has a good chance to achieve its goal of limited production increases with higher tax revenues per barrel produced, even though this will mean further declines in its position in world oil trade. In the longer run, as buyers tend to switch to other fuels, including synthetics, and as cartel solidarity inevitably deteriorates, the future of Venezuelan oil may be more problematic. The true resource base is no doubt substantially greater than the 13.9 billion barrels of currently estimated proved reserves, but much of the additional oil to be found and developed will probably be higher-cost oil with a high sulfur content. The enormous reserves of tar sands in the tar belt, which are estimated to contain 700 billion barrels of oil content, may eventually yield 35 to 70 billion barrels of recoverable oil, but recovery costs will be high.[47]

NOTES

1 Barrows, G.H., *International Petroleum Industry*, New York, 1967, Vol. II, p. 16
2 Hartshorne, J.E., *Politics and World Oil Economics*, New York, 1967, p. 252
3 *International Petroleum Encyclopedia*, Tulsa, 1969, p. 178
4 Barrows, p. 34
5 *World Petroleum Report, 1973*, p. 97
6 Barrows, p. 11
7 *World Petroleum Report, 1973*, p. 96
8 Ibid., p. 97
9 Barrows, p. 97
10 *World Petroleum Report, 1973*, p. 96
11 Barrows, p. 7
12 Ibid., p. 8; also, *World Petroleum Report, 1973*, p. 96
13 *World Petroleum Report, 1972*, p. 94; also Barrows, p. 8
14 *World Petroleum Report, 1973*, p. 97
15 Mikdashi, Z.M., *The Community of Oil Exporting Countries: A Study in Governmental Cooperation*, Ithaca NY, 1972, p. 119
16 *World Petroleum Report, 1973*, p. 97
17 Barrows, p. 29
18 Ibid., p. 36
19 Hartshorne, pp. 251-2

Henry Steele

20 Barrows, p. 37
21 *International Petroleum Encyclopedia*, 1970, p. 182
22 *World Petroleum Report, 1972*, p. 96
23 *World Petroleum Report, 1973*, p. 18
24 Barrows, pp. 43, 45
25 Hartshorne, p. 250
26 *World Petroleum Report, 1972*, p. 98
27 *World Petroleum Report, 1973*, p. 100
28 Barrows, p. 46
29 Hartshorne, p. 249
30 Barrows, p. 51
31 Ibid., p. 52
32 *World Petroleum Report, 1973*, p. 101
33 Hartshorne, p. 307
34 *International Petroleum Encyclopedia, 1973*, p. 158
35 Hartshorne, p. 307
36 Barrows, pp. 56-7
37 Oriente is Ecuador's New Frontier, *Oil and Gas Journal*, 24 September 1973, pp. 188-9
38 Barrows, p. 60
39 *World Petroleum Report, 1972*, p. 101
40 *World Petroleum Report, 1973*, pp. 102-3
41 Tanzer, M., *The Political Economy of International Oil and the Underdeveloped Countries*, Boston, 1969, p. 69
42 Barrows, p. 67
43 *World Petroleum Report, 1973*, p. 104
44 Barrows, pp. 71-2
45 Hartshorne, p. 301
46 *World Petroleum Report, 1972*, p. 102
47 Hartshorne, p. 305

M. V. POSNER

Before October, economists at the OECD were confident of an 8 per cent growth rate in European real output in 1974. Now, the fear is recession, stock markets have panicked. A doubling of oil prices could translate into a 5 per cent increase in producers' prices, increasing the already high rate of inflation. Britain is suffering catastrophic trade deficits; France and Italy are likely to see trade deficits. Six European countries have banned Sunday driving; most have ordered gasoline stations closed on weekends. Speed limits have been reduced, air services cut, and lights dimmed. British coalminers have added a crisis of their own, throwing Britain into a three-day work week.

The American, Canadian dollars, and gold are rising relative to European currencies, signaling that any prolonged embargo will have a much more significant impact on Europe than on North America. Against these short term events, Posner discusses the energy balance in Europe to 1980.

Past European policies stressed the need to switch from high-cost indigenous coal to low-priced oil imports – only now to find oil high priced and increased coal unavailable. Recent discoveries of oil and natural gas in the North Sea will alleviate the problems of importing energy for Britain (who will become a net exporter in 1980), but the rest of Europe will likely remain dependent on imports for over 60 per cent of its energy supply.

Western Europe represents nearly 30 per cent of the world's energy demand. Unless nature has been more generous than we presently know, European energy policy will be dependent on outside events – outside supplies and external prices.

Yet, since Europe represents a large proportion of Arab oil sales, it is ob-

vious that co-ordinated policies, perhaps even co-ordinated with the US
and Japan, could have a profound effect
on the price of oil. Public statements
emanating from Western European capi-
tals in December give the impression
not of co-ordination but of rampant
self-interest. The price of oil would appear to include foreign policy statements. Individual European countries
are scrambling for oil – witness France's
major contract with Saudi Arabia announced in early January. As long as
each consuming country acts in its own
self-interest, while producers are co-
ordinated, the price of oil will 'proceed
by leaps and bounds.'

This paper should be read in conjunction with Adelman on world oil, Crandall and Mabro on the Middle East, and
Homet on oil diplomacy.

M. V. POSNER

Western Europe's energy policies

This article is concerned with OECD Europe – that is, geographical Europe excluding the Warsaw Pact countries. Unless otherwise stated, all facts and estimates are
drawn from the sources cited in the footnote.[1]

Table 1 shows primary energy requirements and their sources from 1960-80:
the estimates for 1980 are to be read as an 'unconstrained forecast.' We deal with
possible constraints and policy changes reflecting these constraints later in the
article.

Since the early 1950s Europe's energy policy has been to shift (with degrees of
speed varying among countries) from indigenous coal to imported oil. The only
brake on this process has been the concern of many countries, for 'social' or
'balance of payments' reasons, to continue protection for coal. Conventional
wisdom throughout the recent past has stressed the availability of cheap imported oil, and the economic case for switching from indigenous fuel output to
the production of exports required to pay for cheap fuel imports. Despite the
important reservations of Robinson himself,[2] the lesson of the so-called Robinson Report of the OEEC in 1956[3] was that domestic coal mines should be closed
at a speed governed chiefly by the development of alternative employment for
the displaced miners. This policy was followed, with varying degrees of success
in different European countries – perhaps most notably in the United Kingdom,
where employment in the coal mines was cut from 690,000 in 1950 to 285,000
in 1970, with virtually no major industrial dispute during the whole period. Success was less striking in other European countries, but nevertheless the clearest
exposition of the common policy of all Western Europe is perhaps stated in the
British Government's White Paper on Fuel Policy of 1967.[4]

M.V. Posner

The development of indigenous natural gas during the 1960s (mainly in Holland and the North Sea) and the important North Sea oil fields developed at the end of the 1960s and the beginning of the 1970s have strikingly changed this pattern of development, but only, as it were, by the facts of geology: it is not policy that has changed, but rather the unexpected discovery of the benevolence of nature.

Like all other regions of the world, Europe (or the European governmental establishment at any rate) did not begin to question the basic assumption that the world energy position was secure until about 1970. In the three short years since then shock has followed shock, and no country has as yet firmly stated a new energy policy based on the new facts as now perceived. But we can develop some of the arguments and hypothetical facts which must now be in the minds of the authorities, and thus examine the policy options for the next few years.

THE MODE OF ANALYSIS

Let us start with a simple method of setting up the problem – used by this author in his 1973 book.[5] Europe's energy demand represents between one-quarter and one-third of the world's total energy demand. As a relatively small part of the world market it is reasonable for Europe to assume that the world price of energy is very little affected by its own policies (we relax this assumption below). If the world price of energy can be predicted with any confidence, then the policy to be adopted by Europe (or by the several European countries individually) is simple: expand the output of all indigenous fuels until the marginal ton costs the same as the world traded price. Provided that the views of individual energy producers (whether privately or publicly owned) are roughly the same as those of the governmental authorities, moreover, this 'planning optimum' will be identical with what would be achieved by the normal working of the market mechanism. Economic forecasters, wishing to predict the behavior of indigenous supplies or of imports, need only to estimate the responsiveness of indigenous supply to changes in demand – once these 'supply elasticities' are known, home production of all individual fuels and total imports are both determined.

However it must be acknowledged that large expected changes in world energy prices may have some significant effect on indigenous consumption: but it is hard to see how, even in the face of, say, fourfold increases over 1972 price levels, the consumption figures in table 1 could be reduced by more than 10 or 15 per cent.

More important is the problem of time scale: while it might be possible to halt the decline of coal output foreseen in table 1, it is highly unlikely that the supplies of natural gas, indigenous petroleum, or nuclear-based electricity could be increased between now and 1980 materially above their estimated levels. The

182

TABLE 1

Europe's energy balance 1960-80 (million tons oil equivalent)

	1960	%	1970	%	1980[1]	%
INDIGENOUS PRODUCTION						
Coal	354	58	273	26	194	11
Oil	16	3	23	2	179	10
Natural gas	11	2	68	7	203	11
Hydro	26	4	35	3	48	3
Nuclear	1		10	1	125	7
Total	408	67	409	39	749	42
NET IMPORTS						
Oil	183	30	597	58	934	53
Coal	21	3	33	3	46	3
Natural gas			2		28	2
Total	204	33	632	61	1008	58
GRAND TOTAL	612	100	1041	100	1757	100

1 1980 is an unofficial estimate.

SOURCE: OECD 1973

major policy options therefore refer necessarily to decisions to be made now that might have some effect in the 1980s.

But of course neither the authorities nor private decision makers can make confident estimates of world energy prices. Moreover even estimates of the elasticity of supply of home energy resources are themselves uncertain. The technological basis for nuclear energy is not properly established; future coal productivity depends on geology, and the availability of suitable manpower; and the potential output of unproved oil or gas reserves is notoriously difficult to estimate. Hence the quantitative estimates in energy plans based on extrapolations of table 1 are inherently uncertain and insecure, and energy policy is moving away from emphasis on such projections; rather it is attempting, against a background of alternative assumptions about the world energy supply picture, to adopt strategies for indigenous output that may in some sense be optimal – strategies, not output targets.

THE FUTURE OF COAL

In 1960 coal represented two-thirds of Europe's energy consumption; by 1970 it was only a quarter; and table 1 suggests that by 1980 it may be as low as 10 per cent. The absolute level of output has fallen by more than one-third over the last decade.

Details of this story vary from country to country, but the experience of the UK (which accounts still for one-third of Europe's total output) is fairly typical. Although productivity in coal mining rose in the postwar period in the United Kingdom by an annual compound rate of over 3 per cent (at about the same rate, that is, as GDP (Gross Domestic Product) per head), coal's competitive position steadily weakened relative to that of oil: this was due in part to a slow but steady decline in the real cost of imported oil to the UK economy, and in part to a slow but steady increase in the non-labor element in coal costs. The money wages of coal miners kept pace more or less with money wage movements generally in the UK, keeping the real labor cost per ton of coal fairly constant: but throughout the 1960s for the ordinary industrial user fuel oil was available (even after a heavy tax charge) at prices 20 or 30 per cent below the thermal equivalent quantity of coal.

It is, however, fairly well established that the cheaper half of coal output (the cheapest hundred million tons or so) was produced at a resource cost well below that of oil, and it was this fact which led continually to pressure on the authorities and on the National Coal Board to curtail output of the more expensive coal, closing many marginal collieries, and allowing normal labor 'quits' to reduce manpower by up to 30,000 men per year. The number of collieries was halved; many seams were permanently sealed off; and, although major reorganizations of efficient collieries in favorably geological conditions were widely attempted throughout the postwar period, by the end of the 1960s the output of coal was firmly on a declining trend which it will now be very difficult to arrest. At the time it seemed to many observers that this decline was a result of the trend of demand, and the availability of cheap oil; but it is now apparent that the depletion of existing seams and the working out of readily available reserves have produced a state of affairs where output will be supply-constrained for at least the next five or ten years. The time lag between investment and the coming into operation of new capacity is at least as long in coal mining as in other energy fields, and the gloomy demand prospects of the sixties have led to the gloomy output forecast for the seventies. Blame for this state of affairs rests on those commentators (including this author) who urged the Coal Board to contract at a time when it appeared that cheap oil was with us for a very long time into the future.

The question now, however, is what increase in coal output it would be reasonable to expect if oil prices, and energy prices generally, were in the 1980s three or four times above their 1970 levels. Even after the inevitable time lags have been overcome, what is the long-run elasticity of supply of coal in Europe? This is in part a question of geology, and in part a question of manpower.

Mining in Europe is still predominantly an underground trade - the vast strip-mining possibilities of the western United States do not exist at all. Despite developments in mining techniques (the so-called drift mining) getting coal in Europe still requires the creation of a safe underground environment in which men can work, and the exploitation of seams of coal very much shallower than those existing in other parts of the world. For these reasons cautious mining engineers believe that the elasticity of coal supply, even in the very long run, is less than unity – a threefold increase in energy prices might barely double the amount of coal which is 'economically' producible. Since a substantial margin of European coal output in the early 1970s was 'uneconomic' at the then-existing world energy price levels, it would seem overoptimistic to expect the long-run equilibrium level of coal output in Europe to be much more than double the 1980 estimate in table 1. But an increase of that order of magnitude by the year 1980 is almost certainly impossible, and very considerable efforts and determination would be required to achieve it by 1990.

The second possible constraint on even the long-run development of indigenous coal supplies is the shortage of labor. The correct analytical way of handling this problem is far from clear. At first sight it may appear that a shortage of manpower willing and able to work in the mines will lead to a rise in the average wages of coal miners relative to real wages elsewhere in the economy, and therefore a relative rise in the real cost of coal. This in turn suggests that, just as the world traded price of all energy (in particular imported oil) may be influenced over the next decade by the degree of monopoly enjoyed by the Arab producers, just so the wages of coal miners and hence the cost of coal in Western Europe may be influenced by the trade union power of the coal miners. This interpretation of recent events was vividly emphasized by the leaders of the miners in Great Britain in the winter of 1973/4, who stated that 'we must exercise our bargaining power just like the sheikhs.'

But a more optimistic interpretation of the possible outcome would stress, first, that the miners' bargaining power is not infinite, and that social pressures will limit the extremes of extortionism; and second, that social pressures (to which the miners' leaders have shown themselves extremely responsive in the past thirty or forty years) will also encourage a certain modesty of demands. Moreover, whereas the high price paid to *foreign* suppliers of energy is necessarily a resource cost for Europe as a whole, the high price paid to *domestic* producers is not so unambiguously a resource cost to the rest of the community – it represents more a 'transfer payment' which in any case is subject to various forms of fiscal levy.

My own judgment of this argument is that the availability of miners may indeed represent a physical constraint on coal getting in the next two decades, and that we would be wise to anticipate that coal-mining wages may have to increase

M.V. Posner

TABLE 2

Europe's oil and natural gas: an optimistic estimate for 1980-85
(million tons oil equivalent)

	1980	1985	1980 (from Table 1)
Indigenous oil	294	390	179
Indigenous gas	294	370	203
Total	588	760	382

SOURCE: P. Odell, *Indigenous Oil*

INTERPRETATION: If, for 1980, we substituted Odell's estimates into an otherwise unchanged table 1, Europe's reliance on imported energy would be one-fifth lower, but would still amount to more than 40 per cent of total consumption.

(relative to industrial average wages) by 1 or 2 per cent per year for the next two decades. These considerations alone are not sufficient to place a constraint on the possibilities for coal output additional to, or more effective than, the constraints already discussed above – the constraints of a technological or geological nature. But these technological constraints are themselves so intensive, and so long lived, that I do not feel it possible to expect coal output around 1980 to be very much greater than suggested in table 1. During the 1990s, however, an upward trend in coal output is possible and (against the world energy price assumption already sketched) likely and desirable. These increases will not be large enough to make a substantial dent in the level of requirements for other forms of energy in the decade of the 1980s, but they will significantly reduce the required rate of increase in the supply of these alternatives.

INDIGENOUS OIL AND GAS

The estimates in table 1 may be considered to define the lower limits of the supply of oil (largely from the North Sea) and gas (largely from the North Sea and Holland). Some estimates (in particular Odell's[6]) would increase these figures two or threefold. Table 2 presents an alternative, probably excessively optimistic, picture for 1980.

It is important that we do not pay inordinately close attention to the timing of any particular forecast output of gas or oil. What is essential is to bear in mind a profile through time of the potential production of gas and oil, remembering that the depletion rate of gas fields is highly variable through time, and that, while

186

technological necessity may determine tightly the rate of extraction of oil, it is possible to delay or bring forward in time the date at which the oil first flows: hence, for any particular level of proved reserves, gas and oil output can follow a whole set of different time paths.

Moreover the precise timing of discoveries cannot be predicted. It is probably true that table 1 gives a fair picture of output that would be achievable from known, proved reserves with the geological information of 1973. The pace of subsequent discoveries, however, cannot be predicted with confidence, even though there may be a fair consensus that such discoveries may eventually appear.

For instance, estimates of the possible oil output from the British sections of the North Sea vary from 2 million to 10 million barrels a day (from 100 million tons of oil a year to 500 million tons of oil a year) in the late 1980s. Of these possible outputs, less than one million barrels per day are sufficiently well 'proved' for contract negotiations for their sale to be realistically undertaken. This is a familiar picture in many other oil provinces, as Odell points out, and there seems to be some historic evidence to expect proved reserves to increase with time.

The pace at which oil and gas fields are developed will be, moreover, a question for political decision, moved by political and economic argument. For instance, the development of indigenous gas fields presents well-known problems of conservation and caution. The 'premium' market for natural gas (domestic users, industrial process users, and so on) has a natural growth rate which may not be more than 7 or 8 per cent per year. To use gas more quickly in time than would be justified by premium sales alone implies the use of gas for crude heat purposes. But that in turn implies a shortage of gas for the premium market towards the end of the 1980s, and a foreseen necessity to manufacture gas from crude oil at that time to satisfy the premium market. If future energy prices and availabilities are assumed to be sufficiently severe, then it becomes financially advantageous for a government or gas monopoly to choose a slow rate of depletion and keep the gas in the ground until a later date. For this reason the gas output figures assumed even in table 1 may turn out to be excessively high.

This problem of depletion rates, however, is more general than the particular example just discussed. There is no distinction between premium and non-premium uses for oil (although some extreme conservationists would regard oil as primarily a fuel for transport and as a petrochemical feedstock, holding that pure steam-raising functions are better performed by solid hydrocarbons or nuclear energy). Nevertheless, if producers accept a sufficiently rapid rate of increase in energy prices, it becomes advantageous to leave the hydrocarbons in the ground until the price rise has occurred, rather than sell now and invest or use the proceeds.

187

The critical analytical relationship lies in a comparison between the rate of increase expected in energy prices and the 'rate of return' available in the future from monies invested today from oil sold at today's prices. If this rate of return is smaller than the expected rate of increase in oil prices, the rational producer (be he King Faisal, the British Government, or Standard of New Jersey) will not produce: and the result will be that demand will bid up the available supply of oil to prices that are high enough to dissuade oil hoarders from their conservative approach. The higher today's spot price of oil, the lower will be the expected rate of increase of that price in the future; and this is indeed the mechanism by which future expected shortages lead to conservation of resources today.

These calculations are peculiarly difficult when they are being made simultaneously by many different producers in different parts of the world, with differing political interests. But it is important to note that the future production of indigenous gas and oil in Western Europe depends as much on the expectations of the world energy situation held by European producers and governments as on the geological facts or the present price situation.

NUCLEAR ENERGY

The prospects for nuclear energy in Europe are a microcosm of the problem for the whole of the world. Most of the different types of reactor design have been tried in Europe as elsewhere; both methods of enriching uranium have been attempted; the uncertainties of research and development have been found throughout. Both Britain and France have a highly integrated electricity supply system, and can therefore calculate readily the advantages of putting in nuclear stations to take the base load in future expansions of electricity demand. It is not anticipated that nuclear stations will need to climb into non-base-load positions in the 'merit order' of power stations until the late 1980s; although in France and Italy (where there is extensive use of hydroelectric resources) this date might come earlier in time. It follows that, in the immediate choice of reactor design, the need for good 'load-following characteristics' of nuclear reactors is not overwhelming. However, since in most countries there is now a wish to develop a nuclear investment program that will lead to repeat ordering for a whole run of years, most countries are now urgently seeking a safe and secure design which they will be able to back for a decade or more, and which will take them safely into the 1990s. It follows that some load-following characteristics will be demanded of the nuclear reactors soon to be ordered.

The early nuclear program in the United Kingdom was the so-called Magnox reactor, out of which the AGR (advanced gas-cooled reactor) was developed in the 1960s. But the AGR program ran into considerable difficulties, and none of

the AGR stations so far are fully working. Thus, in late 1973, the British authorities are still hotly engaged in discussion about whether they should
1 order more AGRs, although none are yet working;
2 order the American type of water reactors;
3 order again the out-of-date and very expensive Magnox reactor of the 1950s;
4 possibly switch to the Canadian Candu-type reactor; or
5 step into the unknown with the new reactor systems now under development in Europe – the SGHWR or the HTR.

The details of this choice are as usual plunged into political and technological uncertainty. Seen through European eyes, the choice is starkly between adopting an American design or trying to develop a uniquely European design of reactor. Before the energy crisis of 1973 this choice was coolly discussed in the familiar terms of choosing between indigenous technological development and pure imitation. The advantages of encouraging indigenous design were based on the usual arguments for protection of 'science-based industries' against North American 'imperialism,' while those who favored using the American system could point to the considerable economies in scarce research resources at home.

Even before 1973, however, the question of reactor choice was heavily swayed by the assumed advantage of proceeding with all possible speed to the fast-breeder reactor. The fast-breeder was thought to be both cheaper and less greedy of uranium than the simple fission reactors at present available. The assumed advantages of developing indigenous research facilities in Europe were reinforced by the hope that, out of this investment, would come a viable design for the fast-breeder.

But the crisis of 1973 has concentrated the minds of public authorities throughout Europe wonderfully, as Dr Johnson remarked about the state of mind of a man about to be hanged. If European governments could really be convinced that the American designs are safe and reliable, no nationalistic inhibitions would prevent them from now backing this horse with all their cash. The dilemma, however, for Europeans as for all other energy users in the winter of 1973/4 is that there is no proved design ready to buy off the shelf.

Even if this overwhelming technological constraint were not operative, hard facts of economics and industrial organization would limit the growth of nuclear energy in Europe to the path suggested in table 1 – or something very similar to that. Essentially table 1 assumes (as do most of the national plans) that almost all new generating capacity laid down in the next 15 years will be nuclear (with the exception of some hydroelectric plants). But, even so, the proportion which nuclear power will represent in the total electricity-generating capacity by the mid-1980s could not possibly be more than one-quarter – and possibly considerably less. To go further than this and actually replace or retire existing plant would call for a vast investment in power stations (probably beyond the industrial capability of the construction or heavy-engineering industries) and a vast cost in capital resources. My guess would be that the price of imported oil would have to rise tenfold before this use of nuclear energy to replace existing modern fossil-fueled generating plant became economically viable.

RELIANCE ON IMPORTED ENERGY

It is therefore inevitable that most countries of Europe (with the exception of the Norwegians and just possibly the British) will rely substantially on imported oil until the turn of the century. The attractiveness of achieving autarchy can in any case be exaggerated. These attractions are fourfold:

1 To achieve security of supply in face of political troubles such as the Arab-Israeli war of 1973. Self-sufficiency could only produce such protection if the country concerned was not only self-sufficient in energy but engaged in no balanced two-way trade (this condition would, for instance, exclude the possibility of the UK trading some of its sulfur-free North Sea oil for heavier oils during calm times).

2 To avoid the consequences of some quasi-permanent long-run physical shortage of energy. But if there were such a shortage, throwing the whole western world into depression, it would be of little comfort to a single Western European country to find itself with ample energy but no export market for its industrial products!

3 To avoid paying high prices for imported energy would be attractive, but only if the indigenous supplies were really available at lower resource cost. There would be no advantage, for instance, in developing an enormous and enormously expensive UK coal industry merely to avoid paying enormous sums to the OPEC countries.

4 Of course, if indigenous supplies were really cheaply available, then the advantages of finding a lot of these supplies would be great. But this would be an advantage of enjoying the generosity of nature, not an assumed special economic or political advantage of autarchy.

Hence, although most western governments would love to find a lot of energy, only those who fear a continual recurrence of troublesome political disputes with the oil-exporting countries during the 1980s will now choose deliberately to adopt policies designed to insulate themselves from world markets. And even those countries who do so choose will be able to do so only if nature turns out to be generous.

Only those, therefore, like Odell, who claim that vast untapped reserves of hydrocarbons remain to be discovered in Western Europe expect the dependence of Western Europe on imported energy to be materially smaller than is suggested in table 1.

The minds of decision makers in Western Europe, like those all over the world, will be turning in days to come to alternative sources of energy and alternative methods for economizing in the use of energy. But, as is well-known, the possibilities of such economies (certainly within the so-called comfort margin) are far greater in North America than in Western Europe, merely because energy consumption per head is so much greater in the American continent. My own guess therefore is that energy consumption may be 10 or 15 per cent lower in Western Europe by the middle of the next decade than is suggested in table 1, and therefore the dependence on imported oil may be 40 per cent rather than the 60 per cent suggested by table 1 itself. That change – short of a crisis of far larger dimensions than seems likely in the winter of 1973/4 – is the limit of possible change in the European energy picture over the next two decades from the 'unconstrained' estimate in table 1.

NOTES

1 *Oil: The Present Situation and Future Prospects* (Paris, 1973). P. Odell, *Indigenous Oil and Gas Developments and Western Europe's Energy Policy Options,* Energy Policy, London, vol. 1, no. 1; other useful references are found in the footnotes to Odell's article. European Economic Communities, *The Energy Conjuncture in the Community,* EEC (73) 1289; there are many other EEC Energy Policy Publications, but this is the most up to date. M.V. Posner, *Fuel Policy: A Study in Applied Economics* (London, 1973)
2 In notes in the *Economic Journal* for 1950, and again in 1959, Robinson relied largely on the terms of trade argument for protection. These are, as far as I know, the only serious economist's arguments in favor of protection advanced prior to the present crisis, and it is in retrospect amusing that they were first formulated to justify British protection of agriculture! Most British economists now feel that EEC agricultural protection has gone much too far!
3 *Energy Policy for Europe* (Paris, 1956)
4 *Fuel Policy,* Cmnd. 3438 of 1967
5 *Fuel Policy*
6 Odell, p. 49

EMILIO G. COLLADO

The energy crisis has resulted in many people looking for a scapegoat. It would be comforting for polemicists if such existed; to point the finger of blame is a satisfying substitute for the real effort of fashioning a workable solution to our problems. A typical response to our current situation is to blame the oil industry: 'The oil companies have manipulated us into a crisis.' And in viewing the companies, all hats are not perceived to be uniformly evil. The larger the company, the more evil. The evilest of all are assumed to be the international oil companies – the multinationals. If they are not exactly above the law, at least they are in a position to disregard it.

Such views are both wrong and dangerous. The 'energy crisis' is neither stage one of the apocalypse nor the beginning of a whimpering wind-down of western civilization. It is policy-induced, not evidence of our first severe encoun-ter with a ceiling imposed by the 'limits to growth.' It is true that the oil industry – and particularly the largest multi-nationals – has a significant input into policy formation in many countries. But the policy determination process involves too many actors with diverse interests and has too many external constraints to allow one to credit any single firm or group of firms as the prime mover. The most general and accurate thing that can be said is that the policy advice of the multinationals is sometimes taken – and sometimes ignored. Moreover, sometimes hind-sight indicates that it would have been better to have taken the advice that was ignored, or to have ignored the ad-vice that was taken. But that is com-mon to all advice.

It is also true that the profits of these multinationals has increased markedly in the last year. How can the crisis help these companies? First, not all of the price increases in crude have been tax revenues to host countries. Second, the previous year was a poor one for oil companies. Third, demand is relatively inelastic and therefore cost increases or tax changes are paid by the consumer. Moreover, in this time of chaos and fears over oil shortages, governments and customers suggested they would pay 'anything' for oil. Amid this hysteria, the industry built up profit margins. If prices continue to escalate and price freezes are lifted in consuming countries, profits will increase even further. But we do need the price system to ration demand. As long as we are convinced that these firms are paying the socially correct amount of taxes, profit increases should not worry us. It is these price and profit signals which move resources. But we do not have a socially optimal tax scheme. Though Dr Collado discusses the problem of double taxation, he does not discuss tax avoidance, unearned depletion, and current expensing.

Because the energy crisis is policy-induced, appropriate *policy* responses are called for – not picking on scapegoats. A mistaken view of the facts will lead to policy which will only compound the difficulties. This is particularly true with respect to current international aspects of the problem because the multinational corporations are often the conduit through which pass the global repercussions of unilateral decisions in producing or consuming countries. If we are correct to predict the implica-

tions of alternative policy options, we must better understand the transmission characteristics of this conduit.

Collado describes the international environment in which multinational corporations operate. His basic position is that, speaking from Exxon's experience, multinational corporations are involved in long-term international investment activities which are enhanced by a stable world political and economic scene and good relations between the host and parent companies. Since multinational corporations have committed themselves to international resource mobility, it is not surprising that Collado advocates policies which facilitate corporate planning in that regard. One area in which such policies are important is international financial arrangements. In this connection, the comparison between Dr Collado as a corporate spokesman and Professor Grennes and Dr Winokur is of particular interest. Dr Collado's inside perspective on the multinational corporation should be compared to the outside perspective in the chapters by Professors Adelman and Nye and the view in the chapter by Mr Homet. Dr Collado's paper was given before the Group of Eminent Persons to Study the Impact of Multinational Corporations on Development and on International Relations, United Nations, New York, 11 Sept. 1973.

EMILIO G. COLLADO

Multinational corporations and national economic policy

MOTIVATIONS AND BEHAVIOR
OF MULTINATIONAL CORPORATIONS

National economic policy is often influenced by international events. A major
concern is, quite appropriately, the motivations and behavior of multinational
corporations. In using their resources of capital and management to undertake
new investment, multinational corporations are most interested in carrying on a
viable business operation over time, while earning a satisfactory return on their
investment. These companies are *not* in business, either at home or abroad, to
earn quick returns, recover their capital, and then 'get out' of business in a given
project or country. On the contrary, decisions to make additional investments
for expansion and modernization, for example, are likely to follow the initial
capital commitment, so that the project is in a nearly constant state of evolution.
These considerations – the long-term view of multinational corporations in making investments, and the nearly continuous renewing or enlarging of those investment commitments – are fundamental to a proper understanding of the process
of international direct investment and the motives and behavior of multinational
corporations.

Of course, the overwhelming majority of investments by multinational corporations lead to mutually successful long-term relations between investor and foreign host country. In the case of Exxon, we have carried on foreign operations
for more than 85 years and currently have operations in more than 100 countries.
When we embark on a new venture in a foreign country we intend to remain in

195

that country for an indefinite period – for as long as we can carry on successful business operations.

Why do companies invest abroad in the first place? Generally, they respond to attractive opportunities to invest wherever they occur at home and abroad. When market conditions have indicated investment in a foreign country, multinational corporations have responded to such opportunities. In the case of extractive industries, investments must be made where the raw materials are located and it is economically feasible to produce and market them. Successful discovery of foreign oil resources, for example, generally leads to a chain of investments in producing, refining, transporting, and marketing the output. Beyond the producing stage, these investments generally occur along the economically feasible transportation routes from producing areas to foreign consuming countries. These foreign oil investments have not only provided the world with its major source of energy, but they have also made substantial contributions to the economies of both producing and consuming countries. They have been politically sensitive in producing countries, however, because they relate to an exhaustible resource in the national patrimony.

In manufacturing industries, foreign investment generally occurs in response to competitive cost conditions and other market factors, reflecting, for example, transportation costs, proximity to low-cost material inputs, availability of appropriate labor, particular aspects of foreign demand, and foreign barriers to imports. In responding to competitive cost conditions, multinational corporations do not 'cause' shifts in international trade competitiveness among nations, but generally respond to shifts which are already taking place. In doing so, they promote international specialization in production among nations, and increase the benefits of international trade to both importing and exporting nations. In the process, they help to raise over-all living standards in both host and home countries.

No multinational corporation has unlimited resources of capital and management at its command. Consequently, a multinational corporation must choose carefully among the many investment opportunities which arise, weighing the various risks and prospective returns of new investments at home and in foreign countries. When considering long-term investments outside the home country, multinational corporations are vitally concerned that the basic 'rules of the game' affecting foreign investments remain relatively stable, or at least predictable. Introduction of host country policies which result in substantial increases in taxation of foreign investment, in detailed government regulation of operating decisions, in restrictive foreign exchange controls, or in substantial special privileges being granted to competing enterprises, could make an otherwise successful investment no longer viable. Moreover, investors face the additional risk in some countries of nationalization or forced sell-out of their investments. Such policies may be invoked by host governments to strengthen their national economies. However, if they serve to discourage foreign investors from participating, a reverse effect may well occur.

A recent United Nations background report, *Multinational Corporations in World Development,* appropriately recognized (p. 83) that 'A critical requirement of a multinational corporation is a reasonably stable environment in which growth and profitability is possible.'[1] Within these limits, investors acknowledge that the future is uncertain, and, in the case of specific investment agreements, that there are occasions where both parties will seek agreement on modifications. In any event, it is important that modifications in contractual commitments be made only after full discussion and mutual agreement.

How do multinational corporations view their responsibilities to society, particularly in developing countries? I believe that they generally see their most important responsibility as conducting their particular business well – by producing a high-quality product or service efficiently, offering it at a reasonable price, and being responsive to possibilities for improving the product and the production process. In this way, the activities of multinational corporations will result in economic benefits to workers and consumers, as well as to governments in host countries. Of course, in conducting their businesses well, these corporations should also abide by the spirit and letter of local laws and requirements, and reflect in their general demeanor a recognition that they are guests of the countries in which they operate. These responsibilities are, I think, accepted by most multinational corporations.

The primary importance of carrying out economic functions well, however, does not suggest an ostrich-like approach of 'minding one's own business,' without regard to the impact of business operations on the goals of various groups. Indeed, a second level of corporate responsibilities to society lies in a sensitivity and responsiveness to the indirect impact of business operations on the society at large. Thus, the operations of multinational corporations must be consistent with national goals – for example, with respect to protecting the physical environment, reducing social inequities, improving labor skills, and so on. Multinational corporations on the whole accept these responsibilities and adapt to the host country environment. They advance the national goals of host countries not simply because it is 'the right thing to do,' but to a great extent because such adaptive behavior promotes a successful long-term operation in the foreign host country.

The operations of multinational corporations indirectly affect the host countries in a positive way by introducing advanced technology and training nationals in new technical or managerial skills. The International Chamber of Commerce has published an interesting descriptive report on this subject entitled 'The International Corporation and the Transfer of Technology.' Also, a number of years ago the National Planning Association in the United States published several case studies of multinational corporation operations in individual countries – for example, Sears in Mexico, General Electric in Brazil, and Creole in Venezuela – which describe technology transfers as well as many other direct and indirect results of company operations. In the case of Exxon, we employ the most advanced technology appropriate to the circumstances of a particular host country and the markets being served, combining our own technology with various relevant technologies developed elsewhere in the world.

In our operations we have engaged in substantial training efforts in technical and managerial fields – locally and in other foreign areas. We have also brought foreign nationals to the United States for training. Partly as a result of these activities, foreign nationals currently hold about 60 per cent of our roughly 1000 executive-level positions outside the United States. This proportion is likely to increase in the future, as currently we have an additional 1000 foreign employees on training and developmental assignments outside their home countries, about 100 with Exxon in the United States.

Beyond the areas of conducting operations well, and ensuring that these operations support national goals, most multinational corporations accept a third level of social responsibility. This concerns efforts to enhance the broader social environment in countries in which the corporation or its subsidiary 'lives and works.' Increasingly, these corporations are examining their proper role to include broader areas of positive contribution to the general welfare. Thus, they have provided financial and technical support in foreign host countries for programs in health and education, community development, and for national cultural activities.

Aramco, for example, over many years in Saudi Arabia has attempted to contribute to economic and social progress by providing technical and financial assistance to local businesses, construction of 45 schools and one hospital, assistance for agricultural development, construction of a 500-mile road, and more than $2 million in financial support for research to eradicate a major eye disease. In Venezuela, our affiliate has undertaken similar kinds of activities over decades. In general, when we find and produce oil in a less-developed area, we carry out many projects and activities beyond those directly involved in oil production. In part, such activities may be related to our operations (e.g., construction of a road) or to the well-being of our employees (education and health), but to a great extent they represent efforts to enhance the social climate in the countries in which we operate.

To mention a cooperative activity with which I am very familiar, nearly a decade ago multinational corporations and banks from the United States, Western Europe, Canada, and Japan jointly formed the ADELA investment company. ADELA's major objective is to promote and strengthen national small business enterprises in the developing countries of Latin America by making minority investments in such businesses. ADELA has been successful in this objective. The availability of ADELA financing has often made adequate additional financing possible for these national ventures. Today, ADELA is supported by 235 multinational corporations and banks, and in eight and one-half years has disbursed over $1 billion in loans and investments. Currently, it has about $350 million of outstanding loans and investments to nearly 400 enterprises in more than twenty Latin American countries. ADELA investment activities range from agricultural processing to capital goods manufacturing. Similar cooperative action by multinational corporations in the Far East and in Africa may be an indication of ADELA's success.

Such efforts by multinational corporations are undertaken because they are aware that the future of their operations will be affected by the broader social environment in host countries and, therefore, it is in their interest to improve that environment. There are economic limits to what any single company can do, but the basic goal of conducting successful long-term operations in an individual foreign country has caused a growing number of companies to undertake such 'social improvement' tasks.

MAJOR ISSUES IN RELATIONS
WITH HOST COUNTRIES

Despite the infrequency of actual conflicts, the potential for conflicts in the goals of multinational corporations and governments is a cause for serious concern, particularly among host countries. This is true of industrialized countries as well as developing countries, as evidenced, for example, by increasing European Community interest in policies toward multinational corporations.

The large size of multinational corporations
The large size of many multinational corporations in terms of total assets or sales, particularly when compared to the economies of developing countries, is often cited as evidence of power over national economies. The vast assets and geographical scope of the corporations are viewed by some as indicating virtual immunity from control by national governments, in host and even in home countries. Their substantial wealth and geographical spread is believed to afford multinational corporations great flexibility in marshalling resources to virtually any task. Thus, they have been accused of bringing about the rise and fall of currencies, weakening labor's bargaining power in individual countries, impeding the development of local industry and local research and development efforts, and of causing many other economic ills.

While undoubtedly size confers some advantages, in carrying out effective research and development programs for example, multinational corporations do not have the flexibility or power to elude effective control by governments that has been suggested. They cannot ignore market forces which render a particular activity uneconomic, but in reacting to such changes in market conditions, they have been accused of undermining national goals.

Concerning their alleged ability to escape control by governments, it should be noted that most of the wealth of multinational corporations consists of fixed assets – in the case of the oil industry, production equipment, pipelines, refineries, and service stations – which cannot be summoned to exert pressure on either individual currencies or governments. On the contrary, the fixed assets of such corporations are potential 'hostages' in foreign host countries. To help preserve their role in managing these immovable assets over time, the subsidiaries of multinational corporations must be responsive to national laws and priorities. The many examples of unilateral government action – imposed production and export quotas, price controls, controls on local borrowing and remittance rights, enforced sell-outs, and in some cases expropriations – and the accommodations made by multinational corporations, do not indicate that global size entails substantial power. Even the so-called 'liquid' assets of these corporations cannot be mobilized readily in a foreign exchange crisis, since they consist largely of working capital required to carry on day-to-day operations, and there is no indication that multinational corporations have used their borrowing power to engage in currency speculation. A recent study by the United States Treasury showed that US multinational corporations were not the major factor in US capital outflows during the first quarter of 1973, when expectations of changes in currency exchange rates led to large increases in such outflows.[2]

The success of multinational corporations in operating in many countries over long periods does not reflect an ability to escape control by governments. On the contrary, their long-term success is due largely to their ability to make flexible adaptations to the national requirements and goals of individual host countries, while continuing to carry on effective business operations on an international scale. As national priorities have changed in host countries, multinational corporations have recognized the need to be responsive to such changes. As the desire and capability for local participation in the equity of multinational subsidiaries has grown in some countries, the parent corporations have increasingly accepted such participation. At the same time, they have adapted to changing conditions in the world economy – in the oil industry, for example, by forming joint ventures with other corporations and with governments to share the burden of the huge capital requirements and risks involved in some of today's large natural resource development projects.

'Disruption' by multinational corporations

Multinational corporations are viewed, particularly in developing countries, as a potentially 'disruptive' influence in the host economy. For example, a subsidiary may be seen as such for doing any of the following: paying wages in excess of the going rate in an area; introducing labor-saving technology when there is unemployment in the country; making some national enterprises non-competitive; increasing local incomes, which results in increased imports of consumption goods; remitting substantial dividends to the home country; and increasing the burden on limited infrastructure facilities. While not minimizing the problem of adjusting to the economic changes set in motion by the establishment of new foreign investment projects, these changes (or 'disruptions') ought to be considered in a broader context.

Most of the 'disruptions' are part of the economic development process, which is clearly not a smooth one. Thus, most of them would occur eventually in the development process with or without foreign investment. The introduction by a multinational corporation of labor-saving technology may in some cases seem inappropriate if there is unemployment in the host country. However, the economic benefits of introducing such production methods may be much greater for the host country than the use of a more labor-intensive process, even after taking into account the costs associated with alleviating the difficult social problems of unemployment. Multinational corporations generally introduce the most efficient technology appropriate to the circumstances of host countries, which may or may not be labor-saving. In most cases new foreign investments do create substantial employment in host countries, directly and indirectly.

The balance-of-payments developments associated particularly with substantial foreign investment activity should be viewed in terms of the total balance-of-payments impact of foreign investments, and not be confined to an annual comparison of capital inflows to dividend remittances abroad. Thus, export promotion and import substitution effects must also be considered. With respect to dividend remittances, it should also be recognized that a foreign investor is making an economic contribution to the host country (and paying taxes to the host government) to make such remittances possible.

Without adopting an approach of avoiding the 'disruptions' by promoting a stagnant economy, greater efforts are needed to anticipate and accommodate the inevitable disruptions that accompany the development process. Thus, where there is a potential for significant economic and social disruption, it is important for subsidiaries of multinational corporations to keep host governments informed about their plans and to attempt to work out cooperative solutions to those social and economic problems which seem likely to arise.

Emilio G. Collado

Division of the benefits from foreign investment
Perhaps the major concern of developing countries about multinational corporations relates to the division of the benefits of foreign investment between the corporation and the host country. In some cases - in considering government tax revenues and balance-of-payments effects, for example - this concern is expanded to include the distribution of benefits between the host and home countries. Some of the benefits of foreign investment to host countries, particularly in the developing world, are difficult to measure. The new knowledge and skills acquired by the labor force, and the impetus to the development of industries related to the foreign investment project, fall into this class. However, much of the host country's concern seems to reflect a belief that there is a fixed amount of benefit from foreign investment to be divided largely between the investor and the host country. According to this view, one party can gain only at the expense of the welfare of the other. This belief has led some host governments to attempt to increase the benefits from foreign investment by imposing a variety of restrictions governing the participation of foreign investors in their economies.

Actually, there is no 'fixed' amount of economic benefit resulting from foreign investment, and restrictive policies intended to increase the benefits to host countries are likely to have the effect of reducing such benefits by discouraging foreign investors from participating in that economy. Multinational corporations are likely to make their greatest economic contributions to host countries where government policies toward foreign subsidiaries are well established and predictable, non-discriminatory as compared with those for national enterprises, and not excessively restrictive. In such an atmosphere, multinational corporations will be encouraged to commit their energies and resources freely to attractive investment opportunities. In so doing, the economic rewards to host countries inevitably will increase.

AREAS FOR COOPERATIVE ACTION BY MULTI-
NATIONAL CORPORATIONS AND GOVERNMENTS

Recognizing the potential for tensions and conflicts between mutlinational corporations and governments, there are a number of positive actions which both corporations and governments could take to reduce, if not eliminate, the potential sources of conflict.

Tax policy
An important objective of certain home country governments in their tax policy toward multinational corporations based in their country is that decisions to invest at home or abroad should be relatively neutral with respect to taxation. A major departure from such neutrality would occur if income earned by a foreign

202

branch or subsidiary were subjected to double taxation, i.e., taxed fully by both the host and home country governments. Should substantial double taxation of foreign income occur, the burden of two taxes would be so great that multinational corporations would simply avoid making foreign investments. Generally, home country governments seek to prevent international double taxation either by exempting all foreign-source income from tax (territoriality principle), or by allowing credit for foreign income taxes paid on the foreign-source income subject to tax. However, even where the foreign tax credit is allowed, some distortions may result from differences in the tax policies of host and home country governments. Thus, further intergovernmental efforts are required to negotiate multilateral agreements to achieve greater harmony in national tax policies, and to ensure that international double taxation is avoided. Such agreements should also seek to eliminate distortions arising from discriminatory tax treatment of foreign investment by host countries. A number of recent bilateral treaties contains a provision which precludes such tax discrimination.

Another distortion occurs when host countries grant substantial tax incentives or offer lengthy 'tax holidays' in efforts to attract foreign investment. This raises several problems. First, the availability of substantial incentives, such as 'tax holidays,' may distort the international allocation of investment resources, with related effects on international trade patterns. While some 'distortion' of investment in favor of developing countries may be considered desirable, the competition among countries in providing incentives can become so great that overgenerous incentives are offered. Although host governments are willing to forego some tax revenue in the interest of attracting investment and the resulting economic benefits, this must be carefully balanced against the need to have sufficient tax revenue to meet growing demands for government services. Without careful balancing of investment incentives and future revenue needs, budgetary constraints may require host governments subsequently to deny the incentives and raise taxes substantially on all foreign subsidiaries, thus making some investments no longer economic. Finally, host country incentives may be rendered virtually meaningless from the start if, in the absence of tax-sparing treaties, the home country government effectively denies such incentives by applying the full home country tax rate to all income from abroad. In such cases, the home country simply picks up the tax revenue given up by host countries in their attempts to attract investment.

Such problems can be avoided only by greater international concordance of tax incentives, including agreement on specific upper limits to the extent of incentives allowable by host countries. To make the incentives effective, home countries should provide for tax sparing in developing countries. This can be achieved most effectively by intergovernmental agreements.

Emilio G. Collado

A third major issue in the tax area concerns the international transfer pricing practices of multinational corporations. It has been alleged frequently that multinational corporations are able to reduce substantially, or minimize, their total tax burdens simply by adjusting the prices charged for goods and services transferred among their various affiliated companies. Thus, it has been suggested that they generally 'manipulate' their international transfer prices in order to increase costs (and reduce taxable income) in high-tax countries, and reduce costs (and increase taxable income) in low-tax countries. While there undoubtedly have been some distortions in this area, their extent has been exaggerated.

In general, multinational corporations follow normal commercial practices in their interaffiliate transactions, and prices charged reflect realistically the market values of the goods or services transferred. 'Manipulation' of transfer prices is usually neither feasible nor desirable for a number of reasons, including the following: the decentralized organizational structure typical of many multinational corporations, reflected in substantial autonomy for local affiliate managers; the desirability, from a management point of view, of having an accurate gauge on the current profitability of individual affiliate operations; in some cases, the need to satisfy local minority shareholders; competitive factors; the possible availability of market prices as a check; and, finally, continued government surveillance in this area, so that interaffiliate prices must be substantiated before both host and home country governments. The problems of complying with numerous national laws and regulations relating to tariffs, other border adjustments, and various national tax laws, do not lend themselves to 'manipulation' of interaffiliate transactions. Indeed, the accounts of multinational corporations are often subject to greater public scrutiny in host countries than are those of national enterprises. Moreover, the penalties for using improper transfer prices are severe. When a government decides a corporation's international transfer prices are inappropriate, the unilateral imposition of tax liabilities results in double taxation for the corporation.

Although today the practice of adjusting transfer prices is the exception rather than the general rule of multinational corporate behavior, international cooperative efforts on the part of these corporations and governments could avoid most potential distortions in this area. It is clear that multinational corporations ought consistently to reflect arm's-length or market prices in their interaffiliate transactions. (In fact, current US law requires US-based multinationals to do this.) On the part of governments, it would be desirable to reach international agreement that arm's-length or market prices for interaffiliate transactions be used to determine taxable income, thereby avoiding unilateral government decisions to tax income which has already been taxed by another government.

A voluntary 'code of conduct'
for multinational corporations
Agreement among multinational corporations on a voluntary 'code of conduct'
describing broad principles of acceptable behavior in various areas would undoubtedly contribute to a better climate of understanding for the corporations
generally. It would also serve to discourage some multinational corporations from
the kinds of activities that can generate ill will for multinational corporations as
a group. It would be impractical for such a code of conduct to set forth detailed
legal rules, of course, since adherence to a set of principles does not indicate precise behavior in particular circumstances. However, an investors' code could support positive adaptations to host country social and economic goals, and con-
demn certain undesirable forms of behavior, such as speculative foreign exchange
operations, distortions in international transfer prices, or attempts to circumvent
host government policies. General endorsement of a 'code of conduct' by multinational corporations would probably have a significant positive impact on their
relationships with governments. The International Chamber of Commerce has
made a useful contribution to developing a set of principles for behavior, and
their 'Guidelines for International Investment' ought to receive serious consideration.

International coordination of government policies
toward multinational corporations
Full international coordination or harmonization of national policies affecting
multinational corporations is perhaps not feasible, and in some cases not desirable
for individual countries. However, there are some policy areas in which greater
coordination is possible, and it would result in substantial benefits to both the
corporations and the governments. Tax policy has already been suggested as a
major area in which a greater degree of international coordination would have
mutually beneficial results. Another area of concern to host governments is the
so-called extra-territorial application of home country policies to the international
operations of multinational corporations. There are a number of policies in which
the apparently overlapping jurisdictions of home and host countries result in a
potential for conflict. Perhaps the most common examples today are antitrust
policy and balance-of-payments policies which require remittances of foreign
earnings. Among the more industrialized countries, the importance of conflicts
resulting from the application of antitrust policies is diminishing, as their antitrust policies are becoming more similar. To a large extent, this development
reflects implementation of the common antitrust policy for the European Community set forth in the Rome Treaty. Concerning the general issue of extra-terri-

toriality, however, in those areas where national policies are not likely to be harmonized, it seems clear that greater consultation among governments before the application of policy beyond national borders would greatly reduce the potential for misunderstandings and conflicts.

National policies toward foreign investment on the part of both host and home countries form another area in which greater international coordination would be useful. By this, however, I do not imply support for regional harmonization of host country policies for the purpose of substantially restricting the activities of foreign investors. Efforts toward a united regional policy that is largely intended to impose extensive controls over the operations of foreign multinational corporations may backfire, if the adverse business climate causes them to undertake alternative investments outside such regions. On the other hand, multinational corporations would be encouraged to undertake new investments in developing nations if they had greater assurance that their operations in those countries would not be subjected to substantial new forms of discrimination or controls once their facilities had been constructed. Thus, a measure of international agreement on some maximum extent of discrimination or restrictions affecting foreign investment in various policy areas – taxation and foreign exchange remittance policies, for example – could substantially reduce the investment risks perceived by multinational corporations. In addition, limitations on home country restrictions on foreign investment would probably have a positive effect on both investors and host countries. As the discussion continues among investors and governments, elements of a broad intergovernmental agreement could evolve and be available for individual governments to endorse voluntarily. Such action in various policy areas could have a substantial encouraging effect on potential investors in countries participating in the agreement. Moreover, in the future the distinction between home and host countries is likely to diminish, as multinational enterprises from current host countries develop. Thus, the benefits of an international agreement relating to investment policies are likely to be spread wider in the years ahead.

While agreement may be possible initially in only a few areas, an intergovernmental agreement could include a commitment by host governments to submit foreign investment disputes to the international conciliation and arbitration facilities of the World Bank or ICC. Strict adherence to the 'Calvo Doctrine,' however, would seem to present obstacles to such a commitment. Irrespective of whether elements of an intergovernmental agreement in policies relating to foreign investment are eventually established, a greater commitment by developing host countries to use international conciliation and arbitration machinery in investment disputes would dramatically improve the climate for investment by multinational corporations in these countries. Such a commitment to the existing facilities of the World Bank or ICC would avoid some of the 'confrontations' that have characterized past investment disputes, and would promote the peaceful settlement of future investment problems.

Arrangements for future discussions among multinational
corporations and host and home country governments
It seems clear that a continuing exchange of views among investors and governments would contribute greatly to a better climate for understanding of their respective goals. Some useful exchanges have taken place in recent years in the various UN panels, and a joint discussion of multinational corporation issues is now developing in the OECD. However, it would be desirable to provide for a continuing discussion in which the developing and industrialized countries participate equally along with multinational corporations. It seems to me that a natural way to achieve this is to expand the UN panel on foreign investment and make it a permanent UN activity. I hope that such an effort will receive serious consideration and active support and that the UN will continue in this constructive and worthwhile activity.

NOTES

1 With regard to the UN background report, two general observations are in order. First, in emphasizing potential conflicts among multinational corporations and governments, the report does not seem to reflect adequately the positive role of multinational corporations in promoting national and international economic development, with the resulting benefits for workers, consumers, and governments. Although it is probably natural for the report to focus on problem areas, considering the many years that multinational corporations have conducted business operations in various countries around the world, it seems that actual conflicts with governments have not been common. However, those that have occurred have attracted wide attention. Conflicts so serious as to result in international relations problems between governments have been relatively rare. Although there is potential for conflict among investors and governments, the relative infrequency of actual conflicts suggests that their respective goals are not inconsistent, and to a large extent are probably reinforcing. Of course, there have also been some conscientious efforts on each side to accommodate objectives, in the interest of promoting mutual benefits.

Second, the background report reflects a broad spectrum of ideas from the growing literature on the subject of multinational corporations. This collection of views is undoubtedly useful in provoking discussion. However, since

many of these views are conflicting and not supported by empirical evidence, I believe the report would have been even more helpful if it had included a critical analysis or appraisal of the various assertions and proposals presented.
2 See letter of Jack F. Bennett, deputy under secretary of the Treasury for Monetary Affairs, to Senator Harry F. Byrd, Jr., 20 July 1973. The Business and Industry Advisory Committee has been consulting with the OECD about volatile short-term capital flows, and will soon have available an interesting BIAC report on this subject by W.A.P. Manser, with an introduction by Louis Camu.

Professor Nye sees some of the byproduct of the activities of multinational corporations – or transnationals – as fostering regional and political integration in the world. His prognosis is hopeful. He does not see transnationals as either disruptive or alien to a system of stable and non-violent intergovernmental relations. Some critics of transnational corporations have charged that in the past, home countries have tended to abdicate governmental foreign policy functions to the private foreign policy activities of multinational corporations with respect to host countries. Professor Nye classifies state-corporate international interactions into direct and indirect modes. Direct modes involve private transnational foreign policy. Indirect modes involve government-to-government foreign policy, although the policy positions of governments are influenced by the transnationals. Both direct and indirect effects may exist side by side and simultaneously in any given situation.

With regard to private corporate foreign policy, Professor Nye sees its incidence as less intense and noxious than sensational reports might suggest. Moreover, he sees corporate-state relations which operate indirectly through government-to-government interactions as most significant at the present time – and growing in importance.

This is important. Jargon often substitutes for thought in political and economic discourse. Such phrases as 'administered prices' and 'economic imperalism' role easily from the tongue, but often prove to have little content. Professor Nye provides a framework for thinking about the political and economic consequences of expanding international economic activity in a context which includes both nation states and transnational corporations. Perhaps only economists can take comfort in a situation where the profit motive explicitly and openly operates in the formulation of intergovernmental foreign policy. But if significant transnational corporations are the hostages of policy-makers in both host and home countries, and to the extent that the transnational corporation becomes better off as the host and home countries *both* become better off together, then the existence of transnationals may have a beneficial and harmonizing effect upon foreign policy. This may be especially true if countries are symmetrically (or at least semi-symmetrically) the host and home for different transnational corporations.

Professor Nye's chapter must be compared to the chapters by Dr Collado and Mr Homet. The international commodity agreement for oil which Mr Homet suggests is an example of the indirect government-to-government mode of corporate-state relations defined by Professor Nye. The role of the multinational oil companies in the recent price increases, in the world oil market is an example, in addition to the tariff preference case cited by Professor Nye, of host-country use of transnationals.

Both Professor Nye and Dr Collado realize that transnationals may be caught in the middle between governments. The 'petrodollar' problem discussed by Professor Grennes and Dr Winokur is a case where appropriate intergovernmental actions to promote international economic flexibility (rather than unilateral restrictions) may make both host and home governments and transnational corporations better off.

Dr Collado, Mr Homet, Professor Nye, and Professor Grennes and Dr Winokur are basically all playing variations on a common theme. This is not surprising since they were all invited to contribute to these volumes. But the complementarity of their analyses was neither consciously coordinated nor directly solicited.

J. S. NYE

Multinational corporations in world politics

THE NATION-STATE VERSUS THE MULTINATIONAL CORPORATION

There are currently some 200 large multinational enterprises or clusters of corporations which operate simultaneously in twenty or more different nations and are joined together by common ownership and management strategy.[1] Some observers believe that by the end of the century, 300 giant corporations will account for a large majority of world industrial production. The sovereignty of nation-states is alleged to be obsolete, and the multinational corporation has been described as 'the most powerful de facto political instrumentality of internationalism, of far greater consequence than the United Nations.'[2]

Such statements stimulate skeptics to point out that large international corporations have long been present on the world scene. Moreover, despite the fact that the value added by each of the top ten multinationals was over $3 billion or greater than the gross national product of some 80 member states of the United Nations, even weak states can and sometimes have nationalized the local affiliate of a multinational corporation.

To a considerable extent, however, this competitive 'either/or' view of the relationship between transnational corporations and nation-states is misleading and generates a false debate. The two types of organization are different both in their goals and their instruments of power, and this makes them complementary as well as competitive. Both can grow stronger simultaneously. Indeed, the growth of the transnational organization can stimulate and enhance the growth of nation-states.

This is not to argue that there are no real conflicts between transnational corporations and nation-states. Quite the contrary. What is new about the modern multinational enterprise and distinguishes it from the large international corporations of earlier centuries is its global management strategy made possible by the technology of modern communications. This means that the decision domains of managers of transnational corporations cut across the national boundaries of both home and host countries. Therein lies the potential for conflict. The most honest corporate manager acting rationally within a transnational perspective is bound to have conflicts of interest with the most reasonable of statesmen whose rationality (and democratic responsibility) is bounded by national frontiers.

At the same time, as Samuel Huntington has pointed out, when entities serve different purposes, their 'complementary conflict' does not threaten the existence of the parties, whereas 'duplicative conflict' among similar entities is more often zero sum in character.[3] In addition to their differences in goals, the means or sources of power available to transnational corporations and nation-states are very different. The power of the corporation stems from its control over a package of financial, technological, information, and management resources. For all its economic power, however, it lacks two essential components of power that the nation-state possesses: force and popular legitimacy. It is dependent upon the state for the right of establishment, police protection, favorable tax treatment, and so forth. Where two entities with such different power sources and ultimate goals confront each other, the opportunities for bargained solutions are great.

The terms of the bargains that are struck between multinational corporations and states depend on their mutual perceptions of the alternatives available in each particular case. Both sides are aware that at some level of cost, the corporation can transfer resources (and use sources of information) beyond the jurisdiction of the state. Over time, mutual perceptions of the opportunity costs of this mobility may change. For example, as the development of local capabilities makes managerial or financial resources less scarce or the fixed nature of an investment makes mobility seem more costly, the terms of the bargain struck between state and corporation may shift. In other words, while stemming from different types of resources, the actual power relationship between nation-states and transnational corporations is best thought of as a subtle balance of mutually perceived alternatives. In Vernon's terms, one must remember that such political bargains are always 'obsolescing.'[4]

ROLES IN WORLD POLITICS

While the multinational corporation is not a threat to the existence of the nation-state, this does not mean that it lacks a significant role in world politics. The traditional 'realist' view of world politics assumes that states are the only significant actors, that states act as coherent units, and that military security concerns of states dominate their other concerns. To varying degrees for different types of states, these assumptions are unrealistic. To the extent that these three assumptions are relaxed, the role of corporations in world politics appears more significant.

For example, it is frequently argued that nuclear technology and changing domestic values have made the use of force a more costly option among the advanced industrial societies. While this is not true for all states (or non-state groups), and while some of the shift reflects the current cycle of détente among the superpowers rather than a linear trend, it nonetheless remains true that there are large areas of interstate politics where force is not a useful instrument. In addition, the goals of many states, both developed and developing, have shifted from territorial possession or domination goals to more economic and welfare-oriented objectives. To the extent that these shifts take place, they represent shifts away from the area of weakness of the corporation (i.e., force) and toward the area where the transnational mobility of the corporation is able to strongly affect state objectives (i.e., economic welfare).

One can also question the traditional assumptions that coherently organized states are the only significant actors in world politics.[5] This is certainly not true if we broaden our conception of world politics to include transnational systems in which nongovernmental actors account for a major portion of activity across state boundaries. While not all transnational systems are economic, a large number are, and multinational corporations are major actors in them. The distributional effects of transnational systems are complex. Take oil for example. Transnational corporations are an important component of the system through which oil-exporting countries extract large transfer payments from consumer countries. But some of the transfer payments come from *poor* countries (like India), and others go from poor individuals in rich countries to rich individuals in oil-producing countries (from which, among other things, the funds have gone to finance transnational uses of force against rich countries). As states' welfare objectives become more prominent and there is a greater awareness of the ways that transnational systems allocate resources across borders, the political relevance of such systems becomes more apparent to statesmen. As such transnational systems become politicized, the role of multinational enterprises in world politics becomes more prominent.

In thinking about multinational corporations in world politics it is useful to distinguish (1) a direct role as autonomous actors with private foreign policies of their own, and (2) an indirect role affecting world politics by influencing intergovernmental relationships. The indirect role fits with state-centric concepts of

213

world politics and is represented by the solid lines in the following simplified diagram, while the direct transnational role is represented by dotted lines.

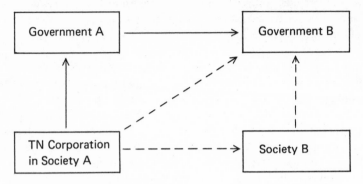

MULTINATIONAL CORPORATIONS AS ACTORS
WITH PRIVATE FOREIGN POLICIES

Certainly the direct transnational role has led to some of the most dramatic instances of the multinational corporation in world politics – witness the case of ITT and Chile which helped to stimulate UN attention. Yet the Chilean disclosures are also informative in that ITT was notably unsuccessful in persuading other multinational corporations to join them in the direct political role. While evidence in such areas is almost impossible to assemble scientifically, it seems on the basis of disclosures that exist that such cases as United Fruit in Guatemala, Union Minière in Katanga, or ITT in Chile represent a very small portion of the state-corporation interactions, and that the indirect effects on government-to-government relations (discussed below) are probably more significant for world politics at this time.

Nonetheless, the direct transnational role does exist, and can be of crucial importance to particular states. If we conceive of a scale of direct political actions by corporations ranging in descending order of intensity from the hiring of private armies, the bribery of host country soldiers or politicians, the legitimate lobby of host government legislators, to advertising to influence the climate of ideas, we undoubtedly find most direct political activities clustered at the lower end of the scale. However, corporations may also use economic means (both inducements and deprivations) in bargaining directly with governments for such political goals as favorable policies or their very survival. In these cases, we are in the political realm of differing power resources and changeable bargains which we described earlier.

When we consider the direct political role of the corporation in world politics, it is useful to relax the assumption that states always act as coherent entities. If

we see that different groups in societies have different interests and that governments are sometimes alliances of competing bureaucracies pulling in different
directions, we can conceive of coalitions for particular policy outcomes that may
be composed of parts of different governments and corporations. [Editors' note:
In the 1950s in the United States, spokesmen for Standard Oil Company of New
Jersey opposed introduction of the mandatory oil import quota system. Spokesmen for Humble Oil Company, a subsidiary of Jersey Standard, favored the program. In the United States government, the Bureau of Mines may favor policies
which the Environmental Protection Agency opposes. Within EPA, some groups
may favor a policy which others oppose.] The theory of structural imperialism
portrays this in terms of the penetration of weak states, or of alliances between
central sectors in peripheral states and corporations from central states. Transnational coalitions, however, are not this simple. For instance, if we look at the
international lobbying over a new seabed regime, we find oil companies and some
elements of the US government allied with some relatively cohesive poor states
against the official US government position. Multinational corporations can affect
the coherence of home governments and societies as well as host countries. Indeed,
Moran has argued from the comparison of Anaconda and Kennecott responses to
Chilean nationalization that the traditional transnational corporate political defense in the form of a transnational alliance with a host country elite may be giving way to more sophisticated economic defenses based on transnational market
and credit networks.[6]

THE EFFECT OF THE MULTINATIONAL CORPORATION
ON GOVERNMENT-TO-GOVERNMENT RELATIONS

We shall consider the effect of the multinational corporation on the agenda, the
instruments, and the outcomes of interstate relations.

A *Setting the agenda*
Why some issues rather than others absorb the attention of statesmen is a question of considerable political importance that has often received too little attention. Even if they played no other role, the effect of multinational corporations
in helping to set the agendas of interstate politics would be a significant role.
    Transnational corporations affect the agenda of interstate relations in one
direct and three indirect ways. First, they may directly affect the agenda by
lobbying for a particular policy of their home government toward the host
country. While this has sometimes taken the form of home government inter-
ventions in support of claims against host governments, there has probably been
a net decline of this type of activity over the past half century. In some cases,

such as lobbying for better tariff treatment of the host country by the home country, the lines of policy influence run in the other direction. Moreover, with a few notable exceptions, there is little evidence that multinational (as opposed to merely large) corporations have an abnormally strong stake in military-industrial production or activities.[7]

This is not to argue that multinational corporations do not create conflicts among states, but that they more often do so indirectly than directly. First, the activities of such corporations by their transnational nature give rise to conflicts of jurisdiction and problems of extraterritoriality in such matters as antitrust, capital controls, trade restrictions, and taxation policies. For example, of 16 conflicts cited by Behrman as arising from corporate activities among the Atlantic nations in the mid-1960s, 12 involved the American Trading with the Enemy Act, one involved computer technology related to nuclear weapons, and three involved enforcement of UN sanctions.[8] In none of these cases did a corporation directly or deliberately provoke or profit from the conflict. In the data assembled by Leyton-Brown on 61 public conflicts in Britain, Canada, and France arising as the result of the activities of multinational corporations, interstate conflicts arose primarily from extraterritoriality problems. In only two cases did a multinational enterprise seek the diplomatic support of its parent government.[9]

A second way in which multinational corporations have affected the interstate agenda is through their effects on changing the nature of various transnational economic systems, particularly trade and money. With international production exceeding trade among the developed countries, and with a significant portion of international trade transformed from 'arms length' to intra-enterprise transactions, a variety of new trade policy questions have been inadvertently put on the intergovernmental agenda by the ability of the multinational corporations to surmount traditional tariff barriers. Similarly, the ability of a few score corporate treasurers, thinking globally and acting rationally, to transfer vast sums with extraordinary rapidity contributed to the problems of the postwar international monetary system, the reform of which has been prominent on the intergovernmental agenda in recent years. [Editors' note: Privately rational maximizing behavior can also be socially beneficial.[9] This is the case if such capital movements are long-run equilibrating shifts. See Grennes and Winokur on this point.]

Third, multinational corporations indirectly affect the agenda of interstate relations by stimulating other groups in societies to press for particular governmental policies. Some groups such as banks, advertising agencies, and some labor groups are stimulated to press for policies of liberalization that permit them to emulate the transnational strategy of the multinational corporation. Other groups which are less transnationally mobile and feel themselves threatened or disadvantaged by the activities of the corporations may press their governments for protective or nationalist policies which subsequently burden the interstate agenda. A contemporary example is the struggle between transnationally mobile corporations and nationally immobile labor over the Burke-Hartke bill affecting the trade and investment policies of the United States.

B *Instruments*

The existence of multinational corporations with decision domains crossing several national boundaries has provided an additional instrument for governments to attempt to use in their relations with each other. For example, as we saw in the cases cited above, the United States has attempted through extraterritorial control of the trading relations of affiliates of US-based corporations to extend its foreign policy embargoes into the jurisdiction of other states. Similarly, the United States used guidelines on capital transfers by multinationals to strengthen its international monetary position.

Manipulation of corporations with transnational decision domains is an instrument available to the host as well as the home government. Fixed investments abroad can be hostages as well as outposts. For example, in two of the 16 nontrivial conflictual issues between the US and Canada which reached the presidential agenda in the 1960s, the Canadian government was able to improve its position by exerting pressure on transnational corporations (obtaining letters of intent from the auto companies in the case of the auto pact; and by obtaining a recognition of jurisdiction from Humble Oil in the Arctic sovereignty case). Finally, it is worth noting that the role of the corporation as hostage has also provided instruments to nonstate groups – witness the guerrilla activities in Argentina in recent years.

C *Outcomes*

We can think of the outcomes of interstate issues in terms of conflict, distribution of power, and political integration. As we saw above, multinational corporations have generated a number of conflicts among states, and have often been used as instruments in conflicts. In answering the question of whether on balance they tend to strengthen the home or host state more, it is useful to specify the time dimension. In the short run of a few years, the net advantage seems to go to the home state. The investment is new and more in demand by the host state. The alternatives probably appear more limited to the host than the home state, and the home state may be more capable of manipulating the transnational decision domain.

In the longer term of decades, however, multinational enterprises help to develop the capabilities of host states, both by introducing general technological and managerial resources and, in some cases, by contributing factors which directly improve the defense capabilities of states. In addition to this absolute contribution, weaker states may improve their relative bargaining position vis-à-vis enterprises as time goes on for the reasons we have stated above. This improved ability to deal with enterprises enhances their reputation for power. Finally, it is worth noting that the home states of multinationals tend to be those most affected by any secular decline in the utility of the interstate use of force. Thus home governments are less well placed to use forceful measures to defend their overseas enterprises. [Editors' note: In this regard, note the remarkable passivity of the US response to the Arab oil embargo.] For these reasons, it is likely that for the longer run Vernon is correct in his judgment that corporations are declining, not increasing, in their utility and availability as instruments for home governments.[10]

Over the even longer run of several decades, it is conceivable that the development of truly geocentric enterprises with strong central strategies and no major home country affiliation will pose a common challenge to states. At that point, statesmen's concern may be less with the way corporations distribute power among states than with the common activities necessary to prevent a distribution of economic power away from all states.

We need not wait for this stage to see some political integrative effects among states as a result of the activities of multinational corporations. In regard to regional integration, multinational enterprises probably on balance strengthen more of the process forces and improve rather than weaken more of the conditions that determine integrative or disintegrative responses by national governments, but this positive verdict has to be checked case by case.[11] In a broader global context, the differences of power, social system, and economic development limit the level of institutional growth or policy coordination that the activities of multinational enterprises may stimulate. Nonetheless, there is a political role for international organization, and it is to this that we turn next.

FUTURE TRENDS AND THE ROLE
OF INTERNATIONAL ORGANIZATION

Of some 193 manufacturing firms that operate transnationally and for which data were available, the recent UN Secretariat Report found only 1.5 per cent had more than 50 per cent foreign content in the ownership of assets; 9 per cent had more than 50 per cent foreign content in employment; 7 per cent derived half or more of their profits from abroad; and some 14 per cent had half or more of their sales abroad. In other words, few corporations that operate transnationally are predominantly multinational on many dimensions.[12]

The trends in corporate development, however, seem to be toward increased multinationality and autonomy of staff. The preponderant American source (some 60 per cent of book value of direct foreign investment in the mid-1960s) is slowly being eroded by the more rapid growth rates of European and Japanese direct investment. Technological improvements are continuing to reduce the costs of communications and enhance the corporate capacity to develop global strategies divorced from identification with the interests of any particular country.

While predictions that 300 giant corporations will run the world economy tend to be based on projection of past trends and fail to take into account diseconomies of scale that appear at later stages of product cycles, even smaller multinationals can make crucial allocative decisions that challenge governments' welfare goals. If we see increased corporate dedomiciling, whether to remote and pleasant tropical islands as some foresee, or simply in the form of shopping among developed states, the willingness of governments to turn to international agreements and organization may increase. There are already some signs of US political attitudes toward foreign investment that resemble those of host rather than home states. If, on the other hand, governments turn to unilateral restrictions to deal with the problems of policy interdependence created by multinationals, this may create such a conflicting maze of regulations that the corporations themselves will drop some of their mistrust of international organization and press for more intergovernmental solutions.

Given deep-seated differences among countries, it is not likely that this evolution will ever lead to a strong supranational organization charged with overseeing the activities of multinationals. Many agreements will be of limited scope, both by subject and number of countries. Nonetheless, there are several possible roles for universal intergovernmental organizations.

A *Information systems*
As we stressed earlier, differential access to information, variable identity, and mobility of resources are key assets of multinational corporations in their bargaining with states. Information that improves governments' information about global corporate activities and governments' knowledge about mutual alternatives can affect the terms of the bargain. Much of the information will be difficult to obtain and equally difficult to assess. Nonetheless, information can be collected, and its usefulness will increase as the staff develops a reputation for fair-mindedness.

B *Technical assistance*
Not all governments have the ability to make full use of the information already available to them. Providing experts in this area, as the Secretariat Report suggests, can be an important function. Technical assistance cannot remove all conflicts from the interaction of weak states and foreign corporations, but at least it

can help to dispel the mistrust that stems from fear of the unknown, and allow the parties to bargain on the basis of more clearly perceived self-interest. The experience of Harvard's Development Advisory Service in helping countries such as Liberia and Indonesia to improve the terms of their contracts with foreign corporations is an instructive example. Again, a reputation for fair-mindedness is essential. [Editors' note: If Harvard could be considered a transnational university, and if a substantial fraction of the funding for the Development Advisory Service comes from the Agency for International Development of the United States government, how would this relation diagram in terms of the solid and dotted lines for direct and indirect relationships discussed above?]

C *Operations*

The foregoing political analysis makes the idea of a supranational corporation seem highly unlikely. If a supranational corporation means a globally chartered multinational enterprise, it is clear that this formally denationalizes the origin but removes none of the real conflicts stemming from the central dilemma of differing decision domains. If one means an intergovernmentally owned enterprise, to exploit the seabed for example, the crucial question is where the seat of management strategy would be within the corporation. The experience of many intergovernmental ventures in high technology have not been encouraging because political criteria have interfered with management.[13] Perhaps a more fruitful avenue for the seabed would be to explore forms of joint ventures between private multinational enterprises able to provide flexible management strategies and an intergovernmental corporation that would set the broad political parameters within which the management strategies would operate.

D *Norm creation and adjudication*

The prospects of a general agreement on multinational corporations are not very high. While it may be possible to create effective norms among limited numbers of states or norms covering a specific aspect of direct investment, the broader the agreement in numbers or scope the less likely this seems. The problem is not only one of collective action among large numbers of states. It also stems from the basic political reality that underlies corporation-state bargaining, particularly between rich and poor. When the basic bargain is political and may be obsolescing over time, poor countries might consider it unwise to institutionalize a set of norms or adjudication procedures that represent a stage in which they are relatively less favored.

These problems do not prevent states at similar levels of development from coming to agreement on certain norms, particularly as the trends described earlier make the origins and challenges posed by direct investment more symmetrical.

Nor do these problems prevent all agreements along a North-South dimension. Bilateral agreements are possible. New access agreements which divorce equity from other parts of the package of direct investment may become more prominent (though they will not solve all of the dilemmas posed by differing decision domains). A general affirmation of Calvo clauses by which corporations forgo the diplomatic protection of their home states might have a useful effect in re-affirming the political trend toward nonintervention that we described earlier. Where economic conflict is inevitable, perhaps the most important normative agreement is to isolate it from the interstate violence system.

CONCLUSION

Multinational corporations, as one of the most dynamic sectors in the world economy and as bureaucracies with transnational decision domains, are playing an important direct and indirect role in world politics. By their very transnational nature they are bound to come into conflict with states, but the conflict is rarely zero sum, and they are not a threat to the existence of nation-states. Given current trends in the utility of force for some states and the importance of economic welfare objectives in the goals of many states, multinational corporations are likely to become even more important. Given trends towards denationalization and globalization of corporate management strategies, political conditions are being created for an international organization role in the assembly of information, technical assistance to weak states, and limited agreements on norms. This is a far cry from a global agreement, but the significance of the multinational corporation in world politics is a challenge that cannot be ignored by a global organization.

NOTES

This chapter originally appeared as a prepared statement before the Group of Eminent Parsons to Study the Multinational Corporation, Geneva, 5 November 1973.

1 'Multinational Corporations in World Development,' a Report of the United Nations Secretariat (New York, 1973). As the Secretariat Report points out, the number of multinationals can be set as high as 7300 if one foreign affiliate is set as the criterion (p. 7).
2 Richard J. Barber, *The American Corporation* (New York, 1970), p. 249
3 'Transnational Organizations in World Politics,' *World Politics* XXV (April 1973), p. 366
4 Raymond Vernon, *Sovereignty at Bay* (New York, 1971)

J.S. Nye

5 See Robert O. Keohane and Joseph S. Nye, Jr. (eds.), *Transnational Relations and World Politics* (Cambridge, Mass., 1972). The general theoretical perspective underlying this statement was developed jointly with Professor Keohane.

6 Theodore Moran, 'Transnational Strategies of Protection and Defense by Multinational Corporations: Spreading the Risk and Raising the Cost for Nationalization in Natural Resources,' *International Organization*, 27 (Spring 1973)

7 'Multinational Corporations and World Order,' Special Issue of *International Studies Quarterly*, 16 (December 1972), edited by George Modelski

8 J.N. Behrman, *National Interests and the Multinational Enterprise* (Englewood Cliffs, NJ, 1970)

9 David Leyton-Brown, 'Governments of Developed Countries as Hosts to Multinational Enterprise: The Canadian, British and French Policy Experience,' unpublished PHD dissertation, Department of Government, Harvard University, 1973, p. 423

10 'Multinational Enterprise and National Security,' IISS Adelphi Paper #74 (London, 1971), p. 16

11 See J.S. Nye, 'Multinational Enterprises and Prospects for Regional and Global Integration,' *The Annals*, 403 (September 1972)

12 Ibid., p. 128

13 M.S. Hochmuth, 'The Effect of Structure on Strategy: The Government-Sponsored Multinational Joint Venture,' unpublished doctoral dissertation, Harvard Business School, 1972

222

PART TWO

Energy and the Environment

Economists, like most people, want a cleaner environment. Economists, however, do not discuss the *absolute* level of *cleanliness* but the *relative* level. Environmental degradation should be limited to the point where the benefits of limiting emissions equal the costs of emission controls. Economists then generally do not call for clean air (a vacuous phrase) but for air clean enough, where the costs of making air cleaner would exceed the benefits. All-or-nothing decisions are not economic decisions.

The question then of energy and the environment is not one of energy versus the environment, or of limiting energy consumption to protect the environment. The choice is between the price of energy and the degree to which environment degradation due to energy discovery, production, transportation, and consumption is reduced.

As Dewees shows, there are substantial costs to society associated with all facets of energy production and consumption. Oil tanker spills and automobile emissions – such environmental side-effects must be reduced to the point where the costs of reduction equal the benefits. *But* we seldom have any knowledge of the costs of control or the benefits from controls. What are the benefits of reducing the level of particulate emissions from burning coal and gasoline? We have little adequate knowledge of the harm to individuals; we *think* these entail cleaning costs and illness. We have little information on air currents and the ways in which nature dissipates emissions at various wind and atmospheric conditions. On the other side, little is known of the technology of emission control and the costs of emission reduction are not well known.

What policies should society thus adopt to bring about an unknown but desired reduction in emissions when control costs and benefits are uncertain? As Dewees elucidates, wise men faced with such difficult decisions will move slowly. Moreover, incentives must be given to improve technology and to reduce emissions to the correct degree. Absolute prohibitions or fixed standards can only do so if both the costs and benefits are well known. In other cases (which are most cases) taxes on emissions are the best public policy. If the tax is set at the likely level of benefits (and readjusted as more information becomes available), then the least cost method of emission control is ensured. Reasonable, flexible environmental policies would ensure that the trade-off between environmental quality and the price of energy would move in society's best interests.

DONALD N. DEWEES

Energy consumption and environmental quality

INTRODUCTION

Concern over the health effects of sulfur dioxide emissions leads to restrictions on the sulfur content of coal burned for generating electricity, which causes a shift to oil and natural gas. Because of concern over automobile emissions, pollution controls are required which increase automotive fuel consumption, and delay construction of new refineries until it is decided whether unleaded fuel will be required to protect catalytic mufflers. Concern for the natural environment delays for several years the construction of major pipelines and halts exploration and drilling for oil in offshore areas near population centers. The result of these and other events is a sharp increase in the price of oil, natural gas, and electricity, combined with occasional shortages of gasoline and other petroleum products. Pessimists conclude from these facts that improving environmental quality requires reducing energy consumption.

As world demand for petroleum products rises, and as oil is produced from ever more remote locations, ocean shipment of petroleum increases. Simultaneous increases in the size of oil tankers and the number of tankers traveling are accompanied by a great rise in the frequency and severity of oil spills. The oil discharged from these tankers into the sea blackens miles of coast line, killing wildlife and eliminating recreational activities, in some cases, for years. The continuing demand for coal is satisfied in part by strip mining which converts thousands of acres of forest and rolling countryside into desolate wastelands of jagged rock piles and eroding mud banks. An alarmed public concludes that increased energy use will inevitably reduce the quality of the environment.

Donald N. Dewees

We can test the validity of these conclusions by examining the technological alternatives for protecting environmental quality, the alternatives for energy production and use, and supply and demand conditions for the several fossil fuels. This information can provide the necessary linkages between energy consumption and environmental quality, in both the short and the long run. We will investigate the relationships between energy and environmental quality in two categories: fuel production and transportation, and energy consumption. The analysis will be confined to the fossil fuels – coal, oil, and gas – and to nuclear power for electricity generation.

ENVIRONMENTAL CONSEQUENCES OF
FUEL PRODUCTION AND TRANSPORTATION

A major environmental problem associated with coal production and transportation is the disturbance of the land surface caused by strip mining. The least-cost means of strip mining is to tear off the soil and rocks (or 'overburden') above the coal seam, and pile it in long rows adjacent to the current excavation. In this operation all top soil and vegetation are lost, and the landscape appears as if it had been deeply tilled by a giant plow. Frequently, little or no vegetation grows for years or even decades after such mining, during which time the soil is washed into nearby streams. Rain water falling on the spoil banks may leach acid out of the ground, causing further water pollution problems in adjacent river basins.[1] The destruction of the affected land is total, and to nearby waterways may be quite severe.

This widely deplored rape of the landscape is not, however, an inevitable consequence of strip mining. In Germany the common practice is to remove top soil and store it separately from other overburden so that it can be replaced on top once the land is restored. After the coal is removed, the overburden is replaced in a level condition, the top soil distributed, and new vegetation planted. In five or ten years it is frequently difficult to tell that an area has been strip mined. The cost of this reclamation in dollars per acre is very high. However if the seam of coal being extracted is reasonably thick, the increase in the cost per ton of coal may range from 25 per cent down to a small percentage.[2] While a single operator who is forced to adopt such reclamation standards would probably be driven out of business by his competitors, a uniform requirement for all strip-mine operations would probably reduce total coal extraction by a small percentage. In short, the cost of nearly complete restoration of strip-mined areas is substantial but certainly not intolerable for the industry as a whole.

When coal is taken from deep shafts rather than stripped from the surface, other environmental problems arise. Water can leach acid out of deep mines to

226

pollute nearby streams just as in strip mining. In addition, surface subsidence can occur if insufficient coal is left for support. Great piles of refuse are removed along with the coal, and can cause aesthetic and erosion problems if not properly disposed of. All these problems can be solved, but at a cost.

Production of crude oil involves several environmental problems. There is a danger that oil under natural pressure may burst through the well or surrounding formations causing a blowout. On land this leads to a risk of fire, although the direct environmental damage is usually not large since dikes or other measures can contain the oil flow. In offshore drilling operations, a blowout will cause pollution problems of the water surface and adjacent beaches and shoreline. Alternatively the undersea pipelines which bring this oil ashore can rupture. Fish and shellfish may be killed directly by the oil, or die out because of damage to spawning areas. The Santa Barbara channel spill is a classic example of an offshore oil seepage.

As in the case of strip mining, several technological approaches can reduce this kind of risk. Different drilling methods can minimize the danger of blowout or casing failure. The installation of automatic chokes on the well can permit rapid closing of the well in case a blowout occurs, thereby minimizing the amount of oil spilled. While these measures might be expensive, they are technologically feasible, and can greatly reduce the risk of environmental damage. On the other hand, it is very expensive to inspect undersea pipes.

In recent years the spillage of oil transported in ocean tankers has become a serious environmental problem. Part of this pollution results from using sea water as ballast in tanks which had previously contained oil and which therefore contaminate the water before it is pumped back into the sea. Several methods are available for reducing the oil discharged from this source. The more extensive problem is that of spillage occurring when loaded tankers are damaged by natural causes or by collision with other ships. These risks can also be reduced by improving navigational equipment on the tankers and on shore in heavily traveled waters, by improving the maneuverability of large tankers, and by modifying their design so that they can better withstand occasional abuse.

Even surface transportation of oil through pipelines is not entirely without risks. The risks are minimal in temperate climates where leaks are unlikely to develop, and the damage from a leak can easily be contained. In Arctic areas, however, the vegetation is so fragile that an oil spill may leave scars on the landscape for years or decades. Furthermore, the high oil temperature, necessary to keep it moving in cold climates, can melt the permafrost on which the pipe is laid, leading to erosion and destruction of this layer of the ground surface.

The probability of leakage from pipelines can be reduced by conservative pipeline design. The damage from a given leak can be reduced by more frequent installation of emergency shut-off valves. And the permafrost damage can be reduced by insulating the pipeline and carefully designing its location and support structures.

In all cases it appears that environmental risks can be greatly reduced by expenditures which reduce the probability of spillage, and reduce the damage once a spill occurs. Even if these risks cannot be eliminated, it should be possible to find a degree of protection which adequately balances the expenditure on protection against the reduction of environmental risk. In no case does it appear that a substantial reduction in risk would come close to doubling the delivered price of the petroleum. The choice is not between energy production and environment but between cheap energy production and the environment.

ENVIRONMENTAL CONSEQUENCES
OF ENERGY CONSUMPTION

Burning coal as a source of heat causes emissions of particulates, sulfur dioxide, and oxides of nitrogen. Particulates are the fine pieces of ash or dust which constitute most visible smoke from power plants; 40 to 60 per cent of these particulates can be removed by mechanical collectors, and up to 99.5 per cent by electrostatic precipitators. The cost of controlling particulates increases much more rapidly than the degree of control. For example, increasing precipitator efficiency from 90 to 99.5 per cent more than doubles the cost of installing and operating the precipitators. Still, the total cost of 99.5 per cent efficient controls on a new coal fired plant would add only a few per cent to the final cost of the electricity generated.[3]

The production of sulfur dioxide, when the sulfur in coal combines with oxygen during the fuel burning process, is much more difficult to control than the particulate problem. It does not appear technically or economically feasible to remove sulfur from the coal before it is burned. Yet, separating the sulfur dioxide gas from other stack gases is both difficult and expensive. The most promising technology involves scrubbing stack gases with a mixture of water and a crushed limestone.

This can remove up to 75 per cent of the sulfur oxide in stack gases but it has several drawbacks. First, it cools the gases so that instead of rising as previously, they fall rapidly to the ground. This can actually increase sulfur dioxide concentrations near the smoke stack, as occurred in the power station at Battersea, England. Second, the process generates an enormous volume of limestone slurry which must be disposed of in some way. Third, the probable cost of this system is tremendous; it may cost as much to clean the stack gases as it does to purchase the coal itself.[4] Even if this process becomes technologically feasible, which it is not now, it would greatly increase the price of electricity.

228

The only alternatives to this technologically unproven and high-cost scrubbing are the use of tall smoke stacks to disperse the fumes, or conversion to lower-sulfur fuels. While tall stacks are a popular solution in less densely populated areas, it is not clear whether they reduce the problem, or simply spread it around so it is not as perceptible in any one location. Such dispersal can reduce or eliminate the killing of sensitive plant species by these gases, but the acid rains which result from precipitation in sulfur dioxide atmospheres are less powerfully acidic, but more widely spread. Before tall stacks are accepted as a solution it must be shown that they actually reduce total damage rather than spreading the same damages over a larger area. Low-sulfur coals are less readily available than those with high sulfur content and generally are not as conveniently located for the major North American power plants. The Appalachian coals, widely used by power plants in the northeast United States and eastern Canada, are generally high in sulfur content. Switching to lower-sulfur fuels may dramatically increase fuel costs.

Finally, modern high-temperature electrical generating stations produce oxides of nitrogen when burning coal, or even oil and gas. These oxides form because of the high boiler temperatures, and particular design configurations in the combustion and boiler area. While factors determining their production are not well understood, it appears that redesign of new boilers can substantially reduce production of these gases at low cost. It does not appear feasible to redesign old boilers for controlling these gases.

The environmental problems with oil burning are reduced by the fact that virtually no particulates are produced. In some cases a small quantity of oily soot is produced, but the volume is insignificant compared to particulate emissions from coal combustion. Therefore the only attention given to the problem for oil boilers or furnaces is to improve design of the burner itself, to reduce production of solid emissions.

Where the oil has a substantial sulfur content, as is the case with many residual oils, the same sulfur oxide emission problem arises as with coal. The technological options for stack-gas scrubbing are the same as in the case of coal, and therefore quite unattractive. For oil, unlike coal, there is another alternative: reducing the sulfur content of the oil before it is burned. Refineries can, and many currently do, include a desulfurization stage in the refining process, which allows production of a low-sulfur residual oil. While this process substantially increases refining costs, the percentage increase in the price of oil is relatively modest. It seems clear that, for oil-burning installations, removal of sulfur from the fuel is far superior to stack-gas scrubbing under current technological conditions.

Another major air pollution problem associated with fossil fuel combustion is emissions from automobiles. Automotive exhaust contains hydrocarbons, carbon monoxide, oxides of nitrogen, and usually lead where this is present in the fuel.

Donald N. Dewees

Automotive pollution control programs in the United States began reducing carbon monoxide and hydrocarbons in 1966 for California and 1968 nationwide. Since 1973, oxides of nitrogen have also been controlled, although to a much more limited extent. Current technology can apparently reduce hydrocarbons and carbon monoxide to one-quarter their initial values or less at a relatively modest cost, perhaps a few per cent of the total cost of operating the automobile. Controlling oxides of nitrogen is substantially more expensive, and has resulted in fuel consumption increases for recent years.

As with other pollution controls, the greater the degree of control, the higher its cost per unit.[5] For this reason earlier legislative standards reducing automotive pollutants to between 5 and 10 per cent of their pre-controlled values has been postponed and may be postponed and modified again. Still, with the average life of an automobile at almost ten years in North America, holding present controls for several years would result in continuing improvement of air quality as old cars are removed from the highways. And, over time, we can expect that abatement technology will improve, allowing further reduction at reasonable costs.

The use of nuclear power in electrical generating stations poses new and relatively unknown problems. As fuel is used up, there are radioactive wastes to be disposed of. With the low volume of nuclear power used until now this has not been a serious problem but in the future it may become more serious as the wilderness areas in which such wastes can be buried without danger of leakage or environmental contamination are exhausted. There is also the danger of explosion, which, though apparently very small, is not entirely zero. Presumably, design considerations can, and perhaps already have, reduced to an acceptable level the risk of explosion and the hazards that might result.

Any time that fossil fuels or nuclear power are used for electricity generation in steam boilers, waste heat is produced. Since the efficiency of modern thermal generating stations is about 35 per cent, at least 65 per cent of the heat value in fuel is discharged to the environment as waste heat. Usually this appears in cooling water discharged to a stream or lake. If the heat addition is large relative to the capacity of the water body, substantial temperature increases can occur. In some cases these temperature increases are damaging to aquatic life and reduce the quality of the water.

The alternative to waste-heat discharge into water is discharging the same heat into the air. Recently, many power plants have been required to install air-cooling towers to reduce heat load in adjacent waters. This clearly raises the question whether, at the time when warm waters are a problem, increased air temperature and humidity may not also be undesirable. If both are undesirable, there is really no possibility of a 'cure.' This is a problem which will continue to get worse as the density of power stations increases, and will be worst of all with nuclear power since its thermal efficiency is somewhat lower than that of fossil fuel plants. It should be noted that fossil fuel combustion in internal combustion engines such as the automobile also produces waste heat in even higher proportion to the usable heat energy. Where the climate is frequently warm, and any increases in air temperature are unfavorably regarded, waste heat disposal may impose serious limits on total fuel use within such areas.

It should be noted that economies of scale are generally experienced in pollution-control facilities. If a million tons of coal are to be burned either in a single electricity-generating station or one thousand small furnaces, it is far less expensive to apply a given degree of particulate control to the large boiler than to the many small furnaces.[6] This is one reason why coal has frequently been banned for domestic use although the local power-generating stations continue to use this fuel. The power station can economically install particulate controls where the homeowner can not. If a city which included thermal generating stations, industrial boilers, and home furnaces had to allocate coal, oil, and gas to minimize environmental problems, they would do best to concentrate coal-use in the largest power plants and boilers, oil-use in the next largest, where moderate smoke stack height can disperse such pollutants as are emitted, and gas or a clean heating oil for domestic purposes where pollution controls are uneconomic.

The above discussion indicates that several serious environmental problems are associated with fuel production, transportation, and consumption. It is also clear that in most cases we have technological alternatives to reduce the risk or impact of these problems. Except in the cases of sulfur oxides and waste heat, a large percentage reduction in environmental damage can be achieved with a small percentage increase in the cost of using the fuel.[7] We can, therefore, increase our consumption of energy without adverse environmental consequences if only we are prepared to pay more for that energy than we would pay if environmental consequences were entirely unchecked. The important trade-off to consider is not between the environment and energy, but between the environment and the *price* of energy.

ALTERNATIVE POLLUTION POLICIES
AND THEIR IMPACT

How much environmental protection?
It is sometimes suggested that environmental consequences from fuel consumption should be entirely eliminated. As a practical matter is often impossible to achieve this goal. We do not have the technology for 100 per cent removal of sulfur oxides or oxides of nitrogen from stack gases. A total prohibition on

Donald N. Dewees

emissions would eliminate the use of most energy sources and stop the production of many goods, necessities as well as luxuries. Most pollutants resulting from fuel use have a lower threshold below which they are not perceptible or not harmful or cannot be distinguished from naturally occurring levels of the pollutant. Money spent eliminating a harmless and imperceptible degree of pollution is money wasted.

The question is not whether to allow pollution, but how much pollution to allow. In a society which must satisfy its needs from limited resources, we must decide how to allocate these resources among many competing needs. No single goal such as environmental quality, no matter how meritorious, can command unlimited quantities of these resources. The protection of environmental quality must therefore depend on the cost of protecting it and the benefits which are derived from it. Economic theory suggests that a proper rule would be to reduce pollution until the marginal cost of an additional unit of reduction is just equal to the marginal benefit which that unit of reduction will provide. While measuring benefits of pollution reduction is extremely difficult, equating marginal costs and benefits is still a desirable goal.

The problem is that in the absence of pollution regulation, energy users impose costs on other members of society, through pollution or environmental damage, for which the energy user need not pay. The environmental costs of energy production and use are not borne by energy users, nor reflected in the price of energy. Thus energy is indirectly subsidized by those who suffer from the pollution. If we require reasonable pollution controls, or require polluters to pay for damage they cause, this will impose the costs on the individuals causing them. Energy prices will rise to reflect these full social costs. This price rise will have the beneficial effect of reducing energy consumption, which will further reduce environmental damage. Thus, energy price increases associated with reasonable environmental protection policies should be viewed not as an added burden on the consumer, but as a correction to a defective price system and an added incentive to reduce environmental damage.

When evaluating pollution-control policies it is important to distinguish between stocks and flows of pollutants. The flow is the hourly or daily emission of pollution into the air, while the stock is the total amount in the air at any moment of time. Some energy-related pollutants are removed rapidly from the environment, as large particles which fall from the atmosphere, or as sulfur dioxide is precipated in rain water. They do not accumulate over time so that a reduction in the emission rate improves environmental quality at once. Other pollutants, such as oil spilled on land or water, or some very fine particulates, remain in the environment for a long period. They are not as durable, however, as mercury or DDT which may move through the food chain to contaminate plant and animal

232

life for many years after emissions have terminated. For these pollutants the harm results not from the daily discharge, but from the stock in the environment which has built up over a period of years. A reduction in the emission rate will not necessarily reduce the stock; it may only reduce its rate of growth. The long-run solution for such conservative pollutants may be to reduce their emission almost to zero, to avoid further accumulation.

How fast a clean-up?

When a pollution problem is recognized, and sufficient public support collected to pass control legislation, there are usually strong pressures to solve the problem as rapidly as possible. This may lead to the establishment of rigid standards designed to achieve the desired equilibrium environmental quality within a year or two. If there is an immediate danger to human life, as in the case of mercury, or if the destruction of a species seems imminent, as in the case of DDT, such precipitate action may be defensible and desirable. But usually, where the harm is less severe and less immediate, there are several advantages to a more gradual approach.

First, we noted in the previous section the difficulties of estimating the benefits and costs of a particular degree of pollution control. If we were to require today that five years hence some source of pollution must reduce emissions by 90 per cent, we run the risk that half-way to that goal rising costs may have outstripped public demand for further improvement. If, on the other hand, we embark upon a program certain to bring significant improvement in environmental quality each year over a substantial period of time then we can be assured that at least things are getting better, and that they are not going to overshoot the point at which further investment is unjustifiable. Thus, a gradual clean-up permits the trial-and-error method of determining the desired degree of environmental quality.

A moderate rate of improvement has other advantages. If the pollutant is being controlled for the first time, there is every reason to expect that better and less expensive means will gradually be found to achieve a given degree of control. If we require a high degree of control quickly, very high costs will be incurred. If more time is allowed to reach the same goal, that goal will generally be reached at substantially lower costs. If there is sufficient pressure on the industry to promote invention and technical progress, then relatively few expensive and inefficient devices will be installed.

Furthermore, short-run economic dislocations can be minimized. The sudden imposition of pollution controls can cause the closing of some plants using particularly dirty fuels, if little time is allowed for adjustment. Since fossil fuels are close substitutes in boiler use, sudden demands that cleaner fuel be used are likely to cause massive shifts in fuel use. Generally, supplies can adjust only slowly so that prices will rise very substantially in response to short-run demand shifts. In the longer run, however, the supplies can adapt much more widely, so that price changes resulting from fuel switching should be less if that switching is accomplished over a period of several years then if it is imposed in one or two. If we calculate the cost of a fuel-switching program based on current prices, and the program results in large shifts in demand for cleaner fuels, the cost of the program will be understated since the fuel price increase for cleaner fuels will be much greater after the program than before. A gradual program would allow discovery of this situation and modification of the policy to suit actual resulting costs.

Regulation or taxation?
By now it should be clear that predicting the cost of a given degree of pollution control is quite difficult. When new technology is involved, as is the case with sulfur dioxide pollution, oil tanker spills, and protecting the arctic environment from pipeline leaks, years of experience may be required before precise protection costs can be established. One solution to this problem is the gradual approach just suggested wherein standards are raised over a period of many years as experience accumulates regarding costs and benefits.

Another approach is to replace standards with economic incentives. If we do not know the cost of stack-gas scrubbing for sulfur oxides and therefore do not know how much control is actually desired, we can establish a tax on sulfur oxide emissions rather than imposing regulations. If the tax reflects some rough estimate of the benefits to be gained from reducing sulfur oxides, or a reasonable amount to be spent on controlling them, then it will provide an incentive for polluters to adopt controls which cost up to the amount of the tax. Extremely expensive controls will not be demanded by a tax of reasonable proportions. And whenever control costs fall, as they tend to do over time, then the degree of control will be increased.[8]

Such a tax has two advantages over standards. First, it avoids enormously wasteful expenditures on controls which were not anticipated at the time of legislation. Second, it creates a positive financial incentive to develop new and better means of pollution control since new devices which are more efficient can reduce the amount of tax. Since technological progress offers our best promise for reconciling energy and environmental demands, it is a vital characteristic of these policies that they promote technological progress.

Effects of policies
Substantial limitations have been placed upon the emission of sulfur oxides from fossil-fuel combustion in the past few years, and further regulation is likely. This has led to extensive research and development on technologies for scrubbing stack

gases, but none of the resulting devices has proven to be technologically or economically feasible at present. Thus, the primary effect of sulfur oxide restriction is to reduce the demand for high-sulfur fuels and increase demands for low-sulfur coal, oil, natural gas, and nuclear power. These demand shifts have already contributed to substantial relative price increases for the lower-sulfur fossil fuels. Already we can see agencies which established control programs on the assumption of stable relative prices retreating somewhat from planned further restrictions because of the much higher cost of fuel switching given the new relative prices.

The high cost of current sulfur-control programs might have been avoided if, instead of absolute restrictions on fuel sulfur content, a tax on that content had been imposed. A tax set at a reasonable level would cause consumers to shift to low-sulfur fuels until their relative price exceeded that of dirtier fuels by the amount of the tax. The magnitude of the tax would place an upper limit on expenditures for pollution control, and thus limit the swings in demand for various fuels resulting from many independent environmental policies. If the tax were reduced when pollution controls were installed, then a continuous incentive would be provided to develop and install stack-gas scrubbing technology whenever that became available at a reasonable price. There would be no requirement to install it before that time. Proper design of a tax could thus achieve reasonable improvements in environmental quality without unreasonable costs being imposed, and without adding excessively to the chaos in energy markets.

Automobile pollution controls have substantially reduced pollution levels since 1968 in North America, and are scheduled to go still further in the future. One side-effect of reducing pollution levels has been that fuel consumption has increased, primarily because of lower compression ratios necessary to eliminate oxides of nitrogen. Further reductions in fuel economy are likely when the next round of standards is imposed. In addition, the 1975 standards will probably require widespread use of catalysts in the exhaust system, which means unleaded gas. This in turn means that less gasoline is produced from each barrel of crude oil, raising still further the amount of crude necessary to produce a vehicle-mile of transportation.

It is most unlikely that these energy consequences were anticipated when the schedule of pollution abatement was written into law. The rigid system of emission standards, however, provides no means to adapt to the higher costs implicit in fuel-economy losses except for a one-year delay of effective implementation dates. If some lessening of the speed or severity of regulation were desired, this could be achieved automatically by a more flexible auto pollution control policy. If the standards were enforced, not by a prohibitive $10,000-per-vehicle fine, but by a payment related to the excess emissions, then manufacturers and consumers would retain some choices. If unforeseen by-products of pollution control raised costs unexpectedly, cars could be manufactured to some less stringent standard at the penalty of paying the additional tax or charge. If this charge is properly selected, it would impose substantial pressure to develop cleaner and less expensive technology, but would not require the installation of unreasonably expensive technology. Unforeseen developments like rapid fuel price increases could be adapted to by slowing the rate of control, and paying a higher charge instead. This mechanism might therefore automatically balance the benefits of pollution control against the costs which are unknown until almost the date of manufacture. Once again, environmental policies may have unnecessarily exacerbated energy problems.

The environmental problems caused by strip mining have led to legislation which requires a degree of reclamation of strip-mined land. This has increased the cost of producing coal. Here, however, there is less need for a flexible policy. The cost of reclamation can be estimated with some accuracy since the technology is reasonably standard. Changes in the price of fuels will not directly affect the cost of this environmental protection. If the improvement to the environment is judged to be worth the anticipated cost of some degree of reclamation, then it is perfectly reasonable that the coal companies bear this cost, and pass it on to their customers. In this way restoring the environment becomes a natural cost of producing coal, the benefits of which exceed the reclamation cost if the policy is a wise one. If the cost of reclamation can be estimated with reasonable accuracy then the kinds of regulations which have been adopted in the past are a perfectly appropriate means for control in the future. Only if these costs are uncertain or highly variable would there be some need to move to a pricing or tax-incentive system to provide flexibility. Since it appears that reclamation methods are available which can restore the land very close to its initial condition, there is no need to ban strip mining entirely.

Protecting the environment from oil spills during production and transport of oil involves some current and some unknown technology. Because the drilling methods and transport methods are themselves new and innovative, the means for protecting the environment from them must also be new and relatively unknown. Therefore it is difficult to estimate the cost of achieving various degrees of protection from this hazard. The damage, however, unlike air pollution which can gradually be corrected by the self-cleansing action of the atmosphere, may endure for many years. Shellfish beds which are destroyed by oil pollution may not return to full production for a long time. Thus the potential risks may be quite high.

In a mixed case such as this it will require astute policy-making to develop regulatory institutions which can adequately protect the environment from unknown risks without imposing excessive costs on the oil industry. Perhaps these policies should include changes in liability laws so that producers and transporters of petroleum products will bear the full social cost of any spills that occur. Perhaps further regulation of marine activities and safety standards is necessary. Undoubtedly further research is called for into the extent of these risks and the cost of avoiding them. However, assuming that policies are adopted which reasonably relate the environmental protection cost to the harm it has avoided, the extra cost of oil production and transport should happily be borne by producers and then passed on to consumers as a natural cost of using this oil.

CONCLUSION

Some people have opposed protecting and improving environmental quality because it raises the price of energy. This argument is entirely fallacious. If we place a positive value on environmental quality, then the question is whether a particular environmental protection program achieves benefits which are greater than the costs it imposes. If it does it is entirely appropriate to pursue that program, and to impose the environmental protection costs on the polluter. The energy price increase in such cases is outweighed by the benefits of less air and water pollution. If the price of energy rises, it further reduces environmental damage by reducing total energy consumption. Proposals to grant subsidies or tax-concessions to energy producing or consuming firms to offset the costs of controlling environmental degradation are preposterous, because they defeat an important effect of the control program: reducing the activity which causes the environmental degradation.

Some people have suggested that energy growth should be limited or prohibited in order to save environmental quality. It appears, however, that even with existing technology there are many ways to preserve environmental quality and enjoy increased energy consumption. With future technological progress we can probably enjoy still more of both. Since large percentage reductions in environmental damage can be achieved by small percentage increases in energy cost, the choice is not energy or environment but cheap energy or environmental quality. If modest price increases can buy much more environmental protection, *and* tend to conserve energy resources, they should be widely approved.

Because technological progress offers great hope for further improving the energy-price/environment trade-off, this progress should be encouraged. If we are worried about environmental quality we should regulate this quality directly, rather than using indirect methods such as limiting or restricting energy use. By operating directly on the parameter in which we are interested, we will encourage the maximum technological progress to reduce or eliminate the problem.

Our failure to achieve a better combination of environmental quality and energy use in the past is undoubtedly due to a failure to develop and adopt better techno-

Donald N. Dewees

logy. This results in turn from a failure to adopt the administrative mechanisms which are necessary to call forth the most vigorous technological and economic responses to these problems. If we can adopt more sophisticated, reasonable, and flexible environmental policies, we should greatly improve the trade-off between environmental quality and energy prices for many years to come.

NOTES

The support of the Inland Waters Directorate of the Department of the Environment through a grant to the Institute of Environmental Sciences and Engineering is gratefully acknowledged.
1 G. Garvey, *Energy, Ecology, Economy* (New York 1972), chap. 4
2 Ibid. estimates that a 10 per cent coal price increase would pay for restoration of strip mining operations *and* protect against subsidence and acid drainage from deep mines.
3 US Department of Health, Education, and Welfare, Public Health Service, *Control Techniques for Particulate Pollution* (Washington 1969)
4 One estimate shows scrubbing costs of over $0.50 per million BTU when the coal itself cost only $0.35 per million BTU. Commonwealth Edison Company, 'Memorandum Regarding SO_2 Removal Experience and Cost Estimates,' 20 Dec. 1972; revised 8 Feb. 1973
5 For an analysis of auto pollution control costs see D.N. Dewees, *Economics and Public Policy: The Automobile Pollution Case* (Cambridge, Mass. 1974)
6 These economies of scale are discussed in US Environmental Protection Agency, *Control Techniques for Particulate Air Pollutants* (Research Triangle Park NC 1969), chap. 6.
7 A general review of the costs of reducing pollution from fuel burning is contained in *The Economics of Clean Air,* Report of the Administration of the Environmental Protection Agency to Congress (Washington DC 1972). Substantial reductions are estimated to add small percentages to the prices of final goods.
8 The arguments for effluent charges are well presented in A.V. Kneese and B.T. Bower, 'Causing Offsite Costs to be Reflected in Waste Disposal Decisions,' in R. Dorfman and N.S. Dorfman, eds., *Economics of the Environment* (New York 1972)

The persistent theme of these volumes is that the current 'energy crisis' is essentially a short-run phenomenon resulting from inadequate planning and poor policy execution. Energy shortages have not resulted from a fundamental change in the relationship of man and nature. If this view is correct, and if we are able to solve our immediate problems, then energy consumption can be expected to continue to increase on a world-wide scale. But will this expected increase not itself create climate changes which themselves may result in a fundamental change in the relationship between man and nature?

Dr Kellogg reviews the prospects for such developments which might occur as a result of man as a factor in climate change. His overall view is quite sanguine. Throughout its history, the earth has been subject to many substantial changes in climate. Man, in the view of Dr Kellogg, is not likely to cause incremental climate changes beyond the ranges of either previous world experience or man's ability to adapt. Dr Kellogg reaches this conclusion after examination of a base case which does not include increased efficiency in energy use or any economic-environmental benefits from such possible technical advances as cost-effective use of direct solar energy.

The chapter by Dr Kellogg should be compared to the environmental chapters by Stoel & Waverman and Dewees, and to the Roberts chapter on the 'limits to growth' hypothesis, and chapters on the problems of nuclear power by Kneese and Carnesale & Elleman, and the chapter on energy and growth by Barnett. It should also be noted that, if the basic theme of these volumes is wrong, if it is not technically and economically possible to increase world energy consumption on the scale assumed in this chapter, then the problem examined by Dr Kellogg is of less immediate concern. We do not believe this to be the case.

WILLIAM W. KELLOGG

Mankind as a factor in climate change

The thought of mankind tampering with the climate of his planet is an explosive
one. There is currently a kind of tribal guilt complex concerned with anything
we do that changes nature, and this is sometimes referred to as 'the environmental ethic.' Considering all the fuss generated by the proposal to build one nuclear
power plant on a marsh in Maine or one airport at the edge of a famous swamp
in Florida, one wonders how much fuss the environmentalists are going to raise
when they realize that we may be toying with the mechanisms that control ice
ages. Actually, we have already started, as will be pointed out later.

There does not yet seem to be a very great public furor over this matter, probably because, first, the changes are almost certainly going to be pretty slow
when measured in units of the term of office of a president or other politician,
and, second, because we are not able to be very definite about what to expect. It
is hard to get excited about slow and uncertain changes when we are faced with
so many near and certain crises at home and abroad.

The purpose of this brief report is to convey a feeling for the time scale and
magnitude of the climate changes that man seems likely to cause, and to emphasize the large uncertainties in *any* prediction of climate change at this stage of
our knowledge. Not only are we just beginning to understand the physical factors that govern climate, with a long path ahead of us before we can make any
sure predictions, but these uncertainties about the physical world are com-
pounded by the uncertainty about what mankind will do in the next century.

There would be no purpose in even attempting a prediction of the role that
man may play in altering the climate were it not for the fact that we have gone
far enough in the development of mathematical climate models and a 'theory of

William W. Kellogg

climate' to be able to isolate some of the factors to a certain extent. We conceive the atmosphere-ocean-land-ice system as a highly interactive and complex one, with many feedback loops in it that amplify or suppress a change; and it is influenced by a variety of *external* forces that may be subject to change, such as the sun, volcanic activity, the circulations of the deep ocean – and now mankind. While a prediction of climate change in an absolute sense is still beyond the capability of our climate models, we can say something about the consequences if some specific boundary condition or external input to the system changed.

In order to do this, we will introduce the climate system and some of the factors that govern it, and then discuss the conceivable limits of societal growth, in terms of energy production, as a gauge of the changes that mankind might be able to cause. We are mainly interested in an *upper* limit to this growth, since this puts a kind of upper limit to its effect. If a reader does not agree with our estimate of society's possible growth – and some will surely not – he is free to scale the effect to suit his own taste. It is doubtful if he will arrive at a grossly different conclusion, however.

INGREDIENTS OF A CLIMATE PREDICTION

Let us consider what are the main factors that determine the climate of any part of the earth and of the earth as a whole, and identify which factors mankind can have some influence on. After all, there are not too many levers that he *can* reach in this massive earth-atmosphere-ocean-ice system.

The key to the matter lies in the heat available to the system, and in the internal processes that transfer energy from one part to another. Indeed, since the atmosphere (and to a lesser extent the ocean) is a large heat engine, it makes good sense to focus on the heating and cooling processes that drive it.

Solar energy input to the system
First, there is the solar radiation that provides the heat for the whole system. We can neglect all other *natural* sources of heat, including geothermal heat, but, as we will show, not necessarily *man-made* heat. This solar source of heat is a sort of standard against which we can compare any other energy inputs to the system, so here are a few numbers to keep in mind.

While the flux of solar radiation that hits the earth has a power density of about 1400 watts per square meter (w/m^2), the average over the sphere of the earth is $\frac{1}{4}$ of this, and slightly less than $\frac{1}{3}$ of that is reflected back to space by clouds, snow and ice, the atmosphere itself, and the earth's surface. Thus, about 240 w/m^2 is the average flux of energy retained by the earth. About 65 per cent of this solar heat is absorbed at the surface, or 155 watts/m². A latitude-by-latitude analysis by Budyko (1963), taking into account the fact that the continental land masses are generally distributed at middle latitudes and have a higher albedo than the oceans, shows that the continental heat flux that is absorbed is only 65 per cent of the average, or about 100 watts/m². So remember 150 watts/m² as a round number to define the average solar heat absorbed by the earth's surface (including, of course, the ocean surface).

Multiplying this by the area of the earth (5.2×10^{14}m²), the *total* rate of solar energy absorption at the earth's surface is about 8×10^{16} watts, or 8×10^7 G watts, which will be a convenient round number to use later on. (A G watt, or gigowatt, is equal to one billion watts.)

Ways that mankind can modulate solar heat input

It is well known that there are several ways by which we can change or modulate the amount of solar energy that is absorbed and retained by the earth-atmosphere-ocean-ice system (henceforth to be referred to simply as 'the system'), and these have been discussed by a number of authors, for example Mitchell (1971, 1973), Schneider and Kellogg (1973), and the SMIC Report (1971). I therefore propose to review them only very briefly here.

One way to change the heat balance is to introduce some infra-red absorbing gas into the atmosphere that will stay there for a long enough time to accumulate (Schneider and Kellogg 1973). Carbon dioxide is the celebrated case in point, and Figure 1 prepared by Lester Machta and included in the SMIC Report (1971) shows the buildup of CO_2 from 1860AD to the present, and that which can be expected to the year 2000 as a result of our burning of fossil fuels all over the world. Using the convectively adjusted global average radiation model of Manabe and Wetherald (1967) or the similar model of Rasool and Schneider (1971), we find that this would by itself cause an increase of about 0.5°C in the surface temperature by 2000AD. Clearly, if we went on burning coal for another thirty years or more there would be a continued increase in CO_2 in the atmosphere and a continued rise due to this effect alone. One of the difficulties with such a prediction is the uncertain rate of absorption of CO_2 in the oceans and the biosphere, which would have an influence on the amount remaining in the atmosphere. In any case, it seems that this will be an effect tending toward an increase in mean surface temperature of 1°C, or perhaps a bit more, by the middle of next century.

Another man-made addition to the atmosphere that has resulted in a long-term trend at many places is the addition of smoke and smog particles, or aerosols (suspended particles). These aerosols also influence the radiation balance, and recent studies of the effect of aerosols on surface temperature by Rasool and Schneider

William W. Kellogg

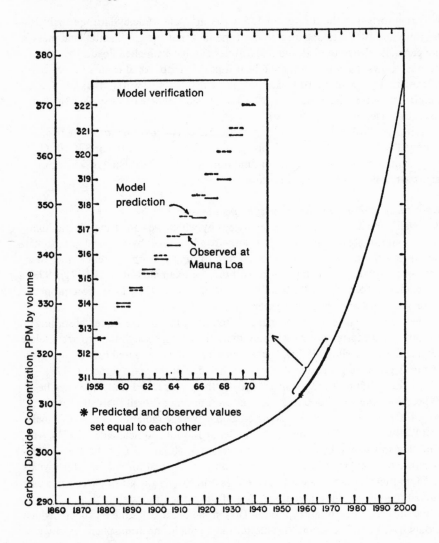

Figure 1 The observed increase in CO_2 concentration in the atmosphere, observed at the Mauna Loa Observatory in Hawaii for the period 1958 to 1970, is compared to a model calculation by Lester Machta that estimates the change from 1860 (the start of the industrial revolution) to 2000AD. For a description of the model see the SMIC Report (1971).

244

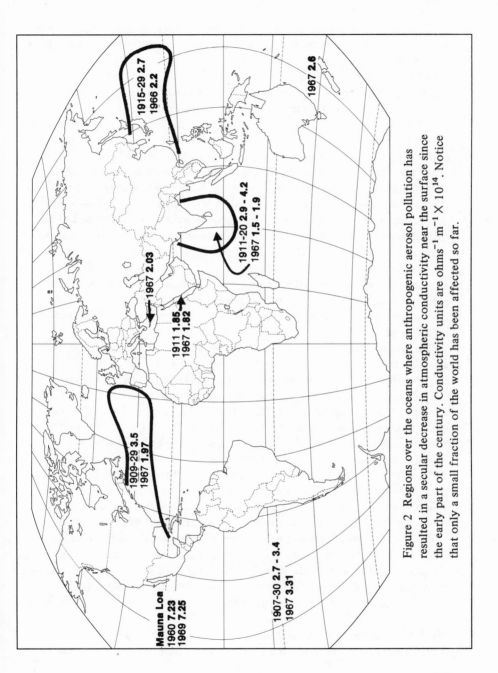

Figure 2 Regions over the oceans where anthropogenic aerosol pollution has resulted in a secular decrease in atmospheric conductivity near the surface since the early part of the century. Conductivity units are ohms^{-1} m^{-1} $\times$ 10^{14} . Notice that only a small fraction of the world has been affected so far.

245

William W. Kellogg

(1971) and Yamamoto and Tanaka (1972) strongly suggest that in regions where aerosols increase due to human activity there will be an increase in the over-all albedo (on the average) and a consequent cooling.

This subject is complicated by the fact that we do not now know enough about the optical properties of various kinds of aerosols, and this has to be known in order to make a good estimate of their effects on heat balance. We will not quarrel with these sets of calculations, which are the best that can be done now. However, we must point out that any estimate of an aerosol effect that assumes a *uniform global* change of aerosol content must be in doubt, and point to the recent paper by Cobb (1973). (See Figure 2.) Aerosols in the lower atmosphere have a mean life of from three days to a week, according to Martell (1971), so it is not surprising that Figure 2 shows only a few areas over the oceans where significant changes have occurred, presumably because of the industrial and agricultural activities of man. While aerosols may have some effect in large regions, as suggested by Bryson (1967), it is hard to imagine any growth of industrial activity that could cause a very marked *global* increase in aerosol loading of the atmosphere. Furthermore, efforts are being made in many parts of the world to curb particulate pollution, and as more nuclear power comes on line the relative amount of fossil fuels to be used to power our society will decrease. But more on this later.

There is one other man-made aerosol that might conceivably have a significant effect on the solar input, and that is the 'smog' that might be created in the stratosphere from very large numbers of high-flying jets (ssts). The scep Report (1970) suggested that this might cause an increase in stratospheric temperature, and a much smaller decrease in surface temperature. In spite of a considerable effort to improve this early estimate, sponsored by the us Department of Transportation's Climatic Impact Assessment Program (ciap), there is little more that can be said by way of a prediction at this time.

The smic Report (1971) also discusses the kinds of human activities that change the earth's surface and its *reflectivity*. There are large areas where urbanization, irrigation of deserts, and deforestation have indeed changed the character of the surface, but we have never seen a study that showed what the *net* effect of all these changes has been or will be. One gets the impression from the smic Report that the trend is toward a lower albedo due to these changes, e.g., especially urbanization and irrigation of deserts, and hence a warming, but this is not established. (We shall ignore any considerations of *purposeful* changes of the albedo, such as the much discussed suggestion of spreading soot on the Arctic ice.)

Mankind's additions to solar heat input
A mathematical climate model must include, as we have indicated, estimates of

246

the natural heat inputs to the system and how this heat is redistributed within the system. So far we have talked about ways that man could modulate the main input, namely sunlight, and our climate models, such as they are, can give a rough indication of how the temperature should change as a result of these changes in input, 'all other factors being constant,' to echo Reid Bryson (1968).

The disturbing fact is that we now see a new term in the future heat balance equation that cannot be ignored: the direct release of heat from all the activities of man. In order to get a handle on this term we must first construct another pre-dictive model – a 'people model.' Since no model can be constructed without stating some basic assumptions, let us start with our assumptions.

The approach to a people model depends on whether you are a pessimist or an optimist, a Malthusian or a believer in the eventuality of a post-industrial society, a member of the Club of Rome or a technological optimist. It is not our purpose to analyze these opposing points of view in any depth, but one simply cannot talk about the twenty-first century without identifying oneself and where one stands.

The Club of Rome, whose viewpoint is expressed in the stirring 'Blueprint for Survival' (1972) and whose prophets are J.W. Forester and his colleagues D.H. and D.L. Meadows, is perhaps the most eloquent exponent of the Malthusian doctrine. Forester's book *World Dynamics* (1971) presents an ingenious com-puter model of the world and uses it to simulate the sequence of events that may come to pass if we continue to behave more or less as we are behaving now. The results of his model have been reproduced so often that they are well known by now. They generally predict a temporary continuation of trends in population, quality of life, energy production, and so forth, followed in about fifty to a hun-dred years by a decline of society as natural resources are depleted. Some predic-tions are more disastrous than others, depending on the assumptions introduced, but the message is decidedly gloomy.

Many people, including Forester himself, were quick to point to some of the difficulties with any such simplified model for society and its resources, and the most incisive comments are those of Boyd (1972). Boyd reproduced Forester's model and then added one new parameter and a corresponding set of relation-ships. The new parameter was something called 'technology,' and technology was a parameter that went up with capital investment, and which improved food production, decreased dependence on fixed natural resources by exploiting alter-natives, and reduced pollution. He also assumed that the birth rate would go down as the material standard of living increases, which is borne out to some ex-tent by current trends in the most developed countries such as the US, Japan, and Northern Europe. His computer models show society achieving a more or less stable state at a level well above the present in terms of population and

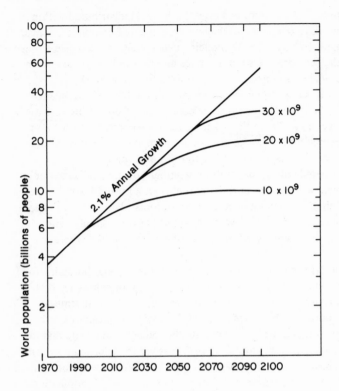

Figure 3 A set of possible world population projections that
start with the current 2.1 per cent annual growth rate and
asymptotically approach a steady state. These are obviously
more realistic than a continued exponential growth, but should
not be taken as 'predictions.' (Courtesy of the Hudson Institute)

quality of life. [Editor's Note: The paper by Roberts in this volume analyzes in
detail the computer simulation model of Forester and Meadows.]

While both Forester and Boyd make it clear that these models are only as good
as their assumptions, and therefore any predictions based on them are suspect,
the lesson to be learned from these studies is that we should not be overwhelmed
by the power of the exponential compound interest formula, which extended too
far inevitably over-predicts the future, but rather that there are ways of slipping
off such an exponential curve in a sensible way, as shown in Figure 3. One can

248

conceive of reasonable models (such as Boyd's) and reasonable scenarios of the future course of events that lead to a more or less stable society – though the definition of what can be considered as 'reasonable' often stirs up a heated debate.

One can draw a curve describing the future worldwide energy production, which in 1970 was 6 to 8 $\times$ 10^3 G watts and was increasing at a rate of 5.7 per cent per year. Such a growth rate, if it continued, would mean an increase, by a factor of more than 5, in thirty years, or by 2000AD, by a factor of 25 by 2030, by a factor of 125 by 2060, etc. (See Figure 3), if one believed in continued exponential increase – which, as we have said, is obviously impossible to sustain indefinitely. There may already be forces at work to slow the growth (Hammond 1972). The interesting question is where the curve will level off, and this is one that we can try to grapple with.

We will draw at this point on the results of a study by the Hudson Institute that approaches the future of mankind, not by a computer model (which they are quite capable of constructing if they had any confidence in one, which they apparently do not), but rather by a set of scenarios that probe the limits of what would be a credible course for society to take. In Herman Kahn's 'Prospects of Mankind and a Year 2000 Ideology' (unpublished) assumptions are stated and a complex chain of reasoning leads finally to 'the basic surprise free scenario' of a post-industrial society of the future that might evolve by the end of the twenty-first century. The conclusion is that the planet Earth *could* support a population of 20 billion with an average per capita income, measured in 1970 dollars, of $20,000, or about four times the current US average. (We have dubbed this 'Herman's 20-20 vision.') Incidentally, this is only slightly larger in terms of world-wide consumption than an independent guestimate by Weinberg and Hammond (1970), who point out that nuclear fuel could power such a society more or less indefinitely.

The main point made in substantiating this 20-20 vision is that it appears to be possible, even with present technology, to design ways to feed, clothe, house, and power such a society. Furthermore, technology itself progresses in such a way that for a considerable period of time one can expect an almost exponential growth in the ability to find alternative solutions to the problems facing society, but with a time lag from the research and devlopment stage to the commercial availability of massive new facilities of several decades (Starr and Rudman 1973). (Unfortunately, this cannot be said now of the population growth and the problem of crowding.) Since power is such a crucial commodity and is the main issue where heat production is concerned, it deserves a special justification in view of the *short-term* limits that we perceive during the current very real 'energy crisis.' In addition to the Weinberg and Hammond report already referred to, an extensive study by the Mitre Corporation on 'Energy, Resources, and the Environment,' as summarized by Zraket (1972), reveals that we can look forward to an amplification factor of 10^6 to 10^9 of our current sources in terms of resource availability for energy generation. This would be achieved by: restraint and conservation, leading to more efficient use of what we have; investment money to encourage new facilities to be built; new choices, stemming largely from improved technology such as breeder reactors, fusion power, coal gasification and liquefaction, solar energy, geothermal energy, etc.; and new discoveries that will open up fresh supplies of nuclear and fossil fuel.

One concrete example of such an amplification factor is the availability of refined uranium oxide (U_3O_8), which at the current cost of $8 to $10 per pound is in such short supply that it is estimated that US ore reserves alone can only keep our non-breeder nuclear plants supplied for the next twenty years. But if we were to let the price of U_3O_8 triple, at a trivial increase in the cost of the electricity generated by it, the supply would go up by a factor of ten times or more, because at that price lower grade ore could be mined profitably, and there is at least ten times more U_3O_8 in the lower grade ore. This should carry us through until breeder reactors can be accepted as safe and practical for gigowatt-size power plants, which will probably be some time after 1990, or until fusion power becomes practical.

We should mention that this conclusion of the Mitre Corporation is at odds with a recent study sponsored by the Atomic Energy Commission (AEC, 1973), which is not as optimistic about the added U_3O_8 to be available with an increase in the price per pound. In that study a doubling of price would only double the US supply – though even this would probably see us through until new technology in the form of fast-breeder reactors or thermonuclear power becomes available.

So much, then, for this digression from geophysical models to people models. To summarize, we may take as a reasonable guess (an upper limit?) for the future world-wide production of power a calculation based on Herman's 20-20 vision, and then see what this implies. The amount is the product of population times per capita energy consumption (in terms of the energy that goes into making electricity plus everything else, such as transportation, heating, manufacturing, etc.). Average per capita energy consumption in the US today is about 10kw, and we have said that the per capita income would be about four times the present US income, so we may scale the per capita power by the same factor. (One can argue that the efficiency of energy use would be greater, so the factor might be smaller, and we could not disagree.) The world-wide total is then $20 \times 10^9 \times 10 \times 10^3 \times 4 = 8 \times 10^{14}$ watts $= 8 \times 10^5$ G watts. (Weinberg and Hammond (1970) arrive at 4×10^5 G watts in their discussion.) Compare this number with the present 6 to 8 $\times$ 10^3 G watts, an increase by a factor of a bit over 100. [Editors' Note: This factor is based on the assumption that man continues to produce power in ways that heat the environment rather than through such means, for example, as direct use of solar energy.]

MAN'S POSSIBLE INFLUENCE ON THE FUTURE CLIMATE

We now turn to some climate models and ask them to predict, first, what the over-all change in mean temperature would be as a result of the various changes that mankind can make in the heat budget of the system. If Q is the total heat input, then a fractional increase $\Delta Q/Q$ can be related to a mean temperature change, ΔT, by the two independent models of Sellers (1969, 1973) or Budyko (1969), and for a 1 per cent change in Q they give a ΔT of 2° to 3°C, or two-thirds this much if the 1 per cent change refers to surface heating alone – say, 2°C. Furthermore, the Sellers model shows that the change at the pole is about twice as large as the average change, which agrees in general with the empirical evidence for the past few decades. For example, while the hemispheric average change in the decade 1960-70 was 0.13°C, the change at latitudes higher than 60°N ranged from 0.4°C to over 1.0°C, or three to seven times larger than the average. There was virtually no change below 40°N (SMIC 1971).

Depending on whether we take as our value for solar heat absorbed at the surface the global average (150 watts/m²) or just that absorbed by the continents (100 watts/m²), where the man-made energy would be liberated for the most part, the $\Delta Q/Q$ due to the 20-20 society is 8 $\times$ 10^{14}/5.2 $\times$ 10^{14} $\times$ (150 or 100), which turns out to be 1.0 or 1.5 per cent. (At present it is only 1/100 of this.) Thus, the average global temperature increase would be 2° to 3°C; and it would be several times this in the polar regions, perhaps more than 10°C.

The implications of such a change in the average temperature are, of course, very great. One would certainly expect patterns of agriculture and transportation to be directly affected, particularly in the higher latitudes of the northern hemisphere. Such questions are, however, beyond the scope of this paper.

One of the effects which would occur is the shrinkage of glaciers and other permanent ice fields, which would suffer more rapid melting in summer. The large-scale climate models of Sellers (1969, 1973) and Budyko (1969, 1972) give some insight into the mean extent of polar ice, which now comes down to about 72°N in the northern hemisphere. Budyko claims that this would vanish with an increase in total heat available 'by several tenths of a percent,' whereas Sellers finds that his most recent model would require on the order of a 10 per cent increase in heat available. As he states, 'differences in the sea ice parameterization are obviously involved here' (Sellers, 1973, p. 252).

William W. Kellogg

The floating Arctic Ocean ice pack has attracted a great deal of attention in the past few decades, because it seems to represent a rather sensitive link in the system (SMIC 1971; Budyko 1971). It is on the average less than 2m thick, and grows in winter and partly melts in summer. Maykut and Untersteiner (1971) have studied the thermal response of the Arctic Sea ice by means of a model that takes into account the flow of heat in and out of the ice from solar radiation, infra-red radiation, conduction to or from the air and underlying water, and snowfall and evaporation. While it represents the most complete model of the sea ice that we know of, and while Maykut and Untersteiner used their model to see what changes in the reflectivity of the surface for solar radiation could do to the thickness (a 20 per cent reduction in surface reflectivity or albedo, for example, resulted in complete disappearance of the ice during the third summer after the change), it was not used to test what a change in the mean air temperature would do to the ice. The extra man-made heat would be transported to the north polar regions by the large scale circulations of the atmosphere, and some of this heat would be transmitted to the sea ice. The critical question is the increase in rate of melting during the summer months. The numbers in the model calculations suggest that a modest input of sensible heat from the atmosphere would eliminate the ice pack after a few years, but a careful calculation has still to be made.

In the realm of conjecture, however, imagine what would occur if the Arctic Ocean lost its ice pack and became an open sea. It would absorb more solar radiation in summer and deposit it in the top few hundred meters. The freshwater layer that covers the top 20 to 40m of water under the Arctic Ocean ice pack would be gradually mixed by currents and wave action so that the present great stability of the top layers would be destroyed, permitting mixing of the deep waters with the surface layers in winter. In short, it can be argued that once the ice pack has disappeared, it will be impossible for the Arctic Ocean to freeze over again until the world gets a great deal colder or something else happens to the ocean circulations.

There are some arguments against that being the case, one being evidence to the effect that the Arctic Ocean has never been ice-free at any time during the last few hundred thousand years. Be that as it may, if mankind can heat up the system enough to remove the Arctic ice pack, then the temperature change around the Arctic due to this alone would be striking. An application of the Mintz-Arakawa general circulation model by Warshaw and Rapp (1972) to a situation with the Arctic Ocean ice out predicts rises in winter temperature around the Arctic of 10° to 15°C when the ice is removed. Unfortunately, this model does not keep track of precipitation, so we cannot tell what the corresponding winter increase in snowfall and continental snowpack would be – though it must be very appreciable due to the large amount of moisture that the air would pick up from the open sea. Even more important, in all likelihood, would be the rate of melting in the summertime. A popular concern is a dramatic rise the level of the oceans if the polar ice cap melted. However, if the Arctic ice melts, there will be no significant change in ocean levels (ice melting in a full glass of liquid does not cause the glass to overflow). Only if the Greenland ice cap were to melt would ocean levels increase significantly. Current models and data make predictions about the Greenland ice cap relatively more uncertain, but the available evidence suggests that the man-created increases in the world average temperature would not be sufficient to melt the Greenland or Antarctic ice caps, except on a time scale which must be measured in centuries.

CONCLUSION

In a very condensed form we have tried to describe each of the main ingredients of a climate prediction, including a prediction about how mankind will behave. Both our understanding of the physical factors involved in climate change and our view of mankind's future are matters of considerable debate at this time.

In spite of all our uncertainties, we must try to make a stab at anticipating what the longer-range future holds for mankind, and that is what we have tried to do. Our best guess is that our great-grandchildren will live in an extraordinarily vigorous and highly technological society, and that by 2050AD, or at least 2100AD. climate changes *due to mankind* will be very evident, especially at high latitudes (unless some natural forces come into play in the opposite direction). Before then we should understand enough about the climate system to know whether this will lead to another ice age because of increased snowfall on land, or to an opening of the Arctic to agriculture and other uses because the climate will be so much more favorable than it is now.

Finally, we should not jump to the conclusion that this change will be a disaster. It could mean some large changes in the way of life for many people, but not a disaster for mankind – certainly not for the planet. After all, taking a geologist's point of view for a moment, an ice-free planet, with no permanent ice at all at the poles, would be the situation that has been 'normal' for 90 per cent of the last 500,000,000 years.

REFERENCES

AEC 1973. *Nuclear Fuel Supply,* US Atomic Energy Commission Rept. WASH 1242 (Washington DC).

Boyd, R. 1972. 'World Dynamics: A Note,' *Science,* 177, 516-19.

Bryson, R.A. 1967. 'Possibilities of Major Climatic Modification and Their Implications: Northwest India, *Bull. Amer. Meteor. Soc.*; 48, 136-42.

William W. Kellogg

Bryson, R.A. 1968. '"All other factors being constant ...": A reconciliation of several theories of climatic change,' *Weatherwise*, 21, 56-61.

Budyko, M.I. 1963. *The Heat Budget of the Earth* (Hydrological Publishing House, Leningrad).

Budyko, M.I. 1969. 'The Effect of Solar Radiation Variations on the Climate of the Earth,' *Tellus*, 21, 611-19.

Budyko, M.I. 1971. *Climate and Life* (Hydrological Publishing House, Leningrad).

Budyko, M.I. 1972. 'The Future Clime,' *EOS*, 53, 868-74.

Club of Rome 1972. 'A Blueprint for Survival,' *Ecologist*, 2, 1-43.

Cobb, W.E. 1973. 'Oceanic Aerosol Levels Deduced from Measurements of the Electrical Conductivity of the Atmosphere,' *J. Atmos. Sci.*, 30, 101-6.

Fletcher, J.O. 1965. *The Heat Budget of the Arctic Basin and Its Relation to Climate*, RAND Corp. Rept. R-444-PR (Santa Monica CA).

Forrester, J.W. 1971. *World Dynamics* (Wright-Allen Press, Cambridge, Mass.).

Hammond, A.L. 1972. 'Energy Needs: Projected Demands and How to Reduce Them,' *Science*, 178, 1186-8.

Manabe, S., and Wetherald, R.T. 1967. 'Thermal Equilibrium of the Atmosphere with a Given Distribution of Relative Humidity,' *J. Atmos. Sci.*, 24, 241-59.

Martell, E.A. 1971. 'Residence Times and Other Factors Influencing Pollution of the Upper Atmosphere,' in *Man's Impact on the Climate*, ed. W.H. Mathews, W.W. Kellogg, and G.D. Robinson (MIT Press, Cambridge, Mass.).

Maykut, G.A., and Untersteiner, N. 1971. 'Some Results from a Time Dependent, Thermodynamic Model of Sea Ice,' *J. Geophys. Res.*, 76, 1550-75.

Mitchell, J.M., Jr. 1973. 'A Reassessment of Atmospheric Pollution as a Cause of Long-Term Changes of Global Temperature,' in *Global Effects of Environmental Pollution*, ed. S.F. Singer (Reidel, Dordrecht, and Springer-Verlag, New York; revised edition in press).

Mitchell, J.M., Jr. 1971. 'Summary of the Problems of Air Pollution Effects on the Climate,' in *Man's Impact on the Climate*, ed. W.H. Mathews, W.W. Kellogg, and G.D. Robinson (MIT Press, Cambridge, Mass.).

Meadows, D.H., Meadows, D.L., Randers, J., and Behrens, W.W. 1972. *The Limits to Growth* (Universe Books, New York).

Rasool, S.I., and Schneider, S.H. 1971. 'Atmospheric Carbon Dioxide and Aerosols: Effects of Large Increases on Global Climate,' *Science*, 173, 138-41.

SCEP Report 1970. *Man's Impact on the Global Environment: Study of Critical Environmental Problems* (MIT Press, Cambridge, Mass.).

Sellers, W.D. 1969. 'A Global Climatic Model Based on the Energy Balance of the Earth-Atmosphere System,' *J. Appl. Met.*, 8, 392-400.

Sellers, W.D. 1973. 'A New Global Climatic Model,' *J. Appl. Met.*, 12, 241-54.

SMIC Report 1971. *Inadvertent Climate Modification; Report of the Study of Man's Impact on Climate* (MIT Press, Cambridge, Mass.).

Starr, C., and Rudman, R. 1973. 'Parameters of Technological Growth,' *Science*, 182, 358-64.

Warshaw, M., and Rapp, R.R. 1972. *An Experiment on the Sensitivity of a Global Circulation Model: Studies in Climate Dynamics for Environmental Security*, RAND Corp. Rept. R-908-ARPA (Santa Monica CA).

Weinberg, A.M., and Hammond, R.D. 1970. 'Limits to the Use of Energy,' *Amer. Sci.*, 58, 412-18.

Yamamoto, G., and Tanaka, M. 1972. 'Increase of Global Albedo due to Air Pollution,' *J. Atmos. Sci.*, 29, 1405-12.

Zracket, C.A. 1972. *Energy, Resources and the Environment*, Mitre Corp. Rept. M72-180 (McLean VA).

ALLEN V. KNEESE

A. CARNESALE AND T. S. ELLEMAN

In its original form, the first of these
chapters bore the somewhat abstract
title, 'Benefit-Cost Analysis and Unscheduled Events in the Nuclear Fuel
Cycle.' The Atomic Energy Commission had asked for comments on one
of its documents, noting that environmental statements for a power reactor
should contain a cost-benefit analysis
which, among other things, 'considers
and balances the adverse environmental
effects and the environmental, economic, technical and other benefits of
the facility.' In response to the invita-
tion, Allen V. Kneese, director of Resources for the Future's program of
studies in the quality of the environment, submitted the remarks which appear here. Dr Kneese's statement was
initially reprinted in the September
1973 issue of the Resources for the
Future bulletin, *Resources*. In that version, Dr Kneese's opening sentences
were: 'I am submitting this statement
as a long-time student and practitioner
of benefit-cost analysis, not as a spe-
cialist in nuclear energy. It is my belief
that benefit-cost analysis cannot answer the most important policy questions associated with the desirability of
developing a large-scale, fission-based
economy. To expect it to do so is to
ask it to bear a burden it cannot sustain. This is so because these questions
are of a deep ethical character. Benefit-
cost analyses certainly cannot solve
such questions and may well obscure
them. These questions have to do with
whether society should strike the Faustian bargain with atomic scientists and
engineers, described by Alvin M. Weinberg in *Science.*'

These questions about the long-term
environmental effects of nuclear wastes
are not ignored by nuclear scientists
and engineers. Members of what might
be called the nuclear establishment are
neither intellectually homogeneous nor

environmentally callous. (Dr Kneese, of course, does not suggest that they are.) One of the consistent subthemes of these volumes is that policy analysis does not make very much progress if the approach used is that of trying to sort out the participants in the debate into 'good guys' and 'bad guys.' In the long run, this subtheme may be most important with regard to our (the world's) nuclear strategy.

Professors Carnesale and Elleman agree that discussion of the Faustian bargain (they originally thought of titling their chapter 'Mephistopheles' Response') is not simply a technical question. However, the discussion must proceed from a technical basis. The social trade-offs cannot be adequately discussed until the technical trade-offs are known. Professors Carnesale and Elleman appear to disagree with Dr Kneese about the relevance of benefit-cost analysis. But this disagreement is more apparent than real. Dr Kneese was warning against the use of superficially quantified benefit-cost analysis which may produce some numerically fictitious coefficient of greater or less than unity. But Dr Kneese urges us to use our judgment about benefits and costs. So do Professors Carnesale and Elleman. That judgment is not yet final and is not irreversible – whichever way it goes.

These chapters should be especially compared to the Gordon chapter on coal, to the Houthakker chapter on energy problems, the MacAvoy chapter on policy disharmonies, and the Homet chapter on oil diplomacy and 'Project Independence.'

ALLEN V. KNEESE

The Faustian bargain

If so unforgiving a technology as large-scale nuclear-fission energy production is
adopted, it will impose a burden of continuous monitoring and sophisticated
management of a dangerous material, essentially for ever. The penalty of not
bearing this burden may be unparalleled disaster. This irreversible burden would
be imposed even if nuclear fission were to be used only for a few decades, a mere
instant in the pertinent time scales.

Clearly, there are some major advantages in using nuclear-fission technology,
since it has so many well-intentioned and intelligent advocates. Residual heat is
produced to a greater extent by current nuclear generating plants than by fossil
fuel-fired ones. But, otherwise, the environmental impact of routine operation
of the nuclear fuel cycle, including burning the fuel in the reactor, can likely be
brought to a lower level than will be possible with fossil fuel-fired plants. This
superiority may not, however, extend to some forms of other alternatives, such
as solar and geothermal energy, which have received comparatively little research
and development effort. Insofar as the usual market costs are concerned, there
are few published estimates of the costs of various alternatives, and those that
are available are uncertain. In general, however, the costs of nuclear and fossil
fuel energy (when residuals generation in the latter is controlled to a high degree)
do not seem to be so greatly different. Early evidence suggests that other as yet
undeveloped alternatives (such as hot rock geothermal energy) might be economically attractive.

Unfortunately, the advantages of fission are much more readily quantified in
the format of a benefit-cost analysis than are the associated hazards. Therefore,
there exists the danger that the benefits may seem more real. Furthermore, the

conceptual basis of benefit-cost analysis requires that the redistribution effects of the action be, for one reason or another, inconsequential. Here we are speaking of hazards that may affect humanity many generations hence and equity questions that can neither be neglected as inconsequential nor evaluated on any known theoretical or empirical basis. This means that technical people, be they physicists or economists, cannot legitimately make the decision to generate such hazards. Our society is confronted by a profound moral problem, in my opinion the most important in the history of man. In a democratic society the only legitimate means for making such a choice is through the mechanisms of representative government.

For this reason, during the short interval ahead when dependence on fission energy can still be kept within bounds, I believe Congress should make an open and explicit decision about this Faustian bargain. This should follow full national discussion at a level of seriousness and detail that the nature of the issue demands. An appropriate starting point could be hearings before a committee of Congress with broad national policy responsibility. Technically oriented or specialized committees would not be suitable for this task; the Joint Economic Committee might be appropriate. Another possibility would be for Congress to appoint a select committee to consider this and other ethical questions associated with developing technology. The newly established Office of Technology Assessment could be useful to such a committee.

Much has been written about hazards associated with the production of fission energy. Until recently, most statements emanating from the scientific community were reassuring on this matter, but several events in the past few years have re-opened the issue and revealed it as a real one. I think the pertinent hazards can usefully be divided into two categories – those associated with the actual operation of the fuel cycle for power production and those associated with the long-term storage of radioactive waste. I shall discuss each briefly.

The recent failure of a small physical test of emergency core cooling equipment for the present generation of light-water reactors was an alarming event. The failure casts doubt upon whether the system would function in the unlikely, but not impossible, event it would be called upon in an actual energy reactor. But it also illustrates the great difficulty of forecasting the behavior of components in this complex technology, where pertinent experimentation is always difficult and may sometimes be impossible. Other recent unscheduled events were the partial collapse of fuel rods in some reactors.

There have long been deep but suppressed doubts within the scientific community about the adequacy of reactor safety research vis-à-vis the strong emphasis on developing the technology and getting plants on the line. In recent months the Union of Concerned Scientists has called public attention to the hazards of

nuclear fission and asked for a moratorium on the construction of new plants
and stringent operating controls on existing ones. The division of opinion in the
scientific community about a matter of such consequence is deeply disturbing to
an outsider.

No doubt there are some additional surprises ahead when other parts of the
fuel cycle become more active, particularly in the transportation of spent fuel
elements and in fuel reprocessing facilities. As yet, there has been essentially no
commercial experience in recycling the plutonium produced in nuclear reactors.
It is my understanding that the inventory of plutonium in the breeder reactor
fuel cycle will be several times greater than the inventory in the light-water reactor fuel cycle with plutonium recycled. Plutonium is one of the deadliest substances known to man. The inhalation of a millionth of a gram – the size of a
grain of pollen – appears to be sufficient to cause lung cancer.

Although it is well known in the nuclear community, the general public is perhaps unaware of the magnitude of the disaster that would occur in the event of a
serious accident at a nuclear facility. I am told that if an accident occurred at one
of today's nuclear plants, resulting in the release of five per cent of the more volatile fission products only, the number of casualties could total between 1000 and
10,000. The estimated range apparently could shift up or down by a factor of ten or
so, depending on assumptions of population density and meteorological conditions.

With breeder reactors, the accidental release of plutonium may be of greater
consequence than the release of the more volatile fission products. Plutonium is
one of the most potent respiratory carcinogens in existence. In addition to a
great variety of other radioactive substances, breeders will contain one, or more,
tons of plutonium. While the fraction that could be released following a credible
accident is uncertain, it is clear that the release of only a small percentage of this
inventory would be equivalent to the release of all the volatile fission products in
one of today's nuclear plants. Once lost to the environment, the plutonium not
ingested by people in the first few hours following an accident would be around
to take its toll for generations to come – for tens of thousands of years. When
one factors in the possibility of sabotage and warfare, where power plants are
prime targets, not just in the United States but also in less-developed countries
now striving to establish nuclear industry, then there is almost no limit to the
size of the catastrophe one can envisage.

It is argued that the probabilities of such disasters are so low that they fall into
the negligible risk category. Perhaps so, but do we really know this? Recent unexpected events raise doubts. How, for example, does one calculate the actions
of a fanatical terrorist?

The use of plutonium as an article of commerce and its presence in large quantities in the nuclear fuel cycles worries a number of informed persons in another

connection. Plutonium is used in the production of nuclear weapons, and governments, possibly even private parties, not now having access to such weapons might value it highly for this purpose. Although an illicit market has not yet been established, its value has been estimated to be comparable to that of heroin (around $5000 per pound). A certain number of people may be tempted to take great risks to obtain it. AEC Commissioner Larsen, among others, has called attention to this possibility. Thus, a large-scale fission-energy economy could inadvertently contribute to the proliferation of nuclear weapons. These might fall into the hands of countries with little to lose, or of madmen, of whom we have seen several in high places within recent memory.

In his excellent article, Weinberg emphasized that part of the Faustian bargain is that in order to use fission technology safely, society must exercise great vigilance and the highest levels of quality control, continuously and indefinitely. As the fission-energy economy grows, many plants will be built and operated in countries with comparatively low levels of technological competence and a greater propensity to take risks. Increased transportation of hazardous materials will probably occur, and safety will become the province of the sea captain as well as the scientist. Moreover, even in countries with higher levels of technological competence, continued success can lead to reduced vigilance. We should recall that three astronauts were incinerated in a straightforward accident in an extremely high-technology operation where the utmost precautions were allegedly being taken.

Deep moral questions also surround the storage of high-level radioactive wastes. Estimates of how long these waste materials must be isolated from the biosphere apparently contain major elements of uncertainty, but current ones seem to agree on 'at least two hundred thousand years.'

Favorable consideration has been given to the storage of these wastes in salt formations, and a site for experimental storage was selected at Lyons, Kansas. This particular site proved to be defective. Oil companies had drilled holes over the whole area, and there had also been solution mining which left behind an unknown residue of water. Comments of the Kansas Geological Survey, however, raised far deeper and more general questions about the behavior of the pertinent formations under stress and the operations of geological forces on them. Solid earth geophysics has limited ability to predict for the time scales required. Only now are geologists beginning to unravel the plate tectonic theory. Furthermore, there is the political factor. An increasingly informed and environmentally aware public is likely to resist the location of a permanent storage facility anywhere.

Because the site selected proved defective, and possibly in anticipation of political problems, primary emphasis is now being placed on the design of surface storage facilities, intended to last a hundred years or so, while the search for a permanent site continues. These surface storage sites would require continuous monitoring and management of a most sophisticated kind. A complete cooling system breakdown would prove disastrous and even greater tragedies can be imagined. Consider the following scenario. Political factors force the federal government to rely on a single above-ground storage site for all high-level radioactive waste accumulated through the year 2000. Some of the more obvious possibilities would be existing storage sites like Hanford or Savannah, which would seem to be likely military targets. A tactical nuclear weapon hits the site and vaporizes a large fraction of the contents of this storage area. The weapon could come from one of the principal nuclear powers, a less-developed country with one or more nuclear power plants, or it might be crudely fabricated by a terrorist organization from black-market plutonium. I am told that the radiation fallout from such an event could exceed that from all past nuclear testing by a factor of 500 or so, with radiation doses exceeding the annual dose from natural background radiation by an order of magnitude. This would bring about a drastically unfavorable and long-lasting change in the environment of the majority of mankind. The extent of the disaster is uncertain. That massive numbers of deaths might result seems clear. Furthermore, by the year 2000, high-level wastes would have just begun to accumulate. Estimates for 2020 put them at about three times the 2000 figure.

Sometimes, analogies are used to suggest that the burden placed upon future generations by the 'immortal' wastes is really nothing so very unusual. The Pyramids are cited as an instance where a very long-term commitment was made to the future and the dikes of Holland as one where continuous monitoring and maintenance are required indefinitely. These examples are not apt. They do not have the same quality of irreversibility as the problem at hand and no major portions of humanity are dependent on them for their very existence. With sufficient effort the Pyramids could have been dismantled and the Pharaohs cremated if a changed doctrine so demanded. It is also worth recalling that most of the tombs were already looted in ancient times. In the 1950s the Dutch dikes were in fact breached by the North Sea; great property losses and the deaths of over 1800 people ensued. Perhaps a more relevant example of the scale of the Faustian bargain would be the irrigation system of ancient Persia. When Tamerlane destroyed it in the fourteenth century, a civilization ended.

None of these historical examples tell us much about the time scales pertinent here. One speaks of two hundred thousand years. Only a little more than one-hundredth of that time span has passed since the Parthenon was built. We know of no government whose life was more than an instant by comparison with the half-life of plutonium.

It seems clear that there are many factors here which a benefit-cost analysis can never capture in quantitative, commensurable terms. It also seems unrealistic to claim that the nuclear fuel cycle will not sometime, somewhere experience major unscheduled events. These could range in magnitude from local events, like the fire at the Rocky Mountain Arsenal, to a world disaster affecting most of mankind. Are these hazards worth incurring in view of the benefits achieved? Alvin Weinberg has called this a trans-scientific question. As professional specialists we can try to provide pertinent information, but we cannot legitimately make the decision, and it should not be left in our hands.

One question I have not yet asked is whether it is in fact not already too late. Have we already accumulated such a store of high-level waste that further additions would only increase the risks marginally? While the present waste (primarily from the military program, plus the plutonium and highly enriched uranium contained in bombs and military stockpiles) is by no means insignificant, the answer to the question appears to be 'no.' I am informed that the projected high-level waste to be accumulated from the civilian nuclear-power program will contain more radioactivity than the military waste by 1980 or shortly thereafter. By 2020 the radioactivity in the military waste would represent only a small percentage of the total. Nevertheless, we are already faced with a substantial long-term waste-storage problem. Development of a full-scale fission-energy economy would add overwhelmingly to it. In any case, it is never too late to make a decision, only later.

What are the benefits? The main benefit from near-term development of fission power is the avoidance of certain environmental impacts that would result from alternative energy sources. In addition, fission energy may have a slight cost edge, although this is somewhat controversial, especially in view of the low plant factors of the reactors actually in use. Far-reaching clean-up of the fuel cycle in the coal-energy industry, including land reclamation, would require about a 20 per cent cost increase over uncontrolled conditions for the large, new coal-fired plants. If this is done, fission plants would appear to have a clear cost edge, although by no means a spectacular one. The cost characteristics of the breeder that would follow the light-water reactors are very uncertain at this point. They appear still to be contingent on design decisions having to do with safety. The dream of 'power too cheap to meter' was exactly that.

Another near-term benefit is that fission plants will contribute to our supply during the energy 'crisis' that faces us for the next decade or so. One should take note that this crisis was caused in part by delays in getting fission plants on the line. There seems, too, to be a severe limitation in using nuclear plants to deal with short-term phenomena. Their lead time is half as long again as fossil-fuel plants – on the order of a decade.

The long-term advantage of fission is that once the breeder is developed we will have a nearly limitless, although not necessarily cheap, supply of energy. This is highly important but it does not necessarily argue for a near-term introduction of a full-scale fission economy. Coal supplies are vast, adequate for at least a few hundred years, and we are beginning to learn more about how to cope with the 'known devils' of coal. Oil shales and tar sands also are potentially huge sources of energy, although their exploitation will present problems. [Editors' note: The consensus of the authors in these volumes is that even at increased world rates of consumption, potential fossil-fuel reserves can supply world energy demands for an indefinite, but very long, period of time.] Geothermal and solar sources have hardly been considered but look promising. Scientists at the AEC Los Alamos laboratory are optimistic that large geothermal sources can be developed at low cost from deep hot rocks, which are almost limitless in supply. This, of course, is uncertain since the necessary technology has been only visualized. One of the potential benefits of solar energy is that its use does not heat the planet. In the long term this may be of the greatest importance.

Fusion is the greatest long-term hope. Recently, leaders of the US fusion research effort announced that a fusion demonstration reactor by the mid-1990s is now considered possible. Although there is a risk that the fusion option may never be achieved, its promise is so great that it merits a truly national research and development commitment.

A strategy that I feel merits sober, if not prayerful, consideration is the phasing out of the present set of fission reactors, putting large amounts of resources into dealing with the environmental problems of fossil fuels, and pricing energy at its full social cost, which will help to limit demand growth. Possibly it would also be desirable to use a limited number of fission reactors to burn the present stocks of plutonium and thereby transform them into less hazardous substances. At the same time, the vast scientific resources that have developed around our fission program could be turned to work on fusion, deep geothermal, solar, and other large energy supply sources while research continues on various types of breeders. It seems possible that this program would result in the displacement of fission as the preferred technology for electricity production within a few decades. Despite the extra costs that might be incurred, we would have reduced the possibility of large-scale energy-associated nuclear disaster in our time and would leave a much smaller legacy of 'permanent' hazard. On the other hand, we would probably have to suffer the presence of more short-lived undesirable substances in the environment in the near term.

This strategy might fail to turn up an abundant clean source of energy in the long term. In that event, we would still have fusion as a developed techological standby, and the ethical validity of using it would then perhaps appear in a different light.

We are concerned with issues of great moment. Benefit-cost analysis can supply useful inputs to the political process for making policy decisions, but it cannot begin to provide a complete answer, especially to questions with such far-reaching implications for society. The issues should be aired fully and completely before a committee of Congress having broad policy responsibilities. An explicit decision should then be made by the entire Congress as to whether the risks are worth the benefits.

A. CARNESALE AND T. S. ELLEMAN

The devil's advocates

Society can enjoy the benefits of a virtually inexhaustible supply of energy from nuclear fission, but the costs must be borne by present and (perhaps all) future generations. Allen V. Kneese's chapter, 'The Faustian bargain,' provides material for serious thought about the nature and significance of the costs associated with the use of nuclear energy on a large scale. It is our intention to serve here as devil's advocates; that is, to examine from other perspectives some of the issues discussed by Kneese.

A pertinent general observation is that the benefits of a successful nuclear-energy program would be enormous. The current 'energy crisis' dramatizes the precariousness of the balance between energy supply and demand, and it is likely that harder times are yet to come. Estimates indicate that by the year 2000 nuclear energy will be the source of about one million megawatts of electrical energy in the United States; a contribution corresponding to approximately 40 million barrels of oil per day. While it is clear that we should not build large numbers of nuclear power plants without acceptable assurance of safe operation, the magnitude of the potential benefit is such that nuclear power should not be rejected simply because it presents complex technical problems.

A second general observation is that policy decisions concerning nuclear power should be made through the use of benefit-cost analysis, recognizing that some of the most important costs will be expressed initially in terms other than financial. A degree of hazard and a long-term commitment can be accepted by society as costs if the benefits are judged to be sufficiently great. We share Kneese's concern with the limitations of benefit-cost analysis, but we see no realistic alternative.

The objections to nuclear power raised by Kneese can be summarized as follows:

1 Nuclear reactor technology is new and our experience is insufficient to determine whether or not important problems will develop.
2 Nuclear power plants, with their long lead times for construction, can make only a very limited contribution to energy supplies in the near term.
3 A reactor accident involving the release of significant amounts of radioactive materials could pose a substantial hazard to the public.
4 The proliferation of nuclear power plants would increase greatly the prospects for accidents associated with the transportation of nuclear materials.
5 Large-scale use of nuclear energy would provide increased opportunities for acts of sabotage resulting in releases of radioactive materials.
6 Nuclear power plants reject more waste heat to the environment than do conventional power plants.
7 Nuclear power plants currently have little if any real advantage in cost over conventional power plants.
8 It is not known how the radioactive waste materials from nuclear reactors will be stored, and the methods now being considered commit future generations to a caretaker role.

Each of these objections is worthy of public consideration in depth. We can only touch upon them here.

Experience with nuclear power plants is limited, but not negligible. Reactors have been operating for over twenty years. As is the case with any device or system employing a new technology, it is likely that unanticipated problems will arise in operation. Care must be exercised to assure that catastrophic events are not among the 'unanticipated problems.' Safeguards are effected at all stages in the design, construction, and operation of a nuclear power plant, with the intention of protecting the public against all credible contingencies. In the judgment of most experts working in this field, the interest and well-being of the public are being protected adequately.

Because the lead time for construction of a nuclear plant (8–10 years) is a few years longer than the lead time for a conventional plant, nuclear plants are at a disadvantage in dealing with near-term energy problems. However, the longer lead time for the nuclear plant is a result primarily of elaborate quality control procedures and complex review and licensing regulations, all of which are designed to assure the protection of the public and to minimize adverse impacts on the environment. As nuclear plants become standardized, the lead times can be expected to approach those of the conventional plants.

Discussions of the implications to the public of a major release of radioactive fission products from a nuclear reactor are often based upon the report of a study performed in 1957 at Brookhaven National Laboratory (US Atomic Energy Commission Report WASH-740). This study examined a hypothetical accident involving a 1000-megawatt reactor. It was assumed that: (a) a loss-of-coolant accident occurs, (b) all safety systems (including the emergency core cooling system) fail simultaneously, (c) the reactor containment is breached (either by an open air-lock or by a missile penetration), allowing a significant release of radioactive materials, (d) the reactor is located in the middle of a city, (e) atmospheric conditions are as unfavorable as possible, and (f) no action is taken by the public after the accident to reduce the adverse effects. A more recent report (WASH-1250) questions the credibility of the accident described in the earlier report and presents a more realistic analysis of the consequences of such an accident.

The hypothetical reactor accident cited most frequently is a double-ended rupture of the pipe carrying coolant water to the reactor, accompanied by a failure of the system designed to cool the reactor core under such emergency conditions. Once isolated from coolant, the reactor core could melt. Concern about this accident sequence has been heightened by the failure of a simulated emergency core cooling system in a small-scale apparatus. Many argue that conditions in this small-scale test (a nine-inch vessel containing electric heaters) were not representative of conditions in an operating reactor; nevertheless, the results of these experiments contributed to a decision to reduce allowable power levels in some operating power reactors.

Experiments on larger systems simulating more closely reactor operating conditions are in progress, and additional ones are planned. It is doubtful that such experiments will resolve the issue. They probably will indicate that emergency core cooling systems perform satisfactorily under the conditions selected, but they will tell us little about the performance of the systems under operating conditions other than those selected and nothing about the likelihood of the occurrence of a loss-of-coolant accident. In this connection, it should be noted that those who favor a moratorium on reactor construction pending completion of the experiments now in progress could be satisfied only if these tests indicate that the safety systems will not work. Successful tests would, in their view, demonstrate only that further testing is needed.

An increase in the number of operating nuclear power plants certainly would render more likely the possibility of an accident associated with the transportation of nuclear materials. Shipping containers are designed to withstand most anticipated accidents. Even if a container were ruptured, the contamination would be local and could be removed safely by known methods. An important

but rarely emphasized point is that, because radioactive material is easily detected and located, there is little difficulty in defining an area requiring decontamination and in determining when decontamination has been effected. Plutonium, a particularly hazardous material, would be shipped in solid form in order
to minimize the possibility of its contaminating water supplies.

The possibility of sabotage at a nuclear power plant cannot be discounted;
however, the task of blowing up a reactor and thereby spreading radioactive
materials would not be an easy one. Reactor buildings are designed to withstand
flying turbine blades, earthquakes, and many other accidents and natural phenomena. The reactor core is housed within a steel pressure vessel about eight-inches
thick. This pressure vessel is inside a containment building designed to withstand
the pressures generated in a loss-of-coolant accident. Personnel entry to the containment building is controlled. Offhand, it would appear that the saboteur might
more easily cause havoc and destruction by poisoning a major water supply, dis-
persing nerve gas, or initiating an epidemic.

Present nuclear power plants are less efficient than conventional power plants,
and therefore must reject more waste heat to the environment. For each unit of
electrical energy generated, a nuclear plant rejects about 40 per cent more heat
than a conventional plant. The environmental impact of the waste heat from
existing nuclear plants is amplified because they reject virtually all of the waste
heat to surface waters, whereas conventional plants divide the rejected heat between the surface waters and the air. Recent indications are that many future
nuclear plants also will divide the heat rejection (through the use of cooling
towers). Thus, it appears that in the future the problems associated with waste
heat rejection from nuclear and conventional power plants will be more nearly
comparable.

The issue of the relative costs of energy from nuclear plants and from conventional plants apparently has been resolved to the satisfaction of most power companies. In making the transition from fossil-fueled to nuclear power plants, these
companies are abandoning a familiar system in favor of one which employs new
technologies, involves extensive government regulation, and requires new skills
on the part of operators, engineers, and managers. It would appear that only a
clear-cut advantage in cost could bring about such a transition.

The cost to the power company represents only a part of the full 'social cost'
of energy; but nuclear energy appears to have the advantage in other areas of cost
as well. The mining and refining of uranium are accomplished apparently without
adverse effect on our surroundings, and a nuclear power plant releases virtually
no pollutants to the environment. In contrast, the mining of coal and the release
to the atmosphere of undesirable gaseous and solid combustion are recognized as
placing considerable burdens on both the environment and our health.

Of all the costs associated with nuclear energy, none presents deeper moral questions or more difficult technical problems than the storage of high-level radioactive wastes, and none is more deserving of full examination by the public. Kneese has reviewed clearly and accurately the hazards associated with such storage. We share his concern.

To place the waste problem in perspective, it is helpful to have some indication of the volume of material to be stored. Projections indicate that the volume of high-level waste to be consigned to storage during the year 2000 would cover a football field to a height of less than one foot. This volume is quite small in comparison with the volumes of other solid wastes generated by our society, and more elaborate methods of disposal need not be dismissed. It may be useful to note also that the duration for which the wastes must be stored is to a great extent a matter of choice, and is not prescribed by some unalterable characteristic of the material. Estimates of required storage times on the order of tens or hundreds of thousands of years reflect the fact that reactor wastes contain relatively small amounts of long-lived isotopes of plutonium, americium, and curium. Separated from the waste material, these isotopes would be of significant value; and, free of these long-lived isotopes, the remaining waste material need be stored for hundreds (rather than tens of thousands) of years. Removal of the long-lived isotopes is technically feasible, but costly. A waste storage methodology involving storage times of tens of thousands of years is one we have elected (perhaps unwisely, but not yet irreversibly) as economically attractive.

Finally, it must be recognized that the Faustian bargain is one which would be struck by all mankind. The United States cannot by itself control the destiny of nuclear energy. Other nations, including Canada, England, France, West Germany, Italy, Sweden, and the Soviet Union, have sizable nuclear energy programs of their own. A complete abandonment of nuclear energy by the United States would decrease only slightly the world's inventories of nuclear fuels and radioactive waste materials, and could place the United States at a significant disadvantage in a world in which the competition for energy resources becomes ever more keen.

Potential advantages of solar, geothermal, and fusion energy are cited often in support of a policy of developing these energy sources rather than of constructing fission reactors. These may well be the more attractive sources of energy, and well-funded research and development programs aimed at harnessing them should be pursued vigorously. But these forms of energy will not be available on a significant scale before the year 2000. Until then at least, the only sources available to us in significant amounts are fossil fuels and nuclear fission, and the value of our irreplaceable fossil fuels is increasing daily. In our judgment, the benefits of nuclear energy exceed the costs, and it will play an important role in the energy economy of the United States.

PART THREE

Policy

HAROLD J. BARNETT

Scarcity is one of the basic themes underlying economic analysis. In the face of scarcity, we have experienced growth. This is in general because we have been willing to trade off lesser current benefits for greater future benefits. Economists are therefore generally very unsympathetic to 'cataclysmic' literature. To many, it appears that most of the contributors to this literature have merely rediscovered scarcity. This discovery, in itself, might be unremarkable except for two things: first, the 'analysis' in the cataclysmic literature is often at best naive; second, the instant policy prescriptions which alarmists leap to are apt to do more harm than good. In the long run, this latter point may be muted because bad policies have a way of being winnowed out. But this winnowing process may take a decade or a generation. To the extent that we now have social problems amenable to policy solutions, these solutions must be based upon sound analysis.

Professor Barnett notes five specific problems with regard to the Forrester-Meadows thesis. First, the undisputable fact that the world is finite is suddenly presumed to have more relevance than at any time in the past; in fact, the world is less limited now than it was for our ancestors. Second, 'collapse models' do not characterize modern societies. Third, economic resources must be measured in economic terms. Fourth, there is little evidence as yet that the production of environmental quality is subject to decreasing returns to scale. And fifth, technology can be (has been! will continue to be?) a positive factor for human welfare.

This last point is especially important. Professor Barnett chronicles a long history of decreasing real costs for extractive industries. To set this in perspective for the energy industries, consider that it is less than 100 years since the first commercial electric power generation station went on line. When the Standard Oil Trust was broken up, early in the twentieth century, the principal use of its refinery output was as illuminating oil. It is uncomfortable (and foolish) to forecast in terms of millenia, but, in our judgment, technology will be a more important factor over the next millenium in the development of human society than the limits to growth as defined by Forrester and Meadows. A fortiori, these limits are irrelevant as guides to specific policy formulation for ourselves or our grandchildren.

Professor Barnett's observations are relevant to all the other chapters in these volumes. Of particular complementary interest are the chapters by Roberts on the limits to the limits to growth, Adelman on real costs in the world oil industry, and Dewees and Stoel & Waverman on environmental considerations.

HAROLD J. BARNETT

Energy, resources, and growth

RESOURCES, ENVIRONMENT, AND GROWTH

In this paper we shall inquire into the compatibility among economic growth, availability of natural resources, and quality of environment. By growth we mean possible increase in population and increase in output and consumption, both total and per capita. The questions are whether scarcity of natural resources and limits of environment increasingly impede growth, and whether economic growth uncomfortably presses upon the natural resource base and environment. What are the problems for society from such pressure, and what are their solution?

There are two forms in which natural resource problems may emerge. One is that we shall face diminishing returns or increasing costs as growing population numbers and consumption press upon the limited resource base. That is, economic welfare per capita will decline as additional numbers of people seek to wrest improved living from the limited resources. We might visualize this increasing cost problem as a *quantitative* reduction in welfare – that is, fewer goods and services for each member of the growing population [1 Ch. iii].

We focus on real costs of resource products as the measure of economic scarcity and availability of resources, rather than on volumes of specific ore reserves or number of acres. Real costs measure the difficulty in getting resource products, in terms of labor and other inputs which must be diverted to such production. If real costs per unit of resource product increase, then we are less well off, because we must work harder to have the same amount of goods. Or else we must reduce consumption of these or other goods. If real costs per unit of resource product decline, then, for any given volume of effort, the bounty on our tables and in

Harold J. Barnett

our homes can be greater. Meaningfully we can say that resources have been economically more plentiful. In summary, the significance of a threat of resource
scarcity is the prospect of higher real costs and fewer goods for our consumption
and investment.

The second problem is that quality of our physical environment will deteriorate
as it becomes polluted from increasing numbers of people and increased economic
activity and wastes. Roughly, we can characterize the pollution problem as a *qualitative* reduction in welfare [1 Ch. XII]. The pollution problem contrasts with my
case of diminishing returns or increasing costs just mentioned, which causes quantitative reduction in welfare. The distinction between quantitative and qualitative,
however, should only be taken as suggestive. In fact, the question of whether we
face increasing costs is *the* basic question. For example, inadequate quantities of
goods could reduce quality of life by leaving us hungry; and large output could
give us tools to improve environmental quality.

Resource availability and costs
I shall first report from a major study on the question of costs [1]. We examined
economic growth from approximately the Civil War to the late 1950s in the
United States, a period of almost a hundred years. The US had very great population growth during this period, both from natural increase and immigration. We
tested the historical record for the possible appearance of increasing costs in those
economic sectors which depend strongly upon natural resources. That is, we examined the cost of incremental products from the extractive sectors – agriculture,
minerals, forestry – in an effort to learn whether in fact scarcity of natural resources had caused diminishing marginal returns to labor and capital during this
period of great US population growth. If so, then the unit cost of extractive products would be increasing. It would take more labor and capital to get each
pound or ton or other unit of agricultural, mineral, and forestry products. We
could not measure cost in dollars and cents since overall inflation or deflation
would move these up or down irrespective of real costs. We therefore measured
costs of the extractive products in terms of days of labor and other input. We
did this for agriculture, minerals, and forestry, and for individual products within
each of these sectors.

In agriculture the cost per unit of products in terms of real units of labor and
capital, after making appropriate allowance for purchased materials, declined. By
1957 it had fallen by more than 50 per cent from the average real cost in the period 1870-1900. (In index terms, if we set real cost of a unit of agricultural product at 100 in 1929, then the level in the period 1870-1900 was 132, the level
in 1919 was 114, and the level in 1957 was 61.) This decline is evidence *not* of
economic resource scarcity and diminishing returns relative to growth, but of

278

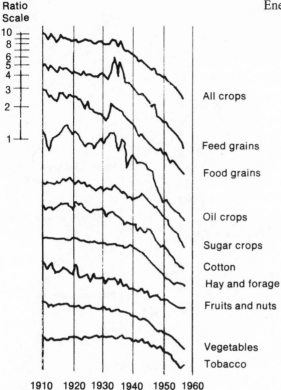

Ratio Scale

10
8
6
5
4
3
2

1

All crops

Feed grains

Food grains

Oil crops

Sugar crops

Cotton

Hay and forage

Fruits and nuts

Vegetables

Tobacco

1910   1920 1930 1940   1950 1960

Figure 1 US agriculture: labor cost
per unit of output in all crops and
nine major commodities, 1910-57

increasing returns. It says that we get our additional units of agricultural commodities at declining cost per unit – that we became richer, not poorer, in goods
available. Figure 1 shows the time series of labor cost per unit for various agricultural products. Declining cost is pervasive over the whole agricultural sector, contrary to the increasing scarcity hypothesis.

We asked the same question for minerals. What has happened to the cost of
mineral commodities as the nation has grown and mineral use has increased forty-
fold? We find that here also diminishing returns did not appear. By 1957 the cost
per unit of mineral products had declined by three-quarters from the turn of the
century. (The index numbers (1929=100) were 210 in the years 1870-1900, 164
in 1919, and 47 in 1957.) This evidence is strongly contrary to the concept of
increasing economic scarcity of resources relative to growth.

279

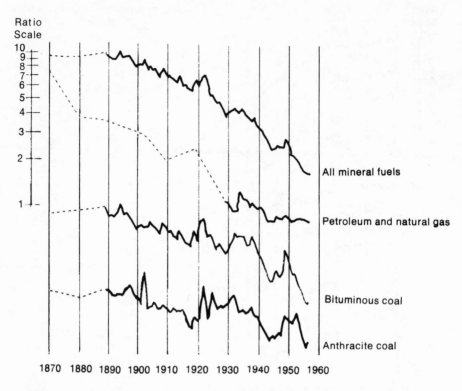

Ratio
Scale

All mineral fuels

Petroleum and natural gas

Bituminous coal

Anthracite coal

1870 1880 1890 1900 1910 1920 1930 1940 1950 1960

Figure 2 US minerals: labor cost per unit of output,
1870-1957

Figure 2 presents the data on labor cost per unit in all minerals, metals, and non-metallic minerals. Declining unit cost is pervasive, and is very rapid for some products.

In forestry we *do* find an appearance of diminishing returns. As the economy grew, the cost of forest products, measured in days of labor and units of capital goods, with appropriate allowance for purchased materials, increased by approximately one-half from the late 1800s to 1957. The index numbers of forestry-products cost were 59 in the period 1870-1900, 106 in 1919, and 90 in 1957.

If we appropriately combine all of these extractive products just described – agriculture, minerals, forestry – we can arrive at a measure of cost of extractive products as a whole. We made such a combination giving each of the sectors, and each of the products within sectors, their weighting of economic importance. The real cost per unit of extractive goods overall declines by more than one-half – that is, the industry shows strong increasing returns, *not* diminishing returns. The in-

280

dex of the unit cost of extractive products (1929=100) falls from 134 in the period 1870-1900, to 122 in 1919, to 60 in 1957.

We then divided the period of almost 100 years from the Civil War to 1957 into two parts. We characterize the subperiod from approximately the Civil War to the first World War as one in which the physical US was still expanding, even moving its frontier. It was not pressing strongly upon its resource base. We then hypothesize that the period from 1919 to 1957 was a case in which the nation's resource base was more fixed, in which there would seem to be less physical accommodation to growth. The results are surprising.

The favorable record of declining unit cost of extractive products improves in the second subperiod as compared with the first subperiod. In agriculture and minerals, the two major resource sectors, unit costs declined only moderately from 1870-1900 to 1919, but precipitously from 1919 to 1957. By way of illustration, in minerals costs declined by approximately 25 per cent in the first subperiod and by about 70 per cent in the second subperiod. Note the slope of the curve in Figure 2. Similarly, in agriculture the decline was less than 20 per cent in the first subperiod, but almost 50 per cent in the second subperiod. See the slopes of the curves in Figure 1. Forestry tells the same story of a more favorable record in the second subperiod than in the first. In the first subperiod the unit cost index of forest products rises from about 60 to about 106, but in the second subperiod the unit cost index declined slightly, from 106 to 90.

These then are the results of a careful quantitative test of the 'increasing scarcity hypothesis,' that economic welfare is threatened by diminishing returns as population and output grow. In the US this has not been true historically; and increasing returns, contrary to the hypothesis, in fact have accelerated since World War I. The hypothesis fails most strongly in the case of minerals, where it could have been reinforced by depletion.

Why has the diminishing-returns hypothesis been wrong in the US during the period of my study and, from a preliminary review of the evidence, to the present? Essentially the reason is that the progress of civilization persistently improves the availability of resources in economic terms. As measured by real cost, resource availability improves exponentially, at a rate of several per cent a year. This more than offsets exponential growth in population and per capita consumption. Unit costs of agricultural goods have declined as rapidly as unit costs in the overall economy, and unit costs of minerals have declined even faster.

Let us now consider the future – the outlook for US growth, resources, environmental quality, and costs during the next thirty to fifty years. Since World War II there have been three major studies in these areas: the five-volume Report of the President's Materials Policy Commission (Paley Commission), which projected resource availability and costs to 1975[16]; the massive Resources for the Future study of ten years ago, which projected resource availability and costs to the year 2000[10]; the 1972 research report of the President's Commission on Population Growth and the American Future (Rockefeller Commission), which projected resource availability and costs, pollution, and costs of pollution abatement to the years 2000 and 2020[14]. We also have the important Third Annual Report (1972) of the President's Council on Environmental Quality, which projected costs of environmental improvement to 1980[15].

The major findings of these rather large studies relevant to our topic are as follows:

1 There are strong propensities toward economic growth in our economy. The tendency is for growth in output and income per capita of 2 to $2\frac{1}{2}$ per cent a year.

2 The tendencies concerning population growth are more ambiguous. Projections range from 2.1 to 3.1 children per woman. The first figure, 2.1 children, is equivalent to zero population growth; 3.1 is equivalent to population growth at $1\frac{1}{2}$ per cent per year.

3 Extractive products – agricultural, mineral, and recycled materials – will be available in sufficient quantities to sustain such economic growth, without significant increases in real costs. That is, resource availabilities in economic terms are expected to keep pace with increases in demands. There will be substitutions away from commodities with unfavorable cost trends toward more favorable commodities. Overall resource availabilities will accommodate increased demands without slowing growth.

4 Active policies of pollution abatement will be successful and expensive; but they can be accommodated without significantly slowing rates of economic growth.

Environmental quality

I now elaborate on the question of pollution abatement and environmental quality, drawing upon the recent research by the Rockefeller Commission and the Council on Environmental Quality [14 15]. In 1970 annualized costs of pollution abatement, both public and private, were about $10 billions. At this level of outlay the public believed it had unsatisfactory levels of stream, air, and land pollution. Moreover, if the policies and technology of the 1960s continued to the year 2000, air pollution emissions would *triple* and stream pollution emissions more than *double* as the economy grew. Two or three times as much emissions into the air and water which envelope us as in 1970 would be quite unacceptable to most of us.

Prompted by this outlook, proposals have been made or accepted for more active abatement policies. These are officially put forward in the 1973 water and

1975-6 air emission standards recommended by the Environmental Protection Agency (EPA). They are all technologically feasible without any dramatic technical breakthroughs. But of course they entail costs, rather substantial costs. [Editors' note: In the winter of 1973-4, some pollution abatement efforts in the United States were curtailed. These curtailments, however, were the result of a short-run emergency caused by policy failures, not a reversal in the long-run trend of real resource costs.]

In annual terms such policies would raise abatement costs from the $10 billions in 1970 to about $30 billions in 1980. Costs would then rise to $35 or $45 billions per annum in the year 2000, depending on the rate of population growth. Put another way, pollution abatement costs would rise from 1 per cent of the nation's output (as in 1970) to 2 or $2\frac{1}{2}$ per cent. Large though these figures on pollution abatement costs are in absolute terms, they are small relative to our economic growth. We would have to give up only a tenth of a percentage point in annual growth of national output to pay for this active abatement policy [14, p. 26].

What would we get for this large absolute but small relative payment? As compared with pollution generated and emitted in 1970, we would get: 86 per cent reduction of particulates put into the air; 65 per cent reduction of hydrocarbons; 40 per cent reduction of oxides of nitrogen; 75 per cent reduction in biological oxygen demand in streams; 80 per cent reduction in suspended solids; but 110 per cent increase in dissolved solids.

As noted, these figures on environmental improvement in the year 2000 result from applying standards which have been adopted or are being recommended by EPA in public policy for introduction by 1975-6. The probable situation is more favorable than I have described. Some technical breakthroughs in pollution control are likely to occur (as they have in the past), some cost reductions will occur, and improved policies can be adopted as necessary.

In summary, improvements in environmental quality of air, streams, and land are quite compatible with economic growth. Indeed, once we accept that we do not face diminishing returns we see that growth in per capita income and improvement in technology provide the social interest and the economic and technical means to seek improvement in the environment.

Comment on Forrester-Meadows (F-M) thesis
A diametrically opposed thesis has recently been presented by a group of computer specialists, led by J. Forrester and D. Meadows and sponsored by the Club of Rome [9 11]. In this view, mankind now faces doomsday. We are fast running out of agricultural and mineral resources, rapidly poisoning ourselves to death by pollution, and crowding ourselves to suffocation. Moreover, the crisis of near ex-

tinction is virtually unavoidable. These adverse developments reinforce each other, and some, such as excessive birthrate, exert baneful effects over very long periods. Mankind is very near to the point of no-return, if indeed we have not passed it. How do I reconcile my own views and data, presented above, with those of Forrester-Meadows? [See 6 for major book reviews.]

F-M do not present detailed support for their conclusion. In essence they present, rather, a classical, mathematical idea of grandeur, ultimate truth, and absolute power. It is that no world of physically finite resources can contain physical resource pressures if these expand exponentially through infinite time. When viewed in the cosmic perspective of the beginning of creation to the end of man's time, there is little ground for quarreling with this view. The Forrester-Meadows error is to assert that this ultimate truth is relevant and specifically descriptive for present and near-term societies. They give no evidence, nor even indication, that they are aware of relevant knowledge, analysis, reading, or data.

F-M further trap themselves in a minor notion of limited validity, which is also inapplicable to contemporary human society. This is the concept that an exponentially growing social variable approaches a ceiling at full speed, without brakes. It smashes at the ceiling limit and then catastrophically declines. This is not a general truth. It is at variance with evidence of social resilience and adaptation. For example, in economics, when supplies of a commodity become short, we shift to others; in engineering, when a technology becomes obnoxious, we choose another; in politics, when a ruler's power becomes oppressive, we neutralize him or remove him peacefully or by force. 'Collapse models' do not characterize modern societies.

A third F-M error is in the definition of the mineral and agricultural resource limits which are relevant for economic analysis. F-M fail to see that economic resources must be measured in economic terms, not in acres or tons. They assert, for example, that mineral resource availability is limited to the stock which was known in 1900, and is likely to last 250 years. This is not economically sensible. Real costs of incremental supplies and of substitutes and alternatives determine resource availability, not acres of Iowa farmland, tons of Arkansas bauxite, pounds of egret feathers or whale blubber, or board feet of Virginia cherry wood [1 Ch. VIII; 6]. Had F-M seen that the economic limits relate to costs and substitutes, they would have found that resource availability has been improving, rather than the reverse, and that economic welfare has been advancing. In the year 2150 there will be more economic resources available than in 1973, as in 1973 there were more than in the year 1900. Knowledge, technology, capital, and need create resources [1 Ch. XI; 10]. Using F-M methodology, a study performed in 1700 would probably have shown that mankind would have exhausted resources by 1900!

A fourth error is the absence of economic thought and evidence from their economic analysis of pollution. They think that pollution control will persistently require sharply increasing costs, absorbing ever increasing fractions of the national product. They think that these costs may be beyond our capacity to bear, with the result that length of life will decline. The fact, as shown earlier, is that only small fractions of the annual *increase* in output will be required to maintain environmental quality. We can have both cleaner air and water *and* enlarged economic welfare [1 14 15].

Finally, in summary, F-M fail to see the full significance of technological advance, in association with affluence, enlarged capital and knowledge, improved labor, and substitutions among inputs and products. They see only that technology spawns more products, more capital, more waste discharge and crowding. They have not noticed that technology and affluence also provide desire and means to limit births; to maintain or improve environment; to create and supply substitutes for scarce agricultural and mineral resources; and for avoidance of other resource limits as these become visible. Moreover, our improved technology and productivity have been growing exponentially, and the rate gives no signs of retardation.

ENERGY AND GROWTH

We turn now to questions of energy and growth: Does energy have any special significance in the connections between natural resources and growth? How do energy demands relate to growth? What has been the historical trend in real costs of energy? What is prospective availability of energy for economic growth; is it likely that US economic development will be impeded by energy scarcity? Does our analysis yield insights into some of the energy questions which have become prominent during the past few years?

Special significance of energy
Many people, perhaps most, feel that 'energy' plays a very special role in society. The very concept of 'energy' is a broadranging one. It is pervasive in basic drives for food, activity, sex, and rest; fundamental in physics and engineering; major in technological change, industrial development, and substitution of inanimate energy for the strength of men and beasts; and a keystone in our comfort and convenience – at home, in our vehicles, in our recreation, and in our meeting and working places. In each of these various respects 'energy' is important. And the importance is magnified by semantics. We use the same word for varied phenomena, and the sense of importance in each 'spills over' to all the other meanings of energy.

Harold J. Barnett

Beyond these generalizations energy has a special significance in our concerns over natural resources and economic growth.

Consider minerals production. We normally prefer to extract out metals, materials, and chemicals from high-grade ores – that is, from ores with large percentages of the desired elements. We prefer ores of 5 to 15 per cent copper, 60 per cent iron, and bauxite over leaner ores. Also we prefer ores which are easily accessible – on or near the surface, close to consuming centers, on dry land. But the fact is that low-grade, distant, and less accessible ores and sources can be economically utilized if technology, capital stock, and energy availability permit. In this sense, energy availability is a key to whether we avert minerals scarcities. Energy has played an important role in averting natural resource scarcity, as we have substituted taconites and porphyrys for higher grade iron and copper ores. In the same sense, energy is key in going to much lower yield materials, indeed down to the plenitude of metals in sea water solutions and ordinary rocks of the earth's crusts [7].

Now consider food and fiber production, and possible scarcity of agricultural land. Food and fiber plenitude can be assured provided there is adequate availability of minerals and chemicals, energy capital resources, and a vital technological environment. And so, to avoid food and fiber scarcity, energy availability plays a key role as it did for minerals and chemicals. Already in our present society, energy and chemicals have made possible enormous increases in land productivity of food supplies. If the US had to rely on work animals for its farm 'horsepower,' their feed might require fifteen to thirty times as many acres of cropland as are cultivated today. If synthetic fibers from energy and minerals were replaced by cotton, the additional land required would exceed acreage now planted to cotton.

Beyond energy's role in processing leaner ores, providing chemicals and nutrients for agriculture, and in substituting for agricultural land, energy is indispensable in yet another aspect of economic growth. In economic growth, capital goods are substituted for labor in production processes. Capital goods require energy input, heat or power, to operate. The substitution of capital goods for labor implies a substitution of inanimate energy for men and beasts. Here also we have a sense of a special significance of energy availability.

And in still another sense we tend to think that energy plays a unique role in economic growth: in meeting the direct demands of the consumption sector. We think of automobiles and air travel, temperature control in buildings, TV and other household appliances.

These are some of the reasons that concerns for availability and real costs of energy grip us strongly. It is generally appreciated that our market system, technological know-how, and ability to provide capital goods work strongly to avert natural resource discontinuities during economic growth. An important question is whether energy availability can support and accommodate the processes of change and growth.

Energy demands to 1965
The foregoing generalizations suggest increased intensity of energy use during economic growth. This is because of recourse to lesser grade or access of minerals and land, need to heat and drive enlarged producer facilities, substitution of energy for men and animals, and energy for household and vehicle consumption. These suggest that economic growth tends to require more than proportionate growth in energy use [7].

This was general belief and my own initial hypothesis in the late 1940s when I first investigated US energy use relative to national product (real Gross National Product or GNP). However, my 1950 research monograph revealed surprising results, and uncovered a relationship which apparently had not been ascertained before. Over a quite long period, beginning at least about the time of World War I, US energy use grew less rapidly than real national output. I projected this would continue during the next generation [2].

The ratio of Energy/National Product (GNP) is shown in the solid line of Figure 3, reproduced from the original monograph [2, Chart D]. The decline in energy use per unit of national output was quite persistent over more than three decades, at a bit less than 1 per cent per year; but there are also irregularities, such as a subnormal level in World War II and a rise in 1947 [2 p. 6].

I revised my initial judgment and hypothesis as follows. The level of energy requirement was primarily determined by the level of real GNP. It was indeed subject to increase from the circumstances described above. But not all of the technical changes and substitutions of energy for other inputs act to increase energy per unit of product. Some of the innovations were 'output-increasing' or 'energy-neutral' or even 'energy-saving.' Moreover, the ratio of energy to GNP was subject to secular fall because of efficiency gains in energy utilization. These included advances in combustion efficiency, use of insulation, higher temperatures, utilization of exhaust heat. Since the most modern energy techniques at the time of my study (1948-50) were much more efficient than the average of energy use techniques in use, I thought it possible that the downdrift in the use of BTU per unit of national product might well continue. Obviously an omnibus mechanical projection would not be economic analysis. The bulk of the monograph cited was an effort to decompose the energy aggregate. I projected to 1965, separately, the demands and efficiencies of each of the several energy-consuming sectors for each of the several energy commodities, with appropriate regard for economic characteristics [2 pp. 6-47 and Tables 1-28; also see 4 re projections generally].

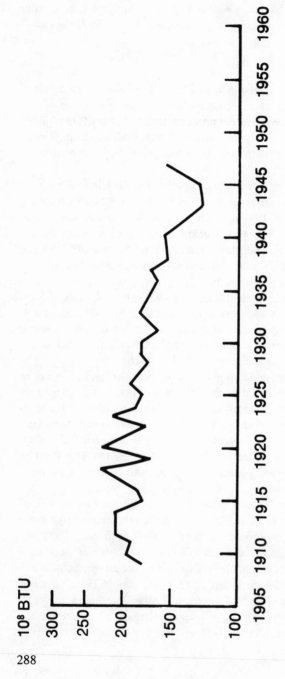

Figure 3 Energy produced and imported per unit of National Product

288

The results of the individual projections from 1947 to 1965 appear in some hundreds of figures relating to energy functions, consuming sectors, activity in consuming sectors, energy commodities, and energy efficiency [2 Tables 26, 27, 28]. After these were all tabulated and combined, they gave an increase in demand for energy commodities only about half as great as the contemplated increase in national product. In effect, the projections resulted in a ratio of BTU to real national product indicated by the dot '.'

The forces leading to improved efficiency in energy utilization, as projected for 1965, including dieselization of railroads, quite overcame the tendencies toward increased energy utilization by households, electro-metals and electro-chemicals, and from other causes. With the passage of a generation, the actual 1965 figure for BTU/GNP turned out to be within 1 per cent of my projected figure: by 1965 the BTU/GNP ratio had declined to about 78 per cent of 1947. (However, my total energy consumption projection was much too low, from error in estimating that real GNP growth would be 3 per cent per year; the actual was 4 per cent per year.)

Prospective energy demands
All of the foregoing concerning the BTU/GNP ratio is prelude to the question of present and prospective demands for energy. Should we expect energy demands to continue to grow more slowly than real GNP as they did for the half century following World War I? If so, then the drain against the long-term supply curve of energy will be moderate. Energy would have to increase by only 3 per cent per year to accommodate a national product growth rate of 4 per cent. Or should we expect that the long-term BTU/GNP relationship has changed, and that energy demands will grow as fast as or even faster than national product?

The question has given added force since 1967 because in that year the BTU/GNP ratio turned upward and continued to increase during the next few years. The ratio increased by a total of 10 per cent during about four or five years. Does this rise manifest a reversal in the long-term declining trend, or is it merely a short-term phenomenon?

The significance of concern over the BTU/GNP ratio can be made clear by the following numerical illustration in Table 1. Assume real GNP growth of 4 per cent per year from 1970 to the year 2000. This is a figure now conventionally used in economic projections and is approximately equal to US experience during the past generation. Now observe the results in the following table, depending on whether the BTU/GNP ratio declines by about 1 per cent per year as in the long-term trend, or holds constant, or increases by about 2 per cent per year, as it did between 1966 and 1970.

Harold J. Barnett

TABLE 1

Alternative levels of annual US energy consumption
(Assuming real GNP increases at 4% per year, 1970-2000)

	1970 (actual) 10^{15} BTU	2000 (projected) 10^{15} BTU	Per cent increase, 2000 over 1970
If BTU/GNP declines at 1% per year from 1970 to 2000	67.4	162	+140
If BTU/GNP is same in 2000 as in 1970	67.4	219	+225
If BTU/GNP increases at 2% per year from 1970 to 2000	67.4	396	+488

As the table shows, the need for energy availability is $2\frac{1}{2}$ times as great under the latter assumption as under the first. The increase in annual needs is $3\frac{1}{2}$ times as large in the latter case as in the first. Which BTU/GNP ratio we use in our estimating equations really does make a very large difference for the question of energy demands and the availability of energy supplies to satisfy them. The differences in results from the alternative BTU/GNP ratios are much greater than our probable error in projecting GNP.

I have not carefully analyzed the details of energy demand in the past two decades, nor have I made detailed energy projections since my 1950 study referred to above. But I can offer views based on the lesser evidence available to me. First, the four years of rise in the BTU/GNP ratio justify questions but not a conclusion of reversal in a fifty-year trend. It is simply a very short period; and on several previous occasions the BTU/GNP ratio has turned briefly upwards. Already, preliminary 1971 figures show a slight decline from the 1970 ratio. Second, a number of unusual events occurred in this four-year period to cause a temporary increase in the BTU/GNP ratio. For example, a shortage of electric power capacity caused heavy use of inefficient stand-by and peaking facilities; and initial difficulties with large generators caused reduced and inefficient utilization, relative to modern design. Third, two detailed projections by the Department of Interior along the lines of my earlier projections study, in which each sector of demand is estimated separately, indicate a decline in the overall BTU/GNP ratio [8 12].

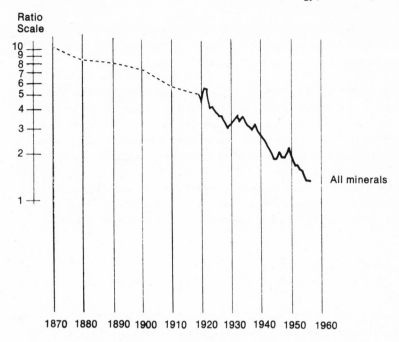

Figure 4 US mineral fuels: labor cost per unit of output,
1870-1957

At this time I conclude that it is more probable that the BTU/GNP ratio will decline or be constant during the next generation than that it will rise. I do not expect the rate of increase in energy demand to exceed that of real GNP.

Energy real costs: historical
As we did in the earlier section of this paper we can address economic availability
by examining real costs. That is, we look at what it costs in labor man days to get
energy output.

Figure 4 shows what we found. [1] The story is the same in fuels as it was for
other minerals. Labor input per unit of fuel has declined in each of the fuel commodities, although more slowly in anthracite than in bituminous coal, petroleum,
or gas. The cost in man days per unit of energy output in 1957 is less than one-
fifth of the 1900 level. Scarcity in long-term economic availability of mineral
fuels as measured by real cost has not occurred in US economic history. [The
measure of output is 'net'; that is, gross output has been adjusted downward to

291

allow for (exclude) purchased materials. I would have preferred to include capital as well as labor in calculating real cost per unit of energy output. But suitable data on real capital inputs were available only for larger industry aggregates, such as agriculture, minerals, and the overall extractive sector. See Reference 1, Ch. VIII, particularly the charts. These show that labor plus capital cost per unit of net output declines as persistently as labor costs, but a bit slower, in each of agriculture, minerals, and extractive industry overall. The upper two curves in Figure 4, above, relating to the extractive sector overall, show the characteristic relationship between labor plus capital cost and labor cost alone in the sectors for which we have data.]

Our interest, however, is not historical, particularly in view of the current and alleged future energy crisis. And so we now turn to the question of long-term availability of energy supply and its accommodation of economic growth.

Energy availability: long-term supply

It is useful to distinguish at this point the economic concepts long-term supply vs short-term supply.

Short-term supply is what would be forthcoming at various prices from existing energy facilities (mines, well, tankers) and the present labor resources which are suitable and readily available. In the energy industries short-term supply tends to be rather inelastic, except for off-peak demand in utilities and in mines and wells operating below capacity. A good part of the present energy difficulties is short-term supply deficiency, due to limited energy-producing capacities and the recent prohibitions in use of high sulfur fuels. Here, as indeed in the entire discussion so far, I concentrate on long-term supply and availability and do not consider the short-term.

Long-term energy supply is what would be forthcoming after completion of new facilities – construction of refineries, tankers, and electric power plants; exploration and development of new mineral resources; recruiting and training of labor force; and technological advances which are visible or suspected on the horizon. The gestation of new facilities in energy is rather long. It takes up to fifteen years for such things as nuclear power plants, development of new oil resources and transportation in remote regions, development of new mines. In energy we might roughly characterize the short-term as (say) five years or less, the long-term as (say) fifteen years or more, and view the range from five to fifteen years as an intermediate gray zone. There is no sharp dividing line between short-term and long-term nor even of the intermediate zone in so large and complex a sector as 'energy.' It would be reasonable also to say that the intermediate zone between short and long is the range from three to twenty years.

Our question, now, is 'what is the availability of energy supply for economic growth over the long-term of fifteen to fifty years?' Numerous studies of this question have been made during the past generation or so.

The early investigations – Barnett (1950), Ayres and Scarlott (1952), Paley Commission (1952), Putnam (1953), and Brown (1954, 1957) – projected demand and supply to 1965 or 1975 or somewhat beyond and found energy resource supply quite elastic. The major studies of the 1960s, such as those by Schurr, Netschert et al. (1960), Landsberg, Fischman, Fisher (1963), and Morrison and Readling (1966), projected energy demands and supplies to year 2000 and/or intermediate points, and also found elastic energy supply. Contemporary studies by National Petroleum Council (1972), Dupree and West (1972), and Darmstadter (1972) project to year 2000 or beyond and find the same results. Virtually all of the competent studies find physical availability of energy ample to meet US demands over the long-term periods considered here. Of course, most of them also identify possible social policy problems, relating to foreign trade, conservation programs, monopoly forces, tax policies, national security, or innovations. But there is no doubt in these studies of physical resource sufficiency within present and prospective technology adequate to meet projected US demands.

In most of the serious applied economic research, it is not useful to project beyond fifty years, if so far. The uncertainties are too great. Wholly unforeseen developments can enter. Nevertheless, there is interest in the question of energy adequacy in the coming centuries and millenia, and I'll contribute a few words at this level of speculation.

The famous Pinchot and related writings of the Conservation movement were pessimistic on energy sufficiency: 'We have anthracite coal for but 50 years, and bituminous coal for less than 200. Our supplies of iron ore, mineral oil, and natural gas are being rapidly depleted, and many of the great fields are already exhausted' [13 pp. 123-4; 1 Ch. IV]. The appearance of controlled nuclear energy has changed this outlook. The available energy resources in uranium and thorium are many times larger than in coal, oil (including shale and tar), and gas. And, because of the character and plenitude of fission materials, cost per unit of power produced would tend to be constant or, more likely, decline from the occurrence of technological advances. There is also solar energy to supplement fission power in space heat. And even beyond fission power and solar energy, 'There is in the long run the possibility of producing power from thermonuclear reactions – from fusion of hydrogen as distinct from fission of uranium. No one as yet sees very clearly just how this is to be done, but it is nevertheless a very real possibility' [7 pp. 111-2]. With the waters of the sea as the source of hydrogen, there would be no practical natural resource limit to the availability of energy.

293

Harold J. Barnett

CONCLUSIONS

Concerning environmental quality
I have presented in stark and simple form the historical and prospective answers
on whether economic growth is compatible with a fixed natural resource base.
I have also answered on whether growth is compatible with maintenance and
improvement of the quality of the natural physical environment. From the
physical and economic cost circumstances there simply is no reason why economic growth cannot proceed. There is no prospect of diminishing marginal returns to real inputs of labor and capital in the acquisition of extractive goods.
And there is no necessity for decline in the quality of the natural physical environment from air pollution, water pollution, and solid waste disposal. Growth,
adequate resource availability, and a healthful environment are all fully compatible, if society has the will and the wit to solve the related social problems. Our
problems are not in economic or physical incompatibility of growth, environment, and resources.

Our so-called problems of growth and environmental quality are really a me-
lange of social problems:
1   the fact that the market economy and the government sectors do not properly
assess the costs of pollution when the environment is free for the dumping of
wastes;
2   the fact that there is incompatibility between our traditional strong individ-
ualism and the popular support of greatly enlarged central political decision-
making;
3   the fact that monopoly forces and market controls are growing rapidly in the
natural resource sectors, and these are damaging rational decisions, efficiency,
and social relations;
4   the fact that we are confusing natural resources and environment with quality
of life.

On this last point, I offer two quotations and a closing comment: 'The grass is
rich and matted, you cannot see the soil. It holds the rain and the mist, and they
seep into the ground, feeding the streams in every kloof. It is well tended, and
not too many fires burn it laying bare the soil. Stand unshod upon it, for the
ground is holy being even as it came from the Creator. Keep it, guard it, care for
it, for it keeps men, guards men, cares for men, Destroy it and man is destroyed'
(Alan Paton, *Cry the Beloved Country*).

'For man is of a quickening spirit and the earth, the strong, incoming tides and
rhythms of nature move in his blood and being; he is an emanation of that jour-
neying god the sun, born anew in the pale South and the hollow winter, the slow
murmur and the long crying of the seas are in his veins, the influences of the

294

moon, and the sound of rain beginning. Torn from earth and unaware, without the beauty and the terror, the mystery, and ecstasy so rightfully his, man is a vagrant in space, desperate for the inhuman meaninglessness which has opened about him, and with his every step becoming less than man. Peace with the earth is the first peace' (Henry Beston, *Herbs and the Earth*).

We seem to be pouring into the environmental quality-bottle all our individual and social yearnings for peace, stability, and quiet, for social justice in the world, and for more meaningful lives. To these we have added our passions for reform of values and improved quality of life generally, and our antagonism toward modern industrial growth and abuses by private enterprise. We may be misled by the beauty and simplicity in the quotations. Environmental quality is only part of our problems, not the whole of them [3 5].

Concerning energy
There are two major energy problems, in my view. The oil and gas industry, nucleus in the overall energy market and gradually absorbing it, is the greatest aggregation of effective economic and political industrial power which the world and nation have ever known. With only minor lapses, market and political power has been persistent as in no other major industrial sector for almost a century. It began in the days when Rockefeller created the first great US industrial 'trust.' It continued through the period of international 'oil diplomacy'; through domestic cartelization by oil companies, Texas, and the federal government; through 1957, when Britain and France opened a war in the Middle East to preserve oil supply and Suez transportation; through almost two decades of quotas on US oil imports, at cost to consumers in excess of $5 billions per year. The most recent measures involve 'muscling in' on and increasing oil monopoly profits by Middle East and other export countries, the state of Alaska, and the governments of US and Canada, and the reaping of enormous economic rents in natural gas by these countries, the Soviet Union, and domestic natural gas producers. The qualities of political and economic power in the oil and gas industries abroad are indicated by their partnerships with national governments in the United Kingdom, Netherlands, France, Italy, Japan, and other countries, and in the US by unusual influence in the federal government. The latter includes leading powers in the congressional establishment and committees; depletion and other tax subsidies beyond those of other industries; major and special advisory and staffing roles in the National Petroleum Council, Interior Department Office of Oil and Gas, Petroleum Administration for War and Petroleum Administration for Defense (independent of WPB and DPA which controlled *other* industries during World War II and the Korean War, respectively), Cabinet Committee on Energy Policy, and other agencies – all of these with senior, high quality, dedicated, patriotic

people who firmly believe that what is good for the oil industry is good for America.

There are many difficulties visible in the overall energy market. They include environmental pollution, mine safety, capital supply, perfection of synthetic technologies, and expansion of electric power capacity. In all of them one can see a high probability of working out rational, sensible solutions which are consistent with a goodly degree of economic and political freedom. But one is less confident of the outcome when looking at the super concentrations of monopoly economic and political power in oil-producing companies and governments, and the trend of increase in such power. This is one energy problem.

The second major problem began thirty years ago and intensifies year by year: the accumulations of potent nuclear materials. Already the 'nuclear club' has expanded from two to six or more nations with respect to nuclear weapons and their wastes. The world is hostage to increasing numbers of political and military leaders in avoidance of use and accidents. Now we are moving to a very large and wide-spread use of nuclear power. The numbers of fission and hot waste sites and the volumes of materials will expand enormously. All nations are joining this club. The probabilities of illicit use of weapons and wastes and of accidents escalate. In scores of nations subject to thousands of leaders in each century there will accumulate great stocks of fission materials and endlessly growing stocks of hot wastes, potent for a hundred thousand years.

How to use nuclear energy and yet avoid nuclear catastrophes – this is the second energy problem.

REFERENCES

I am grateful for suggestions and criticisms to my colleagues, Professors A. Jones, D. Heathfield, P. Sturm, and M. Weidenbaum. None of them is responsible for the errors which remain.

1 Barnett H.J. and C. Morse, *Scarcity and Growth* (Baltimore 1963, 1965)
2 Barnett H.J., *Energy Uses and Supplies – 1939, 1947, projected 1965.* IC 7582 (Washington, DC 1950). The monograph with minor additions subsequently became Chapter IV, pp. 70-168, in H.J. Barnett, Atomic Energy in the United States Economy (Harvard University, unpublished doctoral dissertation, 1952)
3 – 'Environmental Policy and Management,' in *Social Sciences and the Environment,* ed. M. Garnsey and J. Hibbs. (Boulder, Colorado 1967); 'Pressures of Growth upon Environment,' *Environmental Quality in a Growing Economy,* ed. H. Jarrett (Baltimore 1966)
4 – 'Natural Resources in the Changing US Economy,' in *Planning for Diversity and Choice,* ed. S. Anderson (Cambridge, Mass. 1968); 'Specific Industry Out-

put Projections,' *Long Range Economic Projections* (Princeton 1954)

5 – 'Population Problems: Myths and Realities,' *Economic Development and Cultural Change*, July 1971; 'Population and World Politics,' *World Politics*, July 1960

6 Boyd R., 'World Dynamics: A. Note,' *Science*, 14 Aug. 1972, pp. 516-19; H.J. Barnett, 'Book Review of *World Dynamics*, by J.W. Forrester,' *Journal of Economic Literature*, Sept. 1972, pp. 851-4; R. Gillette, 'Book Review of *Limits to Growth* by D. Meadows and Others,' *Science*, 10 March 1972, pp. 1088-92; T. Humphrey, 'The Dismal Science Revisited,' *F.R. Bank of Richmond Monthly Review*, March 1973, pp. 2-13; C. Kaysen, 'The Computer that Printed Out W*O*L*F,' *Foreign Affairs*, vol. 50, July 1972, pp. 660-8; A. Kneese and R. Ridker, 'Book Review of *Limits of Growth*, by D. Meadows and others,' *Washington Post*, 2 March 1972; T. Oerlemans, M. Tellings, & H. DeVries, 'World Dynamics: Social Feedback May Give Hope for the Future,' *Nature*, 4 Aug. 1972, pp. 251-5; M. Shubik, 'Book Review of *World Dynamics*, by J.W. Forrester,' *Science*, 3 Dec. 1971, pp. 1014-15

7 Brown H., J. Bonner, J. Weir, *The Next Hundred Years* (New York 1957, 1963); also see Brown, *The Challenge of Man's Future* (New York 1954)

8 Dupree, W.G. Jr. and J.A. West, *U.S. Energy through the Year 2000* (Washington 1972)

9 Forrester J.W., *World Dynamics* (Cambridge, Mass. 1971)

10 Landsberg, H.H., L.L. Fischman, J.L. Fisher, *Resources in America's Future* (Baltimore 1963)

11 Meadows D.H. et al., *Limits to Growth* (New York 1972)

12 Morrison W.E. and C.L. Readling, *An Energy Model for the U.S. ... to the Years 1980 and 2000.* IC 8384 (Washington 1968)

13 Pinchot, G., *The Fight for Conservation* (New York 1910)

14 US Commission on Population Growth and the American Future, vol. III, *Population Resources and the Environment*, ed. R.G. Ridker (Washington 1972)

15 US Council on Environmental Quality, *Environmental Quality*, Third Annual Report (Washington 1972)

16 US President's Materials Policy Commission, *Resources for Freedom*, 5 vols. (Washington 1952)

RONALD S. HOMET

The US Cabinet Task Force on Oil Import Control began its deliberations in the early summer of 1969 and submitted its report in the early spring of 1970. At that time, imported crude oil was landing on the east coast of the United States and in Montreal at laid-in prices around $2.00-$2.25 a barrel. US crude oil in the southwest Gulf coast was selling for over $3.00 a barrel for sweet crude, with other US crude selling at discounts from that figure according to location and quality. Canadian crude oil was selling at comparable figures, and the eastern Canadian market was served by imported crude oil. Canada was the dominant source of oil for the upper Midwest market in the United States. Prudhoe Bay had just been discovered and exploration was picking up in the Canadian Arctic and off Newfoundland and Nova Scotia.

It was in this context of circumstances that the Cabinet Task Force Majority Report recommended abolition of the mandatory oil import quota and its replacement with a tariff and strategic stockpiles. In addition, there was considerable concern that steps be taken to create an explicit rationalization and integration of US and Canadian policies into a cohesive North American energy policy.

Since that time, the roof has fallen in. The acrimonious debate in the United States about the Trans-Alaska Pipeline delayed both serious discussion of a Mackenzie Valley pipeline and discovery and development of additional Canadian Arctic and Alaskan reserves. Instead of energy policy relations between the United States and Canada being harmonized, new tensions were created. Failure of the United States to resolve its regulation-induced natural gas shortage contributed to the creation of a two-tier natural gas pricing system in Canada. Failure of the United States to resolve policy issues critical to the investment decisions about the creation of new refinery capacity resulted in a shortage of US refined products and increased US dependence upon imports of refined products from Canada. The repercussions of this led to Canada limiting its exports to the United States. Instead of a cooperative North American energy policy developing, the United States is talking about 'project independence,' and Canada is building a pipeline to Montreal and debating the feasibility and desirability of self-sufficiency.

What is happening with respect to energy policy relations between two contiguous and usually compatible neighbors is happening on a grander scale in the world at large. It seems clear that for the current decade, at least, world energy markets are moving to a new equilibrium. It is unclear exactly what that equilibrium will cur-

tail, but it is clear that price expectations have been radically revised upward from the levels prevailing just one, two, three or so years ago. It is also clear that uncertainty about the new market equilibrium and the policies through which it will be implemented and administered have created various economic dislocations. In view of all this, Mr Homet recommends a step to introduce some stability into world oil markets. His proposal is for a formal international commodity agreement with respect to oil which is explicitly negotiated and ratified at the governmental level. This recommendation is made in the context of continued and expanded world trade, including US imports, of oil.

In addition to comparing Mr Homet's chapter to the chapter on multinational corporations by Dr Collado, this chapter should also be compared to those by Professors Adelman and Nye.

RONALD S. HOMET

Oil diplomacy

Controversial issues of public policy tend in the main to be settled not by the force of reason but by the perceived logic of events. Thus when the Cabinet Task Force in 1970 advised that US energy self-sufficiency was attainable only over long lead times and at a substantial increase in price, it was not proposing that such self-sufficiency be made a policy goal.[1] The actual recommendations of the task force majority – that the oil import quota system be replaced by a closely monitored system of tariff restraints with preferences for more secure sources – was premised on a perception of inescapable energy interdependence in a risk-fraught world.[2] Now that the perceived risks of an Arab oil boycott have come to pass,[3] the question of an appropriate long-term response has been posed by the president's message of 7 November 1973: 'Let us set as our national goal, in the spirit of Apollo and with the determination of the Manhattan Project, that by the end of this decade, we will have developed the potential to meet our own energy needs without depending on any foreign energy sources. Let us pledge that by 1980, under Project Independence, we shall be able to meet America's energy needs from America's own energy resources.'[4] The thesis of this chapter, simply stated, is that the proposed national goal runs counter to the national interest, and that the logic of events will sooner or later compel its abandonment. What remains uncertain is the nature and structure of international oil arrangements that will succeed the present instability.

As short-term rhetoric, of course, the president's proposal had obviously meritorious purposes: to warn the Arab States that the United States at least intended to pursue an independent diplomatic course in the Middle East and was prepared to face the costs of doing so. It was also a back-handed recognition of the fact that international oil politics have at long last entered into the official diplomatic equation – a theme to which we shall return. But there are audiences other than the Arabs to take into account, both domestically and internationally; and it is their interests that will force revision of the rhetoric.

What after all does 'Project Independence' mean? It must mean that the United States is prepared to pay any cost, both environmental and inflationary, to develop oil shale and coal conversion and other synthetic and non-fossil fuels to the point where 'we shall be able to meet America's energy needs from America's own energy resources.' For simplicity, let us leave out of account the likely domestic resistance to this policy, and assume somewhat arbitrarily that it results in a long-term direct oil-equivalent energy price of around $7.00 or $8.00 a barrel. (The exact price does not matter, so long as it is clear that a substantially higher-than-present domestic price plateau would be reached.) What international economic and political consequences would follow?

First, it is conceivable that the Arab and other OPEC states would be content to let the US price set the world price, and would, with the aid of their oil-company partners, operate the cartel to achieve this. They have certainly learned that the supply-price equation has a second side, and that at higher prices they can achieve their revenue goals at lower levels of production. The Europeans and Japanese would incur energy costs bearing a rough parity with those of the United States (albeit at much greater balance-of-payments outflows) as a result of what the producing states could piously label 'market conditions.' The heavy losers would be the larger developing nations – India, Pakistan, Brazil – which are short both of domestic energy resources and of foreign exchange.

Second, it is at least equally conceivable that, with prospects for entry to the US consumption market withdrawn, the physical oversupply of world petroleum resources would become so irresistible as to precipitate an eventual competitive producer scramble that would reduce steeply world crude prices. It is not within my province to weigh the prospects for this outcome,[5] beyond noting that 'Project Independence' would restore the secure US profit center for the international companies which underlay the world price differential of the 1960s. If such a differential were to re-emerge, the by-then heavy research-and-development commitment of the United States to higher energy prices would quickly force re-imposition of rigid oil import quotas or prohibitive tariff barriers. This would in turn impose a severe handicap on the international competitiveness of highly energy-dependent US industries, leading to pressures for exceptions and special arrangements such as those that provoked the Cabinet Task Force study.

Third, no matter which way world crude prices should trend, the United States would find itself at serious political cross-purposes with our European and Japanese friends and allies. This has already emerged in the immediate post-boycott jockeying for position. The White House has declared its dissatisfaction with NATO performance during the US re-supply of Israel (although the North Atlantic Treaty contains no obligations whatever on the subject);[6] the solidarity of the European Community has been splintered at least temporarily on the rock of Dutch disdain; and the Japanese have been driven to incur official US dismay by endorsing the Arab position. The fact is that there is no 'Project Independence' available to the Europeans or Japanese; unless the North Sea contains producible resources far vaster than anything thus far documented, these countries will remain inescapably dependent on the Arabs for the bulk of their energy supplies; and the single-minded pursuit of energy self-sufficiency by the United States alone could be taken to mark a severe breach in allied cohesion, whose consequences would prove very difficult to repair. It is not too extravagant to remark that the fomenting of such a division in Western ranks has been at the forefront of Soviet foreign policy objectives for the past quarter century. To be sure, an energy-autonomous United States could retain its own capacity to counter Soviet objectives in the Middle East, but we could well find that in arming ourselves for that struggle we have lost far more important economic and political support.

It is comforting that the present logic of events has at least temporarily shifted control over oil diplomacy from the international oil companies to official governmental channels. The upper echelons of the career US foreign service are well aware of the risks entailed in divorcing ourselves from our allies, and it is now clear that there cannot be any settlement of the Middle East conflict which does not concern itself with a resumption of the Arab oil trade. This will have to enter into the equation along with the questions of secure borders, resettlement of the Palestinians, the status of the holy places, diplomatic recognition, and all the rest. None of these questions will yield to quick or easy resolution, but none will go away until it is resolved. And there is reason to believe that, given the forcing of all these questions into the open by international stalemate, there will never be any time more propitious than the present for seeking durable solutions.

Thus despite the 'Project Independence' rhetoric, the United States has the opportunity and indeed the necessity to work collaboratively with other consuming nations in facing the energy problem. The measures taken can certainly include cooperative research and development into alternative energy sources, as well as more efficient utilization and conservation of energy – but not in disregard of price. They can and should also include concerted emergency measures for pooling of available resources and for increased storage of petroleum and products. The essential thing is to treat these energy problems as what in fact they are: *common* problems, which present the 'West' with a grave challenge to its own unity.

The question remains as to what sort of diplomatic settlement of the Arab oil question should be sought. Given past history, there will doubtless be a strong temptation to leave all details to the international companies, and to limit any intergovernmental accord to one that rescinds the boycott. But this would impose too much of a burden on the companies, and achieve too little in the way of future energy stability. If nothing else, the events of 1973 have proven decisively that the days of the international companies as political 'buffers' are gone. Price and production have both been intensely politicized and the international companies acting in concert have shown themselves less and less capable of arranging secure agreements. Even a full and lasting settlement of the Arab-Israeli conflict, assuming one arrives, will not markedly change this situation.

In these circumstances, careful thought should be given to strategies aimed at devising an international commodity agreement for crude oil. Unattainable as that may now seem, and undesirable as some of its attributes may now appear, there is reason to believe that it may be preferable to any other arrangement that could be obtained. At the root of the present uneasy cartel, history suggests, there lies a deep-seated fear of destructive competition among both the producing countries and companies. One familiar thesis[7] has it that the encouragement of such competition would be highly desirable, in that it would increase production and lower price; and that the way to achieve it is to get the international companies out of the crude-oil marketing business so that the producing countries will compete directly for market share among themselves. This is an appealing proposition, but it appears to give insufficient attention to at least three points.

First, what the international companies appear to do best is distribute supplies to consuming countries on a basis that is generally perceived to be equitable to each of these countries. Wherever one of these companies has ports, refineries, pipelines, or retail outlets, it is subject to tax and regulatory and other pressures to meet the product needs of that country. The only way the international companies can meet and balance all of these consuming-country pressures is to produce reasonably satisfactory assurances that they are in fact behaving fairly. The emergence of nationally owned oil-purchasing companies in various of the consuming countries presumably operates as a further spur to such behavior.

Second, removal of the 'majors' from international distribution would in all likelihood not result in head-to-head competition for sales among the producing countries. The gap would instead be filled by European and Japanese nationally owned companies, which would be quite content to continue propping up the OPEC cartel so long as they could get sufficient supplies for their home markets. Indeed, the evidence assembled by Professor Adelman[8] shows that the scrambling for position by these companies to date has had the result of *increasing* prices above existing cartel prices. Opening further crude-oil purchasing opportunities to them would only intensify the 'seller's market' psychology that underlies their scrambling. And the division of crude supplies by such national companies is not designed to be, and would not be, fair as among all markets.

To be sure, the producing countries can form their own companies, and several have expressed interest in entering into 'downstream operations' in consumer markets. But they have been slow to follow up these expressions with concrete actions. Evidently they are prepared to proceed one contract at a time, and on a joint venture basis with the international oil companies. These matters are being negotiated within the framework of the cartel. Too little attention appears to have been paid to a 1972 Middle East Institute colloquy on this point with the Saudi Arabian petroleum minister, Shaykh Yamani:[9]

Q Minister Yamani, historically the downstream operation has negligible or in some cases non-existent profits. Why is the government of the Kingdom of Saudi Arabia interested in investing surplus funds in business that may bring in a return of less than the interest of money in the bank?
A Well, I hope you aren't asking me to reveal some of the agreements we have made with the oil companies on the disposal of crude ...'

The OPEC countries show no disposition to dispense with the international oil companies as partners (or pawns) in effective cartel activities. Nor are the capital-exporting countries likely to agree on the necessary legislation to remove their national or international companies from such participation. The risks of the unknown, the fear of cheating, the ideology of free enterprise – all operate as formidable barriers to any such agreement. The one thing the oil-consuming countries might be able to agree upon is the opening up of the evolving operation of the cartel to greater public scrutiny and direction.

This then yields the third and perhaps most hard-to-accept point: the inescapable political content of oil arrangements. Whenever and wherever oil has been perceived to be in excess supply, political steps have been taken to cartelize its control. OPEC itself drew its announced inspiration from the market-demand prorationing instituted with federal approval by the Southwestern States of the United States. The producing regions ritualistically proclaim their natural right to control the rate of exhaustion of their non-renewable resources, while the consuming regions display their anxiety to do nothing that may prejudice access to so vital an asset. Price seems always to have been regarded as secondary, unless and until it places a clearly discriminatory burden on some particular industrial or geographic sector. It is in part because of the very real risk of such price discrimination against US industry that the United States cannot afford to 'go it alone' in developing and relying upon alternative energy sources. But it also cannot expect the international politics of oil, as practiced on one side by OPEC, to disappear. The remaining alternative is to try to make those politics multilateral and intergovernmental.

There is after all another US precedent for dealing with monopolistic tendencies, and that is to accept and regulate them. The first Interstate Commerce Act, restraining rail (and later other forms of transport) competition, antedates the Sherman Act's injunction against industrial restraints of trade. Regulatory restraints have been adopted in the avowed interest of consumers, not to yield them the same price benefits as unbridled competition but to assure them adequate services or supply. At the international level, the same objectives have been sought through international commodity agreements.

Stability of supply, we should now be prepared to agree, is not a value to be disregarded. It is what the OPEC - international company cartel has professed as its objective. But the system is not working when prices can be raised to levels that threaten to reduce output below demand, or that place prospectively intolerable strains on balance-of-payments flows. And the system is not working when it provides no representation for consumer interests, or shields from public scrutiny the details of key arrangements. What we have now are *de facto* international commodity agreements reached in private, and without any public mechanism to deal with their supervision or enforcement. It should clearly be in the consuming countries' interests to translate these arrangements to the intergovernmental sphere. Doing so would provide a forum in which to place all the price, production, foreign-exchange, and other trade-offs on the public table, where they could be examined and appropriate conclusions drawn. And it would remove the necessity for officially sanctioned private collusion among the international companies, which in the United States at least breeds strong suspicion of private profiteering.

Why might the OPEC nations be willing to join in a publicly ordered cartel? First, it should be clear that this would not involve a 'confrontation' between consuming and producing blocs. Voting rights and other procedures could be drawn so as to protect their vital interests. Indeed, the very formation of a multinational oil authority would serve as a kind of legitimating recognition of the producing countries' interests. Second and more important, the producers too have an interest in reasonable price and supply stability. If it was concern for each other's behavior that led the OPEC members to join together, it should be fear of undue volatility outside their ranks that leads them to join a wider organization. Losing prospective markets and stirring up great-power rivalries is not conducive to economic or political well-being over any appreciable period.

A multinational oil authority would be quite compatible with research and development of alternative energy sources. Room might appropriately be made for the oil-exporting nations to invest some of their earnings in such technologies if they wish. A price plateau well below the oil equivalent of our arbitrary $7.00 or $8.00 a barrel would still leave room for synthetic-fuel and other developments. Reasonable stability of price and supply would also allow for planning of additional security measures, such as reserve production and pipeline capacity or storage, by both the United States and other consuming countries. And all this could be done without threatening the sudden or arbitrary closing of consumer markets to petroleum.

It is, of course, possible that the world is in too contentious a frame of mind to allow agreement on any such international ordering of affairs. Certainly it is too much to expect that all energy problems would be permanently resolved by such an arrangement. But the alternatives in prospect do not appear superior, and there may never come a better time for putting this plan on the agenda.

Furthermore, the very effort to achieve such a goal would be likely to yield important interim or partial benefits. It would put the United States – Canadian energy relationship, which has always been troubled by Canadian fear of bilateral subjugation, in a wider multilateral setting, where such strains should be substantially dissipated. It would give the Europeans and Japanese tangible evidence of US concern for their energy predicament, and allow them to participate constructively and without 'confrontation' in the resolution of that predicament. And it would provide at least an exploratory forum for oil-exporting nations divorced from the Arab-Israeli dispute (Indonesia, Iran, Nigeria, Venezuela) to examine the merits of intergovernmental cooperation among producers and consumers. Some useful understandings, even if well short of a full-blown multinational oil authority, would in all probability emerge from such exploration.

The Arab states would have to participate if the ultimate objective were to be achieved, and that could only take place in the context of a durable Middle East settlement. But economic 'recognition' for the Arab states may be every bit as important to their future as security assurances are for the Israelis. And the United States at least would be truer to its global necessities, let alone responsibilities, if it shifted its announced policy goal to something more closely resembling 'Project Interdependence.'

NOTES

1 Cabinet Task Force on Oil Import Control, *The Oil Import Question*, February 1970, para. 233
2 See especially Cabinet Task Force Report, para. 213c
3 See e.g., Cabinet Task Force Report, para. 415
4 Text of President Nixon's Energy Message, *Washington Post*, 8 Nov. 1973, p. A13

Roland S. Homet

5 Compare Akins, *New Myths and Old Prejudices in Energy Supply,* with Adelman, *Is the Oil Shortage Real?,* in Hearings on Foreign Policy Implications of
the Energy Crisis before the Subcommittee on Foreign Economic Policy of
the House Foreign Affairs Committee, 92d Cong., 2d Sess. (1972), pp. 401-
423
6 Article V of the North Atlantic Treaty calls for concerted measures by the
treaty partners only in case of 'an armed attack against one or more of them
in Europe or North America.'
7 See Adelman, House Hearings, pp. 407-423
8 Ibid., pp. 419-420
9 House Hearings, Appendix B, p. 372

AFTERWORD

Diplomacy is a process with its own momentum. This chapter was written in
November 1973 and is being proofread in January 1974, by which time (1) the
main lines of the central proposal appear to have been adopted by the Administration and (2) the average of domestic and imported US oil prices has been
allowed to settle at about $7.00 to $8.00 a barrel. The forces at play remain
the same, so that the analysis retains whatever validity it can command.

If the current 'energy crisis' is in fact policy-induced, then prospective policy responses will determine how well the world copes with its problems. Good policy can result in a dramatic turnaround; poor policy can prolong the current situation. Some of the ways to make poor policy include having poor data, having a poor predictive model, or using the wrong data in the wrong model and believing the results. The balance of payments is a subject of considerable mystique. In discussions of energy policy, it is frequently asserted that this or that cannot or should not be done 'because of balance of payments considerations.' The total balance of payments effects are rarely specified in complete detail, nor are the reasons why such effects might be 'bad' completely developed. Moreover, offsetting benefits and possible adjustments are often ignored.

Professor Grennes and Dr Winokur attempt to put the balance of payments issues involved in US energy policy in perspective. Because the United States is such an important factor in both the world financial community and the world energy economy, these issues are equally important to other countries as well. In addition, the same economic principles apply. The major conclusion of Grennes and Winokur is that we should not allow the balance of payments tail to wag the energy policy dog.

The Grennes and Winokur balance of payments chapter should be compared to the Collado and Nye chapters on multinational corporations. This is another area where mystique may tend to override good judgment. Also, because of the current topicality of self-sufficiency, this chapter should be compared to the McDonald chapter on conservation regulation, the Gordon chapter on the US coal industry, the Starratt and Spann chapter on the natural gas shortage, the MacAvoy chapter on inter-fuel energy policy interrelationships, the Homet chapter on the foreign policy implications of US self-sufficiency, the discussion in the Waverman chapter on the US-Canadian energy interface, and Hyndman and Bucovetsky on Canadian tax policy (discussing revenues from the recently imposed Canadian export tax on oil).

THOMAS J. GRENNES AND HERBERT S. WINOKUR, JR

Oil and the US balance of payments

Many observers consider the balance of payments an important constraint on United States oil-import policy. Although mandatory oil-import quotas were removed in the first half of 1973, tariff and subsidy questions remain unsettled. Recent trade and business literature is replete with arguments for oil protection offered by the US oil industry and some government spokesmen. These arguments concentrate on the adverse balance-of-payments effects of current and projected oil imports. The general issue of free trade versus protectionism has always been with us, but recent events involving oil have given it a greater sense of urgency. A new consideration is that currency exchange rates have become much more flexible since 1971, and this has altered the relationship between oil and the balance of payments.

The paper considers three general propositions concerning trade in oil. The first section discusses the proposition that free trade which results in heavy dependence on imports is not the best policy for the United States. The second section considers the contention that current and projected oil deficits will result in intolerable balance-of-payments problems. The last section considers the proposition that oil-exporting nations will accumulate large stocks of dollars (petrodollars) and use these hoards to destablilize world currency markets.

1 OIL PROTECTIONISM

Net oil imports for the United States were $3.9 billion in 1972 and they are expected to grow rapidly in the near future. Some government and industry forecasts predict deficits of $20-25 billion by 1980 and $30 billion by 1985.[1] There

Thomas J. Grennes and Herbert S. Winokur, Jr

TABLE 1

Net exports of selected items for the United States

	1960	1970	1972
	(billions of dollars)		
Machinery	+3.8	+0.5	+5.5
Grains and preparations	+1.8	+2.6	+3.5
Chemicals	+1.0	+2.4	+2.1
Soybeans	+0.3	+1.2	+1.5
Petroleum	−1.1	−2.3	−3.9
Automobiles and parts	+0.3	−2.3	−3.1
Iron and steel	+0.2	−0.8	−2.1
Coffee	−1.0	−1.2	−1.2
Meat	−0.2	−0.8	−1.0
Overall trade balance	+4.9	+2.2	−6.9

SOURCE: Data from *Statistical Abstract of the US,* 1962, 1971 and *Survey of Current Business,* July 1973.

is widespread concern about large oil deficits, and the president and many members of Congress have recently called for a movement toward self-sufficiency in oil. Let us consider the benefits and the costs of importing oil.

A *Specialization*

The traditional justification for international trade is that all trading countries benefit from specializing in production and buying from the lowest-cost source. In terms of its balance of payments accounts each country would show surpluses for its low-cost products and deficits for its high-cost products. Thus the principle of specialization implies that an observed deficit for a particular product should not be interpreted as a measure of a country's failure but rather as a measure of the gains from trade. For example, an oil deficit of $10 billion means that, in the absence of trade, domestic resources worth more than $10 billion would have to be diverted from other uses in order to maintain the same volume of oil consumption.

Recent trade data for the United States show the magnitude of certain imbalances (see table 1). In 1972 the United States was a substantial net exporter of machinery ($5.5 billion), grains ($3.5 billion), and chemicals ($2.1 billion), and a large net importer of petroleum ($3.9 billion), automobiles ($3.1 billion), and steel ($2.1 billion). Although each industry is understandably concerned about the balance for its product, it is not clear why national policy ought to be more

312

concerned about the oil deficit alone than the automobile or steel deficits or the surpluses for machinery, grains, and chemicals. A country cannot obtain the gains from international trade without encountering deficits for some items and surpluses for others.

Two other points should be noticed about the structure of the trade balance. First, it changes over time in response to changes in comparative cost and demand. The surpluses for machinery, grains, chemicals, and soybeans each increased by more than $1 billion between 1960 and 1972, in spite of a worsening of the overall trade balance of nearly $12 billion. During the same period automobiles and steel changed from small surpluses to deficits of $3.9 billion and $3.1 billion, respectively, and the oil deficit increased by $2.8 billion. Second, items in the trade account are interrelated to such an extent that a policy which restricts the demand for some import X may simply switch demand onto another import Y, without much impact on the total trade balance. This is one of the lessons which appears to be emerging from US trade policy in the 1960s.

B *Vulnerability to supply restrictions*
The gains from trade depend not only on the cheapness of imports but also on their reliability. Critics of free trade concede that there are potential benefits from oil imports when they are cheaper than incremental domestic supplies, but they emphasize that foreign oil supplies are unreliable, especially those from the Middle East. A policy of free trade in oil may make the US economy vulnerable to two kinds of supply restrictions. First, there may be sudden, but temporary, interruptions which will impose short-run costs on the United States because of the difficulty of shifting quickly to alternate sources of energy or rapidly expanding domestic production. The cause of the interruption may be either a deliberate embargo by exporters, whose purpose is to extort political concessions, or it may be an accidental side-effect of a civil or regional war involving Middle Eastern exporters. This literature emphasizes that the relevant governments are either hostile toward the United States or, if friendly, politically unstable.

The second kind of problem caused by heavy dependence on imports is that it makes the United States vulnerable to the pricing policy of the international oil cartel. A rationale monopolist may never find it prudent to impose a total embargo on his customers, but he will find it prudent to restrict supply judiciously to achieve a monopoly price. Thus, even if exporting nations were politically stable and were not hostile toward the United States, it would be in their interest to improve their terms of trade and national income by selling oil at a monopoly price. The two problems caused by dependence on imports are standard economic problems: the first is based on the economics of uncertainty and the second on the theory of cartels.

313

c *Temporary supply interruption*
The cost to the United States of a supply interruption depends on the probability
of an occurrence, the severity of the supply restriction, and the adaptability of
the domestic economy. These costs of depending on uncertain imports must then
be weighed against the benefits of consuming imported oil and diverting domestic
resources to more highly valued uses.

How likely is a temporary supply interruption? If the interruption is caused by
a deliberate embargo on the part of exporting countries, then the probability depends on the political gains (difficult to measure) and the more easily measurable
costs. [Editors' note: Since this paper was written, the Arab oil embargo, growing
out of the 1973 Mideast War, was imposed.] The direct cost to oil-exporting countries is the oil income forgone during the embargo and the future revenue lost by
driving importers toward self-sufficiency. The loss of revenue would appear to be
especially painful to most exporting countries because of two characteristics: (1)
their low incomes; and (2) their high degree of specialization in oil production.
The two major producers in the Middle East, Saudi Arabia and Iran, had per
capita incomes of less than $400 in 1969 when the US figure was $4,234 (see
table 2). [Editors' note: As of 17 November 1973 the embargo shows some signs
of easing after being in duration approximately one month. See the discussion on
stockpiling below.] Dependence on oil imports may present a problem for the
United States but dependence on oil exports for income is a much more serious
problem for these countries because the ratio of export revenue to GNP is much
larger for them than the oil import to GNP ratio for the United States.

The severity of an embargo depends on how many suppliers participate. An
embargo faces the standard cartel problem of enforcing member discipline. But
this is more difficult for the oil cartel because the members of an ordinary, profit-
oriented cartel share a common goal, but the political diversity of the oil cartel
prevents them from sharing a common political goal. A further complication is
that the international oil-logistics network is now controlled by international oil
companies.[2] As table 2 indicates, there are many oil exporters, none of whom
dominates the market. The oil-exporting countries are not all Arab countries,
and there are considerable political and economic differences even among Arab
states.[3] Market shares are volatile, and new producers such as Libya and Nigeria
can emerge quickly and old producers such as Venezuela decline. In the presence
of adequate stockpiles for insurance against short-run interruptions, the major
long-run issue would be stability of the cartel. In this connection the 1980 pattern of outputs, revenues, and market shares would be of interest. But as the
numbers in table 2 indicate, these measures are too unstable to be projected with
confidence.[4]

314

TABLE 2

Crude petroleum production and per capita income

	Thousands of barrels per day 1962	Share of world pro- duction 1962	Thousands of barrels per day 1972	Share of world pro- duction 1972	1969 GNP per capita in dollars
United States	7257	0.30	9437	0.19	4234
USSR	3660	0.15	7795	0.16	1200
Saudi Arabia	1388	0.06	7470	0.15	380
Iran	1242	0.05	4829	0.10	350
Venezuela	3253	0.13	3166	0.06	1000
Kuwait	2017	0.08	3036	0.06	3320
Libya	213	0.01	2292	0.05	1510
Nigeria	68	0.00	1941	0.04	100
Iraq	954	0.04	1475	0.03	310
Canada	626	0.03	1461	0.03	2650
Indonesia	469	0.02	1235	0.03	100
World total	24,097		49,620		

SOURCE: *Oil and Gas Journal,* 2 September 1963 and 8 August 1973, and *World Bank Atlas.*

What would be the cost to the United States of a temporary interruption of supply? A rough measure is the elasticity of demand for oil from those sources which are affected, and this elasticity will be larger and the cost of an interruption will be smaller the easier it is for the United States to switch on short notice to alternative sources of imported crude or products, or to substitute other sources of energy for imported oil. This will be easier (*a*) the more elastic is the demand for oil; (*b*) the more elastic is the domestic supply of oil from new production, private inventories, and government stockpiles; and (*c*) the more elastic is foreign supply from those sources not participating in the embargo. Thus the more adaptable is the pattern of oil flows in the world economy to a temporary US shortage, the smaller is the cost of a shortage, and the more difficult it is to justify programs such as tariffs, import quotas, or production subsidies which provide insurance against an embargo. Some tentative evidence exists on the short-run adaptability of the pattern of world oil flows. As a result of the policy-induced[5] energy shortage in 1973 in the US economy, spot shortages for certain fuels in certain markets developed. The response was a draw-down of inventories, a relaxation of the oil import restrictions on products and then crude, and a flow of products from such unconventional sources as Brazil and western Europe. [Editors' note: The draw-down of inventories and the temporarily increased reliance on product imports from unconventional sources made the United States more vulnerable to the Arab oil embargo. As a result of domestic policy failures the United States had no strategic reserves and very little flexibility when confronted with an international crisis.]

There appears to be some agreement that the demand elasticity for crude oil is small (the Cabinet Task Force on Oil Import Control used –0.1), especially in the short run. The domestic-supply elasticity has two components, new production and inventories, and the latter appears to be more important in relation to temporary embargoes. Because of supply uncertainty it is profitable for users of oil (the Defense Department as well as private users) or specialized middlemen to stockpile oil in case of a supply interruption. This profit motive exists for middlemen only if the oil price is permitted to rise during a shortage. It has been argued that, because the government will freeze oil prices in the event of a shortage, private inventories will be too small. Uncertainty about government policy could be reduced by announcing in advance the government's willingness to let prices adjust during a crisis. Alternatively the government could subsidize private inventories by fiscal incentives or rely on government stockpiling of oil as alternatives to self-sufficiency.[6] [Editors' note: The discussion of rationing in 1973 confirms the judgment that the government will act to hold prices down. Even those who want prices to rise in order to ration oil usage advocate use of a sales tax to accomplish this end. This does not encourage the private sector to hold additional inventories. Moreover policy failures had led to private inventories being lower in the winter of 1973-4 than they would otherwise have been. In addition, contrary to the recommendations of the Cabinet Task Force, new government stockpiling strategies had not been implemented to deal with this type of problem.]

D *Uncertainty of all supplies*
Uncertainty about foreign supply due to political disturbances, cartel restrictions, or acts of God exists for all imports, not just oil. If a special trade policy toward oil is to be justified, it must be shown that the consequences of an oil shortage will be more costly than shortages of steel, automobiles, rubber, coffee, or other imports. The United States is already heavily dependent on imports of many minerals such as copper, iron, lead, zinc, and aluminum, and by 1985 the US Department of the Interior projects that import shares will range from 34 per cent for copper to 96 per cent for aluminum.[7] In the case of exhaustible resources, oil import barriers offer a curious kind of insurance. since the more heavily the country depends on domestic supply for current needs, the sooner that supply will be exhausted and the sooner the country will become dependent on for-

eign supplies for future needs. The rate of oil-import dependency has been increasing and the likelihood of an embargo-induced oil-import shortage may be higher than for other materials. Nevertheless the same principles apply. These factors do, however, affect the size of the necessary stockpile.

The supply of imported oil is somewhat uncertain, but so is the supply of domestic oil and substitute sources of energy. Sudden, unanticipated changes in energy policy have radically altered costs of production and the entire pattern of demand for sources of energy. Important changes have occurred recently in policy toward natural gas, coal, electricity, transportation, as well as oil, and those domestic policy changes may have been a more important cause of the current 'energy crisis' than the behavior of any foreign governments. If this were true, then the option of importing oil would be a source of stability to the US market rather than a cause of instability. For example, if changes in environmental policy raised the cost of producing domestic oil, the resulting shortage at the initial price would be smaller, and the new equilibrium price would be lower if oil were freely imported than if it were not. One might ask whether American consumers should be subjected to the uncertainty created by a capricious policy toward domestic oil production when they might be better served by a relatively stable supply of foreign oil.

E *Monopoly supply restriction*

Just as a rational monopolist does not price his product out of the market, neither does he refuse to sell to his customers at a profitable price. Similarly, if the object of an oil cartel were to improve the terms of trade and income of its member countries, it would reduce exports not to zero but to the level which yielded a monopoly price. Even if oil-exporting countries behave as rational monopolists, they may accumulate dollar balances. This problem is discussed in a later section. A second argument against relying on imported oil views the Organization of Petroleum-Exporting Countries (OPEC) as a cartel which attempts to exploit foreign consumers.

This second view of the foreign oil supply is more amenable to economic analysis via the theory of cartels. It does not require the assumption that political motives dominate economic motives. Even if the Arab-Israeli dispute were to disappear, oil exporters may behave in generally the same manner as they are now behaving. The rational-cartel model merely assumes that each government is concerned about its national income and is aware that competition is less profitable than monopoly. There is ample precedent for this kind of government-sponsored cartel: for example, the wheat, coffee, tin, sugar, and olive oil agreements.[8] This view also implies that the cartel members will be aware that excessive belligerence may force its customers into substitutes and self-sufficiency.

To US policy-makers the problem of confronting a profit-motivated oil cartel is quite different from the problem of facing periodic oil embargoes. If a successful foreign oil cartel confronted Americans with a monopoly price, consumers would still have the option of buying domestic oil. This constraint on the monopoly price would provide some built-in protection against the cartel. Whereas consumers would be better served by a competitive import price, importing at the cartel price cannot be more expensive than self-sufficiency in oil. There is some price high enough to induce self-sufficiency, and, as long as oil continues to be imported, the cartel price must be below that price, and some gains from trade will remain.

Of course the domestic oil industry is not adversely affected by a monopoly oil price, and industry spokesmen do not complain strongly about the high price of imported oil. Concern about the foreign oil cartel is more frequently expressed by government spokesmen and private economists.[9] Indeed a successful cartel must share its monopoly rents with the domestic industry, since foreign and domestic oil must sell for the same price in the absence of trade barriers. A foreign oil cartel and oil import barriers can be considered two alternative (but not mutually exclusive) ways to protect the domestic industry. Import barriers may be a more visible form of protection, since the domestic price will exceed the foreign price, while with the cartel no such gap will result. In terms of visibility the domestic industry may prefer this less obtrusive form of protection to import barriers, but, because of the historical instability of cartels, they may provide less durable protection than import barriers. Unlike the case where imports are sold at competitive prices, the cartel provides the foreign and domestic producers with certain common interests.

The allocative effect of the cartel is that total world production and consumption of oil will be smaller (shifting demand to other energy sources) and domestic production will be larger than is the case with competition. World income will be smaller because of the substitution of inferior sources of energy in consumption, and the substitution of inefficient sources of oil in production. The distributive effect of the cartel is to transfer income from oil consumers to oil producers. Part of this is an international transfer from the United States to oil exporters and part of it is purely a domestic transfer between US producers and consumers.

The cartel imposes two kinds of burdens on the United States. The first is the international transfer itself, which is no more burdensome than other forms of aid to less developed countries which the US government has either implemented or advocated, although the same set of countries may not be involved and the 'aid' may not be used for the same purposes. In the past the United States has encouraged and participated in several commodity agreements, and recently it has endorsed the policy of trade preferences for the manufactured products of less developed countries. The unofficial OPEC commodity agreement in oil does not appear to differ in kind from these other policies which the United States has supported.

The second burden is the loss to consumers for which there is no offsetting gain to cartel members. This is a deadweight loss for the world as a whole, and it results from the pricing of oil at more than its marginal cost, which induces socially wasteful substitution by consumers. Cartels, optimum tariffs, and export taxes are inefficient devices for transferring income since the same real transfer could be accomplished by a direct money payment at a lower cost to consumers. Because of this inefficiency consumers should be willing either (*a*) to bribe the cartel to sell at competitive prices, or (*b*) to spend an amount up to the transfer plus the deadweight loss to dismantle the cartel.[10]

F *US monopsony power*

This discussion has assumed that oil exporters can improve their terms of trade by acting in concert. Conversely the United States may possess some monopsony power as a significantly large buyer of oil, so that a decrease in US demand would lower the foreign currency price. This is the traditional argument for an 'optimum tariff' to improve a nation's terms of trade. The monopsony issue has interesting implications for domestic environmental policy with respect to oil. A tax on the consumption of oil may raise the dollar price by less than the tax and lower the foreign currency price, the exact proportions depending on the degree of monopsony power. The cost of a cleaner environment will be shared by Americans and foreign oil exporters. If auto-emission controls and similar demand-reducing policies have the same effect on demand as a consumption tax,[11] they will shift part of the burden onto foreigners by improving the US terms of trade. However another set of environmental policies has the effect of taxing US production of crude oil and refining, and these policies will increase the demand for imported oil and worsen the US terms of trade. Price increases for Libyan sweet crude are an example of effects which worsen the US terms of trade. Arguments to maintain or increase the special tax incentives enjoyed by the US domestic petroleum industry would be an example of policies which would decrease the world price of oil and improve the US terms of trade.

2 OIL DEFICITS AND THE BALANCE OF PAYMENTS

The oil policy chosen by a country depends on the capabilities of the country, the constraints imposed by the domestic and international environments, the objectives of oil policy, and the trade-offs between oil policy and other policies.

319

Thomas J. Grennes and Herbert S. Winokur, Jr

Historically partial self-sufficiency in oil has been taken as an objective of US oil policy for reasons of national security. Pursuit of this objective led to protection of the US producing industry through mandatory import quotas. A new dimension of oil policy now takes as its objective the contribution of that policy to the balance of payments and the value of the dollar. Those concerned with the value of the dollar concede that there are gains from importing some cheap oil, but that balance of payments considerations must limit the volume of those imports. Presumably a $20 billion oil deficit could, in principle, be offset by surpluses on other products but this would be difficult and costly. The literature concerned about deficits seldom offers specific statements about the adverse effects of large deficits, but presumably these would include the following:[12] first, international reserves would be drawn down to dangerously low levels as a result of defending the value of the dollar in currency markets (in effect paying for oil imports with gold); second, as reserves are exhausted, import restrictions (tariffs or quotas) must be imposed in spite of their adverse effect on national income; third, to defend the dollar deflationary monetary and fiscal policy might be imposed which could ultimately reduce employment and real national income. Thus, were it specific, the argument might conclude that programs which reduce the oil deficit to the economy are justified because they obviate the need to resort to these more costly devices.

A *Offsetting surpluses*
If imports differ from exports, a given dollar exchange rate will remain in equilibrium as long as there is offsetting lending or borrowing. Thus a zero trade balance is not a requirement for an economy – even on average for periods as long as 25 years or longer. For the postwar period, 1946-71, the rest of the world had trade deficits every year which just offset the US trade surpluses. The requirement for long-run equilibrium is that the foreign exchange market be in equilibrium so that the government neither gains nor loses reserves persistently. Thus the dollar market can be in equilibrium at the current exchange rate in spite of a large oil deficit if there is either an offsetting surplus for other products or net foreign lending. One form of lending is dollar accumulation by foreign central banks.

Even if a $20 billion oil deficit is realized by 1980, it is possible that at current exchange rates offsetting surpluses will be large enough to yield overall balance. On the export side the outlook for agriculture and machinery is especially promising (and discussions of further trade liberalization are going on under GATT auspices). On the import side automobiles, steel, and textiles had been under strong pressure from imports, and the full benefits of the 29 per cent depreciation of the dollar since 1971 have not yet been fully realized. Already the trade deficit has decreased steadily throughout 1972. A small surplus appeared in the second quarter of 1973 and increased in the third quarter. For the first nine months of 1973 there was a trade surplus, in spite of the energy crisis. In addition to the lagged effects of dollar depreciation, the US trade deficit should also decline in the future because of strong import demand from both industrial countries and oil exporters which have recently accumulated reserves.

B *Measuring and interpreting the oil deficit*
An exchange rate is a price which rations foreign exchange, and, if there is a shortage at the current exchange rate, that rate will tend to rise and the dollar will tend to depreciate. It is as serious a mistake to think of the dollar price as immutable as it is to think of the oil price as immutable. Even though the post-war international monetary system has been based on fixed exchange rates, a member of the International Monetary Fund is permitted, indeed obliged, to change its exchange rate when that rate is in 'fundamental disequilibrium.' Thus, if the United States faced a large and persistent payments deficit in 1980, the pre-1971 IMF rules would oblige the government to devalue the dollar instead of imposing trade controls or deflationary monetary-fiscal policy.

Devaluation raises the dollar price of oil and all other importables which encourages consumers to buy less and domestic producers to produce more. Devaluation also raises the dollar price of exportables (for given foreign currency prices) which encourages domestic consumers to buy less, releasing more for export, and producers to expand output. To see that these substitution effects of devaluation are strong and that their cost is not exorbitant, notice the dramatic improvement in the trade balance during 1972-3 at a time when real income was growing rapidly, unemployment was falling, and the volume of trade was growing.[13]

One should exercise caution in interpreting forecasts of future oil deficits, but this warning does not mean that such forecasts are not useful. They can be interpreted as measuring the magnitude of an oil transfer problem. The traditional transfer problem involves the question of how a country making a money payment could achieve an equal trade surplus to accomplish a real transfer. Specifically it asks whether a gift or loan of $X to a foreign country would, by altering home and foreign spending, induce a trade surplus of $X for the home country which would accomplish the transfer in real terms. If not, a transfer gap exists which would require currency devaluation or other measures.

In the case of US oil imports one can ask whether an increase in the demand for oil by 1980 will induce enough additional foreign spending on US goods (and less US spending on foreign goods) to pay for those oil imports in real terms. If not, there is a transfer gap, and the size of the gap helps to estimate, *ceteris paribus*, the magnitude of the devaluation or other policy actions necessary to close

TABLE 3

US oil transactions and the balance of payments

	1972	1980
	(billions of dollars)	
Oil imports	-3.8	-13.4
Induced US exports to oil countries	+1.3	+3.6
Earnings on earlier US oil investment	+3.1	+4.5
New US investment in oil countries	-2.5	-7.7
Totals	-1.8	-12.9

SOURCE: Herbert S. Winokur, Jr., *Balance of Payments Flows Resulting from Oil Imports,* Mimeo, 1973.

the gap. This gap has been estimated for 1980 (see table 3) by considering four components of oil payments: (1) oil imports; (2) induced foreign spending on US goods; (3) US oil-related investment in producing countries; and (4) US income from previous oil investments.

The oil import deficit is expected to increase from $3.9 billion in 1972 to $13.4 billion by 1980. The increased income of oil exporters is estimated to increase their imports from the United States from $1.3 billion in 1972 to $3.6 billion by 1980. This assumes that their marginal propensities to import from various countries remain the same as in the recent past. This assumption understates US exports somewhat since devaluation makes US goods considerably cheaper. Income on previous oil-related US investment is estimated to rise from $3.1 billion to $4.5 billion in 1980. Finally the flow of new oil-related investment is estimated to rise to $7.7 billion, and the total deficit for the four categories of oil transactions is $12.9 billion. The estimated gap of $12.9 billion is based on the exchange rate prevailing in January 1973, and, in the absence of foreign lending or off-setting surpluses on other specific goods, the gap must be closed by other policy measures such as devaluation. This estimate abstracts from changes in any other exports or imports, except those directly induced by purchases from oil exporters.

Estimates of the future oil deficit have received much attention, and it is important that they be properly interpreted. An estimate of the oil deficit for 1980 is not a balance-of-payments estimate for 1980, since such an estimate would require comparable estimates for all other traded goods and capital flows. If the projected oil deficit is $13 billion, there will be neither upward nor downward pressures on the dollar if there are offsetting surpluses for other products or capital inflows totaling $13 billion.

Oil has received more attention from trade forecasters than other products, but early trade estimates indicate that US export and import substitutes will be increasingly competitive in the future and that foreign investment in the United States should increase. For example, the Chase Manhattan Bank estimates that net exports of three agricultural products – soybeans, feed grains, and wheat – will be $8 billion by 1980.[14] The trade balance for all agricultural products is more sensitive to trade controls, but one estimate for 1985 is a $7 billion surplus if present trade controls persist and a $13 billion surplus with freer trade.[15] As more evidence about trade in other products is assembled, policy-makers will be better able to assess the significance of a given oil deficit. With current limited information a $13 billion oil deficit does not preclude an overall payments surplus.[16] As a guide to further research better forecasts of trade in other products might be more productive than further refinements in forecasting the oil deficit.

c *Exchange rate flexibility*
One reason to be less concerned about payments deficits today than in the past is the greater flexibility of exchange rates. Since August 1971, when the dollar ceased being convertible into gold at $35 per ounce, there has been considerable rate flexibility among all major currencies. Governments have intervened occasionally in currency markets, and the system is probably best described as managed flexibility. The stated policy of the Bank of England and others has been to attempt to reduce deviations from the trend in their currency values without interfering with the trend itself. Since the period prior to the Smithsonian realignment of exchange rates in December 1971, the major industrial currencies have appreciated by a trade-weighted average of 29 per cent relative to the US dollar (as of 1 August 1973), with the German mark gaining the most, 55 per cent, and the Canadian dollar gaining the least, 1 per cent.[17] In addition the currencies of nearly all the major oil exporters have appreciated relative to the dollar (see table 4). If the relevant time period for planning oil policy is measured in years rather than months or days, then exchange rates can be taken as effectively flexible for planning purposes. Forecasts of oil deficits for five or ten years in the future can best be interpreted as forecasts of the behavior of exchange rates.

If a large fraction of the future US oil demand can be satisfied most cheaply by imports, these must be paid for by some combination of more exports and less imports of other products. Depreciation of the dollar accomplishes this adjustment of the trade balance by increasing exports and decreasing imports over the entire range of traded goods. Alternative policies, such as restricting oil imports through tariffs, quotas, or subsidies to domestic production, concentrates the entire adjustment burden on one product.

323

Thomas J. Grennes and Herbert S. Winokur, Jr

TABLE 4

Exchange rates of oil exporters (units of local currency per US dollar)

	1970	1973 (April)	Percentage appreciation
Saudi Arabia	4.500	3.730	+17%
Iran	75.700	68.200	+10%
Kuwait	.357	.296	+17%
Venezuela	4.400	4.200	+5%
Libya	.357	.296	+17%
Nigeria	.357	.658	-84%
Iraq	.357	.296	+17%
Indonesia	374.000	374.000	0

SOURCE: *International Financial Statistics,* 1972 supplement

Since exchange rates are relative prices, depreciation of the dollar implies appreciation of all other currencies. In oil-exporting countries the local currencies will appreciate (as they have in fact; see table 4), and the prices of imports will fall. For given dollar prices of oil local currency revenue will fall. As governments seek compensation through higher prices in the form of revised tax, royalty, and participation arrangements, American-produced oil becomes relatively more attractive. Exchange rates affect not only the pattern of trade, but also the location of direct investments, and dollar depreciation will affect the location of refineries. Exchange-rate adjustment will discourage capital outflows by providing incentives to construct new refining capacity in the United States to serve the domestic market.

3 OIL IMPORTS, PETRODOLLARS,
  AND MONETARY INSTABILITY

The third argument for restricting oil imports is that oil-exporting nations will accumulate large stocks of dollars, and this will threaten the stability of the international monetary system, especially the position of the dollar in that system. This threat is summarized by the warning of Hubert Humphrey that 'the sheiks of Arabia will control the dollar.'[18] However even under fixed exchange rates and growing oil exports oil-exporting countries did not generally accumulate reserves. Under flexible exchange rates such accumulation is even less likely.

A *Dollar accumulation by oil exporters*
The first part of the argument is an empirical proposition about the demand for dollar reserves by oil-exporting countries. In its crudest form it says that this de-

TABLE 5

Ratio of international reserves to imports for major oil exporters

	Mean 1950-59	Mean 1960-69	1971
Saudi Arabia	NA	1.2	2.4
Kuwait	0.5	0.3	0.4
Libya	1.1	0.4	3.7
Iraq	1.0	0.8	0.9
Iran	0.8	0.3	0.3
Venezuela	0.6	0.5	0.7
Nigeria	1.2	0.4	0.3
Indonesia	0.4	0.1	0.1

SOURCE: *International Financial Statistics,* 1972 supplement

mand is insatiable in spite of the opportunity costs of holding reserves. Some observers treat these costs as minor because most oil-rich nations 'don't need the
money.'[19] This argument is startling, since all the major oil exporters are underdeveloped countries by World Bank standards, and, except for the three million
people of Kuwait and Libya, the per capita incomes are extremely low (see table
2). Reserve accumulation is a considerable luxury for those in poverty.

A less extreme hypothesis about reserve accumulation by oil exporters is that
countries will not add all of their incremental income to reserves, but they will
raise the ratio of reserves to imports relative to their past behavior. Table 5 presents some evidence on reserve behavior by comparing the reserve-imports ratio
at the end of 1971 for major exporters with the means of those ratios for the
decades of the 1950s and 1960s. Of the eight countries considered, six are not
behaving differently than they did in the 1950s and 1960s. The two countries
which have accumulated dollars are Saudi Arabia and Libya, but there is no general pattern of reserve stockpiling.

The reason that accumulation of dollars has been limited is that there is an
adjustment process. Under fixed exchange rates a trade surplus tends to increase
aggregate demand, which increases imports, decreases exports, and tends to re-
tard reserve accumulation. In addition there is upward pressure on the exchange
rate of surplus countries which also stifles accumulation. In fact, the currencies
of six out of these eight have appreciated relative to the dollar since 1971.

B *The dollar overhang and monetary stability*

In fact most oil-exporting nations have not been adding substantially to their
dollar hoards, but if they did so in the future, what problems would this create

325

for US policy-makers?[20] Would this not aggravate the problem of dollar overhang and destabilize world currency markets? In analyzing the effect of oil exporters on currency markets, it is important to distinguish between a convertible dollar and an inconvertible dollar. The dollar was convertible into gold at the price of $35 per ounce for foreign banks until 1971 but it has been inconvertible since then. Much of the popular concern about monetary instability relates only to the convertible dollar and is of little relevance under current monetary arrangements.

The term 'dollar overhang' refers to the excess of dollar liabilities held by foreign governments over gold and other reserves held by the US government. Because of the fractional reserve arrangement small conversions of dollars could be accommodated, but massive conversions could not, and this presented a real threat to US reserves until 1971. Monetary, fiscal, and commercial policy could not be formulated without considering their impact on reserves. The United States was concerned about both the size of foreign dollar holdings and their distribution among governments, since some had higher propensities to hold dollars than others. It was difficult to quantify the threat to US reserves because the commitment to fixed exchange rates gave all private speculators an indirect claim on US reserves. Private speculation against the dollar would cause an excess demand for foreign currencies, and foreign governments were obliged to accumulate the excess dollars to prevent their currencies from appreciating and these dollars became eligible for conversion into US reserves. Thus sales of dollars by any US or foreign resident or private business firm could contribute to a gold drain as long as foreign governments were unwilling to accumulate dollars indefinitely. The magnitude of the overhang defied measurement because everyone was potentially a speculator against the dollar (including those who owned no dollars).

This threat to US reserves ended when the dollar was declared inconvertible in August 1971, and concern about the overhang problem lost most of its importance. Since then dollars have been worth as much or as little as sellers could obtain in private markets, and American policy-makers have been freed from a major constraint. At the same time there was a worldwide shift in exchange-rate policy away from fixed rates, and this general policy shift was quite independent of the dollar overhang. There were many reasons for the shift, but the immediate one was the increased mobility of capital between countries, and this affected all countries, not just the United States. The currencies of countries such as Canada and Japan are not held by foreign governments, yet their currencies were floated because of speculative capital flows under fixed rates. In summary, the abandonment of fixed rates reduces the importance of the dollar overhang problem and the contribution to the overhang by oil-exporting countries.

With an inconvertible dollar and more flexible rates the dollar overhang cannot threaten reserves but it may affect the variability of exchange rates. This depends on foreigners behaving differently from Americans, and one hypothesis is that, for any given stock of dollar assets, the dollar exchange rate will be more variable the larger the fraction held by foreigners and the larger the fraction held by oil exporters. An alternative hypothesis is that, if oil-exporting countries behave like well-informed speculators, they will consequently contribute to increased stability of exchange rates around their long-run equilibrium values. The quantitative significance of both of these hypotheses depends upon the assumption that the dollar holdings of oil-exporting countries are a relatively large fraction of total world dollar balances. In this connection a stabilizing transaction is defined to be one which moves an exchange rate toward its equilibrium value. If a government is supporting a disequilibrium exchange rate, then transactions which we would view as stabilizing might be viewed by that government as destabilizing.

Sometimes the literature characterizes Middle Eastern governments as greedy speculators who are anxious to manipulate their dollar holdings to increase their wealth. However, as long as they have pecuniary motives and are well informed about currency markets, they will disturb market stability no more than the treasurers of IBM, Standard Oil, or any private corporation which deals in currency markets and is obliged to satisfy greedy stockholders. If the dollar temporarily depreciates, well-informed speculators will perceive the transitory nature of the movement and buy dollars at the low price and sell them later at a higher price, with the combined effects of (1) reducing exchange-rate variability and (2) earning profits. Contrary to the instability hypothesis, this kind of speculation will stabilize currency markets. These governments do appear to have pecuniary motives, in view of their aggressive and tenacious bargaining with western oil companies; and, if government officials are not well informed about currency markets, they are in a position to hire the most knowledgeable portfolio managers in the world. This discussion of stabilizing behavior also applies to multinational corporations.

The same governments are sometimes portrayed as zealous nationalists who are willing to sacrifice considerable wealth to achieve political goals. They are said to believe that the threat of massive sales of dollars at critical times will accomplish these goals. If such sales occurred they would have two effects: (1) the government involved would lose money; and (2) exchange rates would be disturbed no more than by the operations of poorly informed private speculators. For example, if the dollar temporarily depreciated, malicious governments would sell dollars at low prices to push the dollar lower, and later, when the dollar recovered, they would have to buy at high prices to replenish their reserves.

This process would be partially self-correcting since they would lose money and their impact on the market is likely to be small, since well informed speculators would be delighted to offset their actions by buying dollars at bargain prices. In spite of frequent allegations no governments have been observed to behave in this way.

It should be noted that the dollar holdings of the relevant governments are a tiny share of the total currency market. The combined reserves of the eight largest oil producers (excluding the US, USSR, and Canada) were only $10 billion at the beginning of 1973, a figure which was exceeded by the reserves of a number of individual countries such as Germany, Japan, and France.[21] In addition, the US Tariff Commission estimates that multinational corporations possessed $268 billion in liquid assets which they could readily mobilize for speculative purposes.[22] The currency operations of oil-exporting countries are so small relative to those of other governments, international banks, multinational corporations, and private speculators that they can be safely ignored by those constructing US oil policy. If oil-exporting countries held all their reserves in the form of gold or SDRs instead of dollars, it would be no easier to maintain fixed exchange rates than it is with the current dollar overhang.

c *Petrodollars and foreign ownership of American business*
Petrodollars have concerned some people because of their threat to the value of the dollar. A more recent concern is that holders of petrodollars may take over major American businesses. Since it is not obvious how Americans suffer from foreign investment, such fears could be dismissed as isolated cases of xenophobia if they were not expressed by people in such powerful positions.[23]

A few facts about foreign investment are appropriate. At the end of 1972 American claims against foreigners exceeded foreign claims against Americans by $50 billion. American investment abroad has resulted in much more direct ownership of business than has foreign investment here. United States investment abroad was 50 per cent direct investment, but foreign investment in the US was only 10 per cent direct, and of this total 98 per cent came from Canada and western Europe.[24] Any new direct investment by oil-exporting countries will begin from a very small base. The US government has actively promoted foreign investment for years on the grounds that it benefits both the investor and the host country, and it would be ironic if the US government restricted foreign investment for fear of foreign domination of the US industry.[25]

Increased interest in foreign direct investment in the US is not directly attributable to petrodollars, although some popular literature has attempted to link the two issues. Devaluation of the dollar has made the US a less attractive export market and a more attractive location for direct investment. The automobile industry has already responded to these forces, with Volvo of Sweden announcing plans to produce in the United States, while German and Japanese producers are actively considering similar plans. The two problems of foreign direct investment and the US oil deficit are logically distinct, and some confusion is avoided if they are evaluated separately and on their own merits. If foreign ownership is judged to be in the national interest, then investment should be welcomed whether the nation has an oil surplus or a deficit.

D *Balance of payments and fixed exchange rates*
Concern about the state of the balance of payments is implicitly based on a system of fixed exchange rates. This is a legitimate fear under fixed rates since the central bank faces the prospect of running out of reserves. This has been impossible since the dollar became inconvertible in 1971, but the fear has survived the change in circumstances. Just as there is no threat to the central bank's reserves under flexible rates, there can be no balance-of-payments problem. The official settlements balance measures the US deficit as the change in US reserves plus increases in the dollar holdings of foreign governments. Inconvertibility means that US reserves will not change, and the behavior of foreign reserves is beyond the control of the US government. If there is an excess demand for foreign currency in the private market, and if foreign governments defend existing exchange rates by supplying their currencies and buying dollars, this will show up as a foreign surplus and an American deficit. Conversely, if rates are flexible, foreign governments need not undertake such involuntary dollar purchases, and all official settlements balances will be zero.

E *Monetary reform*
The present monetary system is not one of freely flexible rates but one of managed flexibility. Active discussions are under way to reform the system and the present system may not survive long in its present form. There are many proposals for reform, but a common element in all of them is greater flexibility of exchange rates than occurred prior to 1971. Even the conservative IMF emphasizes that flexibility of rates is an important part of the adjustment process. The US proposal, as set forth by Treasury Secretary George Schultz, calls for greater flexibility, and it specifies a rule indicating when rates should adjust.[26] The major indicator in the plan is the change in reserves, so that, if an oil-exporting country continues to accumulate dollars, then at a certain point it will be obliged to appreciate its currency.

It appears that policy-makers must accept considerable exchange-rate flexibility as a present fact and a likely future possibility. In such a world it makes little sense to ask about the effect on the balance of payments of some particular

329

oil policy. If oil can be obtained more cheaply from abroad, it is a mistake to limit imports for balance-of-payments reasons. Under flexible rates the balance of payments and the exchange rate will adapt to the oil policy. In the long run the only constraint on a nation's consumption and investment is its production possibilities. The balance of payments is not an additional constraint, and the allocative problem of how much oil to produce at home should be based on standard benefit-cost considerations.

F *Oil and dollar seigniorage*

Those who are concerned about a petrodollar problem view the exchange of dollars for oil as disadvantageous to the United States. This is somewhat paradoxical since a much larger accumulation of dollars a few years ago by European governments was widely viewed as advantageous to the United States and costly to Europe. It was said at that time that Americans were acquiring real resources in the form of imports or European businesses and paying for them, not with real resources, but with greenbacks. This process was called an 'exorbitant privilege' by De Gaulle, and it became known as the 'seigniorage' problem in the economics literature.[27] The hypothesis was that Americans paid non-competitive interest on their foreign borrowing and earned competitive returns on their foreign investment, and pocketed the difference as rent or seigniorage. The question of whether Americans do in fact earn seigniorage is an empirical issue. However, since Saudi Arabia and other oil exporters have access to the same forms of dollar investments as France or any other foreigner, then Americans either earn seigniorage on all foreign dollar holdings or on none of them. Thus, if dollar seigniorage exists, petrodollars are a problem for oil exporters and a cheap source of revenue for Americans, and if seigniorage does not exist, petrodollars are a problem for no one. In neither case are they an American problem.

SUMMARY

Balance-of-payments considerations are an increasingly prominent element in discussions of US oil policy. These considerations begin with the extent to which US oil consumption will be supplied from foreign sources and the terms under which such oil will have access to US markets. The point of departure for these discussions is often some version of oil protectionism. The themes now most often invoked are the balance-of-payments effects (at fixed exchange rates) of expected large imports of oil and the effects of large dollar accumulations by oil-exporting countries on international monetary instability.

The three main conclusions follow. First, strict adherence to the principle of self-sufficiency is unlikely to be the optimum way to respond to any balance-of-payments effects of increased oil imports. Oil protectionism results in worldwide efficiency losses because of misallocation of resources at home and abroad, and it causes an arbitrary redistribution of income between consumers and producers of oil.

Second, preoccupation with the deficit for any single commodity is a restrictive way to view the balance of payments. Such emphasis leads to an inefficient policy which concentrates the burden of adjustment on a single commodity instead of spreading it over the entire range of traded goods. Predictions of large and persistent future deficits can best be interpreted as forecasts of the prospective behavior of exchange rates. More flexible rates are not to be feared, and our experience since 1971 has shown that they are compatible with a growing volume of trade and general prosperity as measured by rapid growth of real income and falling unemployment.

Third, concern about increased international monetary instability as a direct result of dollar accumulation by oil-exporting countries is exaggerated. The tenacious bargaining by oil-exporting countries over their returns from oil sales suggests that they are highly motivated by income. This is supported by the fact that they are generally poor countries as measured by per capita income. In fact, the ratio of international reserves to imports for the major oil-exporting countries has been relatively stable. The management of their dollar reserves has not been significantly different from that of countries which do not produce oil, and they appear to present no greater threat to monetary stability than other central banks and multinational corporations.

NOTES

Thomas J. Grennes is Assistant Professor of Economics, North Carolina State University, Raleigh, North Carolina, and Herbert S. Winokur, Jr, is Director, ICF, Inc., Washington, DC

1 *Oil and Gas Journal* 5 March 1973, 48; and US Department of Commerce
2 See M.A. Adelman, *The World Oil Market* (Baltimore 1972). The question is whether the existence of international oil companies increases or decreases cartel stability among the producing countries.
3 For a discussion of actual and threatened military activities between Arab countries see the Statement by Assistant Secretary of State Joseph J. Sisco before the House Near East Sub-Committee, 6 June 1973.
4 For an example of the difficulty associated with such exercises, see W.S. Salant *et al., The United States Balance of Payments in 1968* (Washington 1964).
5 The contributing policies included, among others, the Federal Power Commission ceiling on the wellhead price of natural gas, the uncertainties (e.g., crude

Thomas J. Grennes and Herbert S. Winokur, Jr

sources, refineries location, and the status of Canada) involved in the imminent modifications in the oil import program, and environmental restrictions
on fuel use, refinery siting, and offshore drilling. Despite the long-run good
intentions behind many of these policies the short-run effect was to help
create the energy shortage of 1973.

6 On coping with a supply interruption see The Cabinet Task Force on Oil
Import Control, *The Oil Import Question* (Washington 1970), 50-5.

7 Data from US Department of Interior, published in *New York Times,*
5 November 1972

8 On commodity agreements see Harry G. Johnson, *Economic Policies Toward
Less Developed Countries* (Washington 1967), chap. 5.

9 See the writings of M.A. Adelman and James E. Akins who share a concern
about the foreign cartel but whose views are quite different.

10 For a program to dismantle the cartel see M.A. Adelman, *Foreign Policy*,
Winter 1972-3.

11 Automobile emission controls are not a simple tax on gasoline because they
increase the demand for gasoline per mile driven by lowering mileage per
gallon. The offsetting effect is the reduction in gasoline demand from the
higher price of driving a mile.

12 For example, an editorial in the *Oil and Gas Journal*, 16 October 1972,
warns that 'By the early 1980's the deficit from energy imports alone may
well reach $20-25 billion. Such a possible drain on US finance has fearsome
implications.' However the fearsome implications are not specified.

13 Real GNP grew at the rate of 6.1 per cent for 1972, and the unemployment
rate fell from 6 per cent at the end of 1971 to 4.5 per cent by October 1973:
Survey of Current Business, October 1973.

14 *International Finance*, Chase Manhattan Bank, 24 September 1973, 7

15 *Business Review*, Federal Reserve Bank of Dallas, September 1973, 8

16 For a more alarmist point of view see Frank V. Fowlkes, 'Trade Report/
"Petrodollar" surpluses loom as problem for monetary system, US energy
crisis,' *National Journal*, 18 August 1973, 1211-17.

17 A trade-weighted index of dollar depreciation is calculated daily by the
Morgan Guaranty Trust and is reported periodically by the *Wall Street
Journal* among others.

18 *Wall Street Journal*, 2 March 1973

19 James E. Akins, director of the State Department's Office of Fuels and
Energy, quoted in *Wall Street Journal*, 10 April 1973

20 The dollar overhang refers to a stock of dollars at a fixed exchange rate. The
flow of dollars into this stock is a function of the real volume of oil trade,
the price of oil, and the exchange rate. For a given volume of oil trade, and

even under fixed exchange rates, it is possible to talk about a potential 'oil overhang.' If the long-run world supply elasticity of oil is high, the demand elasticity low, and the current real market price above the long-run equilibrium real price, then the 'oil overhang' may severely limit the flow of dollars into the dollar overhang. This limitation would be reinforced by flexible exchange rates. See M.A. Adelman, *World Oil Market*, for a discussion of long-run oil price trends, cartel stability, and the real resource costs of substantial increments to world oil supply.

21 *International Financial Statistics*, July 1973
22 Study by US Tariff Commission reported in *Wall Street Journal*, 13 February 1973
23 See the statement by Nelson Rockefeller: 'What is going to happen in these countries – particularly these Arab countries – with these billions they are getting? Are they going to come over here and buy up all our corporations? They could buy the *New York Times*, the *Los Angeles Times* or CBS': *National Journal*, 1972.
24 *Survey of Current Business*, August 1973
25 Congressman John Dent of Pennsylvania has proposed such a bill to Congress; see *National Journal*, 18 August 1973.
26 The US proposal is set forth in the *Economic Report of the President*, January 1973, chap. 5 and supplement.
27 See Robert Mundell and Alexander Swoboda, eds, *Monetary Problems of the International Economy* (Chicago 1969), passim.

PART FOUR

Energy System Modeling

A complex detailed project is now underway at Queen Mary College, University of London. The paper by Professor Deam details the program of work which the research team is attempting. Individual fuels are detailed for each country; production, refining, consumption. Imaginary tankers are built and carry energy around the world. Ports are deepened, prices change. Complex interrelationships follow from seemingly isolated acts within individual areas.

A simple model of a single refinery is given to indicate how a multi-commodity world model would operate. Detailed results of the large model's operations will shortly be available.

For a contrasting type of aggregate world resource model, read Roberts' critique of *The Limits to Growth*. See also the article by Houthakker on energy research.

R. J. DEAM

A world energy model

It has been well established that an oil company system can be reduced to a
mathematical linear programming form which, when solved to optimize some
criterion pertinent to the circumstances, leads to practical meaningful results.[1]
The system is one of economics, the logistics being bounded by sets of constraints
not only physical but also social and political in nature. The world energy system
is similar to the company system, except that the former is more heavily bounded
by political and social constraints; the repeated attempts of national governments
to formulate energy policies are at the same time confirmation of the heavy political and social overtones and of the need for some improved framework for
decision-making if real crisis is to be averted.

It is our belief that world energy is a social/political/economic system, which
can be formulated in linear programming (LP) form, and hence solved, to give all
policy-makers a valid common framework. Thus, through knowledge, better policies may be made, and major painful confrontations avoided.

The oil companies, like other energy suppliers, compete and trade within the
given and future world system, which we believe is determined to a marked degree
by political considerations. Oil, coal, and to a more limited extent gas, are readily
transported on a world scale; the national policy of one country will affect supply,
prices, and hence competition in other countries.

It is our belief that national energy policies can only be investigated within a
world-wide framework, and that this is more, not less, true of the countries which
import, consume, and export large quantities of energy.

The linear programming systems used by oil companies have emerged slowly
over the past two decades. The concepts and techniques built into such large,

integrated systems cannot be described or their lessons learnt fully without a great deal of time and some contact with the industry. The organization of data, the computer routines, the methods of sensitivity analysis, the LP mathematics, all are necessary parts of the whole, and each is a subject in its own right.

Here it is proposed to gloss over the mechanics and to suggest both the uses to which a world energy model may be put and, by inference, the reasons for its development.

Our demonstration model, incorporating two crude sources, two refineries, and three markets, has been described elsewhere.[2] This model shows how such an integrated oil company can be represented in linear programming form which may be solved for minimum cost. Within the system both refineries, although owned by the same group, are competing for the same market which is allocated to each refinery on a minimum cost criterion. For example, the solution gives rise to the cost of each product at each refinery. If one adds the transport cost of each product from each refinery to each market, nowhere is it cheaper to depart from the optimal allocation. Given a perfectly competitive situation – with the allocation of the market to the cheapest source – the framing of the problem and solution would be identical were the refineries to be owned by different companies. The methods and philosophy applied to a single company are almost exactly applicable to the industry as a whole, subject to the assumption of perfect competition. Thus with the added reasonable assumption that competing forms of energy can be described in linear programming form, the great bulk of our knowledge and experience is applicable to a world energy model.

It is not intended to extend that time-horizon of the model, either in its static or multi-time period forms, beyond about fifteen years. It will thus be able to take account of innovations in the employment of resources by existing technology, but not of the possible emergence of new technology. On the basis of our previous experience of planning models we believe that a time-horizon of this order is sufficient to enable the currently necessary decisions to be placed in their temporal context, and that little is to be gained by attempting to foreshadow the decisions of several decades hence.

Political constraints, whether legal or fiscal (eg, fuel oil tax), create a restricted environment within which perfect competition is assumed in our proposed models. An important feature of the model is that it will evaluate these barriers to competition. It is likely that a political constraint imposed by one nation will increase the cost of energy to other nations. For example, the social desire for a low sulfur in fuel oil in New York could have a marked upward effect on fuel oil prices in Europe.

The whole system will thus describe the boundary conditions within which details of a national energy policy can be determined. The over-all economic consequences of minimum coal production will require a world-wide model; the logistics of siting power stations can then be determined in a more detailed national model given the boundary conditions from the world model.

The entrepreneur will no doubt use world energy models to determine his optimum market share and to reveal where prices are significantly departing from the perfect competition or equilibrium condition. The energy models on solution will give rise to equilibrium prices as a matter of routine. Where actual or predicted prices significantly differ from equilibrium ones, opportunity exists to prosper by helping to restore equilibrium.

It is of vital interest to measure the effect of changing the charges levied by the Organization of Petroleum Exporting Countries (OPEC) and to determine the extent to which these charges may rise before painful confrontation occurs. The model could investigate the numerous aspects of this problem. Perhaps the most important use of a world energy model is to attempt to ensure the smooth supply of future energy at reasonable cost. Careful prediction of the nature and timing of fuel substitutions could save much wealth. The damage that could be caused by precipitous or ill-considered national policies to this smooth future supply would affect us all and needs expounding.

The assumption of perfect competition, perfect knowledge of competitors' reactions, plans, and the like, is idealistic. The goodness of fit will indicate the competitiveness of the industry and also highlight those areas where deviation is large. These latter areas could be subjected to physical (eg, installation of new processing plant) and/or political intervention with advantage.

Enough has been said to indicate that the need for a world energy model exists, that most of the methodology and philosophy underlying the project are well known, and some possible uses have been indicated; the major problem is now one of assembling world-wide energy and economic data and not the least vital is a clear statement of political constraints imposed on the energy system. Experiments with the model and analysis of its solutions will soon identify those variables and constraints of importance.

The initial study has been divided into five projects:
a) the role of market mechanisms;
b) the pricing of refinery products;
c) oil transportation studies;
d) energy policies;
e) pollution.

As more staff become available it is hoped to widen the study and establish further projects such as:

1 Use of world energy model to develop methods by which companies can determine their optimum market share by countries.

339

2   Show how an aggregate world energy model and a detailed regional model interact and how these can be decoupled (macro/micro linkage).

3   Combining projects 1 and 2 to further develop methods of determining market share of an individual company by regions within a country (eg, the XYZ Company's equilibrium market share in, say, the Bremen, Cologne, and Munich areas in Germany).

4   Monopoly rents particularly in crude pricing; the effect of competition between OPEC countries in the fields of participation and individual marketing, and the consequent effect on the commodity agreement. The probable future OPEC royalties.

5   Discounted, multi-time period energy models will help establish lags and timing of investment decisions. The timing of probable political law enactment will also be indicated.

6   Risk and time. The use of the model in establishing the way in which odds on decision risks depend on the underlying uncertainties and how these change with time.

7   The individual firm would wish to use the outcome of world energy models in its long-term, then medium-term planning, and eventually in its operational planning. The way it would do this and the operational control it needs to establish needs investigation.

8   Energy flows between countries, and political constraints to these flows, will have important consequences on international financial movements (eg, balance of payments). These interactions can be traced in a world energy model.

THE ROLE OF MARKET MECHANISMS

The model of world energy which is being constructed will represent the resources available for satisfying energy needs, and institutional constraints which govern their use. To apply and interpret the results obtained, information is also needed about the behavioral dynamics of the system. This note outlines a proposed study of this aspect of the problem.

Interpretation of results from the model would be simplest if perfect knowledge and perfect competition could be assumed. The optimal (ie, least-cost) pattern of production and supply, as given by the LP solution, would then be a prediction of how the world energy industry would respond to a given pattern of energy demands and institutional constraints. Furthermore, market prices would be identical with the marginal costs generated by the solution.

This simple view must be modified if either knowledge or competition is imperfect. Imperfection of either would lead to the adoption of non-optimal supply patterns. Effects of this kind will be detected in the first place by applying the model to current demand data. In fact, a major use of the model may be to highlight such non-optimalities and enable them to be corrected.

To use the model predictively, however, we must know more than this. We need to know whether imperfect competition (eg, collusion between suppliers) plays any part in preventing the optimum pattern from being attained. It has often been suggested that oil prices are affected by collusion between suppliers, but no convincing evidence of such effects has been presented. Quantitative information is needed on any obstacles to free competition at present affecting the world energy market. Three main sources of information on this matter will be examined.

Firstly, data on market prices will be compared with related information on marginal costs. Information on bulk prices of oil products in Europe has become increasingly available in recent years. The most important variable marginal cost element relevant to these prices is the spot charter rate of crude oil carriers. Changes in the rates of tax and royalty payments to oil-producing countries have also become important in the recent past. These elements determine the marginal cost of crude oil delivered in Europe. Marginal costs of the main products can be determined from this by applying an LP model of refining and transport to the historical patterns of product demand.

Free competition would imply that product prices are determined by marginal costs only. The relationship would involve time-lags, representing delayed response to exogenous changes. Collusive price-fixing, on the other hand, would result in prices being more closely related to average costs – as represented, for example, by the AFRA charter rate series. Statistical analysis of the relevant time series can therefore be used to compare the predictive performance of the two hypotheses.

A second and related line of investigation will attempt to explain profits of international oil companies in terms of exogenous price and cost determining factors. On the hypothesis that the market is governed by free competition, profits represent the difference between market prices (as determined by marginal costs) and the oil suppliers' average costs. A major element is the difference between spot charter rates for tankers and the operating costs of owned tanker fleets. Published data will be analyzed by fitting models representing effects of this kind. This is a more comprehensive approach than that based on price data, because profitability takes account of a wide variety of price movements at different levels, whereas published prices apply only to the largest bulk product markets.

Thirdly, oil industry profits will be analyzed in terms of return on investment. The hypothesis of free competition requires that this rate of return should be similar to that of other large-scale industrial activities. Conventional methods of financial analysis are not adequate for comparisons of this kind because of the

341

distorting effects of high growth rates coupled with long gestation periods for new capital. In spite of these difficulties, attempts will be made to check whether the hypothesis of free competition is tenable at the large-scale investment level.

If these studies reveal evidence against the hypothesis of free competition, the implication would be that the efficiency of the world energy industry (in relation to the limited time-horizon mentioned earlier) can be improved by international political measures designed to correct any distortions that may be detected. At present there is no reason to anticipate such a result. The contrary conclusion would be that energy markets are freely competitive apart from known political and fiscal constraints. This conclusion cannot be established directly, because increasingly elaborate theories of collusion could be put forward to meet the established facts. It may well be, however, that the hypothesis of free competition can be shown to fit the current behavior of these markets. This would strengthen the case for using a world model based on free competition as a tool for prediction, planning, and control.

THE PRICING OF REFINERY PRODUCTS

One of the purposes of the world energy model is to arrive at a valuation of oil refinery products under the assumption that near-perfect competition exists. If it is true, as we believe, that the mechanisms which determine product prices are in the process of changing and that this change is likely to be permanent, it is important that the influences at work, and the options open to the industry in reacting to those influences, should be represented in the model.

Simplified refinery model
The most important single process employed at an oil refinery is the fractional distillation of crude oil, in which the feedstock is separated into perhaps six streams according to boiling point. For the sake of clarity we here consider the separation of crude oil into three streams. The nomenclature employed is not that which is normally used in the industry.

From the bottom of the fractionation column, a residual stream is taken which for the present purposes may be called heavy fuel oil (HFO). This is material which does not vaporize at the temperature of the base of the column, which is typically about 350°C. It may be used without further treatment as fuel, it is of high sulfur content (at least from most Middle East crudes), and may comprise as much as 50 per cent of the crude oil. Yields as high as this are rare and many of the recently discovered crudes have much lower yields of HFO. The next stream in decreasing order of boiling point we shall term middle distillate. Its boiling range is from about $200°$ to $350°$c and it finds application in such forms as diesel fuel and central heating fuel. The remaining fraction which we shall consider is naphtha, by which we mean all material boiling below $200°$c. Though its main use is as a feed material to motor spirit manufacture, it may be used to supplement the supply of middle distillate.

Although this description is a vast oversimplification of actual refinery practice, it is nevertheless a reasonably close description of the marginal adjustments made in response to marginal changes in demand, and is therefore relevant to a discussion of product prices.

Historical price mechanism

If we assume that naphtha, middle distillate, and HFO are the only products of crude oil distillation and are obtained in yields α, β, and $1-\alpha-\beta$ respectively, then the following relation must hold:

α (price of naphtha) + β (price of middle distillate)
$$+ (1-\alpha-\beta) \text{ (price of HFO)}$$
$\geqslant$ price of crude + fully built-up distillation costs.

Otherwise there would be no incentive to expand refining capacity. Under the assumption of perfect competition the inequality becomes an equation.

It is in practice possible to vary α and β within limits, with consequent changes in the qualities of the products. We shall, however, assume that, given the choice of crude oil, the yields are fixed. The above relation then contains four unknowns, namely, the four prices, and three further conditions are sufficient to specify the system.

Until the late sixties, the overriding influence on product prices was the relative shortage of middle distillate and the relative surpluses of naphtha and HFO (this at least was the case outside the United States; there the demand for motor spirit corresponds to a relatively greater fraction of crude, and naphtha is in great demand as a motor spirit feedstock). Consequently, naphtha was used to supplement middle distillate production. In practice this can be achieved by varying the cut-point of $200°$c between naphtha and gas oil over a range from $185°$c to $225°$c. Hence, approximately:

price of naphtha = price of middle distillate. (A)

Also it is possible to 'crack' part of the residue from the distillation, that is, to subject it to processes which break up the large molecules into smaller ones, thus producing material in the middle distillate boiling range. Hence,

price of middle distillate = price of HFO + fully built-up cracking costs (B)

R.J. Deam

The marginal crude was Kuwait and its price determined the prices of other crudes. (c)

These three conditions (A to C) complete the price structure.

Of course, this is an oversimplified view. The three materials we have considered are not the only products of a refinery; naphthas from different crudes vary in their potential for being upgraded to motor spirit; middle distillates and fuel oil vary in sulfur content and viscosity. Yet, while many more complex interrelationships exist than this picture acknowledges, the structure of product prices was until quite recently in broad agreement with it.

Price structure in the future
There are several reasons why the historical price mechanism may break down in the future.
1   The demand for natural gas is growing, for reasons of convenience and on environmental grounds. One way of meeting this demand is to transport liquefied natural gas (LNG) in refrigerated ships from the areas where it is found to the areas of demand. This, however, is an expensive method, estimated to result in a landed cost in Japan of gas from the Persian Gulf equivalent to $7-8bbl of low sulfur fuel oil, as compared with the current price of low sulfur fuel oil of about $4.50bbl.

An alternative method is to manufacture synthetic natural gas (SNG) by a process like the Gas Council's Rich Gas Process, employing naphtha as a feedstock. We believe that such a process is likely to be significantly cheaper, and if so, the price of naphtha would no longer be in accordance with equation (A), but would rather be determined by:

price of naphtha = cost of LNG - cost of converting naphtha to SNG.

2   Again on environmental grounds, the demand for low sulfur fuel oil is growing. It will become necessary to introduce a residue desulfurization process which will inevitably result in a lower viscosity product. Many crudes, and particularly the recently discovered crudes, have low yields of HFO. It is fairly certain that the surplus of HFO and the need for cracking will disappear and consequently that the prices of low sulfur fuel oil and middle distillate will converge. Equation (B) would be replaced by:

price of middle distillate = price of low sulfur fuel oil
= price of high sulfur fuel oil + desulfurization costs.

3   It is likely that, as a result of increasing production capacity, Arabian crude could displace Kuwait as the marginal crude, at least until its price reaches the ceiling set by synthetic crude from tar sands and/or shale.

Conclusions

The influences enumerated above, singly or in combination, are likely to result in a rearrangement of the crude and product price structure which has obtained in the past. This would in turn affect investment decisions by oil companies, governmental decisions on anti-pollution legislation, and decisions by the customer as evidenced in the relative demands for distillate and residual fuels.

It is, therefore, our intention to construct the model so as to include the options of natural gas manufacture from naphtha and residue desulfurization and to examine dual values from the solutions to see whether they support the changes in price structure suggested above.

OIL TRANSPORTATION STUDIES

The world energy model will represent the resources available for satisfying the future world energy demands and the physical and political limitations governing their use. Using the technique of linear programming, least cost solutions of supplying world energy demands will be evaluated. As the geographical location of many of the world's crude oil producing areas are not those of high energy consumption, some of the major costs involved in satisfying energy demands will be those associated with the transport of oil by ocean tanker. This note outlines the method by which these costs will be represented in the model and some proposed studies of the world oil transporation system that will be made using the model.

Crude oils and oil products are moved in a number of different sizes of ocean tankers ranging from around 20,000 dw tons up to the very large crude oil carriers (VLCCs) of over 200,000 dw tons. Daily operating costs of tankers increase with increasing size but in terms of tons of oil moved the cost decreases as the size of the vessel increases. There are, however, restrictions to the use of the larger vessels on some routes owing to restricted facilities either at the loading or receiving terminals to handle the vessels or their cargoes. In addition, there are finite numbers of tankers of any particular size available in the world at any one time.

The model will include opportunities for the movement of oil between areas in tankers of several different size categories. The use of these opportunities will be controlled by restrictions of the total tanker fleet capacity for each category. The marginal values generated by solutions of the model against the capacity restrictions should then represent the scarcity values for each vessel size. From these values, expected spot charter rates relating to any particular energy supply/demand situation can be obtained.

It is proposed initially to test the validity of the model's assumptions by correlating actual spot charter rates realized in the tanker market with model-derived

R.J. Deam

values, using past oil supply and demand data. This correlation will enable quantitative assessments to be made of any imperfections in the tanker market and will validate the model for the predictive studies proposed below.

There has been considerable activity in the last few years to improve terminal facilities to enable VLCCs to be more fully used and schemes have been developed such as that at Bantry Bay in Ireland to create entrepot terminals for tankers of 500,000 dw tons or more. With these developments it is likely that the number of VLCCs available in the future will be insufficient to meet the demand for them. In addition, there will still exist a large number of smaller tankers with active lives stretching a number of years into the future. It is suggested that, under these conditions, charter rates for VLCCs will be equal to those of the smaller vessels and that the advantage resulting from economies of scale will go to the owners of VLCCs in the form of a rent. It is proposed to check, using the energy model, the validity of the hypothesis that the smaller tankers will continue to be the marginal tankers (and will thus set the market rate for all vessels). This will be done in the first place using estimates of future tanker capacities. If the hypothesis is correct, then the concern of the Americans over the inability of their east coast refineries to accept VLCCs for the import of the large quantities of Middle East crudes which will be required in the near future could be allayed and plans for expanding port facilities or building entrepot terminals in this and other parts of the world could be delayed for a number of years. Variations in the assumptions of the model will be studied in order to evaluate the effect on the equilibrium values for tankers of changes in the oil supply and demand position.

Further developments of the model to include opportunities and restrictions for building tankers and expanding port facilities should enable estimates to be made of the optimum world tanker fleet composition and which port facilities should be expanded for different future oil supply situations. With the eventual inclusion of time-phasing into the model, the optimal time for port expansions and vessel building can be assessed.

ENERGY POLICIES

There is no unified world energy policy at the moment and the prospect of one evolving in the foreseeable future is remote. Apart from the occasional consideration of their indigenous fuel production, most countries have no comprehensive fuel policies relating to nationalization or conservation. Instead, each country pursues policies which it considers will suit it best economically or will protect its indigenous industries, commercial interest, or social environment.

These policies, especially when they have international implications, do not always achieve the effect desired by the instigating nation. For example, it has been suggested that the American quota system for crude oil imports (designed to protect their indigenous oil industry) in effect reduced the cost of energy to consumers in Western Europe and Japan. This 'inadvertent benevolence,' it is further suggested, could be ranked in importance with the Marshall Plan for European recovery.

The United States is the largest energy consumer in the world and the fuel policies of that country have a significant impact on the rest of the Western world. US energy consumption per capita is almost double that of the UK and nearly triple that of France. However, the US domestic reserves of oil represent only eight years' supply and those of natural gas about twelve years' supply. What effects will this have on world energy resources if, as estimated, by 1985 over 50 per cent of US oil demand will have to be met by imports?

Questions which need to be investigated (in each case under a variety of assumptions) are:
1 How high will energy prices rise in the US; will the price rises be sufficient to make synthetic crude production from coal or shale an economic proposition?
2 Will the shortage of natural gas promote conversion to other fuels, increased imports of gas, or improved technology for gas production from oil?
3 Will increased prices result in a reduction in the demand escalation and a less wasteful economy?
4 Perhaps 75 per cent of US future crude imports will come from Africa and the Middle East. This dependence will put the US in a highly vulnerable position strategically and economically. Will this situation promote moves towards conservation of national stocks or promote new extraction or conversion technologies?
5 How seriously will the US dependence on imported oil affect the supplies to Western Europe and Japan?
6 Will the US be forced to review their restrictions on high sulfur fuel oil consumption? Or will insistence on this increase the value of low sulfur crudes so that residue desulfurization in US or Europe becomes economically viable?

The reserves of the Soviet bloc are second in size only to the Middle East. With a growing dependence on oil and an appreciation of the world reserve situation, will the Soviet bloc be moved to conserve indigenous fuels by importing Middle East oil? Will they compete with the US and Western Europe in this respect? Russia proposes to export oil via a trans-Siberian pipeline to Japan. Will this influence Japan's dependence on Middle East oil?

The Middle Eastern and African supplying nations will be economically and strategically in a very strong position. Will pursuit of national interest, on the part of individual countries, override OPEC policies? There are indications that the OPEC countries will want to conserve supplies, albeit at elevated prices, just sufficiently to supply a revenue that can be usefully absorbed. What levels of supply and revenue do they contemplate and what prices can they go to before they affect world demand?

Most European countries have some sort of restrictive or selective fuel policies that have international ramifications. North Sea oil will probably be the cause of more international squabbling than that between the Middle Eastern countries. What will be the policies of the EEC? If France does not discover significant indigenous supplies of crude then there will be pressure to put North Sea oil on a community basis. Already Norway has become nationalistic about her own oil production; will this attitude affect the whole structure of the European community? Britain, in common with some other European nations, has heavily subsidized its indigenous coal industry. Does this policy in effect give rise to cheaper fuel in all other countries? Italian legislation insists on oil companies installing excess refining capacity. Has this policy had the effect of ensuring cheap energy and low industry profits in Italy? What effect does it have on the rest of Europe?

There are many other national policies which may have significant international effects – German compulsory stock stipulations, French protectionist controls for French crudes, pressures from national and international environmentalists for pollution control including delays to pipelines, calls for low motor spirit lead contents, low fuel oil sulfur contents, and stricter safety controls on nuclear energy production. These policies and many others produce world situations which we intend to investigate and quantify using our world energy model.

POLLUTION

The social desire for low emissions of sulfurous oxide gases from chimneys and of lead compounds from motor car exhausts can be met technically at a cost. The obvious way to achieve the former would be to reduce the sulfur contents of the fuels to be burnt and this could be done by a combination of expedients. Thus crude oils could be segregated and their transportation routes rearranged so that low sulfur crudes are refined in the countries with the most stringent environmental standards and the more sulfurous crudes processed elsewhere. But this would be only a partial or short-term solution to the problem and, as countries tightened their specifications, increasing emphasis would be given to the direct desulfurization of the fuel oils to be burnt.

It is difficult to determine the cost of such sulfur reductions, and particularly the choice of the most economic way of achieving such goals. Besides deciding where the various crudes should be refined, with additional transportation costs as an important side effect, there are many alternative processing arrangements available for sulfur removal. A world-wide energy model should be able to indicate the most economic arrangements for attaining the required goals and also indicate what should be added to the prices of individual fuel oils as the product specifications became increasingly strict. These burdens must be compared with the costs for alternative arrangements, such as the removal of sulfur after combustion, as the sulfurous constituents of the stack gases.

We have expressed the burden of pollution abatement in terms of low sulfur fuels, but we also intend to assess the implications of low lead contents in motor gasoline.

CURRENT POSITION

The program of work is now well under way, and our first results have been published.[3] A world-wide model of the natural gas and petroleum sector is in operation. The matrix we are currently using is over 4000 rows and 14000 columns, and this is yielding some very interesting results which we intend publishing in the near future. Our experience has proved to us that it is impossible, without systems as large as this, to understand the world-wide interactions. It is incredible to find, for example, that Alaskan oil production reduces the world need for small tankers, lowers spot freight on small tankers, and lowers oil prices in Australia. Interrelationships are indeed complex and can only be seen in a complex detailed model.

NOTES

1 R.J. Deam, 'Short Run Programming of Oil Operations,' *The Proceedings of the VIIIth World Petroleum Conference*, p. 269.
2 R.J. Deam, 'Linear Programming in Management Accounting.' *The Accountant*, 23 Sept. 1967
3 Energy Research Unit of Queen Mary College, London. 'World Energy Modelling: the Development of Western European Oil Prices.' *Energy Policy*, June 1973, p. 21.

In a widely read book, *The Limits to Growth,* published in 1971, an inter-disciplinary team at Massachussetts Institute of Technology developed a computer model of the world. This model reaffirmed the dismal predictions of Thomas Malthus – population and production growing at geometric rates will exhaust the world's scarce resources or produce so much pollution as to lower population.

Roberts asks whether *The Limits to Growth* is in fact a superior document to Malthus. Couched behind impressive computer print-outs. Roberts finds the book's conclusions rest on a number of mistaken assumptions, a naive structure, and a general lack of understanding of either the data or the kinds of economic feedbacks which will limit crises in reality. 'The book says that if we assume (1) there are limits and (2) there is nothing we can do about them, then (3) we will bump into them.

Surprise!??'

Papers to read alongside Roberts' dissection are Deam's, Dewees' on environmental quality, and Barnett's 'Energy, resources, and growth.'

MARC J. ROBERTS

The limits of *The Limits to Growth*

'My mind is made up. Don't confuse me with facts.'
Contemporary American folk saying

Recently the view that economic growth is 'bad' has become increasingly prominent within the movement for environmental protection. Perhaps efforts at 'reform' are perceived as having failed. Perhaps there is an impulse to reject the
values of a society which appears immoral and corrupt. Perhaps the continual
encroachment on wilderness areas and the success of the movement to limit
population have each played a role. Whatever the reasons, more and more individuals, both young activists and solid citizens, apparently have come to believe
that the continued expansion of economic activity is not 'worth the cost.'[1]

Into this context, with all the fanfare that a well-organized public relations
effort could provide, came the book, *The Limits to Growth*.[2] It presented, and
drew implications from, a series of alternative predictions about the future obtained by using a computer to manipulate a simple mathematical model of the
world. It had all the right credentials, having been produced by an interdiscipli-
nary team at MIT and funded by a group of European businessmen (the Club of
Rome). Short, well-written, unencumbered by extensive footnotes, *Limits* included lots of dramatic graphs and diagrams which provided 'white space' and
made the book easier to read. Critical reviews and unfavorable comments by
academic experts did little to halt the book's rapid rise to best-sellerdom both
in Europe and North America.[3]

The popular renown of the book provides some reason to focus an essay quite
closely on *The Limits to Growth* itself rather than on growth policy in general.

Marc J. Roberts

What can we make of the surprising conclusion that the growth of industrial capital, as well as of population, must be ended if we are to avoid a 'crisis,' and that very rapid action is required since the crisis is almost at hand? As a first step – and only for the sake of argument – I propose to analyse these results on their own terms. Are they in fact derivable from the model? Even if we accept that the methods used are reasonable – and I question that as well – how adequate is the particular structure of the 'World 3' model used by the *Limits* team?

As the epigraph to this paper perhaps makes clear, my view of *The Limits to Growth* is quite critical. I find no reason to believe that the real world will behave the way the model does. The inevitable and imminent 'crisis' in the simulation analysis is the result of a number of structural and quantitative assumptions which are both poorly supported and implausible. Make different assumptions and you get different results. The model can be made to behave in almost any way one wishes. Although the authors claim that the behavior of the system is 'counter-intuitive,' in fact it follows directly and transparently from its assumptions. Far from revealing 'the basic structure of the world system,' the work primarily reveals the beliefs and prior commitments of those who wrote it. The operation of the model adds little if anything to the simple assertion of its conclusions as an article of faith.

Even if one were to accept the structure of the model, *Limits* itself does not explore in a reasonable manner the possibility that economic adjustments and technical progress will overcome the limits it postulates. In what follows I do hope to exhibit in detail the reasons for this view, and perhaps to persuade the reader to share it, in whole or in part. Before launching into the argument, however, we need to know what we are arguing about. What exactly does the book say?

THE 'LIMITS' MODEL AND ITS IMPLICATIONS

Limits contends that there is only so much land in the world, so much resources, and so much capacity to tolerate pollution. Industrial and agricultural activity use resources and produce pollution. Population requires food. Population and production grow exponentially. Sooner or later, it is said, the growth of production and population will either use up all the world's resources, exhaust the capacity of the available land for food production, or produce so much pollution so as to lower birth rates and food output.

These sectors are also inter-linked. When one meets a limit, it pulls the others down after it. For example, when food production becomes inadequate, a vain attempt is made to bolster it by investing more capital – which eventually causes industrial output to decline. Declining food output per capita also raises mortality

352

rates and lowers population. Ordinary reformist actions, like better technology, only postpone the crisis a few years and makes it worse when it occurs. The pressures of exponential growth will soon transcend the limits of the world's natural systems. The conclusion is offered that the growth of industry and population must be controlled.

The mathematical model of the world used to support the argument includes eleven crucial 'stock' variables; resources, pollution, three kinds of capital (service, industrial and agricultural), three classes of population (young, middle-aged, old) and three land variables (total, available, and urban/industrial). These quantities are tied together by approximately seventy other variables that represent various rates of flow, multipliers, coefficients of adjustment, and so on. Many of these in turn take on different values, depending on what happens to various other stocks, flows, and coefficients in the model. To 'run' the model you insert an assumed set of initial values for all the various parameters, and use a computer to calculate the 'history' of the succeeding years. Population, capital, pollution, resources, and land use all will rise and fall as the various multipliers and coefficients determine rates of production, investment, consumption, population growth, land yields, and so on. To explore the implications of an alternative assumption, just change the model and the computer calculates the new result.

Let us review the major stages in the argument, as derived from the various runs of the *Limits* model as presented.[4]

1 If we do nothing about the growth of world production and population, the diminishing availability of resources will quite soon require us to use more and more of the capital stock for resource extraction. Within forty years this will bring about a decline in worldwide industrial output per capita. Simultaneously, rising population and lower land productivity will result in lower food output per capita. These decreases, together with rising pollution, soon thereafter bring a drop in population and a much lower standard of living.

2 As a way of depicting policies designed to expand the resource constraints of the previous case, *Limits* presents a run in which we double the amount of assumed resources and lower the rate at which resources are used per unit output to one-fourth the previous value. The increased production which is made possible leads to such an increase in pollution that a rapid drop in population follows from rising mortality. Food output per capita declines due to lower fertility (in about forty years) and does so more sharply due to the impact of increased pollution. This drains away industrial capital, so industrial output per capita also begins to decline, only twelve to fifteen years later than in the previous case.

3 To simulate pollution control policies, we are shown the results of assuming that the amount of pollution per unit output is reduced to one-fourth the previ-

ous rate, in addition to the resource-expansion assumptions. Alas, food production per capita still begins to turn down in forty years or so as the limits of available land are reached. Industrial output per capita likewise declines two or three decades later, as capital is diverted to help maintain food output.

4 To explore the effects of the Green Revolution on expanding food output (to circumvent the limit in the previous run) the next simulation assumes that initial land yields are doubled. This is in addition to the resource-expansion and pollution-control assumptions. As a result, industrial production increases so much that the accompanying pollution brings a decline in food per capita in about fifty years anyway (a decline of over 80 per cent within two decades). Industrial output per capita and population also begin to fall not too long thereafter.

5 What happens if instead of increased land yields, we try population policy? Assume that expanded birth control is available but that people desire the same family size. Population growth slows only slightly. The food crisis is postponed a decade or two. When it comes, industrial output per capita and population turn down also.

6 Since no piece-wise approach apparently works, the next simulation combines all the previous limits-avoiding assumptions: double resources, lower resource use, and pollution-generation rates to one-fourth their initial levels, double initial land productivity, and make birth control available. Food per capita still begins to decline in about fifty years, industrial output per capita in about a hundred, and population a decade or so after that. This is taken to indicate that such 'technologic' policies are doomed to failure in avoiding the crisis.

7 Given the failure of conventional policies, the book then turns to less conventional ones. It explores first assuming a suddenly stable population and alternatively a suddenly stabilized stock of industrial capital. Neither averts collapse. In both cases resource constraints catch up with the industrial system.

8 However, all is not lost. Let us assume a stabilization of population in 1975 and of the industrial capital stock in 1990. Resource-use rates and pollution rates are reduced to one-fourth initial values. The target levels of service output per capita and food output per capita are increased to shift the composition of consumption. The durability of industrial capital is increased, and the use of agricultural capital is shifted in the direction of preserving land yields. No constraints then become binding before 2100. The world settles down to a stabilized pattern at average income levels about half those in the US today.

9 Indeed, we can alter some of the very strict assumptions about the size of the population and the industrial capital stock. Suppose people just suddenly start having only two children a family in 1975. Suppose also that we don't try to raise per capita industrial output above current levels. If we also keep the other controls, we still avoid global catastrophe, but are not as well off as in the previ-

ous case. However, if we delay in implementing these policies to the year 2000, we are told, disaster will follow because we have waited too long.

Both directly and by implication, the world is urged to adopt the policies in the 'stabilized' simulation: increased durability for manufactured goods, a change in output composition to less capital-intensive services, and so on. Given the long delays inherent in the feedback systems that govern the growth of population and capital, conscious (and rapid) action is said to be required.

In what follows, we proceed sector by sector to evaluate the model and these results. In order to do so, we must consult the various versions of the technical report of the project, which actually tell you what the model is and how it was derived. To date, these have only circulated in mimeographed form, but book publication is scheduled for early in 1974.[5]

The resource sector
The resource sector of the model is the source of the conclusion that economic growth should be controlled. Note, however, that *the 'stabilized world models' do not avoid the problems of resource exhaustion.* These have merely been *postponed* beyond the time frame of the simulation runs. The cause of resource exhaustion is not *growth* but *activity*. Even a non-growing economy uses resources. If there are only so much 'stuff' in the world and we inevitably use it, then its exhaustion is equally inevitable. Thus, although the authors don't say so clearly, the book strongly supports the view that continued technological progress in economizing on resources is mankind's only hope in the long run.

In this context, there is nothing magical about zero economic growth since the limits postulated in *Limits* will eventually catch up with such a society. Why then stop at 'no growth'? Why not urge a *decline* to postpone the inevitable still further? Or why not allow some further growth even if that accelerates the day of disaster? After all, there is no reason to lower our use of non-renewable resources to zero – they might as well be exhausted already![6] One notable deficiency in *Limits* is the lack of a normative framework which might be used to resolve such questions.

Meadows *et al.* contend they are just trying to depict the general structure and behavior of the world system, and that details of timing are not very interesting.[7] But on the contrary, *timing is one of the key issues.* All the 'stabilized world' allows is a little more time for technical change. The central question then is, do we need that time? Will technical progress occur fast enough anyway or not? Is zero growth, slow growth, fast growth, or negative growth compatible with the moving technical frontiers?

Answering this question requires an estimate of how rapidly we can expect technical progress to expand the relevant resource base or allow us to economize on the use of such scarce inputs. Yet in *Limits* no realistic attempt is made to analyze such possibilities. The *Limits* group has criticized some of their critics for over-optimism, since the latter have suggested that continuing technical change will occur.[8] But surely that latter postulate is more in accord with the facts than the two alternatives *Limits* offers us: (1) no technical change will occur or (2) we will experience a variety of sudden one-shot discontinuities in resource availability or resource use. How can such simulations shed any light on real world options?

In addition, in the real world we are not restricted in the amount of a given resource which we use per unit output. As other critics of *Limits* have pointed out, it largely ignores the effects of the price system in bringing about such substitutions and adjustments. In fact, we can change both the way we make any given good and can produce fewer resource-intensive goods. If steel becomes expensive, we can substitute artificial materials. If fuels become expensive, we can drive slower or smaller cars or wear sweaters indoors. In *Limits* itself, however, no effort is made to include these mechanisms. There are no prices and no supply curves, no self-correcting feedback devices that operate to influence either use or technology.

In the latest version of the technical report, some of these deficiencies are corrected. Simulation runs with continuing and adaptive technology change of various kinds are presented. These runs make it clear that, even granting *Limits'* debatable structural assumptions, whether or not resources are adequate for the next two hundred years depends critically on exactly what technical change you assume.

The structural assumptions themselves, however, are open to serious objection on the grounds that they do not reasonably represent the constraint that resources impose on industrial activity. This constraint, in my view, is formulated in such an implausible and inaccurate manner so as to largely invalidate most of the exercises with the model.

The villain of the piece is a multiplier called 'fraction of capital allocated to obtaining resources' (FCAOR),[9] which is made a function of the fraction of the resource stock remaining. In each period, the world's total capital stock is multiplied by this parameter in order to see how much capital is 'left over' for industrial production. Given this formulation, as resources are depleted, FCAOR will approach one; industrial output, and resource use, will fall to zero; and the amount of industrial capital required per unit of resource production will approach infinity! This peculiar and illogical result comes about because the capital required to extract resources is not expressed as an amount of capital, but as a fraction of the total capital stock.[10] Equally unreasonable, not only is new investment affected by the resource supply situation but rather by the *whole of the existing capital stock.* Thus as resources become scarce, more and more capital is presumably *shifted* from other uses into resource production. How this is supposedly done to plant and equipment highly specialized in other uses is never discussed.

Is it reasonable to assume that as resources decline we both can and will rapidly shift the entire capital stock into the processes for resource extraction, no matter how much capital we have and no matter how low industrial production and resource use fall in the process? Yet this specification is crucial to the behavior of the whole model. It guarantees that, as resources decline, the economy cannot accumulate enough capital both to produce resources and to provide for expanded industrial production.

To say that there is no empirical warrant for this formulation, not to mention the particular values of the function, is to put it mildly. Since 1900 in the United States, the real costs of resources have actually been declining. Technical change has outpaced the effect of previous generations having used the more accessible reserves first. The technical report even presents Barnett and Morse's data which show that the fraction of US capital devoted to mining has been between 1 and 2 per cent since 1900, with the dominant trend of the last thirty years clearly downward![11] (One wonders, therefore, why *Limits* assumes that FCAOR is a minimum of 5 per cent; but that is a small point.) Data on rising oil drilling costs for the US are also presented. But increases in such costs (much of them non-capital) do not imply that a rising fraction of the economy's growing capital stock has been devoted to resource extraction. To my mind we have been offered no support whatever for the formulation of the model.

In the technical report, the *Limits* team experiments with an 'alternative' formulation and announces that the model is not very sensitive to this specification. But the alternative has the same structural form, where the fraction of capital used to extract resources eventually rises to one. Obviously all this does is to postpone disaster slightly and then accelerate it when it arrives.

Another peculiar and unrealistic feature of the model is that only industrial output and not services use resources; yet services include all natural gas and electricity generation and commercial transportation! Because of this assumption (and the equally implausible specification that services produce no pollution) the authors are able to argue that a shift in preferences toward the supposedly less resource-intensive service sector would help avert the 'limits.' This is a clear case of taking one's assumptions too seriously and confusing the model with the world.

The use of resources in the industrial sector is determined by the Per Capita Resource Use Multiplier (PCRUM), which is assumed to be a non-linear function of industrial output per capita (IOPC). The basic justification for the functional form chosen is that: 'At very high levels of per capita output, a larger fraction [of output?] is devoted to services which also consume fewer resources.'[12] This is a funny argument since (i) the model postulates resource use is a function only of industrial output, and (ii) it would have been easy enough to take account of any changes in the composition of output by having the service sector use resources directly. The function relating PCRUM to IOPC is given an S shape so that when industrial output per capita is between $200 and $600 (the model begins at $200 in 1970) per capita resource use is presumed to increase twice as fast as output. This helps to insure that growth will exhaust resources quite rapidly indeed.

The data base used to derive all this is very limited. In the technical report three graphs are presented: US annual copper consumption per capita versus industrial output per capita, US annual steel consumption per capita versus industrial output per capita, and annual steel consumption per capita and industrial output per capita for various nations around the world in 1969. No data on fuels or non-metallic minerals are given, and the authors do not discuss the fact that in the US, for example, copper and steel together account for well under 10 per cent of value added in mining.[13] Furthermore, the data given do not even support the function chosen. US copper consumption per capita, for example, falls discernibly from 1950 to 1968, while industrial output per capita increases 50 per cent. Data from 1970 would have revealed US per capita steel consumption lower than that of Sweden, despite a higher per capita output in the US. Any similar graph of energy use would also have shown that richer societies use less energy per unit of GNP.[14] If resource use did decline per unit of output at high levels of output, the 'crisis' might not occur within the chosen time frame. But since the function, like many in *Limits,* is derived by intuitive techniques, that contingency does not arise. This is just one of many examples of largely irrelevant data being pushed too far in a given direction.

Let us summarize this sector from an economist's perspective. The average cost of resource production rises rapidly toward infinity as reserves decline, regardless of the level of output. Meanwhile, resource demand is totally inelastic with respect to costs but does exhibit a more than proportional increase with output over the most relevant range. And all this is based on the slimmest data, informally manipulated, and on *a priori* arguments about what is plausible!

The capital sector
The industrial capital stock causes problems in the *Limits* model because it is assumed that, regardless of circumstances, only a fixed percentage of industrial output is consumed. The rest is necessarily invested. Depending on the level of industrial output per capita, varying fractions of industrial output are invested in

services or agriculture – with the rest going to the expansion of industrial capital. Unless another limit intervenes first, the industrial capital stock and industrial output will continue to expand, to use up resources, and cause pollution until 'overshoot and collapse' occur.

In the economics literature one finds a large number of alternative specifications for simple growth models.[15] Yet unlike almost all of these formulations, Meadows *et al.* have chosen essentially to discount the possibility that the population and workforce might grow too slowly to make possible an explosive growth in industrial output. It is true that a labor force variable is included, and that in the *Limits* model the ratio of the jobs available to the labor force does affect the capital utilization rate (but *not* the rate of investment). However, the function has been constructed so as to make that constraint irrelevant except in the most sudden and catastrophic population decline. For example, when the ratio of jobs to workers is 4 (i.e., 4 times as many jobs as workers) the capital utilization rate is set at 80 per cent![16]

In effect then, industrial output requires only capital and resources. Furthermore, there is no profit rate or wage rate and no feedback mechanism which governs the rate of industrial capital investment. It is simply a mechanical residual. If the model was constructed so that labor and capital had prices, and if output had to be sold, one would have to confront the possibility that market mechanisms would moderate the rate of growth of the industrial capital stock. The omission of these matters avoids the contingency that such processes might avert the dramatic crisis and make unnecessary dramatic calls for dramatic action.

'World 3' is really a mutant offspring of the basic economic growth model developed decades ago by Harrod and Domar.[17] There are differences. As noted, in World 3 there is no really operative labor constraint. Also capital is nominally divided into three kinds and does depreciate. But it is essentially a one-sector model, since there are no separate equilibrium conditions to be satisfied in the nominally distinct sectors. As is well-known, such dynamic systems are quite unstable. Their behavior is also extremely sensitive to the particular values chosen for the basic structural parameters.[18] In this respect, World 3 in *Limits* is no exception.

Perhaps the most crucial variable is the 'fraction of industrial output allocated to consumption' (FIOAC), which, subtracted from 1, determines how much is reinvested. Throughout the book it has been set equal to .43. Simulation runs of this sector alone, with FIOAC = .35 produced very much more rapid growth, and with FIOAC = .5, little or no growth at all![19]

The value used was apparently based on the simple average of the values calculated for thirty or so countries. The basis for selecting the sample is not clear since it did *not* include any nations in Eastern Europe, nor China, Sweden, or Japan.

Marc J. Roberts

And in the calculation, nations like Honduras were given equal weight with the US! Furthermore, the method of calculation biased downward the results since it was based on the assumption that all agricultural and service output (including all electricity and transportation services apparently!) are directly consumed.[20] If a more accurate (higher) number were used, it seems quite possible that the explosive behavior of the capital sector, which causes such a problem in *Limits*, would be significantly altered.

The other crucial parameters in the capital sector are also derived from limited data and in a casual manner – despite the fact that the model is apparently quite sensitive to their specific values also. These are the lifetimes of service capital and industrial capital, set at eighteen years and fourteen years respectively; and the capital required per unit output in industry and services, postulated as equal to 3 in the first case and 1 in the second.

Consider, for example, the assumption that the capital/output ratio in services equals 1. This is derived as follows. First some very sketchy evidence is used to suggest that the capital/output ratio in industry equals 3. Then the value 1 is picked on the grounds that it is 'reasonable' since the service is less capital-intensive than the industrial sector.[21] Considering that highly capital-intensive activities like utilities, railroads, and housing are part of the service sector, the argument and the conclusion are both quite unpersuasive. Furthermore, one simulation presented in an early draft of the technical report suggests the whole behavior of the capital sector would be much less dramatic if this number were raised to a more reasonable value like 2 instead of 1.[22]

Equally implausible is the allocation of investment among sectors. In the smoothly growing phase of the model industrial output is divided as follows:[23]

agricultural investment	10 per cent
service investment	10
industrial investment	37
consumption	43

Yet in the US, industry (as defined by *Limits*) actually invests *less* in plant and equipment than what is defined as services, even ignoring residential construction or investment by non-profit institutions which also here belong in services.[24]

The low rate of investment in services reflects the quandary of having to make one error because of another. The low capital/output ratio in services simply cannot be made consistent with a realistic specification of the share of services in both investment and output. The effect of the assumptions chosen is to accelerate the approach of the 'crisis.' They help to ensure that services don't 'sanitize' more of the problem-causing industrial capital stock – since by assumption services are said neither to pollute nor to use resources.

360

Considering these parameter values together also does explain the sensitivity of the model to the assumed consumption rate (FIOAC). When this equals .43, and the lifetime of industrial capital is set at fourteen years and the capital/output ratio is 3, industrial output will grow at approximately 5.2 per cent per year – which on the data presented in the technical report is unrealistically high.[25] If FIOAC = .5 instead, the rate of growth of industrial output becomes 2.9 per cent. In less than fifty years the lower consumption rate and higher growth rate leads to an industrial output approximately *twice* that produced with the higher consumption rate and lower growth rate.

The exposition in *Limits* is so brief that it does not fully tell the reader the meaning of the various runs with respect to this part of the model. For example, the point is made, quite explicitly, that it is desirable to increase the durability of capital goods as a device to achieve lower resource use.[26] But by itself such a change in the model's assumptions only serves to accelerate disaster! Since the rate of investment is independent of the capital stock, a longer lifetime for capital only means a more rapid growth in output, resource use, pollution, etc.[27]

Limits misleadingly notes that in the second stabilized scenario, the one with 'looser' controls on population and capital, there is a lower rate of industrial output per capita than in the 'strict' controls run. An unwary reader might well conclude that this results from not being tough in the second case. In fact, in the strict case, industrial capital and output are allowed to increase until 1990, while in the more relaxed and realistic scenario those controls are imposed fifteen years *early* (1975); as a result the capital stock and industrial output per capita never increase quite so far![28]

In summary, in the model, capital results in output which is necessarily not fully consumed and hence which goes to increase the capital stock. This happens so quickly as to rapidly bring about a crisis. But these are largely self-inflicted wounds. A more reasonable capital sector model – or even the World 3 model with more reasonable parameters – might behave very differently. Again, simulating the model adds little if anything to the simple statement of the vision that the world is limited.

The pollution sector
The second 'limit' in *Limits* is provided by the pollution sector. There is some confusion about exactly what is being modeled here. In reading *Limits* it would certainly seem that all forms of pollution are being considered. The discussion mentions waste heat, air pollution from fossil fuels, radioactivity, organic sewage, pesticides, and so on.[29] However, the technical report makes it clear that only *persistent* materials – like DDT and mercury – are being represented. [30] This restriction is used to justify the assumption that pollution, once generated, only grad-

ually goes away. Furthermore, its assimilation rate is presumed to go down as the cumulative stock of pollution goes up. Thus, in the model, once pollution begins to accumulate, it also begins to go away more and more slowly, with obvious results.

In *Limits* and the first technical report, pollution generation in industry was made a function of industrial output per capita. The actual function was apparently fitted by eyeball to data on international variations in energy use.[31] This is clearly inappropriate since in *Limits* electricity and transport are service activities. Furthermore, the major pollutants from energy conversion are not persistent. In the third draft of the technical report, pollution is simply made a direct function of resource use (which in turn does depend on industrial output). This does change the shape of the function slightly, but two scaling constants are included whose effect appears to be to closely match the old and the new relationships.[32]

A similar specification is made with respect to agricultural pollution. In *Limits* this is a non-linear function of the cumulative investment in agriculture, derived in a debatable manner from slim data – the details of which would no doubt only weary the reader.[33] In the latest version, agricultural pollution is simply proportional to agricultural inputs per hectare. Two scaling constants are included and set so that the new function in fact looks quite a bit like the old.[34] However, the numerical values of these constraints are never justified on empirical grounds (nor are the similar ones in the generation of industrial pollution).

The model also assumes that pollution, once generated, does not have its impact immediately. As we go from *Limits* to the latest technical report, however, this delay in transmission is changed from ten years to twenty years without explanation.[35] Intentionally or not this change apparently compensates for the other changes in the rate of pollution generation just mentioned, so that the behavior of the sector looks about the same in both versions.

It seems quite dubious to set the 'pollution appearance delay' even at ten years. Since the delay in question only applies to biological effects, the failure of society to respond rapidly to pollution problems is quite irrelevant. And note that two very different values for the same parameter are said to be 'supported' by the same evidence! Yet even that data, particularly the narrative of events surrounding mercury poisoning from fish in Japan, reveals that the health effects occurred only *three* years after the mercury dumping began.[36] Note too that the effect of adding such delays to the system is to enhance its instability.

The pollution absorption rate is also mainly conjecture. The key assumption is that this rate goes down as the cumulative stock of pollution rises. Suppose we assume instead that the absorption rate is constant? The simulation runs in the latest technical report make it clear that the pollution crisis is then postponed at least beyond the next 200 years.[37] Surely such results should have been reported in *Limits* itself.

Furthermore, in *Limits* the only pollution control policy which is simulated is a one-time 75 per cent reduction in pollution per unit output, which is characterized as unrealistically optimistic.[38] But quite the contrary seems to be the case. For example, fly ash emission from fossil fuel power plants can be diminished by 99.5 per cent with efficient electrostatic precipitators. Good sewage treatment systems can remove more than 75 per cent of organic materials, and automobile emissions on 1976 model cars will be controlled by even more. Furthermore, US over-all DDT use and discharges of mercury to the environment from factories have also declined by more than three-fourths in recent years.[39] The magnitudes are important because even within the World 3 model, the occurrence of a pollution crisis depends on exactly what progress you assume with respect to pollution control.

The one-shot change explored in *Limits* itself is a thoroughly unilluminating characterization of the situation and our options (although the latest technical report is somewhat better). In the former there are no feedback loops that increase pollution control when the situation deteriorates, no scenarios in which control measures steadily improve. No attempt is made to assess in detail what can and cannot be expected for various levels of expenditure on prevention and cleanup. Yet these are the relevant questions for public policy purposes.

Given its arbitrary structural and quantitative basis, the model again tells us almost nothing about the real world. *Limits* says *if* pollution rises with output, and *if* that pollution causes harm, and *if* output rises rapidly enough, and *if* nothing is done, *then* harm will result. Such results do not require a computer simulation. To say that such simulations prove we can 'wait too long' to avert 'the pollution crisis' is pointless. The model is so poorly grounded that it cannot tell us when, *if ever*, 'too long' will be in the real world.

The population sector
The population sector in *Limits* is so constructed as to produce a discernible increase in birth rates and population as industrial output per capita rises. This is yet another destabilizing feedback in the system. How is this presumed to happen? After all, in the real world the richer nations on average have lower birth rates, and in the US the birth rate has gone down as income has increased in recent years.

First, it is assumed that, past a certain income level, desired family size *increases* as industrial output per capita goes up.[40] The impact of this assumption is amplified by the additional postulate that birth rates are a negative function of life expectancy. Since people are presumed to want so many children, they have children more rapidly when mortality increases. Furthermore, high levels of industrial output are assumed to raise mortality in two ways: (i) pollution, and (ii) by making the adverse effects of urbanization (i.e., crowding) on life expectancy more negative.[41] All of these parameters and relationships are specified on the basis of very limited data. Where no data are available, arguments of the 'it seems reasonable ...' form are used.[42]

The sum of all this is that another self-correcting mechanism has been assumed away. In the book that preceded *Limits* in the Club of Rome project, Jay Forrester had included some corrective feedbacks between population and birth rates. When the world got crowded in this model, birth rates slowed down. In *Limits* the model is built so as to reverse these dampening effects.

The agricultural sector

The agricultural sector is the source of yet another limit. Agricultural production is presumed to be driven by the relationship between indicated food per capita (IFPC) and actual food per capita (FPC). When indicated is above actual, investment in expanding food output occurs. Indicated food per capita in turn is said to depend upon industrial output per capita.[43]

The relationship for indicated food per capita appears to be based on two data sources; a graph of national grain production compared with national per capita industrial output for various countries, and a similar graph based on UN data on food consumption and industrial output.[44] However, the relationship that is postulated between indicated food per capita and industrial output per capita on this basis does not seem warranted. Food targets increase steadily until annual industrial output per capita reaches $1600. Yet the US is the only nation in the world with industrial output per capita over $800, and its food consumption (in calories/person/day) is not significantly above that of nations with only 60 per cent of its industrial output (Denmark, Canada, France).[45] Furthermore, at output levels typical of advanced countries, IFPC is set at about 11,000 calories per person per day. Such numbers are only plausible if one assumes that much of this production is being fed to animals. Even considering the effect of increased beef-eating on food demand as incomes rise, the increase in indicated food output beyond US income levels seems both unsupported and implausible.

This formulation helps to insure that the 'limit' on arable land comes into play within the time frame of the analysis. It appears that at current yields, given the population growth forecast in *Limits*, the land constraint ordinarily would not bind before two hundred years have elapsed. However, intensive land cultivation in the short run, as discussed below, is assumed to lead to significant longer-run declines in food output. Thus expanding agricultural production in the short run actually serves to make the long-run 'limit' contract significantly. And any over-estimate of indicated food output per capita helps to bring about investment to increase short-run yields, which in turn leads to lesser productive capacity a few years hence.

Agricultural investment is specified not as dollars of investment, but rather as the fraction of industrial output devoted to investment in agriculture. This is said to depend not on the total food deficit, but rather on the ratio of actual to indicated food output.[46] No evidence is presented to justify the form used, nor are any alternatives considered. The numerical levels in the function are simply advanced as being 'plausible' - no supporting empirical work is presented. The function says when actual food output equals or is greater than indicated food output, 10 per cent of industrial output is invested in agriculture - substantially more than in the US economy even today.[47] On an upswing the effect of this specification is to keep up investment in agriculture even if actual food output should reach 1.5 or 2 times indicated levels. Since investment in agriculture ulti-mately has an adverse effect on agricultural output, this continuation of invest-ment today helps to guarantee that the land limit will bind tomorrow. Once actual output falls below indicated levels, however, the function requires that a significant fraction of industrial output be devoted to agricultural investment. This helps to guarantee that once food production falls due to decreased land yields, industrial output per capita will turn down quite rapidly also.

The function relating land yields to capital shows very sharply diminishing re-turns. Doubling current yields is said to require six times the inputs. The deriva-tion of this is based largely on data about pesticide and fertilizer inputs, whereas in the model agricultural inputs are conceptualized as durable capital goods.[48]

Treating agricultural inputs as cumulative has a similar effect to that of treat-ing all pesticides as persistent; it makes matters worse. Agricultural inputs and high yields in the short run are assumed to have a very strong adverse effect on yields through decreased land productive life. As best one can tell, a single study of soil erosion done in Missouri in the 1930s is used as the basis for this result. Thus if land naturally has a life of 6000 years at a yield to 600 kg of crops per hectare per year, when yields rise to 3600 kg per hectare per year - a six-fold increase - it is *assumed* that land life falls to 60 years, a hundred-fold decrease.[49] Since many long-tilled farming areas have land yields of 3600 kg per year or higher, the function is both implausible and unsupported.

Land yields are also postulated to be diminished by pollution, via the impact of *two* multiplicative variables. First is LYMAP ('land yield multiplier from air pollution') which is made a function of industrial output. This seems question-able since the polluting substance which has the largest effect on fertility - SO_2 - comes in significant proportion from service-sector power plants. Then there is the 'land fertility degradation rate,' LFDR. This is assumed to depend on the cumulative amount of persistent pollution. Both of these functions imply strong effects so that, for example, when pollution and industrial output are both twenty times current levels, land yields from the product of these two factors will only be 50 per cent of what they would be otherwise.[50]

Little justification is presented either for the form of these functions or their specific values. Yet these two variables play a crucial role in system behavior. Being multiplicative, as capital investment, industrial output, and pollution all increase, they tend to produce dramatic drops in land yields which additional capital investment cannot overcome. But why should we believe that the 'crisis' which results is likely in the real world?

Land is also withdrawn from agriculture by being converted to urban/industrial uses. Again, the form and level of the function appears quite arbitrary, and not well supported, even by the *Limits* team's own data. They tell us in one sentence that US urban land use is about .05 hectares/person in 1970, but that 'the land which is taken from agriculture is approximately three times larger ...'[51] Yet their function, at US 1970 output levels, yields neither .05 hectare/person nor .15 hectare/person, but approximately .7 hectare/person.[52]

If a stable population is ever to be able to continue, *Limits* must include some mechanisms for expanding land yields in the face of all these sources of decline. And there is a mechanism by which investments in improved land fertility occur. This is conceptualized as letting land lie fallow. The land fertility regeneration time – which goes down as the fraction of land devoted to land maintenance goes up – is the variable that captures this process. However, it is also postulated that land regeneration declines as output per capita declines.[53] The notion is that the lower the level of output, the less anyone can afford to have land lie fallow. Thus when food gets short, less and less land is improved – the mechanism helps you less as you need it more.

In the model food output can also be increased by developing additional agricultural land. Here again, the key relationships are based more on speculative intuition than hard data. *Limits* assumes first that development costs are a function of the fraction of potentially arable land remaining. Then on the basis of a few observations it is simply assumed that there is a linear relationship between the fraction of potentially arable land still to be developed and the *logarithm* of development costs.[54] This then implies that if farmed land expands by 50 per cent (from 50 to 75 per cent of the available area) development costs will be ten times current world levels. A simple linear function fitted to the same 'data' would have implied costs of not even double current levels. This makes it very difficult to avoid food shortages by expanding agricultural production through land development, just as it is expensive to do the same via higher land yields.

366

In the real world, with given technology and a fixed capital stock, when the weather gods frown, food can become in short supply worldwide, at least in the short run. The argument here, however, is about the long run. How rapidly, and how much, can agricultural output expand to keep up with a growing population? The answer depends critically upon how one portrays the agricultural system. Lacking a defensible empirical basis, the *Limits* model cannot tell us about the extent to which food scarcity will or will not occur given various possible patterns of population and industrial growth. The fact that the model predicts that food output per capita will turn down in the relatively near future is simply an artifact of its questionable assumptions.

And again, the most relevant simulation studies were not performed as part of *Limits* itself. The only technical changes which were considered were a modest set of one-shot improvements in yields. In *Limits*, the processes of land erosion and fertility decline soon overcome these hypothesized changes. No effort was made to explore what various rates of continuing technical change would do to the system. Yet such progress has in fact characterized real agriculture of the last hundred years. To claim that the *Limits* model sheds any light on the potential impact of the Green Revolution seems quite unwarranted.[55]

EMPIRICAL METHODS
AND CONCEPTUAL STRATEGIES

What is perhaps most startling to an economist about the book is the lack of statistical rigor in the inference of relationships. Samples are not systematically chosen. Data are weak or irrelevant. Formal methods are seldom used. Instead, too often the author stares at the wall, and makes a suggestion about what 'looks reasonable.' There are obvious dangers in proceeding in this way. Only a superman could free such guesswork from the influence of his own preconceptions. What one gets out of such processes – to some unknown degree – is not what the data say but rather what the author would like to believe. And remember, the behavior of the model is very sensitive to these specifications.

Not only are the specific parameter values poorly grounded, but so are the essential structural features of the model. Explorations of how the model reacts to changes in a few selected variables, or to slight shifts in the position of a function, are largely beside the point. The crucial assumptions are those concerning what relationships to posit and how the various quantities are defined. No exploration of sensitivity to such deeper structural variations is offered in *Limits*. This makes the significance of its results difficult, if not impossible, to assess. After all, a well-known and very simple economic formulation of how production occurs can generate endless growth even with a finite stock of one input

367

Marc J. Roberts

(e.g., resources). Is such an assumption (the so-called Cobb Douglas production function)[56] or the essentially 'fixed requirements' view of *Limits* to be preferred? This issue is not even posed in the book, still less resolved by relevant data.

Another obvious difficulty is that by and large, only one-shot changes in various parameter values were considered. Neither continuing technical change, nor policies keyed to overcome difficulties as they appear, were explored, though in the latest version of the technical report a number of runs depicting various packages of more complex technical policies are presented. While I have disagreements about the formulation of some of these, they do at least demonstrate one major point. Even the *Limits* world, with its peculiar structural assumptions and doubtful parameters, can enjoy two hundred years of crisis-free growth provided one makes optimistic enough assumptions about what can be done to avoid pollution and resource depletion and to preserve land yields.[57]

The lack of appropriate technologic process is closely linked to the lack of an economic system. There are no plausible responses to changing patterns of scarcity and abundance. For example, neither resource nor labor shortages have any effect on the rate of investment. There is no price system or its administrative counterpart. The allocational mechanisms that govern production in the world today are surely not perfect. But to assume them away completely seems quite unreasonable.

It is, of course, the failure to include such self-corrective mechanisms that allows the *Limits* world system to go shooting off on exponential growth with such abandon. The implausibility of assuming this is what does or will happen in the real world can be illustrated by many famous examples, say, the rate of growth of railroad track in the US or of horse manure in London in the nineteenth century and extrapolated them exponentially; today the entire US would be covered by rails or the city of London buried in dung.

The most fundamental scientific problem with the book derives from the possibility that there are no stable relationships among such highly aggregate variables as those considered in *Limits*. Is it possible to depict a relationship between pollution and land yields without distinguishing among areas and substances? Pollution after all is many different substances that will have very different effects depending upon what material is involved and many other circumstances. Most of the categories and processes in *Limits* subsume an immense number of geographically and substantively distinguishable phenomena. It is very unlikely that any of these classes come very close to satisfying the strict mathematical conditions for consistent aggregation.[58] In sum, it is far from clear that there is enough regularity in the phenomena at the level at which *Limits* proceeds for the results to be worthwhile.[59]

In economics today, for example, a serious model of just the American economy would have many more basic quantities than World 3 contains. It would, for example, distinguish between consumer spending on durables and nondurables, between residential construction and industrial plant and equipment investment, and so on.[60] If one did try to relate consumption-as-a-whole or investment-as-a-whole to some other variables, the postulated relationships would probably not fit the past or predict the future very well. Different components of the aggregate category would in fact exhibit different behavior because each was determined by structurally and quantitatively different processes.

Such aggregation also makes the model not very interesting from a policy viewpoint. Pressing, detailed questions like the management of industrial location, the balancing of costs against benefits in designing sewage treatment systems, or expenditure priorities in energy research simply are irrelevant in such a simplified framework. What are we to make of such aggregates anyway? After all, any given level of world average income, if equally distributed, would mean something very different than if it were passed out on current patterns.

There are two smaller points worth mentioning. First, the graphs drawn in *Limits* are not precisely taken from the computer outputs. Various jumps and aberrations have been smoothed out to make them look more intuitively reasonable.[61] The problem is that when you introduce sudden changes in yields or other rates into the *Limits* model, you get noticeable and implausible discontinuities in some variables. If Meadows *et al.* believe that the world system reacts smoothly, then they should have introduced experimental changes which reflected that property. On the other hand, having postulated one-shot changes which give rise to funny-looking outputs, they do not well serve the cause of informed dialogue by inaccurately depicting the results.

Another and more serious qualm is over the failure to include and display any index of overall consumer welfare. We have food per capita and industrial output per capita. What we don't have is some total of food, consumption, and service outputs which would provide a sense of what was happening to people in the world of the model.[62]

In sum, Meadows *et al.* have misread the significance of their own efforts. They claim to have illuminated the general behavior of the world system. But the behavior of that system is quite sensitive to what one postulates about its parameters, its structure, the future of technology, and so on. The crucial issues are in fact those of timing, quantification, and structural detail. Depending on your assumptions, 'crisis' either is, or is not, inevitable. If the structure and parameter values are in error, and the policy options examined too restricted the whole exercise is of little significance. Even the justification that the model is a valuable warning of what will happen 'unless' is quite unpersuasive. It is at least possible that nothing very much will happen.

The supporters of the *Limits* conclusion have not infrequently made an argument similar to Pascal's famous wager – in which Pascal suggested that if we were unsure whether there was a god, it was in our interest to act as if there were. They argue that even if *Limits* might be wrong, the harm that will result if it is right is so great that we should assume it is correct until proven otherwise. The problem with this conclusion is that there is certain to be great injury if we control economic growth needlessly. The world is still quite poor, and keeping it so is surely not an attractive prospect. All the risks are not on one side. As another French philosopher responded to Pascal, 'Suppose there are two gods!'[63]

SOME CONCLUSIONS

You get out of a model what you put into it. The *Limits* model is constructed so that overshoot and collapse almost always will occur. It is based on structural and quantitative assumptions that, in a significant number of cases, are extremely dubious. Among others, some noticeable examples in this respect are: the relationship of resource use to capital requirements, the definition of the service sector, the derivation of the consumption and reinvestment rates, and the impact of pollution on land yields. In every case the effect of such assumptions is to reinforce the crisis pattern exhibited by the model. It is equally possible to construct optimistic variations on the model, which will tell you that the world is going to converge smoothly to a position of stable affluence with low pollution and a constant population.

What does and does not have to be done? *Limits* provides neither the answer nor a useful basis for finding one. Nor is it clear that any simple aggregate world model would be adequate to the task. The problems may just be too hard for such simple tools. In literally dozens of difficult problem areas we have to make very complex trade-offs. We have to take into account the level and distribution of the costs, risks and benefits of various options.[64] How can we make policy more equitable, effective, and responsive? That is the real task.

I do not accept *Limits'* argument about the problems of material production, but I do not, however, have the same view of the problems of population growth. Clearly the task of improving the lot of all human beings will be made immensely more difficult if population growth is not rapidly and drastically curtailed. Surely one can favor zero population growth without also wanting to limit economic growth (zero economic growth). Of course, there are still many detailed questions to be resolved about what one does and why – which *Limits*, as usual, does not illuminate.

After all, why not try to reform growth instead of ending it? In my view, given worldwide income levels, material output still has great potential social value. If we in the US are so rich, then let us give more away to those who really need it. Meadows *et al.,* however, have a very different view. In later writings the *Limits* team has argued that no growth may be desirable even if it is not essential and characterize this view as a choice of the perspectives of Eastern over Western religious traditions.[65]

A final objection to *Limits* is the limited scope of the variables it considers. There is no culture in the book, no status competition, no alienation, no nationalism, no satisfaction or dissatisfaction from work or consumption, no politics. There is no war, no race prejudice, no sex prejudice. The focus on physical outputs is very much in keeping with the perspectives and traditions of contemporary economics. Yet if one were to try to engage in forecasting for two hundred years, at least in the currently more developed societies, it is likely that such social factors will become increasingly important in determining how people view their own lives.

Nearly thirty years ago, in a seminal article, Professor Abram Bergson argued that economists could worry about how to expand everyone's consumption of those goods and services which were bought and sold, and safely assume that individual happiness would expand as a result.[66] To an extent that proved to be true, and it surely is still true for much of the world's population. But we are going to have to think further about that assumption in the next two hundred years. It is only a shame that *The Limits to Growth* on this, as on so many other important questions, gives us so little help.

NOTES

1 Among the works that have contributed to this view are E.J. Mishan, *The Costs of Economic Growth* (Praeger 1967); K.E. Boulding, 'The Economics of the Coming Spaceship Earth' in Jarrett, ed., *Environmental Quality in a Growing Economy* (Johns Hopkins Press for Resources for the Future 1966); and Herman E. Daly, 'Toward a Stationary-State Economy' in Harte and Socolow, eds., *Patient Earth* (Holt, Rinehart and Winston 1971).
2 By Donella H. Meadows, Dennis L. Meadows, Jorgen Randers, and William W. Behrens II (Universe Books 1972).
3 Some of these reviews were A. Kneese and R. Ridker, 'Predicament of Mankind,' *Washington Post,* 2 March 1972; P. Passel, M. Roberts, and L. Ross, *New York Times Book Review,* 2 April 1972; C. Kaysen, 'The Computer That Printed Out W*O*L*F,' *Foreign Affairs,* July 1972, and 'Homilies for the Club of Rome,' *Nature,* 4 Aug. 1972; R. Solow, 'Notes on "Doomsday Models,"'

Marc J. Roberts

Proceedings of the National Academy of Sciences, Dec. 1972; R. Klein, 'Growth and Its Enemies,' *Commentary,* June 1972.

4 The following summary follows each simulation in *Limits* more or less in order, beginning with Figure 35 on page 124 and ending with Figure 48 on page 169.

5 I have examined two forms of the technical report, whose official title is *The Dynamics of Growth in a Finite World,* the first draft of 7 April 1972 and the third draft of 1973 (hereafter cited as *Dynamics 72* and *Dynamics 73*). The latter is available from Professor Dennis L. Meadows. The authors of the technical report include Eric K.O. Zahn and Roger F. Naill, in addition to those who contributed to *Limits.*

6 I am grateful to Professor Janet Yallen for this point.

7 See their 'A Response to Sussex' in H.S.D. Cole *et al.,* eds., *Models of Doom* (Universe Books, 1973).

8 Ibid., pp. 233-5.

9 See *Dynamics 73,* II, pp. V-43-51.

10 Since the fraction used is independent of the size of the capital stock this amounts to postulating constant returns to scale within each period, and apparently, complete adjustment to long-run equilibrium levels within a one-year time horizon.

11 H.J. Barnett and C. Morse, *Scarcity and Growth* (Johns Hopkins for Resources for the Future 1963).

12 *Dynamics 73,* II, p. V-36.

13 *Statistical Abstract of the United States 1972* (US Department of Commerce 1972), p. 644.

14 On steel consumption see *Statistical Yearbook 1970* (United Nations 1971), Table 168, pp. 533ff. On power see J. Darmstadter *et al., Energy in the World Economy* (Johns Hopkins for Resources for the Future 1971).

15 See F.H. Hahn and R.C.O. Matthews, 'The Theory of Economic Growth: A Survey,' *Economic Journal,* Dec. 1964, reprinted in *Surveys of Economic Theory,* II (St Martins Press 1965); and E. Burmeister and R. Dobell, *Mathematical Theories of Economic Growth* (Macmillan, 1970).

16 *Dynamics 73,* I, pp. III-78, III-79.

17 R.F. Harrod, 'An Essay in Dynamic Theory,' *Economic Journal,* March 1939; E.D. Domer, 'Capital Expansion, Rate of Growth, and Employment,' *Econometrica,* April 1946, and references in n15.

18 Hahn and Matthews, 'Economic Growth,' pp. 27-34, Burmeister and Dobell, *Mathematical Theory,* pp. 38-47.

19 *Dynamics 72,* I, p. III-70, III-73.

20 *Dynamics 73,* I, pp. III-54.

21 Ibid., pp. III-66.

22 Ibid., III-87, III-88.

23 This follows because in smooth growth, where indicated service output and indicated food output are equal to actual outputs, those two activities each absorb 10 per cent of industrial output. See *Dynamics 73*, I, p. III-61; II, pp. IV-57, IV-58.

24 In 1972 in manufacturing and mining, business expenditures for new plant and equipment were $33.6 billion. For transportation, utilities, communication and commercial, the total was $58.98 billion, while residential construction was $53.9 billion. See *Economic Report of the President* (US Government Printing Office, January 1973), Table C-38, p. 236, and Table C-40, p. 240.

25 When FIOAC is .43, and industry and agriculture each take 10 per cent of industrial output for investment, investment in industry will equal 37 per cent of output. With the capital/output ratio is 3, this will produce enough new capital to expand output by 12.33 per cent per annum. If the average life of industrial capital is fourteen years, then 7.14 per cent of the industrial capital stock disappears each year due to depreciation. The net annual rate of growth of the industrial capital stock is thus 12.33 − 7.14 = 5.2 per cent. Meadows *et al.*, on the other hand, choose 2.0 per cent as a 'reasonable' figure for recent historical worldwide growth rates of industrial output. *Dynamics 73*, I, pp. III-48 to III-50.

26 *Limits*, pp. 163-77.

27 *Dynamics 73*, I, pp. III-84, III-85; II, pp. VIII-38, VIII-39.

28 Compare *Limits*, p. 163 with p. 166 where the change is introduced by saying, 'Let us go back in the general direction of the real world and relax our most unrealistic assumptions.'

29 Ibid., pp. 69-87.

30 *Dynamics 73*, II, p. VI-9, VI-28-30.

31 *Dynamics 72*, II, pp. VI-24-6.

32 *Dynamics 73*, II, pp. VI-35-VI-41.

33 It was based on one chart from a study done for the President's Science Advisory Committee report, *The World Food Problem* (1967), vol. 3, p. 174. The chart, whose sources and origins are not explained in this original presentation, shows estimates of *desirable* pesticide use and agricultural investment in order to achieve increased food yields in the developing nations. This is extrapolated to a relationship of what *will* happen to worldwide averages. See *Dynamics 72*, II, pp. VI-30-3.

34 *Dynamics 73*, II, pp. VI-43-6.

35 Compare *Dynamics 72*, II, pp. VI-34-9 with *Dynamics 73*, II, pp. VI-47-54.

Marc J. Roberts

36 *Dynamics 73,* II, p. VI-47; mercury dumping was begun in 1950 and the first case detected in 1953.

37 Ibid., pp. VI-91–3.

38 *Limits,* p. 135, 'Reduction to less than one-fourth of the present rate of pollution generation is probably unrealistic.'

39 On smokestack particulate control, see Bar Association of the City of New York, Special Committee on Electric Power and the Environment, *Electricity and the Environment* (West Publishing Company, 1973). On sewage treatment plant efficiencies see G.M. Fair, J.C. Geyer, and D.A. Okun, *Water and Wastewater Engineering* (John Wiley 1968), II. On automobile air pollution see H. Jacoby, and J.D. Steinbruner, 'Salvaging the Federal Attempt to Control Auto Air Pollution,' *Public Policy* (Winter 1973). On DDT see *Congressional Quarterly,* 13 May 1972, p. 1062, and 24 July 1972, p. 1537. On mercury see *National Journal,* 8 Aug. 1970, pp. 1695-700.

40 There apparently have been some substantial changes in the population sector model between *Limits* and the first draft of the technical report on the one hand and the most recent version of the latter. The relevant parts of the population formulation of the latter are discussed on pp. II-159–84, esp. II-181. The discussion in the text refers to the earlier version. The newer version, for a growing economy, exhibits essentially the same dynamic behavior based on a somewhat different structural formulation. See also *Limits,* p. 115.

41 *Dynamics 73,* I, pp. II-103–34.

42 E.g., ibid., II-125, II-126, II-132.

43 Ibid., II, pp. IV-48–55.

44 Ibid., pp. IV-49, IV-50.

45 *United Nations Statistical Yearbook 1970,* table 160, pp. 504-17.

46 *Dynamics 73,* II, pp. IV-57–8.

47 See *Survey of Current Business* (US Dept. of Commerce, July 1973), vol. 53, no. 7, p. 39.

48 *Dynamics 73,* II, pp. IV-89–92.

49 Ibid., pp. IV-108–12.

50 Both LFRDT and LYMAP lower unit output to approximately .7 of its otherwise achieved value when cumulative pollution and industrial output respectively are twenty times basis levels. Since they are multiplicative, their joint effect is to make yields $.7 \times .7 = .49$ their otherwise achieved level. See ibid., fig. IV-43, p. IV-126, and fig. IV-36, p. IV-97.

51 Ibid., p. IV-114.

52 Ibid., fig. IV-41, p. IV-117.

53 Ibid., pp. IV-136–9.

54 *Dynamics 72*, I, pp. III-38, III-39. As best I can tell, this function too has been modified in the more recent work (*Dynamics 73*, II, p. IV-63). Note that the same data has been said to 'justify' two very different relationships.

55 This is how these runs are characterized in *Limits* (see esp. p. 137).

56 See, for example, Burmeister and Dobell, *Mathematical Theory*, pp. 30-6. And for a related discussion see also Cole *et al.*, eds., *Models of Doom*, pp. 75-9.

57 *Dynamics 73*, II, pp. VII-60-9.

58 See H.A.J. Green, *Aggregation in Economic Analysis* (Princeton University Press 1964). As a simple example of these issues, consider what happens when we have a number of subsystems in all of which an independent variable is linked to a dependent variable by the same non-linear function. Even then we cannot assume that the function in question can be used to predict the average value of the dependent variable on the basis of the average value of the independent variable. Differences in the distribution of values of the independent variable among different subsystems will result in differences in the average value of the dependent variable. There simply is *no* unique relationship among the 'aggregate' parameters in such circumstances – which appear to be typical of the sort *Limits* considers.

59 For a fuller discussion of some of these issues see my 'Models and Theories in Economics,' PhD thesis, Harvard University, 1969, esp. pp. 70-92.

60 For a description of perhaps the most complex of these models see J.S. Duesenberry *et al.*, eds., *The Brookings Quarterly Econometric Model of the United States* (Rand McNally 1965).

61 For example, see *Dynamics 72*, II, p. VII-34, which shows clearly that introducing a sudden doubling of agricultural yields causes, as one would expect, a discontinuous jump in food output per capita. Compare this with *Limits*, p. 138, where in a similar graph, two of the relevant observations on food per capita (indicated by *F*) have been omitted and the curve for that variable smoothly drawn in (the printouts give you five-year averages, so ten years have been glossed over). I suspect similar problems on pp. 140, 165, 168. I have also been unable to figure out what change in assumptions is responsible for some significant behavior differences between the model as shown in *Limits* and in *Dynamics 72*. In particular, in the latter, a sudden increase in land yields is generally succeeded by a decline in food output per capita, after the initial jump, since food output is generally now 'too high'; while in the former food consumption per capita continues to rise substantially in such circumstances.

62 Such an index was presented in J. Forrester, *World Dynamics*, the earlier study in the Club of Rome project (Wright-Allen Press 1971), p. 9.

Marc J. Roberts

63 I am indebted to Professor Robert Solow for this point and to Professor Joel Yellen for the analogy.
64 See my 'On Reforming Economic Growth,' R.N. McKean, 'Growth vs. No Growth: An Evaluation' and R. Zeckhauser, 'The Risks of Growth,' all in *Daedalus,* fall 1973.
65 Meadows *et al.,* 'A Response to Sussex,' in Cole *et al.,* eds., *Models of Doom,* pp. 239–40.
65 'A Reformulation of Certain Aspects of Welfare Economics,' *Quarterly Journal of Economics,* vol. 52 (Feb. 1938), pp. 310–34. See also P.A. Samuelson, *The Foundations of Economic Analysis* (Harvard University Press 1947), chap. VIII, Welfare Economics.

Contributors

M.A. ADELMAN Massachusetts Institute of Technology
HAROLD J. BARNETT Department of Economics, Washington University
A. CARNESALE Department of Engineering, North Carolina State University
MAUREEN S. CRANDALL Department of Economics, Wellesley College
R.J. DEAM Energy Research Unit, Queen Mary College, University of London
DONALD W. DEWEES Department of Political Economy, University of Toronto
T.S. ELLEMAN Department of Engineering, North Carolina State University
EDWARD W. ERICKSON Department of Economics, North Carolina State University
THOMAS J. GRENNES Department of Economics, North Carolina State University
ROLAND S. HOMET Elbert, Homet and Elbert, Washington DC
WILLIAM W. KELLOGG National Center for Atmospheric Research, Boulder CO
ALLEN V. KNEESE Resources for the Future Inc., Washington DC
EMILIO G. COLLADO Exxon Corporation, New York
ROBERT MABRO Oxford Institute of Economics and Statistics, Oxford University
J.S. NYE Harvard Business School, Harvard University
SCOTT R. PEARSON Food Research Institute, Stanford University
M.V. POSNER Pembroke College, Cambridge University
THOMAS G. RAWSKI Department of Political Economy, University of Toronto
MARC J. ROBERTS Department of Economics, Harvard University
HENRY STEELE Department of Economics, University of Houston
LEONARD WAVERMAN Department of Political Economy, University of Toronto
HERBERT S. WINOKUR, JR ICF Inc., Washington DC
ARTHUR W. WRIGHT Department of Economics, University of Massachusetts

Contents of volume 2

Contents of volume 2